Coming late to the United States, the Greeks had more obstacles to face than other, more firmly entrenched immigrant groups. They brought with them a passionate adherence to the ancient cultural entity that was Greece, a church that was oriented toward the East, and a language that was very little heard or known in this country. But step by step the Greeks became part of America, as the straw hat shown here indicates. The photograph is of the author's aunt and uncle, taken around 1910.

THE
GREEKS
IN THE
UNITED
STATES

THE

GREEKS

IN THE

UNITED

STATES

Theodore Saloutos

HARVARD UNIVERSITY PRESS
CAMBRIDGE · MASSACHUSETTS
1 9 6 4

DISTRIBUTED IN GREAT BRITAIN BY OXFORD UNIVERSITY PRESS, LONDON

LIBRARY OF CONGRESS CATALOG CARD NUMBER: 64–13428

PRINTED IN THE UNITED STATES OF AMERICA

DEDICATED TO THE GREEK COMMUNITY OF
MILWAUKEE, WISCONSIN

PREFACE

H ISTORIES of ethnic groups that migrated to this country from southern and eastern Europe are long overdue. Such studies are needed because these people have become a part of the greater American community and the history of this nation, and because they came from a part of the world that is playing a significant role in international affairs.

Much of what we know about American citizens from southern and eastern Europe has been of a fragmentary or an extremist variety. At one pole we have the racist accounts of some pioneer sociologists, sensational journalists, and representatives of "glandular groups" bent upon proving that these newer immigrants were an inferior and hence an undesirable lot. At the opposite pole are the versions of the so-called inferior groups themselves, which, as a rule, glorified the traditions, courage, and accomplishments of their people. These writings have been ultranationalistic, panegyric, and emotional, tending to place emphasis on the discrimination to which they, as a national group, were subjected, to sweep the less complimentary aspects of their history under the rug, and to ignore their own important in-group activities. Often their writings were defensive and resentful.

The Greeks fall within this general description. With only a few exceptions, the accounts of them have been derogatory and abusive. Little effort was made to understand or even provide them with an opportunity to explain what they were doing. The social climate at the time of their arrival was inhospitable and militated against a fair hearing for anyone classified as undesirable. When the Greeks began coming to the United States, antiforeignism and racist thinking was at its peak.

The first and only serious attempt to write about the Greeks in scholarly fashion was that of Henry Pratt Fairchild, whose *Greek Immigration to the United States* was published by Yale University Press in 1911. Fairchild chose to emphasize the worst features: his general thesis seemed to be that the Greeks were a hopelessly degenerate people who were likely to become the dregs of American society. He had no knowledge of the Greek language and consequently was unable to use Greek sources; he failed to give any serious attention to the cultural impact of those arriving from "the unredeemed lands"; and the contemporary character of his study denied him historical perspective. As was common among writers of the day, Fairchild brought the immigrants through Ellis Island, emphasized their poverty, drew some unfavorable comparisons with the older immigrant stocks, and concluded that they were a far cry from the earlier arrivals in terms of physical qualities, intelligence, and capabilities. More realistic and well-rounded study of the Greeks was handicapped from the start by a serious language barrier and by an unwillingness or inability on the part of those with linguistic competence to undertake such studies. Coupled with this were the lagging interest in immigration studies and the even greater lack of concern with immigrants after they were firmly planted in their American surroundings.

My own interest in the Greeks has been of long standing. Both my parents came from Peloponnesian villages during the first decade of the twentieth century, my father from the province of Elias and my mother from Arcadia. Like so many of my contemporaries, I was compelled to speak the language of my parents. I suspect that I had some knowledge of modern Greek before I uttered a word of English. I lived through most of the period I am writing about, knew some of the participants, and at times was involved, in one way or another, with many of the important issues. Those who lived through these years know full well about the two societies between which the Greeks were torn: that of their parents and home and that of the daily non-Greek world in which they had to move. And the gulf that separated the two worlds was wide and deep. One marvels that a fate worse than that of becoming professional men, businessmen, and academicians has not befallen some of us.

Greeks, like members of other ethnic and religious minorities in this country, are a sensitive people who often react sharply to what they think of as unflattering aspects of their past. Many of the "oldtimers" retain their ultranationalistic orientation and feel passionately about the land of their birth. In their opinion, anything worthy of the Greek name must be written in "the spirit of 1821" (the Greek War of Independence) or of OXI Day (October 28, 1940). These are patriotic dates no red-blooded Greek can forget. Anyone who writes in a contrary vein, then, deserves to be branded a "Janissary," a non-Greek, an anti-Greek, an outcast, or a traitor to his faith and nationality.

The reaction to this study in the initial stages were mixed. I was informed that too many people of Greek background were incapable of comprehending the objective approach of the scholar; hence they would be offended at much that appeared in these pages. Some confessed that they had no special pride in their history as an ethnic group and saw no reason for my attempting to write one. The young who felt ashamed of their background saw no point in "pouring salt on an open wound." One fairly well-known journalist thought that the history of the Greek people in the United States would bring little to light that was complimentary about them. Fortunately, these were the sentiments of a minority, and many individuals expressed a desire to know more about themselves, their organization, their parents, and the American background of the church in which they worshiped.

The organization of this study is a compromise between the chronological and the topical. An appreciation of conditions in the native country—political, cultural, spiritual, as well as economic—is basic to any understanding of immigrants in the United States. This provides the key to their behavioral patterns, their organization, their hopes and aspirations, especially during the earlier years. The impact that events in the Old Country had on the immigrants in the United States, and, in turn, the reciprocal effects that these self-same immigrants had on Greece, is one of the persistent themes of this study.

My research was based on extensive library work and lengthy interviews with journalists, clergymen, organization leaders, business and professional men active in Greek-American affairs, and the ordinary people who came to this country as immigrants. Interviews and protracted correspondence revealed the temper of the times, experiences and reflections that otherwise might have remained unrecorded. For such immigrant people have sentiments that run deep and frequently go unrecognized and untold.

My indebtedness to individuals who have assisted me in various stages is great. First and foremost, I am deeply obligated to Demetrios Calli-machos, a penetrating and fearless observer of the Greek-American scene, the dean of Greek journalists in the United States, and an unfailing friend and counselor. Before his untimely death, Stavros Skopeteas, Director of the Library of the Chamber of Deputies in Athens, was an instructive guide in helping me to locate materials in the Greek press and in enriching my personal knowledge of the immi-grant. George C. Vournas, with his insistence that the truth be told, provided me with numerous helpful leads and the benefits of a keen and critical mind. My only regret is that I did not get to know him earlier. George P. Skouras was helpful in acquainting me with relief activities in the United States and Greece; his assistance was exceeded only by his magnanimity. George Perros placed at my disposal materials pertaining to Greeks in the United States during the nineteenth century. Venetia Vidalis was unstinting in her cooperation in placing materials at my disposal. George E. Phillies was a most enthusiastic correspondent and supplier of materials on the church and the Justice for Greece Committee. Peter Topping proved to be a very congenial colleague as the director of the Gennadius Library in Athens.

Other individuals who have assisted me in one way or another include Frank Agnost, Kostis Argoe, John Cavarnos, Vladimir Constantinides, Nicholas Culolias, George Demeter, Paul Demos, Constantine Dukakis, George Eliades, Alexander Georges, Judge James A. Geroulis, James Harakas, Peter T. Kourides, George J. Leber, Mike Manatos, John L. Manta, Demetrios Michalaros, Anastasios Mountanos, Dimitri Parry, Adamantios Th. Polyzoides, Constantine Poulos, John Poulos, Stylianos Spiridakis, Stanley Stacy, Mayor James Vouvoulis. Roger Daniels and Charles Moskos read portions of the manuscript and gave me the benefit of their criticisms. I should also like to thank Carl Wittke and Oscar Handlin for the encouragement they have given me.

My indebtedness to the personnel of the various libraries in which I worked must also be acknowledged. They include those of the Greek Chamber of Deputies, the Gennadius, and the Benaki of Athens. In the United States I worked extensively in the Library of Congress, the National Archives, the New York Public Library, and the library of the University of California, Los Angeles. Also helpful were materials in the Widener and Houghton libraries of Harvard University and in the libraries of Yale University, the University of Chicago, and the University of California, Berkeley.

This project could never have been undertaken had it not been for the timely assistance of the Research Committee of the University of California, Los Angeles, the American Philosophical Society, the Social Science Research Council, and the Fulbright Awards Committee.

Lastly, I cannot overlook the members of my family—Florence, Bonnie, and Pete—for enduring with me while I labored with the Greeks.

Los Angeles, California   T. S.
August 1963

CONTENTS

CONTENTS

ILLUSTRATIONS

following p. 238

An immigrant couple, about 1910.

King Constantine of Greece (*Illustrated Monthly Atlantis,* August 1913).

Eleutherios Venizelos (*Illustrated Monthly National Herald,* March 1922).

Meletios Metaxakis, Metropolitan of Athens (*Illustrated Monthly National Herald,* April 1922).

Solon Vlasto (*Atlantis*).

Demetrios Callimachos (*Illustrated Monthly National Herald,* April 1922).

A Greek wedding party, Newark, New Jersey (Thomas Burgess, *Greeks in America,* Boston, Sherman, French Company, 1913).

Students of a Greek school, Milwaukee, Wisconsin, 1919.

Volunteer Greek unit of Haverhill, Massachusetts (*Illustrated Monthly Atlantis,* December 1914).

Arrival of Philadelphia volunteer unit to fight in the Balkan Wars, Piraeus (*Illustrated Monthly Atlantis,* November 1912).

Parade commemorating the freeing of Salonika (1912), 1952.

Old Greek Church of the Annunciation, Milwaukee (*Milwaukee Journal*).

New Church of the Annunciation, Milwaukee, designed by Frank Lloyd Wright.

THE

GREEKS

IN THE

UNITED
STATES

1

THE HELLAS
OF THE IMMIGRANT

IMMIGRATION to the United States from Greece was chiefly a product of the late nineteenth and early twentieth centuries. The immigrants came from a country that had a population of slightly more than two and a half million, a land that was scenic and appealing, the possessor of a proud history and traditions, but also a nation of peasants and poverty. A discerning observer could easily detect that Greece during these years had its eyes set on higher goals. He could sense that a craving for economic betterment and an uninhibited nationalism had converged, as though by design, into a massive campaign that would unchain this historic land and its people from their enslaved past.

Evidence of these multiple forces came from many directions. The Greeks, with a passion unequaled since the days of the War of Independence, were waging vociferous crusades for the union of their "unredeemed brothers" in Crete, Macedonia, the Aegean Islands, and other portions of the Ottoman Empire with "Mother Greece." Their songs, literature, and newspapers resounded with the aspirations of a people striving to recapture some of the greatness of the Byzantine era. Their commerce, shipping, and finance, if not their agriculture, were making strides forward. An emerging middle class behaved as though it had been divinely inspired to mold the foreign and domestic policies of an alerted nation. More significant still, Greece's enterprising peasants, who had despaired of a life of unrewarding labor on the soil, were migrating to the towns and cities or embarking for the United States in search of opportunities unavailable at home.

This buoyant and aspiring spirit accompanied the Greeks wherever they went. It guided their thoughts and actions, gave them confidence, comforted them during their lonely hours, kept them attached to their families, church, and country, and put its stamp on Greek communities. One misses the deeper significance of the immigrant exodus to America if he conceives of it as just another chapter in the migration of people from the Old World to the New. It began as something more, for it was part and parcel of what many heralded as a national renascence.[1]

Some of this optimism was reflected in the economic advances that Greece made during the late 1890s. A visitor in Athens at the time would have been greatly impressed by the bustle of events. Business there and in the port of Piraeus was brisk; factories were operating at full capacity; new buildings, hotels, business blocks, and factories were rising; scores of additional structures were planned for the future. As a result of this boom Athens and Piraeus were pinched by shortages of masons and plasterers for the first time in modern history. Thousands found gainful employment who, in previous years, would have been fortunate if they could have worked one day a week.[2]

Late in 1899, drought, crop failures, and a decline in the value of the drachma brought the upward swing in the business cycle to a temporary halt, but in due time the prosperity of the previous two years resumed its course. The gold streaming into Greece from America, good crop years, and the money left behind by the visitors to classical shrines pumped fresh blood into the anemic economy of the country.[3]

Greece owned a merchant fleet that ranked only after those of England, Norway, and Denmark. Some idea of its growing size can be gleaned from the steamers flying the Greek flag; from 1896 to 1904 they increased in number from 107 to 201, and their net tonnage from 86,968 to 214,814. These new steamers were bought mainly in England by shipping firms in Piraeus and the islands of Syra and Andros with money advanced by the Bank of Athens. These figures do not include the sailing ships which, over the same period, declined in number from 1,059 to 899. Piraeus, in terms of ship entries and clearances, ranked after Marseilles and Genoa as the third Mediterranean port.[4]

Equally significant were the foreign capital funneling its way into Greece and the economic ties being forged with the countries of Western Europe. French, German, and Belgian capital was attracted by Greek mines, banks, gasworks, tramways, electric power, and other enterprises. The Banque d'Orient, formed with local and German money, became the representative of Greek and French interests. The more hopeful looked forward to the day when the untapped resources of the country would attract additional investors. Under such conditions the Greeks would reap only a portion of the benefits, yet the willingness of foreigners to invest in Greek enterprises was encouraging.[5]

Although by Western standards the signs of technological progress were few, they were nevertheless conspicuous in a country that was predominantly rural and undeveloped. One significant example of this was the Greek Electric Company, which was designed to provide the greater Athens area with electric power and to stimulate manufacturing in the plains of Attica. Patras and other districts—especially Pyrgos and Tripolis inland—benefited from the installation of an electric railway system that brought with it new industries, capital, and employment.[6]

Important to the economic future of the nation was the completion of the Corinth Canal in 1893. Costing 60 million drachmas, or 2.4 million British pounds, the canal by joining the Isthmus of Corinth with the Saronic Gulf shortened the journey from the Adriatic and the ports of Austria, France, and Italy to the Aegean Sea and the ports of Turkey, Rumania, Russia, and Asia Minor. Thus the attempt of Nero, the prophesy of Appolonius of Tyana, and the dream of Lucan, "to save ships from rounding long Cape Malea," was finally achieved by the modern Greek nation.[7] Perhaps the principal financial undertaking of the period was the railroad linking Piraeus and Larissa. Also noteworthy was the completion of the Peloponnesus Railway along the southwestern coast of the peninsula. This line penetrated an area that was rich in agricultural products and favored with a climate for raising currants, figs, olives, and other export crops. All sections of the Peloponnesus were brought within immediate reach of each other, the rest of Greece, and the outside world.[8]

But to know the Hellas of the immigrant at that time, one must know the rural areas, the villages, and the peasants, more so than the cities, ports, banks, railroads, and public improvements. It was the agriculturalists and, to a much lesser degree, the small manufacturers and merchants, the independent tradesmen, the professional classes, those employed in the transportation and service industries, and government workers who constituted the dominant occupational groups of the country.[9] For this reason the rural background and the hardships to which these people were subjected are relevant. Modern Greece began as a nation with a poor, neglected, and fixed agricultural population. Her productive power was small. Turkish rule had been too ineffective to enforce a system of slavery that would have been profitable to the master; but it was sufficiently awake to the danger of permitting too much profit to a subject people. Of an estimated 120,000 farm families in Greece in 1833, only 20,000 were proprietors.[10]

Land ownership should have been encouraged by the government. But this was not the case. Matters, it appears, became worse when the bulk of the lands once owned by the sultan passed into the hands of the Greek government, which made it difficult, if not impossible, for the people to acquire and cultivate them. As late as 1842, two thirds of an estimated 5 million acres remained untilled. As a consequence, the Greek farmers, the former vassals of "the unspeakable Turk," found themselves at the mercy of an indifferent Greek government. Rather than attempting to compensate the people for their sufferings and repopulate the abandoned areas, the government unwisely chose to retain these lands. Ironically enough, the government extracted higher rents from its subjects than did the hated Turks.[11] Continued pressure eventually forced the Greek government to adopt a policy designed to develop the agricultural resources of the nation. It also displayed a belated appreciation for those who had fought to liberate the country.[12]

The lack of reliable statistics makes it impossible to assert how many of the government lands passed into the hands of the small holders. The passion of the peasants for land, however, was unmistakable; they saved to acquire it, and the holders gradually increased in numbers. On the island of Euboea, where the returns from farming were relatively high, and even in districts where the rewards were smaller, the peasants procured large portions of the land from the original proprietors.[13]

In Thessaly a somewhat different situation prevailed. After the province was annexed in 1881, the new landlords who replaced the easygoing and indulgent Turkish proprietors were for the most part wealthy speculators anxious to manage their holdings on a more businesslike basis. On the other hand, the peasants of Thessaly, unlike their Peloponnesian counterparts who were owner-proprietors, were chiefly hereditary tenants, farming under the metayer system known to many Europeans. Under this arrangement the peasants obtained seedgrain and one third of the land tax from the owners or their agents, in return for a portion of the crop as rent. The owners made no other contributions to the cost of cultivation.[14]

The plight of these hereditary tenants eventually beame the concern of the Greek government. As a means of alleviating conditions, crown lands and private estates were purchased, divided into small plots, and made available to the landlords on reasonable terms. As a result, proprietorships increased. Of an estimated 22,129 agricultural families in Thessaly in 1900–1901, there were some 10,141 owner-cultivators, 10,104 hereditary tenants who paid their rent in kind, and 884 outright tenants or lessees.[15]

Mounting national tensions aggravated these agricultural problems. As a result of political disturbances in East Rumelia, approximately 3,200 Greek families totaling between 17,000 and 18,000 persons found refuge in Thessaly in 1906. Meanwhile Greek nationalists heaped anathemas on the detractors of the Hellenic name and the persecutors of their "blood brothers." The Greek government maintained these political refugees for about two and a half years before it built permanent villages for them; it had no intention of making an outright gift of this property but, since the refugees repaid their obligations on such a small scale, the loan turned out to be a bad debt.[16] Relief for the peasants became a primary concern of many politicians, who joined the leaders of the military coup of 1909 in demanding the expropriation of the landlords. But Prime Minister Stephanos Dragoumis and the Turks reminded the insurgents that the rights of the Moslem proprietors were safeguarded by the convention of July 2, 1881. This restlessness, however, continued until in March 1910 it erupted into bloodshed in Larissa and Karditsa.[17]

Matters became still more complicated after the Balkan Wars of 1912–1913, when another 90,000 refugees fled to Thessaly. Some of the large landowners, as a means of facilitating the rehabilitation and reconstruction program, offered to convert part of their holdings into small plots, provided they received fair compensation for them. The government also sponsored a plan which made it possible for the refugees to acquire land by a system of deferred payment. The hope was that this generous policy and a few good crop years would transform the great plain of Thessaly into the granary of Greece.[18]

On the Ionian Islands, annexed from Great Britain in 1864, a dual system of land tenure prevailed. Under one, the owner supplied the seeds, implements, and manure, and received two thirds of the total produce as his share. Under the other, the tenant furnished his own equipment and in theory paid half of the produce to the landowner. Under the latter plan a fifth of the holding belonged to the tenant and descended to his next of kin, it was almost impossible for an owner to dispossess a tenant, except in the most unusual circumstances. The chief wealth of the islands was their olive groves; they were valued according to the yields estimated by the peasants and the agents of the landowners. But since the agents normally were peasants themselves and sympathetic to members of their own class, it was common practice for them to underestimate the yields. After a harvest it was usual for a tenant to inform the landlord that his trees had been infested with insects or that bad weather had damaged many of them; hence his share would be about half of the original estimate.[19]

Farm laborers as a class were unknown in Greece. When needed they generally were obtained from Albania, Bulgaria, and Montenegro; and they usually worked on an annual or semiannual basis. They received from thirty to forty drachmas a month, plus food and lodgings; in communities where emigration produced labor shortages, wages were much higher. Women and children also worked in the fields at harvest time, and they earned good wages for their efforts.[20]

Taxation had always been a sore point with the Greek peasants. They believed, and with much justification, that they bore the brunt of the burden and received few of the benefits. During the nineteenth century a tenth of the gross produce was requisitioned as a tax. The sovereign was entitled to his share of the crop from the moment it began to ripen; and judging from contemporary accounts, the collection of the one tenth was more important than the interest of the cultivator in the other nine tenths. Since grading was unknown, all crops were lumped together regardless of the quality, and the collector took what he saw fit. Good management and labor, as a consequence, rarely benefited from efforts to improve the quality and raise an early crop.

To expedite matters, the collection of the tax was assigned to private contractors, but this practice tended to aggravate abuses and contributed to the general restlessness. The collector usually set the day when the crop was to be harvested; to him it made little difference whether it was green or ripe. Or the peasant, after cutting his wheat, would carry it on pack animals, in some cases for miles, to the public threshing floor where he waited until the collector found time to see it threshed and collect his levy. This process could take weeks or months. Frequent complaints were voiced against these primitive methods of taxation, but proposals for reform were deferred for one reason or another.[21]

The war with Turkey in 1897 and the construction of numerous public works inevitably led to the imposition of higher taxes. In keeping with past practices, a disproportionate share of the burden was thrust upon the poor rural classes. Tax money obtained from the agricultural population was spent lavishly on public buildings, street cars, light and power systems, and port facilities for Athens. But marshes in need of draining and roads requiring construction in the outlying districts were neglected. The politicians rarely visited the provinces— they lacked firsthand knowledge of local problems, and as a rule they ignored pleas for constructive action. These disparities were aggravated by the arrogance of the educated and privileged minorities of the cities, especially in Athens, "toward the ignorant, downtrodden, and neglected peasantry." [22]

The hostility of the peasants and the wide distribution of the rural population posed problems for the tax collector. Delinquency in payments was one consequence. Between 1882 and 1891 the Greek government was 75,278,420 drachmas in arrears, though later collections reduced the amount. Minor reforms and better times alleviated conditions for a while, but the passage of the Arable Land Law of 1911 created widespread dissatisfaction. Based on a Cretan law and having the support of the government of Eleutherios Venizelos, this Arable Land Law replaced the old tax on plow animals with a new tax on the produce of arable lands. Opponents who made no secret of their dislike for the measure likened it to the hated tithe of earlier days. Fortunately, the improved economic conditions of the country persuaded the authorities to suspend its application until the middle of 1913. In this year the communal authorities were empowered to assume the tax-collecting responsibility that previously had been assigned to private contractors.[23]

Equally burdensome were the interest rates. Since Greece was a capital-starved nation and the returns from farming were small and uncertain, moneylenders found themselves in a position of extracting rates ranging from a minimum of 10 percent upward. This business proved so lucrative that villagers who emigrated to the United States often became moneylenders upon their repatriation in Greece.[24]

Agriculture, as an occupation, held a low status in Greek society, and the tendency was for the more ambitious to enter one of the professions. Parents anxious for the welfare of their sons felt obliged to direct them into law, medicine, and the study of philosophy, for these denoted status and culture. Small wonder, then, that Greece in 1907 had one lawyer for every 828 persons and one doctor for every 888 persons.[25] Despite the general dissatisfaction with farm life, Greece maintained its predominant agricultural complexion. In 1879, almost fifty years after the War of Independence, about 82 percent of the Greek population lived in communities having less than 5,000 inhabitants. As late as 1928, despite the inroads of urbanization, commerce, and manufacturing, the rural class still comprised 67 percent of the total population.[26]

In view of the rural character of Greece and the nation's general poverty, it is hardly surprising that commercial relations with the United States were virtually nonexistent. During the late 1890s, when immigration was on the increase, trade consisted chiefly of petroleum shipped from the United States to Greece and quantities of black olives and Peloponnesian root shipped from Greece to the United States. American merchants and manufacturers, feeling the pressure of English and German competition in the world market, were anxious to exploit the commercial possibilities of Greece. In fact, the persistence of some Americans to make sales was so relentless, and their knowledge of the Greek market so small, that they repeatedly had to be cautioned by consular representatives against burdening the Greek mails with catalogues and other advertising matter printed in the English language. Consular officials, alerted to the possibilities of trade, recommended establishing "a live agent" or representative in Greece and a steamship line that would connect the United States with ports in the eastern Mediterranean. Such facilities promised to eliminate expenses normally incurred by the transfer of freight, losses from delays, and profits pocketed by middlemen.[27]

Statistics on the value of goods imported into Greece from the United States are misleading. For instance, in 1897 and 1898 the United States ranked seventh and eighth among importers. But perhaps four or five

8

times as many dollars worth of American watches, sewing machines, machinery, and various other manufactured goods were sold in Greece as products of English, German, French, or Italian origin.[28] Consular officials realized that the Greeks had a preference for the higher-quality American products, and that long and vexatious delays in transportation discouraged them from placing orders with American firms. Freights that could have reached Greece within eighteen to twenty-five days by means of a direct steamship line required from thirty-five to sixty days to arrive by circuitous routes. Only after the United States had built a fleet of ships capable of carrying the products of its own merchants would freight rates decline and foreign shipping companies cease discriminating against American goods.

The sales and credit practices of American business firms also hindered trade. Greek merchants wanted prices quoted as delivered at Greek ports, but the Americans persisted in quoting prices f.o.b. The Americans also had to reconcile themselves to the European practice of granting long-term credits.[29] Establishment of direct communications in 1902 between New York and Piraeus seemed to mark the dawning of a new day in commercial relations. A ten-year contract was signed by the Hamburg-American and the Levant lines, which guaranteed monthly ship departures from Greece that would be increased if business warranted. Each ship, according to the agreement, contracted to haul freight, to carry between four hundred and five hundred passengers in steerage at a cost of forty dollars per person, and to make the trip between Piraeus and New York in eighteen days.[30] However, in this same year the United States consul in Athens sadly related that not a single ship flying the American flag had appeared in Greek waters. He urged Americans to patronize the new company, to ship directly to Greece, and to avoid middlemen charges and the reshipment of goods at foreign ports with the consequent delays and losses. He also pleaded for the building of still more ships.[31]

There were other signs that the interest of the Greeks in the United States had been aroused. In 1885 the United States consul in Athens, De Witt T. Riley, informed the State Department that "there is here at Athens Mr. Demetrius Constantine who keeps what is called the American store. He has spent nine years in America, learning the profession of a merchant."[32] In 1900 Daniel E. McGinley, the consul, acknowledged the publication in Athens of a small volume by C. N.

Maniakes, the acting attorney general of Greece, entitled *America and Greece*. "Mr. Maniakes," wrote McGinley, "is an enthusiastic admirer of the United States, its people and institutions, and on the occasion of the American Thanksgiving Day in 1898, and again in 1899, wrote a number of articles for the Greek press of Athens, Constantinople, Smyrna, Alexandria and Cyprus, eulogizing the United States and its inhabitants." [33]

Greeks had been expressing their affection for the United States ever since the Greek War of Independence and the days of Samuel Gridley Howe. But one of the most dramatic manifestations of this occurred on the eve of the Spanish-American War. Rumors had been circulating that the United States would accept foreign volunteers in its army and navy. As a consequence, the United States consulate in Athens "was besieged day and night, by hundreds of would-be volunteers." [34] The military commandant of the province of Sphakia in Crete wrote the consulate that the Cretans were convinced that the sinking of the *Maine* was going to force the United States into a war with Spain. The commandant, speaking in behalf of the Christian population of Crete, felt that it was his duty to express the appreciation of his people for the many "services and kindnesses" that the Americans had displayed toward the Cretans in their struggles with the Turks, and to state that the Cretans were prepared to cross the ocean and fight alongside "the liberal and noble American soldiers." Sphakia had no fear of being attacked by the Turks, continued the commandant, "so it declares through me its fervent wish to be allowed by the Government which you so worthily represent, to send a small body of volunteers with the Cretan dress, to fight with the soldiers of the noble American nation." [35]

Still another communication received by the consulate was one bearing the signatures of the military chiefs, deputies, and other local leaders of the province of Cydonia. It likened the Cuban struggle with the one the Cretans had been waging for their freedom:

Five hundred warlike men, who have many times faced the brave but barbarous Turks, have offered their services and wish to go under the command of the undersigned and fight together with the brave American soldiers.

We beg of you, dear friend, to inform us if it is possible to go and fight in Cuba and if it is possible for a steamer to pass and take us. [36]

The consul in Athens expressed gratitude for the friendly sentiments that prompted so many Cretans to offer their services to the United States, but he stated that he had no authority to accept volunteers or otherwise act in the matter.[37]

Another strong influence on the future of Greek immigrants in the United States was the domestic politics within Greece in the late nineteenth and early twentieth centuries. Political controversies reached floodtide proportions at a time when immigration was at its peak. The result was a clash between royalist and liberal factions, which was to have violent repercussions on Greek communities throughout the world, especially in the United States. To understand these changes a recapitulation of the main events is in order.

Greece, it should be recalled, belonged to a group of Balkan nations that developed in a different manner and at a later time than the nations of western and central Europe. While the European countries were freeing themselves gradually from the bonds of feudalism, Greece and the other Balkan states remained under the Ottoman yoke. The Greeks, and the other people of southeastern Europe, were blanketed with a singular spiritual and economic medievalism whose influence was felt for years after their physical liberation.

The Turks differed from the ruling monarchical, ecclesiastical, and aristocratic classes of western Europe in that they were a nomadic people, devoid of an urban middle-class culture. The conquered Greek, as a result, failed to develop a thriving, well-integrated, and influential midle class capable of initiating political reforms comparable to those initiated by the middle classes of western and central Europe. The revolution culminating in Greek independence was a product of a movement spawned by Greeks in the lands beyond the Danube and the Pontus and by the military classes that fought an implacable Ottoman foe. The actual uprising within Greece that led to the outbreak of the War of Independence (1821–1829) was engineered by rebels who subsequently assumed positions of leadership in the liberated country.

We have already noted that the population was composed chiefly of farmers who furnished the manpower of the nation in times of peace as well as war. The artisan, maritime, and retail classes were relatively small in numbers; large capitalists, manufacturers, and factory workers were nonexistent. Other segments in Greek society included the "kotsambasides," who had been the unofficial leaders of their compatriots in Turkey; the "phanariotes," who were members of the diplomatic corps; and, finally, the military.

The rise of the revolutionary leaders to political leadership after the War of Independence was inevitable. The middle classes were in no position numerically, financially, or psychologically to assume such a role; and the kotsambasides, and the phanariotes, because of their earlier associations with the Turks, were distrusted. But the military leaders who led the embattled nation to a victory found that the farmers were willing to follow them in peace as they had in war. Finding themselves in control of the government through default, these men were realistic enough to capitalize on the energies, learning, and experiences of the kotsambasides and the phanariotes in the technical administration of the state. This coalition made up the ruling classes of new Greece, and for a time it discharged its duties with some degree of success.

But the deficiencies, inconsistencies, and other shortcomings of this coalition finally came to the surface. The courage and heroism of the revolutionary leaders in the field of battle was no substitute for their lack of wisdom and failure to appreciate the necessity of political organization. At the same time, the ideals and capabilities of the kotsambasides and the phanariotes ran counter to the immediate interests of neo-Hellenism. These men who had been reared in an atmosphere that was Byzantine and patriarchal forgot that Greece was "the daughter of 1821," and the past and the present were never productively blended into the new national life. Capodistria, the president of Greece, proved unable to restrain the leaders who were still followed by the agricultural masses. The political orientation of the nation, as a consequence, was both unfocused and unrealistic.[38]

Greece remained under the tutelage of Europe during the first years of its freedom. Lewis Sargeant has pointed out that it was Europe which furnished the money for government by raising a loan in the name of Greece. It was Europe, which sent Greece a king with this money—"a young lad of seventeen, absolutely ignorant of kingcraft, utterly incompetent to govern, capable of nothing but the indefinite increase of the national debt, and escorted by an army of hungry Bavarians."[39] It was Europe in effect which established a virtually bankrupt country, restricted its boundaries with "a cynical indifference" to nationality, excluded from the government men who under genuine freedom could have become statesmen, saddled it with an army of foreigners, and forced upon it a monarch whom it became necessary to drive out by a new revolution. "Few greater cruelties, if such a word can be applied to political blindness, are recorded in the pages of history." [40]

The opposition, which gradually developed into a ruling oligarchy, managed to curb the powers of King Otho (1833-1862) and to strengthen its position with the adoption of the constitution of 1864. It also collaborated with King George I (1863-1912), obstructed the efforts of Prime Minister Harilaos Trikoupis to reorganize the government along more democratic lines, and sought to impose its will on the people in the name of the national interest. The foreign policy of Greece during these years was provincial and contradictory. It looked forward to the possible regeneration of the Byzantine autocracy without providing for the necessary alliances and international agreements to fulfill these ambitions. The Greco-Turkish War of 1897 was one product of this confused and faltering leadership.

Unfortunately, the incompetence of the ruling clique was exceeded only by the power it wielded. The self-sufficient farmers, who constituted the bulk of the population, were unfamiliar with the techniques of political oragnization, and they were used as a buffer against an emerging antagonistic urban minority. It was from this oligarchy that the administrators of state, the military and diplomatic appointees, and those who controlled the Chamber of Deputies were selected. Prime ministers seldom came from the middle classes, never from the agricultural.

The arbitrary policies of this ruling minority were especially apparent in the apportionment of the tax load of the nation. The rural and urban classes paid from 10 to 40 percent of their net incomes in taxes, the small companies paid 5 percent, and the ruling oligarchy nothing. Estimates of the indirect taxes on the prime necessities of life ranged from 30 to 1400 percent. Demetrios Gounaris, a deputy from Patras, conveniently divided Greek society into two classes: those who, through their honest labors, replenished the public coffers; and those who, through mismanagement, squandered them.

But the position of the oligarchy was not to go unchallenged. The reform program of Trikoupis, the advances in communication systems, public improvements, and the growth of constitutional government gave courage to the urban classes. The increase in the national debt after the war of 1897 disturbed the public calm and brought inquiries into the affairs of government. The middle classes grew in number, until in 1907 they numbered about half a million. Professional groups were forming societies to advance their interests; and the peasants, owing to the currant crisis (1898–1906) and the uprisings of the propertyless classes in Thessaly (1905–1910), were attracting national attention.

The rise in the political status of the middle classes was of crucial importance. Their position was reinforced after 1906 by the increasing value of the drachma, the prosperity of merchant shippers, and the influx of immigrants into the United States. These immigrants were living in a country that was democratically governed and middle-class in orientation, and they sent material assistance to the homeland, corresponded with relatives and friends, made periodic visits to Greece, and otherwise gave nourishment to a movement for a representative government in Greece. This kind of activity was a response to the Progressive movement in America, which at this time was reaching its zenith.[41]

The faltering foreign policy of King George gave the middle classes a real opportunity to come to power. The revolt of the Young Turks in 1908 heaped new insults on Greece and intensified the opposition to the ruling dynasty. The economic boycott of Greece by the Turks and humiliations on the diplomatic front were more than influential patriots could tolerate. Matters came to a head in 1909, when the Military League, comprised of insurgents, demanded a drastic reorganization of the Greek army and a thorough reform of the political system of the nation. The Military League, except for its demand to modernize the army and take the command of it away from the princes, had no specific reform program to offer. Its ability to furnish sustained leadership was in doubt; the experienced political hands knew this, and they waited their time patiently. But these army officers either were warned of their limitations or recognized them—for they cast about in search of a capable leader with a positive program of action.[42]

The dilemma of Greece remained unresolved. Everything seemed out of order. The nation was overrun with incompetent administrators; old party leaders, whose names were linked with one scandal after another, were discredited. The Chamber of Deputies was functioning improperly; the countryside was infested with bandits; the position of

14

the peasants, although improving, was far from ideal. Furthermore, the economic boycott of Greece was increasingly embarrassing, and the Turks were amassing new armies on the borders of Thessaly.

This chaotic state of affairs forced the Military League to turn to Eleutherios Venizelos of Crete, whose statesmanlike qualities and excellence of mind were counted upon to avert complete disaster. The significance of this event can hardly be overemphasized. This was a triumph for the middle classes, Panhellenism, and representative government. It marked a significant breakthrough for western European liberalism, which soon was to lock itself in mortal battle with the royalist forces of Greece. Finally, it had a tremendous impact on Greek communities in the United States, and in some cases these communities responded by influencing the politics of the mother country. This was the beginning of a new era, one of hope, triumph, reverses, and disaster.

The attitude of Venizelos toward the Greek monarchy was a burning issue. The members of the Military League and a few politicians assumed that Venizelos was antidynastic, despite his pronouncements that he would work to strengthen the authority and prestige of the Crown. The merchant classes who had wide contacts with the outside world recognized that the royal family, because of its many European ties, was of some value; and they also knew that Venizelos was not antidynastic. They had reason to believe that Venizelos would build on the old foundations, unless he had something better to substitute. But the intemperate militarists interpreted the rise of Venizelos to mean a complete break with the past.

The attachment of the merchants to the liberal movement headed by Venizelos, with its relation to the territorial aspirations and prosperity of Greece, is of fundamental importance. Many members of the merchant classes came from families with fortunes whose foundations were laid in "unredeemed Greece" or in Greek communities in foreign countries. These men "looked upon the Kingdom of Greece not as a mother country from whom they derived their origin and to which they owed their allegiance, but as the means of accomplishing the redemption, the regeneration, the union of Hellas. In Venizelos the merchants saw an embodiment of their ideals, as well as a man whose methods they understood. His achievements in Crete inspired confidence. He came to Athens, in the opinion of many, as "a wise, courageous, energetic, magnetic" leader, a representative of unredeemed Greece who would never sacrifice *Graecia irredenta* to his own fortunes. He was aided by the merchants to the very end in his struggles against the church, the court, and the old-line politicians.[43]

When Venizelos came to power, the Panhellenic movement was at its peak. This age-old crusade to unite all Greeks under one flag was frequently referred to as "the Great Idea." Its lofty aim was to revive the glories of ancient Greece and the Byzantine Empire by building a new Greek empire with Constantinople as its seat, embracing the Balkans, Asia Minor, and the whole Near East: "For the Greeks, Constantinople is the 'Polis,' 'Urbs,' 'The City,' which from Constantine the Great to Constantine XI [A.D. 323–1453], uniting the Hellenic cities and provinces into a nation, permitted them alone to survive among all nations of Antiquity. It is the true historical capital of Hellenism." [44]

According to the census of 1907, the population of Greece was about 2.6 million, or considerably less than half the combined population of Holland and Belgium. Various estimates placed the number of Greeks living outside of Greece considerably in excess of those living within the country. Some claimed that the number residing in Europe and Asia Minor was less than 4.5 million. Ripley, Chisholm, and others estimated that there were more than 8 million. The *Statesman's Yearbook* placed the total number of Greeks at 8 million and distributed them as follows: Greece, 2.2 million; European Turkey, 4 million; Turkey in Asia Minor, 2 million; insular Greece, 650,000.[45]

The patriotic Greek, whether living in Greece or not, believed in extending the influence of his country as far as Constantinople and over the islands inhabited by people speaking the same language, worshiping in the same faith, and adhering to customs and traditions normally regarded as Greek. He was determined to incorporate large portions of the region north of Greece proper, to reclaim islands held by Turkish garrisons, and to annex at least a portion of the seacoast in Asia Minor where much of the commerce, wealth, and influence was under the control of Greeks. "Everyone who has travelled in Greece," wrote Bickford-Smith in 1893, "is familiar with the prophecy, an old one, revived with great earnestness by the Greek priesthood that Greece would win back Constantinople when she should have a Constantine for King and a Sophia for Queen. The marriage of the Crown

Prince with Princess Sophia, sister of the Emperor of Germany, has made it probable that in the course of time the necessary conditions will be fulfilled." [46]

That Panhellenism was a living aspiration was everywhere in evidence. The Society for the Formation of a National Fleet was created for the purpose of collecting money from Greeks all over the world to help build a modern Greek navy. Survivors of the Greek revolution and a number of prominent Greek personalities lent their names to this effort. In 1878 the society contributed a large share of the money for the purchase of the *Admiral Miaoules;* in 1900 the Treasury of the National Fleet was founded in the Ministry of the Marine.[47]

The Panhellenic movement made more headway in 1892, when the Hellenismos Society was founded to further the Great Idea. In 1895 N. Kazazes, a Greek from unredeemed Greece and former rector of the University of Athens, became its head and the most vigorous exponent of its principles. The official aim of the society was to foster the just rights of Hellenism. Translated into plain English, this meant driving out the Turks and reviving the national spirit, which was portrayed by the emblem of the society—a phoenix rising from its ashes. Kazazes went on frequent European missions to persuade his listeners that Macedonia was predominantly Greek and hence should become a part of Greece. At the turn of the twentieth century, the Hellenismos Society claimed more than 10,000 members, who were scattered in various parts of the world, including distant Australia. The membership fees were small, but the Greeks contributed with their customary generosity. Branches were formed in the provinces and beyond the frontiers of Greece; its agents were spreading the doctrine of Hellenism throughout the Ottoman Empire.[48]

There was ample proof that the Great Idea had assumed activist if not uncontrollable proportions. During 1906 Greeks bands renewed their guerrilla campaigns against the hated Bulgars. Greeks were still exulting over the marathon race that was won by a fellow countryman in the Olympic Games of 1896, but other, more sober, critics recalled that this victory was followed by a wave of exultation that helped to precipitate the unfortunate war with Turkey in 1897. In 1906 John B. Jackson of the American legation in Athens wrote that "if a Greek should win the race next month, there is certain to be a great revival of the national 'Great Idea' with ensuing increase in the number and activity of Greek bands in Macedonia, and uncertain results. If a foreigner should win the Marathon race I should not be surprised to see him mobbed before he could get out of the Station in which the finish took place." [49]

However, a few weeks later Jackson informed the State Department that the Greeks seemed to be losing heart in Macedonia. He reported that a speech by King Edward of Great Britain in Athens on April 16, 1906, expressed a desire for the peaceful development of Greece. This, combined with the defeat of the Greek runners in the marathon of the Olympic Games in 1906, the first Greek having come in fifth, "occasioned a kind of national stupefaction and depression . . . which may be of lasting benefit. Had a Greek won this race, the general impression is that the national self-confidence would have been increased to such an extent that serious trouble in Macedonia would have been probable." [50]

Equally pertinent to these Panhellenic aspirations was the Greek Orthodox Church. Before the formation of the Kingdom of Greece, the religious leadership of the Greeks was vested in the Ecumenical Patriarch of Constantinople, who was considered the political head of the unredeemed Greeks in the Ottoman Empire. However, in 1833 the jurisdiction of the Patriarchate was renounced when the king was declared the supreme head of the national church; this break was formally recognized in 1850. Meanwhile, the ecclesiastical affairs of Greece were placed under the control of the Ministry of Education; the church government was vested in the Holy Synod, a council of five clerics presided over by the Metropolitan of Athens. [51]

The Greek constitution of 1864 guaranteed religious toleration for all faiths and did not impose civil disabilities on religious grounds. However, a man who was not a member of the recognized religion of the overwhelming majority was likely to be viewed as an alien. The Roman Catholics, who comprised the only significant Christian minority in the country, numbered about fifteen thousand. The Jews, found chiefly on the island of Corfu, constituted still another minority of five thousand. The Moslems lived mostly in Thessaly, which became a part of Greece in 1881.

National sentiment rather than religious conviction was a prime factor in adherence to the Greek Orthodox Church. In Macedonia the portion of the population that recognized the Patriarch of Constantinople was considered Greek, while another group adhering to the

Bulgarian Excharcate was branded schismatic, even though both were in agreement on matters of doctrine. During the Greek revolution, the Roman Catholics on the island of Syros sided with the Turks, while the Moslems of Crete naturally opposed the Greeks.[52] On various occasions the Greek Orthodox Church was as much concerned with political affairs as it was with the spiritual needs of the people. The church gave ample evidence of this during the War of Independence, the Balkan Wars of 1912–1913, the royalist-liberal imbroglio before and after World War One, the disastrous Asia Minor campaign of 1922, and the Nazi occupation of the 1940s. The Greeks, although a religious people, were not fanatical, except over political and religious issues that affected national aims.[53]

Religious festivals played an important part in the life of the nation. Despite the frequent interruptions of work and business, and the criticisms of the more practical-minded Greeks, religious holidays became fixtures in the lives of the people; they were especially observed by the peasant population. Religion, at least on the surface, had a firm hold on the nation.[54] Simultaneously, the passion for politics was insatiable. The desire to be informed on topics relating to the welfare of the country made the Greek one of the most avid newspaper readers in the world. He combed the various papers for scraps of information or arguments to attack or defend government measures. Waiters and domestic servants had their favorite newspapers and discoursed fluently on politics. Animated political discussions were a commonplace in the cafés of the country.[55]

The Greek, in many respects the most individualistic as well as the most nationalistic of Europeans, found it difficult to accept the leadership of others. Popular sayings reinforced and echoed these assumptions. One held that the Greek had the license of the poet and used it whether he had the poetry or not. When two Greeks met, it was said, three ideas emerged. In the navy every Greek was an admiral, in the army every Greek a general; when four Greek soldiers met, five generals emerged.[56]

This ardent individualism, coupled with a mercilessly independent mind, had an undisciplining effect. During the Greco-Turkish War of 1897, a young naval officer telegraphed the Minister of War criticizing his admiral, and the young officer was applauded by several newspapers for his actions. In the political arena a party was held together by the influence of the leader, instead of by organizational rules; defections were common, and as a rule each deputy in the Greek Chamber made his terms with the party leader. Greece was one country on the Balkan peninsula in which the government could not obtain a majority at the polls through pressure.[57]

The individualism of the Greeks was reinforced by the absence of class distinctions; in fact, those assuming aristocratic airs were ridiculed. One man hailed another not by his family name or official title, but by his first name. The lower ranks of the Greek army contained men as well-educated and as well-off financially as the commanding officers. Still these men called their officers "Aleko" or "Georgi" or "Jonni"; and "they met their officers on equal terms off parade." [58]

This, then, was the Hellas of the immigrant—a land of poverty, restlessness, unstable rule, and passionate Panhellenic aspirations. But it also was a country that seemed to be on the threshhold of a national awakening. Agriculture of a primitive and impoverished kind formed the basis of the economy, and large cities were few and far between. But the middle classes were increasing in numbers and influence, and commercial ties were being forged slowly but surely with the United States. Greece's peasants, about to become immigrants, were imbued with the same pioneering spirit that carried the people of other nations to America. They were nurtured in a climate of individualism that was to blend admirably with the native American variety.

PREPARING FOR

THE UNKNOWN

L ITTLE is known about the Greeks who left for America before the
immigrant tides of the late nineteenth and early twentieth centuries. This is partly because of the sporadic character of their
migration, but perhaps to a greater extent because of the concern the
Greek had for winning their freedom from the Turks and the problems
arising from their liberation. What is more, these migrating compatriots formed an unimportant minority which was expected to return
to its homeland. Chroniclers were more interested in the fortunes and
fates of their countrymen—the "free" and the "enslaved"—in the nations
of Europe, Asia Minor, and Africa than in those who had strayed off
to the distant shores of the New World.

The growth in immigration changed all of this. Nationalist writers,
anxious to disprove the notion that the Greeks were an unworthy
people, began chronicling with considerable pride the names and feats
of compatriots who reached the New World during the period of
colonization. At least two accepted the legend that Christopher Columbus was a Greek. Foremost was Seraphim G. Canoutas, a Greek-
American journalist, lawyer, and pamphleteer.[1] A second, a former
member of the Greek diplomatic corps, wrote: "Christopher . . . the
discoverer of America and named Columbus, is not an Italian, but a
Byzantine nobleman, whose real name was Dispatos." [2] Others recount-
ed the exploits of Juan de Fuca, whose name was given to the straits
separating Vancouver from the state of Washington, and the Greeks
who reached early St. Augustine and New Smyrna in Florida.[3] During

1957 representatives of the Greek Orthodox churches of seven Virginia cities planned a pilgrimage to Jamestown in honor of the memory of John Paradise, a member of the faith who lived in Williamsburg in 1787.[4]

None of this alters the fact that immigration did not begin until the nineteenth century. At least three phases stand out clearly in this movement of the Greeks. The first, minor in scope, stemmed from the activities of American missionaries of the 1820s and 1830s; the second revolved around the representatives of Greek-owned commercial firms stationed in various cities of the country during the mid-nineteenth century; and the third had its roots among the Spartans of the late 1870s and 1880s who, for all practical purposes, were "the Greek Pilgrim Fathers."

The work of the American Board of Commissioners for Foreign Missions in encouraging Greek youths to come to the United States was a short-lived humanitarian effort. Its missionaries visited Greece and other parts of the Near East during the War of Independence and immediately thereafter to sponsor American educational methods, win converts to the Congregationalist faith, and inaugurate reforms in Greek ecclesiastical organization. A novel part of the program consisted of persuading promising Greek boys to go to the United States for their formal education. Upon the completion of their studies, they were to return home and contribute to the moral regeneration of their native land.

Perhaps the best known of this group was Alexander Paspati, who came to the United States in 1824. Following his graduation from Amherst College, he returned to Europe where he studied medicine and later established a practice in Constantinople. He retired in 1879 and lived in Athens until his death in 1891. Paspati acquired a reputation as "an almost unrivalled authority on Byzantine history and archeology and an eminent glossologist. Master of sixteen languages, his literary production were mostly given to the world in English, French and Greek." In Constantinople and Athens he became identified with many philanthropic societies and institutions. Paspati "with five other scholars, planted in 1861 the Philologikos Hellinikos Syllogos [Hellenic Philological Society] which . . . reckon[ed] its members by the thousands and . . . planted nearly two hundred schools in the Ottoman

Empire and by its literary contributions . . . acquired world-wide fame." [5]

From an American standpoint, the most important of the young arrivals under the American Foreign Missions plan was Evangelos Evangelides Sophocles, who reached the United States in 1828 from Thessaly. He later became a professor of Greek at Harvard University and a distinguished man of letters. [6]

Commerce also played a part in attracting a few Greeks to the United States. After 1850 commercial firms bearing Greek names established offices in New York, New Orleans, Savannah, and other American cities, where they conducted import-export business. A number of these firms were interested in the cotton trade. One of the most important was that of the Ralli Brothers, whose manager in New York City was Demetrios Botassi, a native of the island of Spetsoi; for many years he was the consul general of Greece and its official representative at the funeral of Abraham Lincoln. Directories of New Orleans show that the head of the branch office there was Nicholas M. Benachi, also a Greek consular agent. [7]

Other prominent nineteenth-century arrivals included John Zachos, a physician, educator, and later curator of Cooper's Union in New York City; Michael Anagnos, the son-in-law of Samuel Gridley Howe and for many years the head of the Perkins Institution for the Blind in Boston; and Lucas Miller, who was brought to this country at a young age and later became a congressman from Wisconsin. [8]

Even though these Greeks were unrepresentative of the rank-and-file immigrants of this period, their status became a source of comfort to their sorely distressed compatriots of a later age, when the menacing hand of American antiforeignism began to be felt. But for all practical purposes, the pace for immigration to this country was set by the Greeks of the Peloponnesus, the islands, the mainland, and the Ottoman-dominated areas who came during the late nineteenth and early twentieth centuries—not by those educated under the auspices of American missionaries or representing Greek mercantile firms. It is with these people, the poor but energetic who arrived in large numbers, that this study is primarily concerned.

The Spartans were the first Greeks in the modern era to give signs of emigrating, even though in the beginning it was for brief periods of time and only to neighboring lands.[9] Heavier emigration from Sparta began during the 1870s and reached a peak between 1890 and 1910, when an estimated three fourths of the male population between the ages of eighteen and thirty-five departed for the United States and, to a lesser extent, for Russia, Egypt, Turkey, and central Africa. Many Spartans viewed this exodus with alarm and believed that their province had been cursed by God.[10]

Triggering the initial flow of immigrants from Sparta was an obscure young man named Christos Tsakonas, born in 1848 in the village of Zoumpaina. This "Columbus of Sparta" displayed the attributes of many of his contemporaries who were to emigrate. After completing two years in the village grammar school, Tsakonas set out for Piraeus in quest of a job. Making little headway there, he left for Alexandria, Egypt, where, after encountering similar experiences he decided in 1873 to leave for America. At this time it was unusual for a man of peasant stock to seek his fortune in the New World. Tsakonas apparently found the United States to his liking. After a brief visit in Greece in 1875, he left again for America, but this time in the company of five compatriots. This group seems to have constituted the nucleus for the succeeding waves of immigrants from Sparta.[11]

Indications at this early date are that the Greek emigration followed the cycle of prosperity and depression. Once the depression of the 1870s gave signs of lifting, the number of emigrating Spartans increased. The first Greek newspaper to take note of these departures was *Sphaira* (The Globe) of Piraeus. Apparently it was unaware of the earlier emigrants, for it wrote that immigration to the United States began in 1877, when twelve or fifteen men left from the village of Tsintsinon. Early in April 1882 about seventy more left from the same general area for Piraeus, where they attired themselves in "European clothes" and boarded an Italian ship bound for Italy; there they took passage for the United States. Still others left Piraeus on a French vessel headed for Marseilles and Le Havre, from these ports beginning the transatlantic voyage. Most of these immigrants were married men aged twenty-five or more. Contrary to popular belief, the district from which these people emigrated was by no means the poorest, even though it was agricultural; the greatest need of the villagers was for liquid capital, which could be had at rates ranging from 15 percent upward. Most immigrants were believed to have had at least five hundred francs in their possession at the time of departure. But few borrowed money for the trip; those in need of funds sold their lands or their animals.

Sphaira noted that for the first time since ancient days the Greeks were leaving for distant lands in large numbers. It suspected that these numbers would increase, but it hesitated to predict what dimensions the exodus would assume.[12] Speculation was rife regarding the future of these people. Most were in agreement that these men left for America to better their economic status, which was understandable and commendable, but there was less agreement over the probability of their return to Greece. Although the married men were expected to become reunited with their families, the future of the young unmarried men was unpredictable. *Sphaira* eventually became disturbed enough over the future of Greece to urge the authorities to find means of bettering "the conditions of life" before the outflow became unmanageable. The opportunities were there. Greece needed the strong arms of her sons to build railroads, dig the Corinth Canal, drain Lake Copais, and cultivate the lands of Thessaly. Improving conditions in the rural communities was the most urgent problem facing the nation.[13]

A similar plea for government action came from *Stoa,* an Athenian newspaper; it compared the departures from Sparta with those from other European countries. Assistance to the classes that composed the major part of the immigrant traffic was the only means of checking the exodus. *Stoa* also suggested that, if the Greek government found it advisable to aid the provinces in northern Greece, it was equally obligated to aid those in other sections of the country.[14] *Aeon,* another Athenian newspaper, adopted a more optimistic outlook. It suspected that these people were taking temporary leave to accumulate capital, improve their status in life, and then return to Greece. Within these limits this was beneficial to the country and the immigrants; for the repatriates would bring back with them "spiritual, ethical, and material capital" to invest in local enterprise.[15]

Distress signals emanated from other quarters as well. From Demetrios Botassi, the Greek consul general in New York City, came warnings to prospective immigrants not to come to the United States. He conceded that every individual had the right to better his position, especially if this opportunity was denied him in his native land. But the Greek immigrants had to keep various things in mind. The United States was a nation of many nationalities, not one. The Irish, Germans,

Swedes, Norwegians, Italians, and Swiss had been in the country for many years, and they had philanthropic and mutual-aid societies to aid them in times of need. Furthermore, these people were equipped to work in the United States, and the language posed no serious problem for them. Many had planned to establish themselves in the heart of agricultural America before they embarked, and they brought their own farm tools and implements with them. The Irish spoke English, while the Germans were numerous enough to converse in their native tongue.

The position of the Greeks, on the other hand, was somewhat less favorable. They often arrived without any clear-cut objectives in mind and without special training, trusting that they would find gold in the streets or that God would provide in one way or another. Many came to the United States during the early 1880s thinking that it was the California of 1846. Greece needed her sons more than the United States did, said Botassi; it was regrettable that so many of them were emigrating. He pleaded with them to take heed of his warnings, to circularize them in Laconia and those portions of the Peloponnesus from which emigration was increasing.[16]

The United States consular officials in Athens were also starting to take notice of the emigrant outflow. Early in the spring of 1885, De Witt Riley wrote: "Today I had a pressing application from ten Spartans, who are going to Chicago, but I refused to visa [sic] and gave them instead a simple note in English stating where they wished to go and asking persons to direct them. Please order me in this matter. In the present depressed condition of trade and industry here the immigration to the United States may increase." [17] William H. Moffett, the American consul in Athens, after obtaining instructions in 1886 to probe into "the extent and character of the emigration," reported that "There is no emigration to the United States or any other country." Moffett added that the Greeks in the United States were chiefly seamen, who had no special desire to establish a home there. "A few agricultural laborers, vaguely reckoned from forty to one hundred or so, have gone from this district within the past four or five years."

Moffett was of the opinion that the conditions under which the peasants and laborers lived in Greece were hardly conducive to emigration. The country was thinly inhabited and undeveloped, and congenial employment could be found: "the Greek . . . knows nothing of the desires and wants which in other countries lead men to give up home and friends in anticipation of better things to be gained in a New World." [18] But during the spring of 1887, Moffett sent a worried communication to the State Department that emphasized the swelling tide of emigration. Those joining this exodus were neither agriculturalists nor mechanics, but young men who "have been told of a great demand in America for Greek laborers, that money is to be had in abundance, and that the American Government will furnish transportation."

Meanwhile a special report on immigration was prepared by A. C. McDowell, a consular agent in Piraeus, who had an intimate knowledge of the Greeks, spoke their language, and was personally popular with them. His findings confirmed virtually everything the Greek press had been saying. The immigrants upon being questioned about why they wanted to go to the United States invariably gave the same answer: the lack of opportunity at home. Usually they left their wives and children behind to plant corn and other crops while they went in quest of employment. McDowell thought that some sort of supervision should be exercised over these people. At this time it was possible for an immigrant to enter the United States without a visa. Hence he seldom, if ever, went to the American consular office in Athens. However, he had to have a passport to leave his own country; so McDowell believed that these immigrants shoud be compelled to present themselves at the American consulate for visas. This would enable the authorities to examine the backgrounds of the immigrants and to determine whether they had means of support or relatives and friends that they could fall back on in the United States. Copies of such information could then be forwarded to the State Department and the collector at the port of entry.[19]

During the spring of 1888, Moffett, again acting on the advice of McDowell, sought action from the State Department on the issuing of visas. He reasoned that a visa would save prospective immigrants from disappointments and losses and aid the authorities in carrying out the intentions of their legislation.[20] Moffett's suggestion met with a negative response. Official correspondence within the State Department made it clear that no action could be taken along the proposed lines.[21]

Letters now began to appear in the Greek press, presenting a discouraging portrayal of immigrant life. It is difficult to state whether these accounts were spontaneous or whether they were part of an official campaign to throttle immigration. Suffice it to say the letters were written—their tone was one of despair, and they were strikingly similar in content.

A letter from an immigrant in Cincinnati, dated March 21, 1888, lamented the departure of so many of his compatriots for the United States. These men were the heads of households and in a position to do as they saw fit; hence he had no intention of advising them. However, if one of his brothers were among those planning to emigrate, the columns of *Sphaira* were asked to plead with him to remain in Greece. "I am unable to help him here. I do not have a shop. I go about the streets selling candy and about August 1 plan to return. We are unable to support ourselves here owing to the masses of people . . . America once was but today it has spoiled." [22]

Another letter from Hailey, Idaho, dated May 17, 1888, painted an even drearier picture of life in that ranching community. The letter, written in poor Greek, said that over a six-year period, from 1882 to 1888, only two men returned to Greece. Both were married and their wives begged them to come home with each letter they received. The rest were bachelors and remained in the United States because they were unable to obtain the return passage. They were uneducated herders who did not know English. Raising the necessary funds was thus very difficult, and there were no well-established Greeks in the far west to come to their assistance. This same regretful immigrant also told of the experiences he and his friends encountered in coming to the United States. In traveling from Piraeus to Marseilles, he and his companions were in a jovial frame of mind; but once they started across the ocean they were overcome with melancholy and began crying and screaming. When they reached New York, they were victimized by gypsies. He was of the opinion that the presidential election that fall (1888) was going to have some bearing on their future. He anticipated that if Cleveland were defeated for re-election, serious restrictions would be invoked against street vendors of Greek, Italian, and other nationalities. "All day we sell candy with a basket tied around our neck, and they call us in American, English, German, dago, that is, beggars, and so many other names that we do not understand. If we did understand them we would be going to jail every day." [23]

Sphaira now began to show mounting evidences of alarm. More and more the newspaper began to emphasize the perils of expatriation.

Those who emigrated had no real knowledge of the language; they knew only how to read and write; and they were in real danger of losing their affection for Greece. More unfortunate was the learning of a foreign language, the developing of sympathies and an understanding for a strange country, marrying women of other nationalities, and, according to the very latest reports, of becoming citizens of the United States.[24]

In essence, this was the pattern of immigration during the 1870s and 1880s, when most of the immigrants left from Sparta. The quest for opportunities, rather than the desire to escape from military service or class discrimination, was the prime motivating force. This marked the close of the initial stage of immigration.

After 1890 Greeks began departing from all parts of the country, but the outflow was the greatest from the Peloponnesus. Emigration from the province of Arcadia began in earnest between the years 1892 and 1894 and increased steadily until it exceeded that from Sparta.[25] It affected the provinces of Argolidos and Corinthias, Achaea and Elidos, Messinia, Attica and Boetia, Phthiotidos and Phokidos, Aetolia and Akarnanias. Immigrants left from the regions around Larissa, Trikkala, and Artis; from the islands of the Cyclades,[26] the eastern Aegean, the Dodecanese, Crete, Cephalonia, and Zakynthos.[27]

The exodus of the 1890s was precipitated by the decline in the price of currants, the principal export crop. Changes in the commercial policies of France and Russia, the big currant customers, dealt a severe blow to the economy. France formerly purchased between 60,000 and 70,000 tons, or about half the entire Greek crop, to supplement its own harvest that had been destroyed by the phylloxera. But when the French vineyards were replanted and their yield increased, France enacted a protective tariff that literally legislated Greek currants out of the market. Russia adopted a comparable policy.[28] The sharp decline in the demand for currants brought disaster to the Greeks who, in the meantime, had destroyed their olive trees to profit from the active currant trade. Restoring the olive trees was a time-consuming process, for many years are required before they reach a productive stage.[29] The response of many Greeks to this depressed state of affairs was emigration.

After the Spanish-American War, emigration reached much higher levels. Even though most left for the United States, sizable numbers departed for South America, especially Brazil, and southern Africa.

This exodus continued after work became plentiful in Greece and wages had risen as high as 100 percent in many places. Labor shortages had become acute even in the depressed currant districts, thus making it necessary for workers to be imported from the neighboring islands and Turkey. These unusual signs of prosperity were due to the actual shortages of help rather than to any increase in the available amount of work.[30]

If the depressed state of the currant trade was the immediate cause of the immigrant wave of the 1890s, the unhealthy state of the Greek economy and the natural disasters that struck Greece over these years were the underlying reasons for the continuing outflow. Need, that painless synonym for hunger, was threatening to expatriate many to that unknown land beyond the Atlantic: "Deprivation and the sole hope for bread is the black flag that directs them afar." [31]

Many felt compelled to leave because an indifferent government squandered public funds on party parasites and ignored the welfare of the peasants.[32] An immigrant in Philadelphia complained that his countrymen paid "taxes on taxes without seeing any improvement" or protection of their lives and property. The Greeks were in danger of being "sold to the Europeans," wrote one inflammed compatriot, unless the politicians who were making a trade of politics were stopped.[33] Even Cretans as late as 1912, fourteen years after they had gained their independence from the Turks, complained that they found themselves in the same depressed state they had known under Ottoman rule. The government had done nothing to find means of transporting farm products to market; until this was done, the agricultural resources of Crete would remain in a paralyzed state.[34]

The Repouli Report of 1912, perhaps the best-known government report on immigration, confirmed the persistence of this demoralized state of affairs. This document, with a deep sense of regret, observed that farmers were advising their sons to abandon agriculture and prepare for one of the more respectable professions. The belief was that the largest segment of the population, the one that bore the brunt of the economic burden, was shunted, despised, and avoided as though it were a loathsome disease.[35]

The inability to borrow money to cultivate the land and purchase supplies was still another basic cause of the exodus. Prosperous citizens were unwilling to lend money without collateral; many cultivators in their hour of financial need were forced into the grasping clutches of the usurers, who lent them money at rates starting at 20 percent. If one added the produce, such as butter, cheese, and wool, that the debtors frequently were asked to deliver to their creditors, interest rates reached levels of 70 and 80 percent.[36] Emigration, judging from contemporary accounts, was responsible for bringing down interest rates in some districts. This is difficult to believe, but in Sparta and other districts in which the exodus was greatest, rates had declined to as low as 4 and 6 percent.[37] The correspondent of *Skrip,* an Athens newspaper, observed that thrifty Arcadians were sending money home in such abundance that private persons lent money at lower rates than the banks.[38]

Military service as a causal factor has been ignored. The Greeks have always been known as a patriotic people who readily spring to the defense of their country. But the unmistakable fact is that some emigrated to avoid military duty. Local and national authorities quickly recognized this; and it became the subject of debate in the Chamber of Deputies.[39] A conference of demarchs in Thebes reported that many were emigrating precisely for this reason. The nomarch of Attica and Boetia advised the Ministry of Foreign Affairs that in many parts of his nomarchia about two thirds of those of military age had emigrated.[40] In the province of Corinth the exodus was so great that priests and schoolteachers were the only adult males left.[41]

Patras for a time became the principal port of embarkation and was the scene of ceaseless immigrant activities. Here many purchased their tickets with money acquired from the sale of currants or other crops. The hotels of the city were crowded, the various offices swamped, the warehouses filled, and the streets lined with immigrants, as ship after ship departed.[42] Finally, in September 1912 the aroused government authorities banned the immigration of all subjects between the ages of fourteen and forty-one until further instructions were issued.[43] Then stern measures were adopted as a means of bolstering the defenses of the country that was about to go to war.[44]

The dowry system, the curse of many a Greek family, also forced some females to emigrate. According to custom, the bride was obliged to provide her betrothed with a dowry; hence father and brothers labored hard to secure money and provide dowries for their daughters and sisters. A duty-bound brother seldom married until after his sisters had obtained husbands. The opportunity of earning and saving money in the United States persuaded many fathers and sons to emigrate, in the hope of meeting these domestic obligations. Women seeking husbands and unable to provide dowries also emigrated, hoping to find suitable mates. The surprising thing is that more women did not take advantage of the matrimonial frontier that emigration opened up. Perhaps this was too venturesome an undertaking for the usually restricted women to attempt on their own, or perhaps they believed that most men would return to Greece and thus spare them the need of going to America.[45]

Representatives of relatives and friends in the United States also helped swell the immigration tide. Once an immigrant reached his destination, he wrote his parents immediately; within a few more days he followed up this initial letter with a small sum of money borrowed without any reference to work or working conditions. This had a chain reaction. It persuaded others to leave for America in the hope that they, too, would obtain ready money to forward to their families.[46] Encouraging letters written after a person obtained a job produced a similar effect. As one immigrant informed his former employer in Greece: "Here the people work much and regularly, and rest only on Sunday, but we fare well. This day that I am writing you is Sunday; I took my bath, had my milk, and I will pass the day satisfactorily. Where did I know life with such order? . . . If you wish, afentiko [master], you can do well to come, and I will send you the cost of the ticket."[47]

A growing belief on the part of some that Greece had been condemned to a life of misery, disaster, and insecurity created such an atmosphere of despair that it caused many to want to leave. These sentiments developed despite the fact that the Greeks, as a rule, loved their country with a devotion and passion that many Americans found difficult to understand. But as one correspondent had earlier observed: "within the twelve months past, or little more, she has rounded a full cycle of calamity—earthquake well-nigh destroying Zante, a constitutional crisis, national insolvency or the next thing to it. And now, in the very throes of her economic distress, she is prostrated by a fresh visitation from Heaven [an earthquake] which is without a parallel in her modern history. . . . It has shaken the solid core of Greece from the Isthmus to Thermopylae, as well as the great island of Euboea—rocked it like a ship upon an angry sea."[48]

Steamship company agents who canvassed the rural districts in search of prospective passengers also aided the movement.[49] For a time the most popular, if not the sole, form of advertising in the village coffeehouse and grocery store was a picture of a transoceanic liner or some other notice regarding the United States.[50] How effective this was in persuading peasants to emigrate is unknown. But advertising must have broken down the resistance of many and "softened them up" for agents that thrived on the immigrant traffic.

Passage to the United States was financed by various means. Many, no doubt, did as the early Spartans did: they sold parcels of land and farm animals or used up small savings husbanded through the years. Many others solicited loans from relatives or moneylenders. Creditors lent money regularly, as long as they were reassured that the borrowers would pay their debts. The first letters of the immigrants portraying the United States as a land of promise often contained the cost of passage.[51]

Greeks emigrating from the Ottoman Empire, especially before 1912, usually left for political rather than economic reasons. This was particularly true of those leaving Macedonia, Epirus, the island of Mytilene (Lesbos), and the Dodecanese. Prior to 1903 the word immigration was rarely heard in Macedonia; peace and a relative degree of prosperity prevailed. But after 1903 this good fortune was shattered by the rivalries among the Bulgars, Turks, and Greeks. In some communities tensions had reached the point where peasants were afraid to go into the fields to farm. Then, beginning in 1908, the new Turkish constitution was adopted which required Greeks in Macedonia and other parts of the Ottoman Empire to render military service. These developments persuaded many to seek homes elsewhere.[52]

Immigration from Mytilene achieved sizable dimensions beginning in 1908 and increased until 1912, when the island was liberated from the Turks. The causes of immigration during these early years were also political and psychological, for the people owned their own plots of land, farmed them at a profit, and were their own masters. But the promulgation of the Turkish constitution of 1908 drew protests from the Greek residents of the island against service with the Turkish forces. Loyalty to Greece made it impossible for a Greek to think of yielding to Turkish demands. Youths of nineteen and twenty years of age, as a result, managed to raise funds in one way or another and worked

33

their way to Piraeus, where they boarded ships for the United States.

Later however, especially during 1914–1915, economic hardship and poor administration compelled many people to emigrate from Mytilene. The effect that the influx of refugees had on depreciating the wages of the island and the decline in olive production encouraged the emigration not only of individuals, but of entire families.[53]

The growth in immigrant traffic in these years was creating concern for American consular officials. In 1903 John B. Jackson of the American legation in Athens inquired of the Ministry of Foreign Affairs if the Greek government would consent to the stationing of American health officers at Piraeus and Patras for the inspection of immigrants. They believed that these were the only two ports worth considering for such purposes, for very few of the immigrants left directly for the United States; most departed via Naples, Marseilles, or some other European port.[54] The response to the American request was pretty much what one would have expected. The Greek minister stated that the laws of Greece forbade the establishment of any foreign health officers in the country, but he suggested that the kind of medical examination sought could be performed by Greek officials, if their certificates of examination were acceptable to the American authorities.[55]

The tedious delays, misrepresentations, and wide assortment of questioning and examinations to which the immigrants were subjected prior to their departure frequently have been overlooked. Early in the spring of 1906, a large number of people left Megara, Thebes, and Corinth for Boston, New York, St. Louis, and other American cities. Most of them passed through the inspection authorities without any difficulty; on May 12 about a hundred reached Hamburg aboard the steamer *Patricia* where, after being searched and questioned, they were forced to return to Greece. Those immigrants said that they did not know why they were turned back while others from the same towns, whose health and finances were not better than theirs, were permitted to proceed. They claimed no knowledge of any work contract that might have been advanced by some agent in their behalf.[56] (A later inquiry revealed that these men were returned to Greece under the provisions of the alien-contract labor law; and that otherwise there was no objection to the emigration of Greeks to any part of the United States.[57])

During this same year, another three hundred immigrants carried by one of the ships of the Austro-Americana Line were turned back; when these passengers reached Trieste, they mobbed the office of the steamship agency and created a near riot. This episode cost the company about fifteen thousand dollars and forced it to adopt a more selective policy in selling tickets. Thereafter, passage was to be booked only after an immigrant had a physical examination; permission to board ship was to be given only after he underwent three physical examinations.[58] Incidents of this kind caused waves of excitement to break out in Greek political circles, and infuriated prospective immigrants stormed the ticket-selling agencies.[59]

Piraeus, at first the major point of embarkation for immigrants from Greece and other Balkan countries, ranked next to Naples as the principal Mediterranean port. Vessels of the Fabre and Prince lines arrived there regularly.[60] Early in October 1907, the much-publicized *Moraitis,* the ship built especially for the Greek immigrant and cargo traffic, reached Piraeus from Smyrna. From there it proceeded to Kalamata and Patras and then set sail for the United States.[61] Patras became the other principal port of direct embarkation, and for a time the most important. To Patras came the ships of the Austro-Americana Line, the Prince Line, the Fabre Line, the Messageries Maritimes—which carried immigrants via Marseilles—and the Greek Transoceanic Steamship Line, the owner of the *Moraitis.* The immigrants leaving from this Peloponnesian port city came largely from the districts of Sparta, Messinia, and Arcadia, the fountainheads of immigration, and in lesser numbers from northern Greece, the Greek islands, Epirus, and Macedonia.

During 1907 a total of 21,207 immigrants left from Patras, Kalamata, and Zante for New York. This sum does not include those who left from Piraeus and the large numbers going by way of Italy, France, and England.[62] In due time the embarkation of non-Greeks from Patras also increased. This became evident during 1909, when a large number of Turks, Jews, Armenians, Albanians, and Macedonians left from this city. The facilities provided by the feeding lines from the Levant promised to make Patras the ranking immigration port of the country.[63]

As late as 1910 Greece had still failed to provide for the medical inspection of immigrants or crew members sailing from her ports. Consequently, this responsibility was assumed by the steamship companies and the consular officers of the United States. At one point the Austro-

Americana Line had forty ticket agencies and subagencies scattered in various parts of Greece where preliminary medical inspections were made. The procedure appears to have been this. A prospective immigrant, accepted by the examining physician at the time he applied for passage, was required to make a deposit on the purchase of a steamship ticket. In return he received a certificate showing that a reservation had been made for him on a steamer. On reaching Patras the immigrant was re-examined by the chief physician of the company and, if found physically acceptable for the second time, was allowed to complete the purchase of his ticket. On the day of departure all immigrants were brought to the office of the company and examined for a third time. As each immigrant passed his physical examination, he was stamped on the wrist with one of seven stamps, the identity of which remained unknown until the morning of the sailing. When the stamp to be used was determined, the ship captain was notified of this in a sealed envelope just before the final inspection started. No one was permitted to board the ship unless his ticket and wrist bore the proper identification mark. Such precautions were taken to prevent the substitution of one person for another, a practice well known at ports of embarkation. The method used in Patras made substitution difficult, since the ink on the stamp was indelible and lasted for some time.

At Patras the immigrants also were required to sign statements about criminal records, the amount of money they had in their possession, and other matters about which they would be examined in the United States. Baggage brought to Patras was placed in a warehouse where it, too, was inspected and thoroughly disinfected before being transferred to the ship. The United States consul or his assistant held the key to the warehouse until the disinfecting process had been completed, and then he issued stamped labels for each piece of baggage. Occasionally ships that would sail from Patras first called at the port of Zante, where the inspection of baggage was supervised by a consular official; but the examination of the passengers was withheld until the ship reached Patras. At Kalamata, where a few immigrants boarded the ship, the inspection of baggage and the medical examination was entrusted to the French consular agent.

The medical examination at the port of Piraeus appears to have been more perfunctory. Representatives of one company stated that about 3 percent of their applicants were refused passage. The explanation for this seemingly small percentage of rejections was that a large number of those sailing from Piraeus came from Thessaly and Macedonia, where the people were presumed to be healthier, and that inspection at this port was preliminary to the more thorough inspection given at Patras.[64]

That the Greek government and influential individuals should have expressed themselves on the subject of immigration is to be expected. For one thing, there was the serious matter of military service. Greece felt harassed by her historic enemy Turkey, which naturally objected to all Panhellenic aspirations that were to be gained at Ottoman expense. Still, the Greek government rarely went beyond expressions of verbal opposition to immigration. It made plain its desire that Greek men remain at home to respond to the call of duty, but beyond this point it would not move. Those deterred from emigrating were probably discouraged by the unfavorable reports circulated by those who were in the United States or had returned; the lack of official sanction served only as a mild restraint. Greek officials preferred their people to believe that those who emigrated would be laboring under great disadvantages, restricted to trifling occupations and handicapped by not knowing the language. "Bear in mind," wrote one first-hand observer, "that the majority go about in the streets with handcarts and sell fruit, and are greatly persecuted by the street urchins, and . . . policemen who do not permit them to stand in any one spot." [65]

However, as a means of keeping departures to a minimum and protecting the immigrants, the Ministry of the Interior and police authorities throughout Greece were required to enforce an order permitting the sale of passage only by well-known steamship companies having permanent offices in Greece, or by agents having written permission from the proper authorities. The Ministry of the Interior also threatened to introduce a measure in the Chamber of Deputies that would prevent the immigration of everyone under sixteen years of age and all others who had not discharged their military obligations.[66]

The Greek press devoted considerable space to the subject. During the spring of 1903, articles appeared in the newspapers of Athens based on the reports of Botassi, the Greek consul general in New York, dealing with the hardships of the immigrants and the proposed tightening of the immigration laws of the United States. Even though little attention was given to this particular charge by the Chamber of Deputies, the authorities continued the policy of discouraging immigration. Their line of argument was that many of the immigrants would fall into the hands of unscrupulous agents and that the military services and labor of these men were needed by Greece.[67] Those most anxious to discourage immigration welcomed the opportunity to magnify the hardships associated with it.[68]

The Greek government kept no records of immigration; permission was not needed to leave the country, although the authorities retained the right to demand military service of the immigrant after he returned from his residence abroad. The only real measure adopted by 1903 to check the outflow was one requiring the Minister of the Interior to instruct the nomarchs that they must acquaint all prospective immigrants of the dangers and privations they would face in a foreign country.[69] However, as a further means of protecting immigrants, the authorities took steps to curb the misleading claims of some of the steamship companies. The Minister of the Interior addressed circulars to prefects throughout the country stating that one line, Gastaldi and Company, was unable to assure immigrants a landing in the United States, as its advertisements inferred. The prefects were instructed to give wide publicity to these circulars in their districts and advise those planning to emigrate not to patronize the steamers represented by Gastaldi.[70]

The legal representative of Gastaldi and Company protested this action and asked for a retraction of both the charges and the order. "We never pretended," wrote D. J. Tsatsos, the attorney, "to guarantee the reception of the emigrants to the United States of America, we only guarantee the return of the passage money in case the emigrants are not allowed . . . to land in the United States." The note branding Gastaldi a "swindling concern," he continued, was the result of an erroneous translation of the advertisement. Tsatsos asked for a fresh note, the recall of the old one, and a redress of the injury.[71]

Meanwhile, the United States was beginning to adopt regulatory measures (they appear mild by present-day standards). Starting on September 1, 1907, a ticket agent or broker was required to post a bond of $15,000 or be excluded from the business. Another proposal was to confine the sale of tickets to accredited representatives of steamship companies.[72] But by 1906 the Greek government, despite the patriotic utterances made by various representatives, had still done nothing to curb immigration. If anything, it displayed a less stringent attitude.

At first the Chamber of Deputies seemed to concern itself with preventing emigration, but now it was seeking the best means of protecting the immigrants from those who preyed on them. This shift in position was best illustrated by Minister of Foreign Affairs Skouses, who after seeing advertisements telling about associations being formed to attract immigrants to the southern states, inquired if it were possible to direct these people to communities that wanted them. This was based on the assumption that they would meet the entrance requirements and not violate the contract labor laws of the country.[73]

The most plausible explanation of this change in attitude is an economic one. The emigrating Greek was considerate of his family, as money remittances indicated—between four and five million dollars were received by families in Greece during 1905 from relatives in the United States. For this reason the Greek government hesitated to choke off the flow of dollars by curbing emigration. The most it was willing to do at this stage was to make military service obligatory at the age of nineteen instead of twenty-one and deny the privilege of emigration to anyone who had failed to discharge his military obligations.[74]

A commission appointed by the Chamber of Deputies in 1906 to study emigration reported that it was increasing at an enormous rate. But it also noted that the districts furnishing the largest number of immigrants were among the most prosperous, owing to the money coming back into the country. Thus the commission asked that the government protect this source of national wealth by supervising the steamship agencies and establishing an office of sanitary inspection.[75] The recommendations of the commission seemed inadequate, however, and many discerning observers expected that the government would sponsor a bill of its own to regulate the immigrant traffic. They believed that such a measure would forbid the emigration of minors under the age of sixteen, unless they were accompanied by their parents or had special permission to leave the country; deny permission for military reasons to those between the ages of eighteen and twenty-one, but permit the emigration of those over twenty-one if they had passports and paid a tax of ten drachmas; restrict the sale of tickets and the embarkation of immigrants to Piraeus, where strict controls could be imposed; require all ticket agents to furnish a bond, be Greek subjects, and conduct their advertising in a manner prescribed by the Greek government; and grant all immigrants a contract, the terms of which would be fixed by royal decree, which would enable them to take legal action against their ticket agents in the event of a breach.[76] According to *Sphaira,* a bill was introduced in the Chamber of Deputies.[77]

The reactions to this proposal were quick in coming. The British legation in Athens planned to make representations against the measure on the grounds that the provision requiring agents to be Greek subjects was a treaty violation. John Jackson of the American legation, asked if he would join the British representations, replied that he had no instructions to do so and that the question was of no practical importance since there were no American agents in Greece. Furthermore, Jackson added that he looked with favor on any legislation that tended to restrict emigration to the United States.[78]

But hard times came along to provide a natural check to the outflow of immigrants. When news of the 1907 financial crisis in the United States reached Greece, emigration literally stopped. The reports of the Greek consuls in New York and other American cities describing the sufferings of the unemployed circulated in the rural areas with a notice from the Minister of the Interior, urging the prefects in the provinces to use all possible means of checking emigration. Even more effective was the drop in money remittances. The building of churches and homes with money sent from the United States came to a standstill. A half-constructed church near Tripolis, awaiting further remittances, stood as a temporary monument to the panic of 1907.[79]

The crisis furnished more ammunition for the foes of emigration. One or two Athenian newspapers carried regular dispatches from the Greek colonies in the United States, citing the unemployment in railroad construction, the steel mills, tanneries, and various other industries. Letters presumably written by the immigrants themselves and published in the local press confirmed these stories of hardship. One communication bearing a St. Louis dateline, addressed to the Greek government, recited in formal fashion how the immigrants in that city expected to find wealth and found poverty instead. The tone of the letter and the literariness of its language suggest that it was inspired by some government agent. Immigrants in the United States also wrote of their misfortunes to parents, relatives, and friends, who in turn repeated them to all who were willing to listen.[80] A Piraeus story, carried in the *Atlantis* of New York, told of one hundred and nineteen "unfortunates," the majority of them unemployed, returning on the *Themistocles.* Among them were people suffering from advanced stages of tuberculosis.[81]

Testimonials of the unemployed, the destitute, and frustrated individuals returning from the United States were seized upon as means of discouraging those who still wanted to emigrate.[82]

But once the financial crisis of 1907 gave signs of coming to an end, the immigrant exodus to the United States resumed its former course. This was inevitable, for the outlook of the immigrant is always one of undying optimism. Others may try their luck as immigrants and be repulsed by a tide of economic misfortune. But a prospective immigrant as a rule wants to have his own chance. The newspaper *Peloponnesos* of Patras recognized the futility of issuing repeated warnings against leaving Greece and did what it considered the only practical thing in the circumstances. It deplored the fact that immigrants boarded the ships "bare-footed, attired in rags, and wretched in appearance." It pleaded with them to dress properly before landing in America, where simple, clean, and respectable dress was considered a sign of good breeding. It was urgent that one's first appearance not create the impression that a man was uncivilized.[83]

As the outflow continued, passionate appeals against it were made by the disenchanted who had returned from America and by the emissaries of the Greek government. This time reasons of health were argued. Too many young men "with redness of their lips and brightness in their eyes" were being urged on by a "damnable fate" to gain a few hundred gold pounds, only to lose their vigor, robustness, the sparkle in their eyes, and the power in their arms. One father was warned that if he permitted his son to emigrate, he might never see him again. If by chance his son did return to Greece, the father would never recognize him: "His face will be different. There will be no color in it. His strength would be impaired and he would be condemned to death by tuberculosis." [84] An enterprising merchant in Crete, who capitalized on the prime fear of the immigrant—that of losing his health or meeting accidental death in a strange land—promised his customers that America would come to them if they used his fertilizers: "You better the quality and quantity of your product and increase the wealth and benefit more than you would by emigrating to America. Instead of going to the United States, we bring the United States to Crete." [85]

The proposals for curbing emigration continued. A rather novel one asked for a systematic eradication of the malaria-infested swamps of

Greece, which would help to invigorate the people, check emigration, and persuade many ambitious immigrants to return from the United States. Another sought the deposit of three thousand drachmas by all underaged youths prior to their departure, as a means of preventing the evasion of military duty. Still another called for a twenty-drachma tax on each passenger ticket and the use of these proceeds for the establishment of a tubercular sanitorium on some uninhabited Greek island. Another asked for the medical inspection of all people returning from the United States and the commitment of those suffering from tuberculosis to a government hospital for treatment.[86]

As might be expected, the trend of events forced the Greek government to use a firm hand. The outbreak of the First Balkan War in 1912 brought a halt to the emigration of all able-bodied males between the ages of eighteen and forty-one. Simultaneously, different categories were established that specified which age groups were free to emigrate and which were not.[87] But once peace was restored in 1913, emigration resumed its course. It appeared certain that emigration would increase once the soldiers, among them many Greek-Americans, were discharged from military service.[88]

Piraeus regained its pre-eminence as a port of embarkation after the Balkan Wars. During 1914 and 1915, a total of 10,969 and 17,804, respectively, departed from the greater Athens area. The gains at Piraeus, however, were offset by losses at other ports.[89] The next major outflow of immigrants occurred right after the First World War. Available statistical evidence indicates that of the 26,386 departing from Piraeus in 1920, some 20,946 left in steerage, 4,632 as second-class, and 808 as first-class passengers. Two thirds of the passengers that year were immigrants from the Greek mainland, the islands of Rhodes and Cyprus, Asia Minor, Albania, Rumania, and Armenia. A large percentage of the second-class passengers were United States citizens of Greek origin who had visited friends and relatives in Greece. The first-class passengers were chiefly relief workers, salesmen, and traders, which indicated the growing interest of the United States in the Balkan countries and the Near East.[90]

Despite all that was said against immigration, the immediate benefits from it were seen in all directions. There was scarcely a village in Greece that did not furnish living proof of what America had to offer. This made an effective reply to many of the charges of injuries, unemployment, hostility, and hardships associated with emigration and life in America.[91] The Greek immigrants gained the reputation quite early of sending more money home per capita than the immigrants of any other nationality. During the early years, the Minister of the Interior estimated that about eight million dollars was remitted; some three fourths of this came from the United States. In some districts the cancellation of mortgages was one of the most important results of immigration.[92]

Much of what the foes of immigration said proved true, but, as we have seen, the determination of the immigrants to find opportunities or easy riches urged them on. Official pronouncements against emigration, the exhortation of compatriots, family members, and friends, could not stem the immigrant tide. The appeal of America, despite the hardships endured in the process of reaching it, was overpowering. The urge to emigrate proved as irresistible after World War I as it had before.

3

EARLY YEARS

E VEN though Greeks came to America early in the country's history, the records of the Commissioner General of Immigration make no reference to them until 1824. During 1848 exactly one Greek arrived, with 91,061 Irishmen and 51,593 Germans; in 1850 two more Greeks reached the United States.[1] After 1880 the picture began to change. More than a hundred arrived during 1882 and, in 1891, more than a thousand for the first time. From then on, the influx increased steadily, until the number of arrivals achieved the dimensions of a movement.

The exact number of Greeks reaching the United States probably will never be known. The Greek government failed to keep a record of departures, especially during the early years, and those it kept later are incomplete. Furthermore, the Greek definition of a Greek is more inclusive than the American—which complicates matters.[2] Nationality, according to the Greeks, is eternal; it cannot be transferred or obliterated. If a man's father is a Greek, he also is a Greek, regardless of where he was born or now lives. The United States, on the other hand, accepts the country of a man's birth as the criterion of nationality. Whereas the American authorities considered persons born of Greek parents in Bulgaria and Turkey as Bulgars and Turks, the Greeks claimed them as Greeks. Nevertheless, compared with that from other European nations, immigration from Greece was small, as the facing table indicates.[3]

Approximately 500,000 Greeks had reached the United States prior to the Second World War.[4] This total includes those arriving from non-Greek territories who called themselves Greeks and wanted to be counted as such. If one considers only those arriving from the Kingdom of Greece, the number would be nearer 430,000.[5] But both these figures, in the opinion of some—especially the ardent nationalists—are far too conservative; they claim that from 600,000 to a million arrived.[6]

Decade	European immigration	Greek immigration
1820–1830	106,508	20
1831–1840	495,688	49
1841–1850	1,597,581	14
1851–1860	2,452,660	3
1861–1870	2,065,272	7
1871–1880	2,272,329	210
1881–1890	4,739,266	2,308
1891–1900	3,582,815	15,979
1901–1910	8,213,409	167,519
	25,528,410	186,204

Even though Greek estimates and American immigration sources differ regarding the numbers, there is general agreement that most of the arrivals were males. About 95 percent of those arriving from 1899 through 1910 were males. In this respect the Greeks were outnumbered only by the East Indians, Turks, Chinese, Bulgarians, Serbians, and Montenegrins. This comparatively high male ratio continued throughout the peak years of immigration.[7]

The immigrant pattern appears to have become quickly systematized. The tendency at first was for the newcomer to head for destinations in all corners of the United States, even faraway Alaska, which gained the reputation of being "a frozen cemetery." But in time the Greeks started forming colonies in the cities of the New England states; New York City; the metropolitan areas of the upper Mississippi Valley, especially Chicago; and, in the far west, San Francisco. Upon reaching this country, the immigrant normally went to the home of a relative or friend; for it was here that he received help in finding lodgings and employment. The chances are that he also had been delegated to deliver some message or token of remembrance from a relative or friend in Greece.[8]

The immigrant, we have seen, was a man of the soil. Though devoid of technical skills and a knowledge of the English language, however, he found it preferable to live in the cities, where he could find ready employment, receive wages at the end of the week, be in the company of his compatriots, and enjoy the social life that would be denied him in the more isolated areas. He brought with him the sturdy qualities of the peasant—perseverance and a willingness to work. These were assets to a person from a land of pastoral quietude, who suddenly was thrust into a seething atmosphere of youth, vigor, and optimism. The tempo of urban life was quick and demanding. He soon discovered that there was "a God named Business" which was to cast its spell over him and many of his compatriots. For the Greek, work, to be in business, to succeed, were moral duties.[9] But as an immigrant he knew that he had to start as a dishwasher, a laborer, a railroad worker, a bootblack, or a street peddler.[10]

Inability to speak English became a major problem, for it was difficult for the immigrant to find his way around the city, seek employment, and receive advice. English did not bear the slightest resemblance to Greek, he soon learned, except for the scientific and academic terms that were unrelated to his everyday needs. This language hurdle was overcome by the more energetic who attended classes in English for the foreign-born. Others learned English slowly by more leisurely methods; still others never learned it, especially the older women. Those men who stuck together had to rely on the few words they learned from each other and their co-workers in factories, mines, and shops. This language barrier explains why in the beginning so many Greeks had to confine themselves to menial tasks.[11]

The earliest arrivals were forced into the petty street trades and sold cigars, flowers, sweets, and other articles; or else they kept lodging and boarding houses or small taverns for seamen.[12] They had no choice but to content themselves with trifling occupations. Most were honest working people. They lived on next to nothing in order to save and send money to their relatives, which they, in turn, would lend out at interest. A sum of two thousand dollars was a fortune; lending this out at 20 to 30 percent interest per year brought in enough to make a living.[13] The resourcefulness of the Greeks as street vendors was confirmed at the start. A Washington correspondent in 1904 wrote: "Not everyone knows that ninety-nine of every hundred of itinerant vendors is a Greek and that every Georgios or Demetrios among them, boy or man . . . is a small capitalist, and carries anywhere from fifty to several hundred dollars concealed about his person." [14]

Their entry into the textile mills of Massachusetts was hardly a pre-

46

meditated affair. During the depression of 1893, peddlers in the Lowell area, finding that their business had faded away, got jobs in the textile mills that paid them not more than four dollars a week; this was less than the wage received by the other operatives. They stood up rather well under the rough work in the picker rooms and dye houses. Seeing that they were reliable workers, the overseers asked them if they knew others who needed employment. Naturally they sought out their compatriots, and in due course Greek immigrants filed their way into the textile mills of New England.[15]

Accurate statistical data on the occupations of the early immigrants is unavailable. In 1907 Demetrios Botassi, the consul general in New York City, estimated that, of the 150,000 Greeks in the United States, between 30,000 and 40,000 were working as laborers in factories and railroad construction gangs. Others were employed as bootblacks, waiters, and clerks in stores that catered to the immigrant trade. Some had become apprentices in various trades; the more ambitious already had become shopkeepers. An undisclosed number owned and managed their own grocery stores, coffeehouses, barbershops, clothing stores, bakeries, carpentry shops, saloons, cleaning and pressing shops, laundries, print shops, meat markets, and brokerage firms. The legal and medical professions were also represented, but in relatively smaller numbers.[16]

Many of the immigrants graduated from the street-vending trades into more fixed employment. Often it was planned that way, for they saved money and looked forward to the day when they would own their own businesses. In other instances, as in Chicago, the vendors were driven out of their itinerant occupations by municipal legislation; in still other cases, as in Lowell, they were forced out by the depression of 1893. Establishing their own businesses gave them a great deal of satisfaction and confidence that they could scale the economic ladder in a country teeming with representatives of other nationality groups. They discovered that they could compete with the Americans, the Germans, or the Irish as confectioners, florists, and hotelkeepers; gradually they abandoned the street-peddling trades to the Italians, the Syrians, and the late-arriving immigrants of other nationalities.[17]

But it is to the common laborer, the unskilled worker, and the performer of menial tasks—not to the small shopkeeper establishing himself in some community—that we must turn for a full knowledge of immigrant hardships. Some of the first occupations lent themselves to easy exploitation.

One of the most notorious forms of exploitation was inflicted by the "padrone system," which was known to the Italians, the Austrians, the Bulgarians, the Turks, the Macedonians, and the Mexicans, as well as to the Greeks. The padrone was the person in authority, the "boss" to whom the immigrant appealed for a job, help in meeting some language problem, or arbitration in a dispute. The decision of the padrone often was law among the immigrants. During the early years, ignorance of the language and of the ways of the country compelled the bewildered newcomer to rely on his employer, who frequently was a labor contractor as well as a compatriot and who had a limited knowledge of English and working conditions. Sometimes this contractor-compatriot provided him with room, board, and an agreed wage, with the understanding that anything he, as an employee, received in excess of this amount belonged to him, the padrone.[18]

Among the Greeks, the padrone system assumed a slightly different form; it is said to have been in operation in almost every city having a population of ten thousand or more. It was confined to the shoeshining trade, to the flower, fruit, and vegetable peddlers in the larger cities, and to the railroad construction workers in the western states.[19] As employed by the Greeks, the padrone system appears to have been a modernized version of the indentured-servant system of the late seventeenth and early eighteenth centuries. The extent to which it existed among the Greeks is difficult to gauge. In all likelihood, the scope of its operations was exaggerated by the antialien press. The system, however, did exist, especially during the earlier years, when the immigrants were less informed about the United States and before aroused Greek community leaders and immigration authorities sought to bring an end to the vicious practice.

The movement to import and employ youth began during the mid-1890s, after the Greeks had started to invade the shoeshining business. For the most part, this field had been confined to Italians and Negroes who had booths, chairs, or stands outside or within short distances of popular saloons, hotels, restaurants, and amusement places. Shoeshining furnished an ideal entering wedge for an immigrant. The requirements were a good pair of arms, a strong back, minimum knowledge of the English language, and a willingness to work at all hours, including Saturdays, Sundays, and holidays. Fixtures, chairs, and supplies were available on credit; hence it became relatively easy for a man with small savings to start his own shop and even branch out, if he had the necessary help.[20]

The Greeks not only did this in increasing numbers, but they began to establish well-equipped, even ornate, shops in the high-rent areas. The more enterprising among them found it profitable to think in terms of organizing chains of shoeshine parlors. A certain Smerlis, operating chiefly in New Jersey, is credited with having had more than a hundred establishments under his control at one time. His success naturally encouraged others to enter the field, and within time every city had a score of shoeshine parlors operated by Greeks.

During 1903 Smerlis and a few others conceived the idea of organizing the shoeshining business into a trust. This, of course, was in line with the trend of the times. If the steel, oil, banking, railroad, tobacco, farm implement, and other interests were combining into larger units, why should not the shoeshine-parlor owners of the nation follow suit? The future of this proposed trust, they believed, was contingent upon the ability of the padrones to control the labor supply. It was the wholesale invasion of this business that attracted a flood of new youth into the country and took the Greeks from the cotton mills of New England to the shoeshine parlors of America.[21]

Finding employees, at least in the beginning, was easy. An enterprising shopowner or padrone wrote letters to relatives and acquaintances in Greece, telling them of his good fortune and the opportunities he was in a position to offer ambitious boys who wanted to come to America. He indicated a willingness to arrange for the transportation of those who came and assured them that adequate provisions would be made when they arrived. Greece offered a fertile field for such recruiting. Parents, weighed down by heavy responsibilities, often were more concerned with the earning power of their children than in educating them. The earning power of the family generally was confined to the males. As a result, parents seldom passed up an opportunity of placing their sons in gainful employment.

Such conditions forced boys in Greece to become apprentices to grocers, restaurant keepers, peddlers, and bootblacks, whom they served for periods of from three months to a year before they started earning salaries of ten to twenty dollars a year. This compensation was considered satisfactory, for in many instances it was enough to defray the expenses of an entire peasant family. These boys worked long hours and sometimes were treated harshly, but they exhibited qualities of patience and endurance. A peasant, offered the opportunity of placing his son in a job in the United States at relatively high wages, considered himself fortunate indeed. He knew little about the rights of employees and the laws of this country. His major interest was his family and its economic security. So he instructed his son, well-trained and obedient, to remain on the job and to follow the advice of his presumed benefactor.[22]

The procedure in transporting the youth to the United States was essentially this. Passage money often was advanced by a relative or friend of the employer, with the understanding that the boy was to remain in his employment for one year. At the same time, a mortgage was placed on the property of the boy's father, showing that he had received in cash an amount equivalent to one year's wages. In fact, all the boy obtained was a steamship ticket to the United States and twelve to fifteen dollars in cash, known as "show money," which he had to declare to immigration officers at the port of entry. The mortgages, negotiated by relatives of the padrone, were drawn up so shrewdly that it was difficult to secure evidence linking them to the padrones. Attorneys in the United States and Greece had instructed them in ways to avoid leaving traces that might implicate them.[23]

The ambitious padrone exploited all the relationships he could in recruiting boys. He instructed his relatives in Greece to visit villages and become godfathers at christenings and best men at weddings for the sole purpose of contracting family alliances. Or a padrone might make a visit to Greece every two or three years and personally exploit all the possible opportunities for becoming a godfather and a best man.[24] Since many of the padrones came from the Tripolis district in Arcadia, a sizable percentage, if not most, of the bootblacks were "Tripolitsiotas." Many had been bootblacks at home. As the demand increased, recruits were drafted from other parts of Greece and even Turkey; the system spread. From the ranks of the bootblacks rose new shoeshine bosses who imposed the rules of the system on their employees.[25]

Cities near the port of entry were purposely avoided as destinations for boys; for the padrone knew that, the closer to the port of entry the destination of the youthful alien was, the more likely he would be detained and subjected to a rigid examination. In such cases, the relatives or friends of the boy were expected to appear before the immigration authorities. On the other hand, the farther the destination from the port of entry, the less rigid the examination was likely to be. The likelihood of compelling a relative or friend to present himself for questioning also was remote.

Chicago was especially desirable as a place for the boy to work, for almost every province of Greece was represented there. In case a boy had no previous commitment, he could head for some saloon or restaurant on South Halstead Street, where he was bound to meet a relative or friends of his father. In fact any unattached boy would find employment in a shoeshine parlor within a week. In some cases, boys were instructed to report to a saloon keeper in Chicago or some other western city, to be directed from there to their final destinations. Some padrones operating in the east and south ordered their boys to head directly for Chicago. This method expedited their admission, camouflaged the tracks of the padrones, and made detection difficult.

The legal action that could be taken against the padrones was at first limited. Under the provisions of the acts of 1885 and 1903, the only punishment for importing labor was a fine of a thousand dollars. Since the resources of many padrones were difficult to reach, the securing of judgments against them for violating the law was useless. However, by the act of February 20, 1907, it became possible to institute criminal proceedings against any padrone for conspiring to commit an offense against the United States. The immigration authorities, under the provisions of this law, succeeded in convicting a number of padrones, whose convictions were given wide publicity in Greece. This discouraged some of the importers of youthful labor and made others extremely cautious. Many decided to import their labor indirectly through relatives in a manner that placed them beyond the reach of the criminal statutes. Some chose to pay attractive wages to boys brought into the country by their parents.

After the act of 1907 was passed, it became common for fathers of boys destined to become a part of the padrone system to accompany their sons, as a means of ensuring entry into the country. But the "pseudo-father" soon made his appearance. He usually was a distant relative or close acquaintance who brought the boy into the United States, either for a fee or as a favor for the father or the padrone for whom he was to work. In such cases, the boy assumed the name of the pseudo-father and posed as his son. Since the examining inspectors often were harassed by crowds and long interviews, they were unable to put the boys through thorough examinations and generally allowed them to enter.[26]

During their first and second years in the United States, the boys were profuse in expressing gratitude to their employers for giving them a chance to earn their bread and some money. Some helpless boys actually believed that, if it had not been for their employers, they would have starved to death; their ignorance of the language and working conditions made it impossible for them to get jobs elsewhere. Some padrones convinced the boys that justice seldom was meted out, that it could only be purchased. Officers of the law were grafters, intent upon extorting money, rather than in performing their duties. For this reason the boys had to depend on their boss for protection and employment.[27]

The workday of these shoeshine boys began early in the morning and continued well into the evening, seven days a week. The shops opened between 6 and 6:30, which meant that the boys had to awake between 5 and 5:30. Those living some distance from their place of work rose as early as 4:30 A.M. They labored until 9 and 10 o'clock at night, and later on Saturdays and Sundays. In the smaller cities the workday was shorter. After the doors were closed, the boys generally mopped the floor, cleaned the marble stand and fixtures, and gathered up the shoeshining rags to take home, wash, dry, and have in readiness for the following day.

The eating schedules of the boys were a curious composite of co-operative living, expediency, and bad judgment. When ten or more lived together, one usually served as the cook. Part of the meal was prepared in the morning and taken to the shop for the noon ration, with the rest left at the house for supper. Almost every shoeshine parlor had a rear room that, though hardly inviting to eye or nose, it served the purpose of a dining room. Every boy took his turn in dis-appearing behind the partition to eat his apportioned share of the food. If a customer arrived, the boy had to postpone his meal. In many instances, especially during the early days when many thought in terms of saving all they could and returning to Greece at the earliest opportunity, the meal consisted of bread and olives or cheese.[28]

During the earlier years, some of the padrones sought to maintain rigid control over the boys. They tried to prevent them from saying too much to inquisitive compatriots coming into the shops, from learning too much English, and from obtaining information about better jobs. In some cases the boys were instructed to refuse to answer questions regarding their ages and work; some of the more ruthless padrones even devised a system of espionage. They tried to impose a censorship on the incoming and outgoing mail as a means of preventing complaints from reaching the outside. The padrones, in fact, were anxious to maintain the good will of the parents and wanted to keep reports of maltreatment from circulating in Greece; for such accounts could circulate from village to village easily and tend to blacklist the employer.[29]

From our present perspective, it may be difficult to believe that such conditions of servitude existed in this country, and even harder to understand why the boys submitted to it. In the first place, this system affected a small percentage of the immigrant population; in the second, those caught in the net of the padrone probably did not view it with the same degree of horror as contemporary Americans would. This was a passing phase in the life of an immigrant youth; the benefits to be gained from coming to America would greatly offset the harsh experiences. Those returning to Greece would have some money for their labors. As for those who remained in the United States, this was part of the price they had to pay for emigrating from a retarded agricultural economy to one that was urban, industrial, commercial. This, in their view, was the entrance into something better, and so they were willing to work for a padrone a part of the time.

Many, perhaps the majority, were able to read and write some Greek, for they came from areas in which compulsory education was beginning to be enforced and where, we have noted, it was customary for boys to be apprenticed out to storekeepers, café owners, and bootblacks. But because they arrived in this country at a very early age and worked from morning until night, the boys had no time to attend either night or day classes. Temporarily they remained ignorant of the language and conditions in the United States.[30] Within three or four years, however, as a result of contacts with customers, these boys awakened to the possibilities of education. They started writing to the Greek newspapers for English primers, and in due time they learned to read and write, often with the assistance of kindhearted patrons. This marked the first step in their emancipation. Other boys, less ambitious, remained condemned to the lot of "bootblack slaves." They lacked good advice or else were unwilling to take it; they suffered mentally, physically, and morally.[31] A statement drafted by Dr. N. Salopoulos, the Greek consul general in Chicago, and a number of other local physicians left little doubt about the gravity of the situation.[32]

The profits from shoeshining with this kind of labor supply were very rewarding to the owners. The padrone paid wages ranging from $80 to $250 per year, the average being $110 to $180. The boys often were obliged to turn their tips over to the padrones by depositing them in the cash register after the customers departed or in a separate container to which the padrone held the key. In a small city and a poor location, the tips could exceed fifty cents a day; in a larger city with a favorable location, they could be considerably more. This meant that the padrone, with the gratuities rightfully belonging to his employees, could pay the boy's annual wage and still retain a substantial amount for himself. Estimates placed the income of the padrone at $100 to $200 a year for each boy he employed, in some cases $300 to $500.[33]

Conscience-stricken compatriots who read about the padrones or *somatoemporoi* ("somatic merchants," or flesh peddlers), and the subsequent accusations leveled at their innocent and law-abiding countrymen, were quick to react. The Foreign Ministry of Greece acknowledged the existence of this illicit traffic, but doubted that it was as widespread as represented by the American press.[34] The Greek government also took action to eliminate the evil by exhorting the people not to become participants in this dishonorable trade. One consul in Lowell, Massachusetts, suspected of being an accomplice, was removed from office.[35]

Atlantis, the most influental Greek-language newspaper of the day, also waged a vigorous campaign against the padrones. It carried accounts from the American press telling its readers of the "flesh emporiums" being conducted by some of their dishonorable countrymen and urged them to use their influence to curb it. Articles and editorials filled the pages of the *Atlantis* throughout 1908 and 1909, condemning the actions of those who were heaping disgrace on the Greek nationality.[36] The crusade against the exploitation of youthful workers continued even after the padrone system had passed its peak. One of these latter-day crusaders was Christos Damascus, the editor of *Saloniki* in Chicago, and he had all the earmarks of a muckraker. As late as 1916, Damascus claimed that he had received letters from bootblacks in Kansas, Minnesota, Montana, Tennessee, and Oklahoma, confirming the charges of inhumane treatment and long working hours; he promised to continue his campaign until these boys were liberated from this form of slavery. "There are certain rich bosses who fill their teeth with gold," he complained, "that they may eat more easily with the profits earned . . . by the sweat and blood of young Greek boys. The Greeks were ready to fight the Turks and Bulgars for enslaving and degrading their countrymen, still they had no scruples about enslaving their own youth in the shoeshining parlors of the United States."[37]

Agitation from these and other quarters caused many concerned shopowners to discuss the problems of their trade with their youthful employees. They recognized the legitimacy of such complaints in the past, but they doubted whether they were now as serious and as widespread. They also pointed to the peculiar nature of their business by emphasizing that they were busy on Saturdays and Sundays, when people did most of their shopping or patronized popular places of amusement, motion-picture houses, and restaurants. It became apparent that some kind of organization or grievance committee had to be established in order to protect the interests of both.[38] By 1916 the Employers' Protective Association had been formed in Chicago; shortly thereafter a comparable organization made its appearance in New York City. Information about the scope and life span of these organizations is unavailable. In Chicago, however, an informal agreement appears to have been reached which provided, at least on paper, better working conditions and higher wages for the boys. The shops were to remain open from 7 A.M. to 8 P.M.; the boys were to be paid ten, instead of five, cents for each shine on Saturdays and Sundays, receive a few hours of free time on Sunday afternoons, sick benefits, hospitalization, and opportunities to attend evening classes.[39] As a further indication of the growing unrest, from Springfield, Massachusetts, where *Saloniki* claimed it had a large circulation and influence, came news that a hundred bootblacks had gone on strike and forced their employers to furnish them with better working conditions.[40]

Despite somewhat better conditions, however, the importance of the

Greeks in the shoeshining business declined, and it was not merely because the padrones had fallen from power. An expanding economy and the immigrants' increasing knowledge of the language and customs of the country opened up opportunities that promised steadier wages, shorter hours, and more satisfying work for shopowners and employees alike. The more prosperous shopkeepers often invested their earnings in enterprises considered more dignified and socially acceptable. The small operators, on the other hand, found it difficult to survive in an era of rising labor costs, especially after immigrant bars had made it impossible for them to obtain labor so cheaply. Furthermore, there was a drop in the demand for shoeshine establishments. The coming of the automobile meant that fewer people walked—hence, the need for cleaning dusty and dirty shoes diminished. The growing popularity of the oxford shoes, as against the full high shoe formerly worn by so many, also made it sure that fewer people would patronize the shoeshine stands of America. In short, some of the ill fortunes of the shoe-manufacturing industry were also visited upon the shoeshiners of the nation.

Similarly subjected to the evils of the padrone system were the first railroad construction workers, though the results were less appalling. These laborers had been persuaded by agents to emigrate with the promise of obtaining permanent work at wages ranging from $1.75 to $2.00 a day. As in the case of the bootblacks, these laborers often were relatives of the padrone, who was better known as the "interpreter" or "foreman." Anyone emigrating under such conditions was subjected to the standard ritual. In exchange for the promise of a job, he was provided with passage and the "show money" he was to declare at the port of entry. In return, the labor agent extracted a mortgage on the property of the prospective immigrant or of a close relative, for a sum equal to three and four times the cost of transportation, with verbal assurances that after three or four months of labor the immigrant would have enough to discharge his obligation.

The exploitation to which such a laborer was subjected was endless and unbelievable. Sometimes he found a job awaiting him, which, as a rule, was in violation of the labor laws of the country; sometimes there was no job. When employed he usually was assessed an interpreter's fee and a labor agent's fee, which was tantamount to a bribe.

About every three months he might be approached for a contribution of one or more dollars to purchase a suit of clothes or as a gift for the foreman or roadmaster. Every spring or fall he might be presented with the opportunity of giving some agent a ten-dollar fee to use his influence to prevent the worker's discharge by the company.[41]

Besides paying bribes, enduring the uncertain fate of seasonal workers, and having to work under the rigors of winter and the agonizing heat of summer, construction workers fell prey to other unscrupulous devices. During the spring of 1915, a gang of one hundred men was transported from Chicago to the scene of their presumed labors near Omaha, Nebraska. After laboring for two days, the services of the men were suddenly terminated and they were ordered to leave. Finding themselves unexpectedly in the prairies of an uninhabited region, without friends or funds, they spent an entire day without food; at night they had to sleep in the open fields. On the following day, in an act of desperation, they began to dismantle the railroad tracks. Representatives of the company summoned the police and had the men arrested without giving them a chance to explain their action. The judge presiding over this case not only freed the employees, but ordered the railroad company to provide them with transportation to Chicago.[42]

Many who worked on the railroads were not contract laborers. They were bona fide employees recruited by agents of the companies needing their services. During the spring of 1913, some fifteen hundred Greeks were reported as leaving Lowell and other small New England towns for Chicago, Omaha, and other western cities where they expected to find employment. Some headed for Pocatello, Idaho, where one of the companies was building railroad cars. These men were provided with transportation and promised wages ranging from $1.75 to $2.00 a day.[43] But, at best, railroad work furnished seasonal employment. It was also highly dangerous. Hundreds of immigrants suffered from crippling injuries or met death in one way or other. The termination of this seasonal work was comparable to the demobilization of a large army; when cold weather set in, thousands swarmed into the Greek colonies of Chicago, San Francisco, St. Paul, Minneapolis, Omaha, and other metropolitan areas, where they spent the winter months in idleness or in search of other employment.[44]

Fruit and vegetable peddling was still another occupation that lent itself to the machinations of the padrone. Chicago became the focal point of such activities. The workday of the peddler began between 5 and 6 o'clock in the morning, sometimes earlier. The duty of the boys employed in this business was to go into apartment houses and flats with samples of the produce, while the padrone watched his stock on the street. Often two boys were employed by the padrone peddler, whose knowledge of English, as a rule, was confined to the names of the various fruits and vegetables and their prices. The employment of boys in this business was desirable, in fact necessary; for the women did not mind letting them into their homes to take orders. They bought the produce from them more readily than from the padrone, who, besides being an adult, was often rough in appearance.

Boys employed in fruit and vegetable peddling, like those in shoe-shining, often lived in crowded basements or poorly kept and unventilated rooms. Sometimes their living quarters were over stables in which horses and wagons were kept. Unsold merchandise was stored in these quarters during the night and placed on display the following day.

Boys employed as flower vendors usually were less than sixteen years of age, fewer in number, and found chiefly in New York City. They were sent to parks and other parts of the city where they tried to dispose of flowers that were unsalable in the regular stores. A few flower-selling companies, with a limited business, also used them. As a rule, the boys employed by regular florists were better-fed and boarded, and they received wages of fifty to a hundred dollars per year. When not employed in peddling, they were used to deliver store orders.[45]

Exploitation at the hands of a fellow Greek was difficult to eradicate, especially during the early years. A helpless and uninformed newcomer, who had no well-informed relatives or friends to turn to, often was forced to fall back on some mercenary compatriot. He might go to him for help in obtaining a peddler's license after violating some municipal ordinance, for filing his naturalization papers, or for assistance in asking the immigration authorities about the prospects of bringing a relative, a friend, or parents to the United States. Every major city at one time or another had some "shyster" who rendered the most routine service for an extortionate fee.[46]

For a time, Greeks gave signs of establishing a "thalassocracy" in America. Thousands of fishermen were scattered in all parts of the country. On the shores of Rhode Island they were primarily lobster fishermen; in Florida they were sponge divers; and on the shores and rivers of California, they caught lobsters and fish. On the Sacramento River, they organized the first Greek fishermen's association in the country.[47]

Farming, cattleraising, and herding appealed to relatively few immigrants. Those attracted to these occupations were found in the western part of the United States, where the mountains, valleys, shores, and skies reminded them of their birthplace. For a brief time, they appeared as farmers and stock raisers in the southern states, but they either found agriculture unprofitable or they encountered local opposition; so they retreated to the cities. As farm laborers, they were exceptions rather than the rule.[48] During the early 1900s, one of the most widely circulated booklets in Greece advised emigrants to settle in the southwestern part of the United States and become farmers. This, they were assured, would be more profitable, for it was agricultural pursuits that were most natural to them. The climate and the work were more in keeping with their training and background, and land could be rented from companies under reasonable terms. They were urged to form small groups and pool their resources to acquire land, instead of spending their money unwisely in New York and Boston.[49] But such pleas generally proved ineffective.

Later, Anastasios Mountanos, editor of the Greek-language *California* (San Francisco), offered similar advice: "Cease having those rusty ideas that you came here to stay three or four years and return to your native country. You will never make enough money to return to your native country, unless you go into agriculture." He pleaded with his compatriots to abandon the cities where life was expensive, exhausting, and filled with many dangers, and to embrace the practical and happy life of the outdoors.[50] Mountanos compared the progress of the Armenians in the Fresno area who had gone into agriculture with the minimal progress made by the Greeks who had gone into cities: "The Armenians came to this country with the intention of remaining permanently and for this reason they went into fields of production such as agriculture. But we [Greeks] came here with the idea of remaining three or four years, 'make what we make,' and then leave." These three or four years, he reminded his readers, passed with few signs of progress. In fact ten years had passed and many still were "slaves of railroads" and of the most menial occupations.[51] Those working in the vicinity of Fresno and Bakersfield, especially, were urged to become farm laborers, save money, learn something about farming, and purchase land.[52]

About a year later, the editor of *California* observed that his countrymen were making some progress in agriculture, and he expressed the hope that this would encourage more to enter the field. He also looked forward to the day when California, once the headquarters of Greek railroad workers in the United States, would not have a single member of his nationality working on construction in the state.[53] During the fall of 1919, he estimated that about 650 Greeks were engaged in agriculture in the state.[54]

But asking the Greeks to enter farming was asking them to revert to a way of life they had already rejected. Many had become city-oriented, for the trend in Greece, as well as in the United States, was away from farming and toward the cities. It was the city, they had learned—the trades, commerce, and the professions—which offered opportunities, not the farm. Farming, they remembered only too well, was an occupation of short crops, debt, despondency, and little hope for the future. It was an agrarian Greece that these people had forsaken, and it was not an agrarian America—more promising though it was—that they wanted to embrace.

Some scholars, who frequently know the American scene better than immigrant psychology, have cited the disappearance of the choice lands or their appropriation by the older immigrant stocks as the chief reason for the failure of the Greeks to enter farming. This, at best, was a minor factor. It fails to take into account that most of the immigrants came to the United States with the sole thought of living and working in the cities. Furthermore, rural life in the United States was different from that in Greece. There the peasants lived in compact villages, were closely related to each other or had been close friends for years, spoke the same language, worshiped in the same church, and observed the same customs and traditions. Farming in the United States was a life of magnificent distances. Farmers in many instances lived miles from their neighbors, who often were of different national stocks, observed different religious faiths, and observed customs and traditions that were alien to the Greeks.

Farming in the United States also was a long-range enterprise that required a high initial capital investment—tools, supplies, managerial capabilities, a knowledge of the language, and a willingness to intermingle with others. This radical readjustment would hardly have appealed to individuals who came with the thought of remaining only a few years. The census returns of the United States confirm the urban orientation of the Greeks. As late as 1940, less than 29,000 lived in rural areas and only 6,511 were in farming or stock raising. Even when setttled in rural communities, the likelihood is that they preferred the commercial to the agricultural way of life.[55]

The Greek colonies in the major cities must have had a fair share of normal-school graduates, public-school teachers, and college students who had been caught by the emigration fever. These individuals had few opportunities to pursue their callings among compatriots in the United States, and virtually none among the non-Greeks. Many probably considered it beneath their station to perform the manual labor normally expected of immigrants, and they consequently could be found in the prominent coffeehouses of the cities, discussing every conceivable subject.[56]

A few physicians joined the immigrant procession; their chances of practicing their profession were better than most. At first, it was relatively easy for a medical-school graduate to gain permission to practice medicine, for the examination could be taken in Greek and translated into English. A doctor also could begin his practice with greater ease than a lawyer, since he was not required to have a command of English if he confined his practice to Greeks. A number of these men established themselves in cities where they pursued their professions with great success.

The reverse, however, was true of the lawyer. His tools had to be the English language and a knowledge of the laws of the country. A member of the legal profession in Greece could practice in the United States only after he learned English, studied in one of the law schools, and passed a bar examination.[57]

Needless to say, these newcomers of the early 1900s faced difficulties from other directions. Their earlier years were made uncomfortable by the older non-Greek immigrant groups, who resented their coming and who visited upon them the same recriminations which their predecessors had suffered. Some recall instances when they could not walk down the street without being pounced upon, assaulted by "unbridled" youngsters, or subjected to the profanity of their parents.[58]

Some of this opposition was brought on by the immigrants themselves through their eagerness to earn a living, coupled with an igno-rance of the language and customs of the country. One episode in Chicago is a case in point. During 1904 a strike had broken out in the diesel shops of the city; many employees left their jobs, which were filled by a fresh and inexperienced group of Greek immigrants. Not knowing what had happened and seeing an opportunity to earn their living, they accepted employment in the strike-bound plant, where they were handled like sheep in a pen. This immediately brought forth a series of inflamed protests from organized labor and segments of the Chicago press, which lost no time in heaping criticism on the Greeks in general. Some small shopkeepers, who already had felt the menacing hand of nativist opposition and were worried by these latest manifesta-tions of anti-Greek hysteria, condemned their strike-breaking com-patriots for their actions and lodged a complaint against the press for indiscriminately attacking all Greeks, including those who were in no way identified with the strike. Community leaders and the various societies and agencies were urged to unite and guide the new arrivals as a means of protecting themselves from attack.

Let us educate ourselves, recognize the fact that the prosperity and welfare of our family depends upon the prosperity and well-being of our neighbors. Our neighbors who are working as we are belong to unions and they are fighting for higher wages to improve the standard of living of the working class. By taking their jobs when they strike, we commit an offense at them and ourselves.

Let us not repeat this blunder . . . Americanization is the star that will guide us to prosperity, success, and progress. Let us adopt this great country as our own. Let us be part of this land of plenty and not remain predatory aliens. America opens her arms to us. Let us embrace her with love and a desire to understand her laws, political and social life.[59]

Anti-Greek outbreaks, plus difficulties in finding gainful employment during these years, became subjects of widespread discussion in the Greek-language press of the country. Special attention was focused on the growing number of the unemployed and reports of compatriots who were being dismissed or laid off from their jobs in factories, mines, and construction gangs.[60]

As the national economic crisis worsened, the animosity of native Americans, employees of older immigrant stocks, and union labor was felt with unmistakable fury. A telegraphic dispatch from Boise, Idaho, told of fifty armed and masked men who reached Mountain View, where some one hundred Greeks were employed, and warned them to leave town within twenty-four hours. Comparable reports emanated from California, Colorado, Utah, and other western states, where labor organizations had some influence and the antiforeign elements were vocal. Many demanded that the Greeks be ousted from their jobs because they were not citizens of the United States and made it difficult to maintain decent wages and working conditions for the other workers. Labor spokesmen warned the public that these foreigners, whether citizens of the United States or not, had come to the United States to work for a brief period of time, save money, and return to their native land.

Many Greek spokesmen realized that the opposition of organized labor was also directed at Italians, Hungarians, Bulgarians, and other nationalities. They urged their countrymen to become citizens of the United States and to seek membership in the American Federation of Labor, which was no more interested in the Greeks than it was in the other recent immigrant arrivals. "Do not stop with the filing of your declaration of intentions. We are Greeks but we want to become Americans; since we have come here, we must adapt ourselves to the customs and traditions of the land." [61]

Antiforeign opposition stemmed from quarters other than organized labor. On July 15, 1907, C. C. Maximos, the acting consul general of Greece in New York, wired Secretary of State Elihu Root about the attacks on Greek stores in Roanoke, Virginia, which the local authorities were unable to restrain. [62] In an exchange of correspondence, Governor Claude A. Swanson informed Robert Bacon, the acting secretary of state: "The local and state authorities are fully prepared to maintain law and order and to protect the Greek residents of the city in their rights and privileges. You will note from the letter of the Mayor that full reparations will be made to the Greeks for any damage sustained." [63] Joel H. Cutchins, the mayor of Roanoke, in a letter to Governor Swanson, accused the Greeks of disregarding the advice of the municipal authorities in a manner that was bound to create trouble. He charged them with showing little regard for the laws and customs and with being contentious and always ready, almost all of them, to fight with their customers rather than to settle differences in a peaceful manner.

I have urged them repeatedly being anxious to give them every protection, to report any person who refused to pay a bill for refreshments, and that I would see that the parties were brought before the Police Court. I have been exceedingly anxious to prevent friction, because this city is made up largely of working men and members of labor organizations, and they are not especially friendly to the foreigners living in the city.

Very few of these Greeks can speak English, and if a customer gets a fifteen cent lunch, and there is a misunderstanding as to the price, there is hardly a Greek in the place that will not upon the least provocation, grab a butcher knife or some other weapon and make for the complaining customer. This action on their part causes our people to be incensed, and it is with difficulty that we can prevent the smashing of their places of business. We have been on the eave [*sic*] of two riots since July, and nothing but the quick, prompt and effective work of the police force prevented trouble.

. . . I am somewhat inclined to believe that they are too presumptious, and if they continue to multiply here as they have during the past year, and do not change their method of collecting bills and settling disputes you will find dead Greeks in Roanoke before another year rolls around.[64]

Meanwhile, President Roosevelt, who had been plagued with the question of Japanese immigration in California, began giving thought to the idea of legislation to regulate the entry of Greeks into the United States. Writing from Oyster Bay on August 8, 1907, Roosevelt asked Root: "Will you glance at the enclosed two letters from Congressman Bennett to Lodge? It seems to me that if we could make some agreement with Greece, a European power, for the restriction of immigration it might be very important in Japanese matters, for such a precedent by a European power would deprive Japan of much of the irritation she feels." [65] Congressman William S. Bennett had written Senator Henry Cabot Lodge, from Patras, Greece, on July 3: "I think that there is a great chance to restrict undesirable immigration just now. The [Greek] government is concerned about the whole subject and, I think would go a great ways to stop, by agreement, such immigration as possible, particularly as they cannot get recruits enough for their army." [66] However, nothing tangible emerged from these efforts, and the contemplated curbs never materialized.

Developments in Greece now touched off a series of incidents that had repercussions in the Greek-language press of the United States. During March 1908, word reached America that the Greek government had appropriated 25,000 drachmas to defray the return passage of immigrants who, according to official sources, were wandering about the streets of New York and other cities "naked and hungry." Some, including the *Hellinikos Astir* (Greek Star) of Chicago, viewed this action as proof that the Greek name was being protected by the mother country, which was anxiously awaiting the eventual repatriation of its sons.[67] *California,* in a front-page editorial, urged that part of the 25,000 drachmas be used for the destitute in the far west and not confined for the use of those in the east. The railroad companies were giving few indications of hiring more help in the western states, and the unemployed immigrants were idling away their time in gambling and dreaming of the future.[68]

Accounts continued to circulate that the United States was a land of ceaseless toil, privation, danger, and "the grave of practically one half the Greek segment." [69] This, it appeared to some, placed a responsibility on those being returned to Greece at government expense: they were obligated to give first-hand accounts to their uninformed compatriots of the dangers involved in emigrating to the United States. The wealth of America was to be had through hard work, not idle dreams and wild hopes.[70] It is unknown to what extent the frightening pictures of immigrant life were subscribed to by the newcomers themselves. Most certainly the immigrant tide was not checked, and it is known that many Greeks in America protested bitterly against the picture that was being circulated about them and their status. *California,* in a stinging editorial entitled "Let Us See," denounced the leaders of the Greek government who were circulating such uncomplimentary portrayals. It also predicted in unequivocal terms that more good would emanate from the immigrants in the United States than from those who had gone to other parts of the world.[71] Greek politicians who found it expedient to speak in sanguine terms against the departure of their compatriots were reminded that it was their disregard for the plight of the peasant classes of Greece that was indirectly responsible for the exodus to the United States, and that this exodus would continue until the Greek government found effective means of alleviating the condition of the rural population.[72]

Perhaps the most highly dramatized clash over this particular issue was one involving Lambros Coromilas, the Greek minister to the United States, and the *Atlantis* of New York. In a blistering article, Coromilas was accused of maligning the immigrants and grossly misrepresenting their position in the United States. In one of his reports he is said to have depicted America as "a living Hell" in which "hunger, wretchedness, despair, decay, idleness, fasting, and we don't know what else, reigned." The Greeks in America were described as dying in the streets from hunger, becoming "rag and bone pickers," leaving for Chile, or depending on the Italians for charity. Not one word was uttered about the many who were gainfully employed or thriving.[73] George Horton, the United States minister in Greece, according to *Atlantis*, upon hearing of this false representation, went directly to the Greek Ministry of Foreign Affairs to register a protest. On his last trip to the United States, Horton had visited various Greek communities and found the people in a prosperous condition. In appreciation, the New York daily devoted a full-column editorial to praise of Horton for coming to the defense of the immigrants and four columns to a merciless attack against Coromilas and his commentary.[74]

Perhaps the most publicized, if not the most flagrant, assault on the Greeks in America occurred in South Omaha, Nebraska, early in 1909. The colony in this suburban community consisted of about eighteen hundred, to which must be added another three thousand living in Omaha proper. It appears that this number was swelled by the seasonal workers who came into South Omaha during the winter months in search of work in the slaughter houses.[75] Some of these men probably were strikebreakers brought in to replace striking employees at a time when jobs were scarce.[76] At any rate, a strong feeling of resentment had been built up against them by some segments of the local population.

Anti-Greek feeling broke out into the open on February 19, when a Greek, in the company of a woman of presumably questionable virtue, killed a South Omaha policeman. On the following day a petition signed by more than five hundred persons accused the Greeks of being outlaws who disregarded the laws and ordinances of the city, "attacked our women, insulted pedestrians . . . openly maintained gambling dens and other forms of viciousness," and created the general conditions that had brought about the murder of a police officer. In response, a public mass meeting was arranged for Sunday afternoon, February 21, 1909, "to adopt such measures as will effectively rid the city of the undesirable Greeks and thereby remove the menacing conditions that threaten the very life and welfare of South Omaha."[77]

The mass meeting assembled at the city hall of South Omaha, with a few city officials and policemen in attendance and with the full knowledge of the municipal authorities, who made no effort to restrain the crowd. Two members of the state legislature and some local politi-

cians were among those whipping the crowd into a frenzy, which—
after being fired with cries such as "One drop of American blood is
worth all the Greek blood in the world" and "It is time we were
ridding our city of these people"—embarked on its mission of avenging
the policeman.[78] Estimates of the size of the mob ranged from several
hundred to several thousand. "Picture in your mind," wrote the
Evening World Herald, "an aggregation of about 400 men, about half
under the age of 21 years. Of these perhaps one fourth are negroes, and
of the balance a majority are unmistakably of foreign birth. About
half carry hammers or clubs." [79] The riot began late in the afternoon
of February 21 and lasted until midnight.[80] The mob seems to have
accomplished its purpose of destroying the property of the Greeks and
driving twelve hundred from the city; in the process it inflicted its
wrath on people from Austria-Hungary and Turkey who were mistaken for Greeks.[81]

Aroused Greek spokesmen lost little time in protesting the brutality
of the South Omaha mob and the indifference of the authorities.
Minister Coromilas, in a communication to the State Department, asked
that "the necessary measures be taken to protect the life, liberty and
property of so many innocent upon whom it is intended to visit the
offense of one criminal. And is it not logical to cause compensation to
the sufferers for all they have undergone and lost . . . because the
authorities of Omaha . . . are all the more responsible as they had
previous knowledge of what would happen." [82] Indignant protests
were also sent to President Roosevelt by the president of the Panhellenic Union, a Greek patriotic organization which claimed one
hundred local chapters and fifty thousand members throughout the
United States, and officers of other groups and communities.[83]

A cable from Robert Bacon of the State Department to Governor
A. C. Shallenberger of Nebraska expressed confidence that the state
authorities would take every precaution to assure protection of persons
and property "guaranteed them under Article I of the treaty of 1837,"
and asked for information on the actual conditions.[84] Shortly thereafter
the State Department notified Coromilas that the trouble at South
Omaha seemed to be over, that the authorities had the matter under
control, and that protection woud be provided his countrymen in
Nebraska.[85]

Atlantis gave wide coverage to the South Omaha riot. In a tone that appeared to be more in the nature of a reprimand to the Greeks than a criticism of the perpetrators of the mass violence, it stated:

The Greeks coming to America aren't capitalists coming to profit in Wall Street. We aren't professional people bringing light from Athens to the American republic. We do not belong to social classes capable of rendering advice or who are independent in their undertakings. We are laborers. We are unable to be independent. It is necessary that we be assimilated by the large laboring population of America. Become citizens and join labor unions. Show a concern for this land which is so great and strong because it has concerned itself with more than 90 million people coming from different lands. America asks you neither to renounce your national heritage nor to become an enemy of your self-interests. It merely asks you to discipline yourselves with the customs of the land, which will prove beneficial to us as they have to others.[86]

From the *Hellenic Herald* of London came accusations that the rule of law and order had broken down in America. The desperado who shot down the policeman deserved punishment, but the authorities were obligated to see that the rioters were punished as well. Nothing was more unjustifiable than the wreaking of vengeance upon those who were innocent of the cause of the violence. The Greeks always had shown respect for all things American: "We hope that the American people who in many respects are as great and civilized as the English will not remain backward . . . for moral principles [are] the crown of a noble and enlightened people." [87]

On May 13, 1909, Governor Schallenberger, in response to a request from the State Department, submitted a detailed report of the losses suffered in the riot and a list of claims totaling $248,418.[88] Meanwhile, Coromilas had called upon Theodore P. Ion, identified as "a professor of international law" at Boston University, to conduct a private investigation into the causes of the South Omaha riot. Ion's preliminary report showed that there was a lack of effort on the part of the South Omaha police to stop the riot that was tantamount to acquiescence. Coromilas, on the basis of these findings, concluded that the murder which triggered the riot "grew out of the fact that a policeman, said to have been drunk, attempted to arrest a man and a woman to whom he was talking on the ground that she was disreputable, and that she now has been proved a virgin." Coromilas found that thirty-six merchants had been ruined, that their claims for compensation would be large, and that he had been inquiring into the policy of the United States in such cases.[89]

Coromilas had learned that in the South American countries, where citizens of the United States had been affected by demonstrations of violence and destruction of property, the United States generally held the government of South American countries responsible for such losses when they failed to provide the necessary protection. However, when the United States was confronted with similar charges of losses for failure to provide protection for the people of other nations, it usually refused to acknowledge such responsibilities, except in some cases in which damages had been paid to Italy. He said that redress through the courts of Nebraska was hopeless; for this reason he was going to write the Department of State, trusting that his representations would receive serious consideration.[90] On December 23, 1909, Coromilas submitted an exhaustive report to the State Department that was prepared by Ion. His findings elaborated upon earlier statements, that the violence would never have occurred had it not been for the mass meeting; after the killing of the policeman, the undercurrent of animosity toward the Greeks became open and plain.

Coromilas, after referring to a resolution of the city council of South Omaha disavowing any responsibility on the part of the city for the acts of the rioters, and stating that the laws of Nebraska denied reparations to those left without protection or defense, asked that the Secretary of State recommend to Congress an appropriation of $153,544 for the indemnification of the victims of the riot. In making this request he appealed "not only to the well-known humanity of the Government and Congress of the United States, but also to [the] lofty principles of justice that have always inspired their acts." [91]

Discrimination against the Greeks emanated from other quarters as well. Late in the winter of 1909, a bill was pending in the Rhode Island legislature, which if passed would have banned noncitizens from fishing for lobsters. This, it was claimed, was aimed directly at the Greeks of Newport, Providence, and Fall River, who were crowding out "the natives in a very profitable and competitive trade" and gaining too much control over the lobster-fishing industry.[92]

Atlantis resented the indiscriminate use of the word "Greek" as employed by many of the newspapers of the country. It protested that too many scandals, crimes, court cases, and other incidents involving Russians, Bulgarians, Hungarians, Syrians, and peoples of other nationalities were being pinned on the Greeks. "After all we Greeks of the United States have plenty of problems of our own without having the Slavs burden us with theirs." [93]

We have seen that the Greeks found their early years in the United States trying. These first immigrants were predominantly males who shunned the rural areas and gathered in the cities where they could obtain ready employment, be in the company of compatriots, and seek help in an hour of need. Like other foreigners, they too were subjected to exploitation, frequently by their own kinsmen. The most popular menial occupations in these years were bootblacking, railroad construction work, fruit and vegetable peddling. Efforts to persuade these men to become farmers proved futile: farm life did not appeal to them; even if it did, the costs of farming were prohibitive. Opposition to the Greeks was strong, especially in periods of economic crisis and in communities where they were formidable competitors as wage earners or shopkeepers. This, combined with an unfamiliarity with the laws and customs of the country, gave them a feeling of great insecurity. Such difficulties could not help but rekindle fond memories of Greece and cause them to want to return. America was still considered only a temporary port.

4

SOCIAL AND
COMMUNITY LIFE

T HE FIRST immigrants attempted to graft the social and cultural
life of the Old World onto the environment of the New. And to
a considerable extent they succeeded. During the early 1900s,
living within relatively compact areas bred a special community spirit.
The Greeks built churches; they sponsored schools, social events, church
programs, theatrical and musical productions; and the men continued
that most ubiquitous and popular of all Greek institutions—the coffeehouse.

The perpetuation of the Greek language became a prime concern.
Community leaders, priests, the press, all joined in the demand that
children born of Greek parents learn the language that "gave light to
the world." This was a mission that had to be carried out, as well as a
heritage that had to be preserved. The missionary zeal shown for the
study of the parent language probably explains why so many children
before the First World War learned to speak Greek before they
learned English.

An immigrant with a family to rear faced the dual task of learning to
speak English himself and of instilling an appreciation for the Greek
language in his children. In this he faced an uphill, and eventually a
losing, struggle; for, despite the risk of antagonizing his children, he
sometimes placed greater emphasis on Greek than on English. In this
respect the immigrant had greater foresight than those critics who
advised him against it, for he himself needed an avenue of communication. He knew that his children could learn English in the public

schools, but who could teach them Greek? With him it was a matter of necessity as much as it was one of culture. This was an unusual situation. For here was an immigrant parent who, for the most part, had little or no formal education, worrying lest his children reach adulthood in ignorance of the native tongue. He was haunted by this fear. Patriotic organizations, the press, the parish priest, and letters from the homeland kept drumming it into his ears. On the other hand, he was harassed by critics, Greek and non-Greek, frequently his own children, who kept telling him that since he had come to the United States he was obliged to speak English and forget Greek.

The church community, as a rule, accepted the responsibility of offering instruction in the Greek language. This occurred as soon as a sufficient number of families had settled in a district, and after a core of small merchants and tradesmen had taken command. The community school normally made its appearance after the church had been established. Often the parish priest served as the first teacher.

Beginning late in the afternoon—after the public-school day had come to an end—and continuing into the early evening, the Greek school was conducted in the most convenient quarters available. Children of various ages, sometimes as young as five and six, gathered in a rented hall, a vacant store, the basement of a church, or a community center to commence their study of Greek. Maintaining the interest of the child was a challenging and frequently frustrating experience, which taxed the ingenuity of even the most dedicated teacher. The objectives of these schools varied little. Most commonly stressed was the need of perpetuating the modern Greek language and of preventing the child from being raised in complete ignorance. The latter was particularly true when so many of the first immigrants still dreamed of returning to Greece. The more patriotic—the ardent nationalists—spoke of the need of rearing the children as Greeks, and as one well-drilled youngster put it: "If you want Greeks give us Greek schools." Another spoke of the urgency "to imbue our American-born children with . . . the greatness of our race . . . teach them the Greek language and impose upon them the Greek character and Greek virtue." This would mark the beginning of a new era, the emergence of a new kind of citizen, one who would be proud of both the United States and Greece.[1]

Sensitive and responsible leaders wanted to avoid misunderstandings with their American neighbors, and they tried to explain the schools' objectives as best they could. The fostering of Greek schools, they claimed, was no more repugnant to the best interests of Americanism than it was to Hellenism. The purpose was to preserve the identity of children born of Greek parents in an all-absorbing American environment, which threatened to eliminate all knowledge of a language that was "universally accepted as a masterpiece of expression." The immigrants, like their compatriots in Greece, were convinced that there was no break between the civilizations of ancient and modern Greece. They wanted to preserve the individuality of their culture in the urban communities in which they settled. They saw nothing inconsistent or contradictory between building Greek-language schools and upholding the ideals of the United States.[2]

A protesting minority objected to the church's assumption of a teaching role. Education in Greece, as well as in the United States, was a public and not an ecclesiastical responsibility. Church-controlled schools, the complaints went, bred ignorance, stifled scientific inquiry, and fostered intolerance. But the community churches seized the educational reins and kept a tight hold on them. The churches, despite their endless feuds and shortsighted objectives, fostered whatever semblance of Greek education there was. No other agency proved capable of maintaining this sustained effort.[3]

Experience bore out that more than oratory and strongly worded resolutions were needed to support the language schools. Finding satisfactory central locations for the schools, securing properly trained teachers, raising the necessary finances, weathering controversies and shifts in policies—these problems taxed the patience of parents, pupils, and priests. When the immigrants began dispersing, the problems multiplied.[4] Finding qualified teachers of modern Greek who understood the needs of children born in the United States was an endless quest. In many instances the classroom teacher was the community priest, whose knowledge of the United States and the English language was about as limited as that of the parents of his pupils. Sometimes a graduate of a Greek gymnasium or, on rare occasions, a former student from the University of Athens was available. For the child, attending public school during the day, in which he was taught by an American-born, American-educated teacher, and then attending a

Greek school in the late afternoon, presided over by a Greek-born, Greek-educated teacher, was often a contradictory and confusing experience.

The Greek school scene in Chicago in 1914, which probably was typical of conditions in other cities, must have been a shock to many people's patriotic sentiments, for very few of the city's estimated five hundred children born of Greek parents participated. The classes were held in dark and dreary rooms; the instruction was dull and uninspired; the children were unhappy over having to attend a Greek school after a full day of classes; cooperation between teachers and parents was lacking. The two Chicago schools were so inadequately equipped with desks and materials that many parents withdrew their children after a brief attendance. In 1915, according to one observer, the two schools graduated one child for every five attending the city's public schools.[5]

The poor quality of the schools stemmed in part from the lack of harmony in the community. Organizations, societies, and fraternal orders were competing for members and funds; parishes were fighting over election results; storekeepers were working night and day to get rich; priests were too busy officiating at weddings, baptisms, and funerals for fees; and newspapers were shamelessly calling each other names. The net result was that the children were being reared without knowledge of the language, customs, traditions, and history of their parents. They were being educated "in a strange language, strange customs, strange backgrounds, and strange mores. When these children finish their education, then goodbye to Hellenism!" A supposedly patriotic people was murdering its own nationality.[6]

The clergymen also were severely criticized for their failure to take the initiative in furnishing religious education for the young people. They were admonished to cast off their cloak of indifference, to display some zeal in teaching Sunday classes, and to make other provisions for the young. It was not enough for them to baptize, marry, and bury the members of the faith; they had to work systematically for the propagation of the faith. Sunday school instruction had to begin at once.[7]

The formation of fraternal societies was as much a part of community life as was the establishment of Greek-language schools. Perhaps the prominence of these societies and the conspicuous role they performed is best illustrated by the comforting letter that a candidate for mayor of a town in Greece received from his son: "Father, do not feel very badly because of your failure to become the mayor of our town, for I have been elected president of our lodge here in America." [8] Here he touched on one of the most delicate phases of community life. The immigrants demonstrated a mania for forming local, or *topika,* societies that many Americans found difficult to understand. It appears that every village and minute parish in Greece was represented in the United States by a society with an impressive array of banners, lengthy constitutions, and high-sounding names. The majority of these organizations, at least in the beginning, were composed of fifteen to thirty people and governed by councils of twelve to fifteen. Gold tassels and buttons adorned the officers' uniforms, which were worn on every possible occasion. An essential part of their equipment was the organization seal, whose use was confined exclusively to the president and the secretary. About one hundred such societies were in existence in the United States as early as 1907; in New York alone there were thirty.[9]

Onlookers undoubtedly found it difficult to understand this zeal for societies. Four, five, and even more persons lived in cheerless rooms and denied themselves the ordinary comforts of life. Yet they formed societies, paid dues, elected officers, carried on endless debates, and raised money to aid their villages. When one curious American asked the meaning of this, the reply was: "Every organization has a president, a vice-president, a secretary, and a treasurer, and that's something." [10] Of course, there was more than the usual quest for status and recognition behind these efforts. They reflected the localism and provincialism of a naturally provincial people, and these traits were transplanted to the United States. Greece was a country of small valleys and plains shut off by mountains, making communications between different parts of the country extremely difficult. This proved contagious, and it bred organizations of a local character in America as well as in Greece.[11]

Sometimes the local societies sprang from the urgent appeals of village mayors and priests in Greece. By hortatory letters, resolutions, petitions, and other actions, these petty officials succeeded in arousing the immigrants' patriotism often to fever pitch.[12] This plethora of organizations unfortunately tended to breed suspicion, mutual antag-

75

onism, aloofness, stubbornness, and a "do it alone" attitude.[13] They helped to isolate members from strangers and to divide Greek from Greek.

The immigrants' organizations were also, of course, characterized by activities: mutual aid, charity, and humanitarianism. These bodies came into existence before many of the members knew how to speak English; they were, as indicated, organized according to villages, towns, districts, and islands.[14] They collected money to build schools, bridges, waterworks, churches, roads, and other public works in their native villages. They also furnished a meeting place for old acquaintances and for the formation of new friendships, entertainment, political activities, and outlets for those floods of oratory that flowed so profusely from every Greek.[15]

The localism manifested in the societies also was reflected in the railroads, mines, and factories in which Greeks labored. A Lacedemonian, a Thessalian, an Arcadian, a Macedonian, or a Cretan could generally be found working with compatriots from the same village or province. The same divisions were observed among the coffeehouses and restaurants; the Lacedemonians had theirs, as did the Macedonians, the Arcadians, the Messinians, the Stereoladitans. The Greeks tended to work, sleep, eat, and drink according to villages, districts, and provinces.

Attempts to break down the barriers of localism were unpopular with the majority of Greeks: the break represented a form of cosmopolitanism that ran counter to local custom and offended the pride, self-confidence, and competitive spirit which the Greeks had in such full measure.[16] In due time the local societies were viewed as obstructions to community progress. At first, they had kept the immigrants from becoming estranged from their language and customs and had furnished aid for their villages. But they soon became mere vehicles for personal aggrandisement. Their mortality rate was high, but so was their fecundity; new ones emerged from the ashes of the old. During the early years, they kept communities divided, fostered antagonisms and hatreds, and impeded unification and cooperation.[17]

Also founded on a local, though more permanent, basis was the *kinotitos,* or community. The kinotitos was the governing body of the group. It provided for the establishment of a church and school; arranged for the election of officers; administered funds; hired and fired priests, teachers, and janitors. This community-wide organization was the equivalent of the New England town meeting (which all patriotic Greeks would agree was Hellenic in concept).

Such a community organization was headed by a board of directors, elected by dues-paying members. In the beginning the actions of this organization were a true barometer of community opinion. But unfortunately they also set the stage for ceaseless feuds that rocked colony after colony to the very foundations; sometimes they resulted in harsh and long lawsuits that left deep scars. These community-wide quarrels on some occasions were instigated by priests; on others, by lay leaders seeking to shape and guide the policies of the community. They usually were fought out in the open, for undercover feuding was foreign to the average immigrant. The disputes revolved around the qualifications of priests, teachers, and board members, the political affiliations of rival leaders, the use of funds, church and school policies, construction projects, the use of the English language, and kindred topics. For a time, these community organizations were never at a loss for issues over which to argue.[18]

A third kind of organization in this era was national and patriotic in nature, such as the Panhellenic Union. The Union hoped to enroll every Greek in the country; its fees were small, its ceremonies simple, and its promised benefits liberal. The branches in every major city of the country furnished a forum for the expression of Greek national interests, and they attracted considerable attention. The Union was founded in New York in 1907, on the premise that most Greeks would return to their homeland; it would help them perpetuate their faith and language in this country and, when the occasion arose, to help to mobilize them for military service. When the Balkan Wars broke out, the Union assumed the characteristics of a semimilitary order. Its local branches attempted to discharge the duties of recruiting offices.[19]

The Union was not as successful in "mustering, organizing and equipping whole regiments of potential soldiers," as has been claimed, or in shipping them to Greece where they were assimilated with better-trained and better-officered military units of the Greek army.[20] Its financial methods came under severe attack. The *Atlantis,* its severest critic, questioned the claim of the Union that it financed the shipment of 7,956 reserves to Greece by reminding its readers that the Greek government had provided for the transportation of 1,000 reserves.[21]

The Panhellenic Union's recruiting was denounced as illegal. Critics charged that it was wrong for an organization known as a philanthropic agency to be used for recruiting purposes and to take advice from the leaders of a foreign government. As soon as the Union committed itself to mobilizing reserves and raising funds for war, it ceased to respect the laws of the United States.[22]

After the Balkan Wars, the Union lapsed into the same state of animated confusion and indecision that had characterized its earlier years. It continued to suffer from loose administration and from an undisciplined and uncoordinated membership. The confused political situation in Greece, the prospect that the United States might enter the war on the side of the Allies, the hesitancy on the part of many to commit themselves to an organization that could be identified with royalist neutralism, and the growing feeling that the immigrants owed a greater obligation to the United States than to Greece—all contributed in reducing the organization to a cipher.[23]

No account of a Greek community would be complete without reference to one of the most widespread of all immigrant institutions, the *kaffeneion,* or coffeehouse. For it was to the coffeehouse that the immigrant hurried after his arrival from Greece or from a neighboring community. It was in the coffeehouse that he sought out acquaintances, addresses, leads to jobs, and solace during the lonely hours. One could frequently hear him say: "I'll see you at the coffeehouse . . . I went by the coffeehouse . . . I heard it at the coffeehouse." [24]

The coffeehouse appeared whenever a sufficient number of Greeks and an enterprising compatriot had settled in a particular neighborhood. Little capital was needed to start one. A store was rented; a few marble-top tables and wire-twisted chairs, several pounds of coffee, a few narghiles, and a dozen or so decks of playing cards were collected; and the coffeehouse became a reality. On the walls the proprietor was likely to hang lithographic portraits of his political favorites and those of his patrons; in communities in which Venizelos was the idol, pictures of the kings of Greece were not to be seen. There might also be posted battle scenes of some Greek victory over the Turks, a map of Greece, a military hero, a revolutionary leader, or some modern Greek Hercules.[25] Coffeehouses bore names such as "Acropolis," "Parthenon," "Paradisos," "Venizelos," "Messinia," "Arcadia," "Synantisis," and

"Lesche." In the rear of the house was the kitchen in which the proprietor brewed the coffee which he himself served to his patrons. Lokum, baklava, and other Near Eastern delicacies were in evidence, as were bottled soft drinks.[26]

The coffeehouse was a community social center to which the men retired after working hours and on Saturdays and Sundays. Here they sipped cups of thick, black Turkish coffee, lazily drew on narghiles, played cards, or engaged in animated political discussion. Here congregated gesticulating Greeks of all kinds: railroad workers, factory hands, shopkeepers, professional men, the unemployed, labor agitators, amateur philosophers, community gossips, cardsharks, and amused spectators.[27]

The air of the average coffeehouse was choked with clouds of smoke rising from cigarettes, pipes, and cigars. Through the haze one could see the dim figures of card players or hear the stentorian voices of would-be statesmen discussing every subject under the sun. No topic was beyond them. European problems were resolved readily, and all were at their peak when the politics of Greece were discussed. On the marble-top tables one could see diagrams of Near Eastern divisions, military strategies, and imaginary advances or retreats. One might find a plan for the bombing of the Dardenelles or a likeness of Eleutherios Venizelos. Quarrels began and amnesties were declared here. When the subject under discussion was not politics, it was the weather, the stock market, the faults of others, the capabilities or limitations of the community priest and teacher, life in the hereafter and what language departed souls spoke, and the possibilities of a Greek's becoming president of the United States. Few listened, and most talked as though they would explode if they did not talk.[28] On visitors, especially those not understanding Greek, such discussions could have an almost terrifying effect; they could easily have been mistaken for quarrels. But they were all verbal; no blows were delivered, "except those received by the tables or chairs." Greeks, like other southern Europeans, accompanied "their words with multiple gestures of hand and head, maybe even the foot, or the whole body."[29]

The coffeehouse served as a recreation center. Tables were filled with players deeply involved in some card game, frequently the intricacies of *skampili*. The game usually was vociferous, with many exclamations and disputes, loud acclaim on the part of the victor and threatened

79

recriminations on the part of the vanquished. After tiring of cards, a new amusement could be found, sometimes music. Perhaps a violin or two would be brought out, "a bellying guitar of powerful resonance, and a zither-like instrument called the 'santouri.'" After a few minor chords, "a waiting and strikingly mournful cadence" became the signal for two or maybe four *palikaria* to step out on the floor and clasp hands. After the tables were pushed aside, spectators would gather round and shout encouragement as the dancers began their steps. The Greek dances consisted of "many gyrations, leapings, stampings, twisting of the body, alternating with many short steps and breaking and reclasping hands with loud slaps. Now and then a dancer would whirl swiftly on his toe, slapping his leg or the bottom of the other foot." A successful rendering of the dance was rewarded by applause, drinks for the performers, and the inevitable call, *Eis hygeia sas* (To your health).[30]

At the peak of the immigration period, some coffeehouses in the more densely populated communities furnished music for their patrons. This was true in Lowell, Massachusetts, where a long line of coffeehouses on Market Street catered to the immigrant throngs. In such places one could find a player or two of the *bouzouki* and the *lagouto*. One popular coffeehouse added a four-piece orchestra which, on three evenings a week, was joined by Helene Antonopoulos, a professional coffeehouse singer from Constantinople.[31]

The coffeehouse offered entertainment of still other Levantine origins. In the larger cities, occasionally in the smaller ones, *karagiozi*, or silhouette performances, were staged on hastily improvised, elevated platforms at one end of the room. Stretched across the top of the platform was a white sheet about three feet wide, behind which were burning candles or electric lights. The figures usually were handled by one performer, who stood behind a white-sheeted screen and reflected them against the sheet; gestures and rapid inflections and modulations of the voice gave them an animated appearance. The chief character, Karagiozi (Black George), frequently was portrayed as a crude and clever, barefooted, gruff-voiced hunchback with a "murderous punch." [32]

A *karagiozopechtis,* or silhouette performer, who lived in the United States from 1899 to 1913, estimated that there were five or six performers in the country during this period who traveled from city to city. Greeks often were portrayed as "God-fearing Christians" and the Turks as *Christomachoi* (enemies of the Christians). The various characters, "the armed Turks and the armed Greeks," would appear on the scene "moving to and fro, gesticulating, fighting, fleeing, singing, and dancing." A more enterprising performer appearing in a community with a substantial anti-Greek clientele would reverse the order and portray the Turk as hero and the Greek as villain.

The compensation of the performer seemed to follow a set pattern. The coffeehouse proprietor usually paid his room rent and provided him with tobacco and coffee. If the profits from the sale of refreshments were substantial, the proprietor might add an additional twenty dollars to have him stay over. But the performer's remuneration, for the most part, came from the patrons, who gave what they pleased during the intermission when the tray was passed among them. On a profitable weekend one might collect as much as a hundred dollars, but this was rare. Silhouette performers had the reputation of being gamblers who lost their earnings as readily as they earned them.[33]

Less important were strong-man exhibitions, floor shows, and Greek cinema productions. The strong-man demonstrations appealed especially to those with a liking for Tarzan pictures and to youngsters, who gaped at the weightlifting and rod-bending antics of the performers. The strong man generally prefaced his performance with a few preliminary remarks to the effect that he wanted to demonstrate, in person, that the Herculean powers of the ancient Greeks had not disappeared. After displaying his physical prowess with gusto, he concluded his performance by talking about physical fitness. What were called floor shows attracted slight attention, but we may note that they were attended by an all-male audience, were Oriental in flavor (of the "belly-dance" variety), and were staged by females of questionable talent and virtue.

Some of the coffeehouses achieved notoriety by becoming gambling houses that were periodically raided by the police.[34] The police files of a number of cities were filled with the names of persons confined for such activities. Many owners and patrons were fined; some coffeehouses were placed under police surveillance; others were temporarily closed. On one occasion Mayor Carter Harrison of Chicago condemned the coffeehouses as centers of vice and evil, classified them with "dime-a-dance" halls, and opium dens, and suggested placing a heavy tax on them. An uninformed and antagonistic general public that gathered its impressions from reading the daily newspapers, as well as Greek compatriots who were hostile to the coffeehouse on general principle, were prone to agree with the mayor. But the picture portrayed by the mayor was obviously out of proportion. Few would deny that coffeehouses catering to the gambling instincts of lonely and frustrated immigrants should be condemned. But those observers who knew about the gambling knew that it was of the petty variety engaged in by young men away from home for the first time, who craved a kind of excitement that would bring them relief from a drab, humdrum existence.

The raiding of the coffeehouses and the arrest of their patrons had a humorous as well as an embarrassing side. Since many of the houses bore historical or classical names, it was amusing to read in the newspapers headlines such as "Parthenon and Seventeen Greeks Arrested," "Acropolis and Venizelos Taken," "The Acropolis Closed," or "Paradise Is Raided." In such instances the ridicule was worse than the disgrace.[35]

Responsible community leaders and newspaper editors admonished the proprietors and patrons to refrain from practices that brought shame upon their nationality. Young men were urged to shun the coffeehouses, to attend night school, and to improve themselves intellectually, vocationally, and physically. At the same time, the proprietors of clean and well-regulated coffeehouses were praised for providing dignified meeting places and recreational opportunities for their patrons.[36] But the attacks to which the coffeehouses were subjected can easily cause one to overlook their constructive features. After all, they were social gathering places where men could meet and discuss a wide variety of subjects, where information and advice could be obtained, and where the otherwise lonely hours could be spent in the company of compatriots. Coffeehouses became veritable places of refuge for many immigrants who worked hard all day and slept in crowded and cheerless quarters. In some cases they were potent influences in keeping the immigrants content with their lot. Few objected to the closing of the more notorious and disreputable coffeehouses, the gambling dens that preyed on innocent and unsuspecting immigrants; but many, perhaps the majority, would have objected to the closing of all coffeehouses. "Let the gambling houses be closed—but not the *kaffeneia*." [37]

In time the coffeehouse lost its appeal. A better-developed family life, an increased knowledge of the United States, the formation of new friendships, the acquisition of some knowledge of English, and the substitution of other forms of recreation helped bring about its decline. The coffeehouse eventually became a shadow of its former self, a memory of early immigrant days, even though in some communities it has survived to this day. One can only conjecture what the social life of the male immigrant would have been had it not been for the companionship and diversion provided by this very special Greek institution.[38]

The observance of religious holidays, at least in these early years, were another important social outlet. Women often found their way to church on weekdays, as well as on Sundays, in observance of a saint's day or some special religious service. If a man also acquired the churchgoing habit, he soon discarded it; for attending church on weekdays meant the loss of a day's wages.

The nameday furnished still another occasion for celebration. In accordance with Old World customs, the nameday rather than the birthday was regularly observed. Friends and relatives visited the homes of the namesake to extend good wishes and share in the hospitality of the day. Music, dancing, and food were inevitable parts of these events. In the beginning the tendency was to celebrate them in a fashion reminiscent of the village from which the host came. With the passage of time, these celebrations were observed with declining regularity; only in the homes of the tradition-bound and the newer arrivals were they observed.

Christmas for the early immigrants was more of a religious holiday than a day of gift-giving and fun-making. Solemnity, the offering of greetings, and the singing of carols depicting the nativity predominated. Gift-giving was kept at a modest level. Unlike Christmas, New Year's Day, or St. Basil's Day, was the day for mirth. The zeal with which this was celebrated varied. In cities with large colonies and where tradition was strong, children carolers sometimes visited homes, coffeehouses, and stores singing "Agios Vasileos." They concluded their caroling by extending good wishes for the New Year and receiving small tokens from the listeners. Cutting the *Vasilopita,* or St. Basil's

Cake, was also common. The eve of St. Basil's Day, and in some cases the entire holiday season, offered the men an excuse for swarming to the coffeehouses to test their luck at the gaming table.

Easter was far and away the most important holiday of the year. In Greece the pre-Lenten season was observed with much festivity and music, but in the United States this was rare, except perhaps in the earlier years. Palm Sunday, or *Vaeion,* was accompanied with the customary good wishes to friends and neighbors. During Holy Week, church services were held every night. At the Thursday evening services the priest read from the Twelve Gospels, and on Good Friday (*Megale Paraskevi*) the churches literally bulged with people. This was the one day of the year when the once-a-year churchgoers turned out en masse.

Good Friday also was the day of the procession of the *Epitaphios,* a flower-decorated bier which depicted the entombment of Christ. In a large colony such as Chicago, the stores of Greek proprietors would be draped in purple and black on the night of Good Friday. At the late evening service, the priest would slowly move amidst the flare of hundreds of tapers held by those in attendance, the smoke of the incense, and the sound of chanting, and sprinkle the crowd with scented water. At the appropriate time the *Epitaphios* would be lifted and carried around the church amidst singing. In the larger cities this funeral procession was held out of doors, sometimes assuming the dimensions of a lengthy parade; but later this phase of the ceremony was eliminated.

The religious services for the week culminated at midnight on Saturday, when the mass was celebrated which ushered in Easter. At the approach of midnight, all church lights were extinguished. At the stroke of twelve, the priest appeared with a lighted candle and chanted to the parish: "Arise, and take the flame from the Eternal Lights, and praise Christ Who is risen from the dead!" "Truly He is risen," was the response. Then the congregation responded with the enthusiastic Resurrection Song. Meanwhile, the worshipers had taken light from the burning taper of the priest and passed it around until all the candles in the church were lighted.

In the earlier days, the singing of the Resurrection Song was the signal for the setting off of fireworks in the neighborhood of the church. Skyrockets and firecrackers were symbolic of all the believers in the faith. Inside the church, services continued. After the ceremony, the customary greetings were exchanged—"Christ is risen" and the response "Truly He is risen." The people then returned to their homes where they broke the Lenten fast with a ceremonial breakfast. The chief dish was *mayeritsa,* a stew consisting of tender liver, kidneys, and the intestines of the paschal lamb, seasoned with butter and thyme and covered with egg and lemon sauce. Salads, *retsina* (a cool resin wine), cakes, and sweets rounded out the annual feast. Before the meal, the family usually cracked red-dyed eggs, symbolizing the blood of Christ. The one whose egg best withstood the cracking was expected to have good luck during the year.[39]

The desire for family security led to marriage as soon as the immigrant felt reasonably secure in his job or business. This, in many instances, furnished a feeling of permanence that made it difficult, if not unthinkable, for one to return to Greece. It became the turning point in the lives of many. During the early years, when Greek women were scarce, the more tradition-bound of the men either journeyed to Greece in search of wives or else had prospective brides, vouched for by relatives and close friends, sent to the United States. This was a logical if not a very romantic procedure. Those immigrants who felt strongly about secure and indissoluble family ties had a natural preference for a mate of their own nationality and religion, plus an abhorrence of the manner in which so many marriages ended in America.[40]

The attitude of some men, especially during the peak of the immigration movement, toward American women or women of other national backgrounds was one of misinformation, confusion, and poor judgment. Some who should have known better created the impression, through their boastful talk, that Greek women had a monopoly on virtue, homemaking, and belief in the family. The spoke of "American women," in particular, as though they were Amazons determined to rule or ruin their husbands. A few other adventurous individuals had ideas, shared by many Americans in addition to the immigrants, which they passed on to friends. Believing that marriage in America was a passing convenience, they married women outside their group. When they tired of married life, they put on their hats and blithely went their way. This behavior was known in other nationality groups, not to mention among Americans, but for some reason the idea spread that this was an old Greek custom. Conscience-stricken compatriots who had been exposed to discrimination and abuse severely censured friends who indulged in such irresponsible talk.[41]

Marriages between Greeks and non-Greeks were more common than suspected at the time, even during the earlier years when matrimony outside the national group was subject to censure. Proof of this is furnished by the number of inquiries made of church and consular officials in the United States and the various ministries of Greece. In response the Ministry of Education and Church Affairs, with the consent of the Holy Synod of Greece, issued a bulletin on the subject. It said in effect that the marriage of a Greek citizen to a subject of another country, and an adherent of a different faith, had to have civil and religious sanctions before it could be recognized. A religious ceremony in itself did not make a marriage valid. The first step taken to make the marriage binding in the eyes of the Greek church and civil law was to obtain a certificate from a consulate in America specifying that all the legal requirements had been satisfied. Then two witnesses, both citizens of Greece, had to testify under oath before the consul that the future husband and wife were not related. On the basis of this certificate, the bishop would issue the marriage permit. A communicant of the faith could marry a Christian of another creed, provided that the religious ceremony was performed by a functionary or priest of the Eastern Orthodox Church.

The failure of the Holy Synod of Greece to provide a bishop for the United States until 1918 posed a problem for those wishing to adhere to the civil code of Greece and the canons of the Orthodox Church. As a means of enforcing these regulations and facilitating the marriage, the bridegroom was required to obtain permission from the bishop of the province from which he had emigrated. Since many in the United States married without having obtained this permission, the presumption is that these marriages were invalid according to the Greek church and state.[42]

Marriage for a Greek woman in the United States meant that, as a rule, her parents were spared the need of providing a dowry. The scarcity of women naturally elevated their status and weakened all efforts to introduce the dowry system into the country. Those exposed to the American scene began viewing the dowry as "a barbarous system" that brought grief, unhappiness, and spinsterhood in Greece, but there were men who, if given their way, would have held fast to the custom. For all practical purposes, however, the tables were reversed in favor of the women.[43]

Wedding receptions were commonplace in many communities. Native dances and music became a standard form of entertainment. The gusto with which they were celebrated sometimes achieved a hilarious note. After one ceremony, the officiating priest was seen with "a shiner on his left eye" and the groom with a head "lumpy from bruises." Originally the custom had been to throw rice at the newlyweds, but for some reason or other hard candy was substituted. Some suspected that the Greek confectioners, who were well represented in the trade, were responsible for this innovation.[44]

Another custom, viewed with mixed feelings and even contempt, in evidence at wedding receptions was the practice of wetting one-dollar and five-dollar bills with the tongue and sticking them on the foreheads of the musicians. Some considered this an ugly and unsanitary practice, which offered the members of the musical group an unusual opportunity for gain. Relatives and friends of the players could easily initiate the proceedings at receptions as a means of expressing their satisfaction with "the screeching, nerve-wracking tunes of the sweating players," hoping to induce the guests to follow suit. And as if these exhibitions were not enough, at the other end would be the violinist, the drummer, or the banjo player quarreling for the money all around them and converting the reception into a comedy.[45]

The status of women was somewhat improved over what it was in Greece, even though matrimony was almost the only career open to them. If custom had been observed, every boy born of Greek parents in this country would have supported his sister, provided her with financial aid at marriage time, and even made provisions for her after the death of her husband. Considering that in Greece women were kept in near seclusion, they adapted themselves reasonably well in this country. They tended to keep within their circle of Greek friends, but became active in charitable and church work. However, unlike women of other immigrant groups, they rarely worked outside the home unless it was in the family business. This was partly because the husband felt that it was a disgrace for his wife, even his sister, to work, and it was a question of his ability to provide for his family.[46]

The Greek mother preferred the services of a midwife at childbirth;

in part this was the result of habit. The midwife usually served as doctor, nurse, and family counselor, which meant preparing the food and caring for the children and husband, as well as the mother and newborn infant. The qualified midwife posed no problem; but those who were unqualified, and they seem to have outnumbered the others, had a demoralizing effect on the useful members of the profession and caused no end of concern to the health authorities.[47]

The father generally was the master of the family, in fact as well as in theory. He believed in exercising his authority: "He is the family head who must be respected and obeyed. Children must submit to his will; womenfolk must uphold his decisions. He . . . governs his affairs according to the precedent laid down by his elders and in strict conformity with the established customs."[48] It was he who put the seal of approval on the prospective marriage of a daughter.

One of the loudest complaints of the immigrant father, especially in the larger cities, were the restrictions imposed on him by American custom and law when he wanted to discipline his children. Many a father wished that he could have momentarily found himself in his native village, where he could handle in his own style an insubordinate son or daughter who had been spoiled by "America." His inability to discipline his children in the fashion he had grown accustomed to and respected, and the social pressures that prevented him from so doing, made him very critical of the "American system of rearing children."

The Greek-language press was a conspicuous and, for a time, very influential part of community life. It carried international news, especially stories about the affairs of Greece, including events in the villages and provinces, as well as about the Greek colonies in the United States. It kept the immigrant with little or no knowledge of English in contact with happenings in the homeland, perpetuated Old World feuds and gave rise to new ones. Greek publishers printed and sold newspapers and books geared to the needs of the people, which filled a useful function as immigrants continued to arrive, communities continued to grow, and the Greek language continued to be used.[49] These newspapers had a rare opportunity to be of public service by acquainting the Greeks with American ways and ideas, but whether they did this is open to question.

In Greece there was a saying: "Either you give me a job or I'll bring out a newspaper." This kind of personal journalism got off to a quick start in the United States, even though newspapers with broader issues were also published. Newspapers, however, did appear for the sole purpose of attacking or praising certain individuals, of exploiting the weaknesses, prejudices, or petty vanities of the naive. Men presuming to be editors wrote vituperative articles against a particular individual, showed these handwritten pieces to rivals of the attacked man, received from them the cost of the newsprint or the salary of the typesetter, and then printed the articles as "newspapers."

There were newspapers engaged in personal journalism of another variety, less venal but equally pointless. Usually having a handful of subscribers, they wrote two- and three-column articles about the wedding of some patron, with laudatory accounts of the bride and groom and numerous other details; or they ascended to unbelievable heights in praising the deeds of some local society or organization. And there were newspapers which on one day would heap praises on Mr. X, calling him a merchant, a man of eminence, a friend of the people, and a patriot, and on the next would denounce him as a nonentity, a traitor, an illiterate, and a bootblack.

These newssheets multiplied rapidly and their activities became widespread. To one observer at least, anyone who knew how to read and write and was unwilling to work issued a newspaper; he cites the ten-line letter of an editor which had more than thirty mistakes in it as proof of this. This same observer, a lawyer and immigrant publisher, adds: "the influence of the press and clergy was so great on the future of the Greeks in America, that were it possible to say who worked most earnestly for the welfare of the immigrants, the latter [the clergy] were not only prototypes of friendly, educated, and progressive citizens, and finally Christians, but virtually angels." [50]

The mortality rate of the Greek-language papers was high. *Neos Kosmos* (New World) of Boston, the first Greek newspaper to appear in America, was edited and published by one K. Fasoularides. The second was the long-lived and influential *Atlantis* of Solon Vlasto of New York City, published first in 1894 as a weekly, ultimately as a daily. *Thermopylae* made its appearance in New York in 1900 under the editorship of Joannis Booras. *Simaia* (The Flag) made its debut in 1905 under the editorship of Fasoularides, the former editor of the defunct *Neos Kosmos;* it merged with *Thermopylae,* under the title

Thermopylae-Simaia, before it finally ceased publication. Satirical publications included *Romaios Metanastis* (Modern Immigrant) and *Paraxenos* (Eccentric). Other short-lived newspapers included *O Hellene* (The Hellene), an antidynastic weekly that directed its barbs at King George I of Greece, and *O Tachydromos* (The Express).[51]

One of the most publicized and ambitious journalistic efforts was *Panhellinios* (The Panhellenic), edited by Socrates Xanthaky, who for ten years was editor-in-chief of *Atlantis.* It appeared in 1908 as a bi-weekly, was converted into a weekly, and waged five years of unremitting warfare against the newspaper Xanthaky formerly edited.[52]

Chicago was a close rival of New York in the birth and death of newspapers. *Hellas,* the fourth Greek newspaper to be founded in the United States, appeared in Chicago in 1902 and was published until the latter part of 1912. The weekly *Hellinikos Astir* (Greek Star) began its existence in 1904 and is still being published. *Athene* began as a weekly in 1908; after the bankruptcy of *Panhellinios, Athene* was transferred to New York in the hope that it would acquire the patronage of the defunct newspaper and that of people dissatisfied with the policies of *Atlantis. Loxias* (The Blade), a weekly, began publication in 1908 and was issued for approximately ten years. Of longer life was the *Saloniki* of K. Salopoulos, which was a product of the Balkan Wars and an organ for Venizelist sentiments. Shorter-lived was the *Nea Hellas* of Speros Kotakis, who, beginning in 1921, also edited *Kathemerini* (The Daily).

Prominent among the newspapers issued in the cities west of the Mississippi River were: *O Ereinikos* (The Pacific), which made its debut in San Francisco in 1906 and later was published in Greek and English as *Prometheus,* under the joint editorship of Alexander Pavellas and George Papageorgiou-Palladius; and the long-lived *California* of Anastasios Mountanos, a royalist, who later became a columnist for the *Atlantis.* Weekly papers appeared in other cities of the south and the middle west throughout these years, attempting to satisfy the reading appetites of a people thirsty for news and controversial topics. In short, there was hardly a Greek colony of any stature in the United States which at one time or another did not claim a newspaper.[53]

Foremost among Greek public men of the earlier years, and especially during the high point of immigration, was Solon J. Vlasto, an importer-exporter of some stature, a New York community leader, and best known to his compatriots as the bearded founder and publisher of the *Atlantis*. The descendant of a prominent Cretan family, Vlasto was born on the island of Syros in August 1852, and educated in the schools of Syros and Athens. His father was a teacher of the Greek language. At the age of eighteen young Vlasto went to work in the banking house of an uncle; and in 1873, at the age of twenty-one, he arrived in New York.[54]

Vlasto's climb was sure but not spectacular. His first job in the United States was in a confectionary factory, as was common among the early immigrants. Within a year he found employment with a well-known firm of steamship agents. Later he entered into business partnership with his brother, with offices in Boston and New York. Vlasto's compatriots soon recognized his qualities of leadership and the value of his contacts with the American business world. They came to his office frequently for advice on establishing a church, hiring a priest, dispensing relief, and other matters of general interest to an immigrant group.

Vlasto started to publish *Atlantis* on March 3, 1894. In 1904 it became a daily.[55] The paper attributed much of its early success to the interest of Americans in the Greek language and the affairs of Greece. It made periodic references to John Stuart Mill, Lord Dufferin, John Stuart Blackie, and teachers of modern languages who believed that to teach Greek in the schools was to begin at the wrong end: "It is only through the living and spoken Greek that the ancient can be mastered." Some American colleges used the paper for reading exercises; special subscription rates were given clergymen, professors, and students.[56] But in the long run the success of the *Atlantis* may be attributed to the patronage of the immigrants.

Socrates A. Xanthaky, a Laconian by birth and a pioneer Greek-American journalist, became editor-in-chief of *Atlantis* in 1897, when it claimed a circulation of 2,500.[57] During his ten years as editor Xanthaky wrote on a wide variety of subjects—community affairs, Greek politics, international issues. While serving as editor-in-chief, he wrote a book, *Guide of the Greek Immigrant,* and saw the popularity of the *Atlantis* increase steadily until it was converted into a daily. But differences over politics and the running of the paper with his domineering and demanding publisher forced him to resign his position in 1907.

The successor to Xanthaky as editor of *Atlantis* was Adamantios Th. Polyzoides, who served in this capacity until 1933 when he launched his short-lived *Neo Vima*. Polyzoides' editorship spanned a quarter century of recurrent crises and community upheavals. During his tenure the *Atlantis* found itself locked in battle with the ill-fated *Panhellinios* of Xanthaky, the *Athene* of Argyros, and its most formidable adversary, *Ethnikos Kyrix*. These were the years of the triumphant Balkan Wars, the civil war between Venizelists and royalists, and the feuding between rival bishops and church factions in Greece and the United States.[58]

When Xanthaky left the *Atlantis* he was determined to establish his own newspaper. In seeking the financial assistance of Greek merchants and others, he left the impression that if he obtained enough financial support he would force the *Atlantis* to its knees and perhaps annihilate it; he argued that a new newspaper was urgent for the Greek national interest. Within ten months he had acquired the necessary funds to launch his *Panhellinios*, which began publication on April 7, 1908.[59] Xanthaky left little doubt of his bitterness toward the *Atlantis* and its publisher, and he seems to have found a number of allies. Many disliked Vlasto and his ruthless ways.[60] Vlasto in turn suspected that his former editor had the support of Coromilas, who had been anxious to unite all Greeks under the aegis of the Panhellenic Union and the Greek consuls in the Uinted States.[61]

Panhellinios got off to an auspicious beginning as a tri-weekly paper; with the October 16, 1908, issue, it became a daily. During 1911 it claimed a circulation of 9,262, as against 17,014 for the *Atlantis*.[62] However, it soon became apparent that opposition to the *Atlantis* in itself was insufficient cause for publication. The termination of the Balkan Wars in 1913, the paper's close identification with the discredited Panhellenic Union, and financial difficulties contributed to its collapse. It ceased publication on April 23, 1913.[63]

Meanwhile, the circulation of the *Atlantis* had increased. It acquired most of its readers from the greater New York area, the New England states, and the Chicago district. For news stories it relied heavily on clippings from the Greek press, but for a time it also had correspondents in London, Paris, and Athens. As a means of attracting readers, it had a page devoted to happenings in the Greek provinces.[64]

Beginning in 1915 the *Atlantis* encountered its strongest opponent,

Ethnikos Kyrix (National Herald), a militant opponent of royalism and neutralism. Better-financed than any previous rival of the *Atlantis,* ably edited, and based on the principles of Greek liberalism in which its founders believed, the *National Herald* advocated the entry of Greece into the war on the side of the Allies. The paper quickly acquired the distinction of being more than a foe of the *Atlantis.* It came into existence at a crucial time in Greek-American history and helped mobilize pro-Ally sentiment in the country.

Perhaps the most dedicated advocate of Greek liberalism in the United States was Demetrios Callimachos, who served as the editor of the *Herald* for twenty-seven years. Few editors could claim the wealth of experience and education that Callimachos brought with him to the United States. Born in "unredeemed" Thrace in 1879, he was educated in the three cultural centers of Hellenism—Constantinople, Smyrna, and Athens. Trained as a clergyman, he nevertheless spent most of his life in journalism, where he expounded his profound feelings for Hellenism with "apostolic fervor." Hellenism was especially strong in the areas in which Callimachos spent the formative years of his life. Late in 1914 Callimachos came to the United States at the invitation of a moribund Panhellenic Union to serve as a coordinator and preacher. But another role, more permanent and far-reaching in effect, was awaiting him, and he became the vigorous editor-in-chief of the newly founded *National Herald.* Making his debut as editor on April 2, 1915, he was to have a great influence on the Greek-American reading public and on community politics.[65]

The short lifespans of the Greek-language newspapers had an unsettling effect on the various communities, often arousing suspicion and distrust. To make matters worse, some outcasts from Athenian society and the world of letters posed as agents for various newspapers published in Greece or America, without the knowledge of the papers. As a result, Greek-Americans suffered from numerous bilkings by paying for their subscriptions in advance. It is apparent that more weeklies and dailies appeared than the public could support.[66]

Some readers became very critical of newspapers that published articles in coarse dialect. Literate and status-conscious immigrants, who believed in preserving the "purist tradition," expressed their distaste for this type of journalism. They warned these publishers of *vlachika* that professors and students of the Greek language read Greek newspapers for the sake of retaining their knowledge of the language or gaining a greater familiarity with it. It would be a sad day indeed when the language of the shepherd became the universal language of the Greeks in the United States.[67]

But despite these criticisms, many of which were justified, the Greek-language press rendered services to the members of the first generation that otherwise would have been difficult for them to obtain. It helped perpetuate the Greek language. It served as an intermediary between the immigrant and the New World; it kept him posted on happenings in the old country, even though the treatment of the news often was slanted; it published information on naturalization procedures, printed books and pamphlets that were of direct concern to the newcomer, and in various other ways came to his assistance. Still the role it played in perpetuating Old World quarrels and in fomenting political strife in the United States cannot be ignored. In any event, no treatment of the Greeks in the United States would be complete without an account of the activities of the Greek press.

Among the best-edited publications in the English language was the *American Hellenic World* of Demetrios Michalaros, a man who came to the United States from Smyrna.[68] Published first as a weekly, it later became a bi-monthly publication.[69] The *American Hellenic World* claimed the distinction of being "the only Greek newspaper published in the United States" for the avowed purpose of strengthening the ties of people of Hellenic descent with their adopted land. It also was committed to the policy that "those people descended from Greece and other Hellenic lands, constituted one of the most virile, progressive and law-abiding elements of our otherwise heterogeneous and polyglot immigrant populations." It denied in most emphatic terms that "the so-called Mediterranean races [were] in any way inferior to the Northern races or unsusceptible to conversion to the ideals which primarily are the prerequisites of the Anglo-Saxon mentality." [70]

Curious, sometimes aroused, readers of a nationalistic frame of mind wrote to the editor to ask why the paper was published in English. The editor replied that there were many good papers published in Greek in the United States and abroad, but few, if any, in the English language. As a result, because they were unable to read Greek, thousands of children born of Greek parents in the United States remained in ignorance of the language, traditions, and ideals of the land of their parents' birth.

Furthermore, many Greeks were married to non-Greek women who had little appreciation of Greek culture and civilization. The aim of the *American Hellenic World* was to bridge this gap. A daily newspaper in the English language would have been preferable, but capital and personnel were unavailable for this.[71]

It is apparent that social and community life, outside the church, whose role will be explained later, revolved around the numerous local societies that came into being, the all-male coffeehouse, the language school, the family and neighborhood ties that were being formed, the numerous weddings and receptions, the religious and nameday celebrations, and the discussions and controversies inspired by the Greek-language press. Everything tended to emphasize the idea of preserving a Hellenic identity. And nothing better demonstrated the effects that these community efforts were having than the readiness with which the Greek-Americans sprang to the defense of the mother country during the Balkan Wars of 1912–1913.

5

FOR GOD AND COUNTRY

A CORRESPONDENT for a Piraeus newspaper once claimed that, of all the many nationalities in the United States, no group was better able than the Greeks to maintain its Old World loyalties. Then in a facetious vein he wondered whether there was any likelihood that Hellenism would overtake Americanism.[1] Ethnic minorities, we are told, often carry their ideals, political rivalries, and traditions with them wherever they settle, and the Greeks were no exception. Being among the last of the European peoples to reach the United States, they were also among the last to cling tenaciously to their faith and traditions.

Part of this may be attributed to their rural background. The Greeks were rooted to the soil and bound by customs that had been handed down from generation to generation. They obtained their living from the family lands which they all helped to cultivate. Beyond the family was the village, which also fastened its hold on them. As a rule, they did little original thinking: "Initiative [was] at a discount; novelty almost a crime."[2]

When the peasant-turned-immigrant reached the United States, he found himself cut adrift from the stratified rural environment he had known. The very influences that had once provided him with stability, he discovered, gave him little opportunity to adjust to new conditions and opinions. In the United States he encountered different social and economic codes. Life was lonely, frustrated, exhausting; he felt lost and tried to stave off social annihilation by seeking the company of compatriots and reaffirming "his Greek faith and country." The fact he came of peasant stock suggested that he would do this; that he was thousands of miles away from home was assurance that he would.

Nor should one underestimate the hold of the Greek Orthodox Church. At home it was the state church, the only church. For years its clergy had been leaders in crusades to unite all Greeks into one nation and under one flag. The parish priest was a constant reminder of Greece, and this tended to attract to the church even those who had been wayward members.[3] The parish priest constantly warned his parishioners that it was impossible for them to remain loyal without being true to the faith of their homeland and parents. The Greek Orthodox Church became the badge of Hellenism in the United States, as it had at home. "Preserve it and strengthen it," was a constant admonition, "or else face the danger of becoming Protestants and idolators."[4]

It was customary for communities to celebrate Greek national, as well as religious, holidays, which gave patriotic parishioners the opportunity to rise to great rhetorical heights. In San Francisco, for instance, one priest in exhorting his listeners about the "national dream" cast a magnetic spell over them and caused many to shed tears as he elaborated on the historic aspirations of the mother country. A thunderous ovation climaxed his sermon, followed by the singing of a patriotic song, "To Greece," and the collection of funds for support of the Holy Synod and the Greek army.[5]

The spirit of national regeneration that had seeped into the political, literary, and cultural life of Greece influenced the lives of the immigrants. They, too, were beginning to stir, shaking off the notion which seemed so prevalent in America that they were a shiftless, helpless, and degenerate people. Their courage, determination, and industry were contributing materially and psychologically to freeing them and the mother country from the political and economic shackles of the past.[6]

The Kingdom of Greece carved out of the Ottoman Empire in 1830 comprised but a small fraction of the nation that the ardent nationalists aspired to build. The annexation of the Ionian Islands in 1864 and the acquisition of Thessaly in 1881 were initial steps in the building of "Greater Greece." At no time had they relinquished the thought of incorporating all lands considered Greek under one flag.[7] The immigrants were expected to contribute in all ways to the realization of this goal. This was evident in each city in which sizable Greek colonies existed. In 1903 a short-lived National Union was founded in Boston, which started soliciting funds for the defense of Greece.[8] A comparable society appeared in Chicago, but it was torn apart by the petty rivalries of the Spartans, Arcadians, Islanders, Athenians, and Greeks from Turkey who found it difficult to forget their local prerogatives and prejudices.[9] These efforts were hindered by localist ambitions, but not by a lack of patriotism.[10]

To cite another example of patriotic feeling for Greece during these years, proud compatriots kept a close vigil lest any aspersions be cast on the Greek name. One sensitive individual took exception to an article in *Collier's Weekly* which referred to the superiority of America's athletes and the inferiority of the Greek entries in the Olympic Games of 1906. "The writer in *Collier's*," he fumed, "displays gross ignorance in comparing little indigent Greece with America." [11] Later that year meetings were held in protest against the activities of Bulgarian agents.[12] In Chicago seventy-five prominent Greeks discussed means of counteracting the "fabrications" that had appeared in the *Daily News* under the caption of "Greeks and Bulgarians." [13]

One New York correspondent observed that the Greek residents of the city brought with them memories of the homeland that were difficult to erase. They were moved by "the patriotism that Byron wrote about and the Turks fought against." As a salesman, he said he found the Greek quiet, polite, and attentive, though inarticulate. "But touched on the point of unreclaimed provinces, he blazes up, regardless of the barriers of etiquette and idiom, and soon your salesman is pouring out to you the miserable story of Turkish rule . . . or talking of suspicious doings of Bulgaria in the provinces still under bondage." [14]

Prior to 1907 the efforts to maintain the spirit of Hellenism in the United States were uncoordinated. They were inspired by local benefit and patriotic societies, the florists or confectioners' associations, the editorials of the *Atlantis* of New York, the *Hellinikos Astir* of Chicago, and other Greek newspapers. The remittances to Greece to aid families and villages also nourished this spirit. But the feeling grew that the immigrants' efforts to aid Greece would be more effective if they were channeled through a single agency specifically designed for this purpose.[15] During 1907 a committee representing the various New York societies sent letters to the heads of all known Greek organizations in the United States, asking them to send representatives to New York on October 16 to prepare the groundwork for a national organization. Shortly afterwards the formation of the Panhellenic Union was announced.

Meanwhile, a dispatch from Greece reported that Prime Minister Georgios Theotokis had issued instructions to Lambros Coromilas, the newly appointed minister to the United States, presumably on matters pertaining to Greek nationals in America. Announcement of the formation of the Panhellenic Union and the appointment of Coromilas were received with widespread enthusiasm.[16]

The story behind the appointment of Coromilas appears to have been this. John B. Jackson wrote to Elihu Root early in 1907 that members of the Greek Chamber of Deputies had been anxious to establish a Greek legation in Washington. At the time the Greek press had been giving a good deal of attention to reports that Bulgarian agents were collecting funds in the United States, and to the effects that immigration was having on Greece. The name of John Gennadius, who had once served as secretary under Rangabe in Washington, was mentioned as a possible appointment for the head of the legation.[17] News that Gennadius refused the Washington assignment came as a blow to those who had hoped that Greece would soon make a number of sorely needed consular appointments.[18] In due course the Greek minister of foreign affairs inquired of Jackson whether Lambros Coromilas, the consul general in Salonika, would be acceptable to the United States. The Greek foreign minister, wrote Jackson, felt that Coromilas' "transfer has become necessary, and the government—in order not to appear to show disapproval—is anxious to give him a new appointment at once." [19]

In September the American legation informed the State Department that Coromilas was coming as "Greek Envoy" to Washington on "a special mission." This particular title became necessary because the Greek budget for 1907 made no provisions for a legation in Washington. However, as soon as the Chamber of Deputies met, the government expected to obtain appropriations that would place the Greek legation in Washington on a permanent basis.[20]

Coromilas, one of the better diplomatic representatives of the day, came to his post well trained. After being educated in the gymnasiums of Greece and France, he studied in the University of Tubingen, where he obtained a doctorate in physics and mathematics; from there he branched off into the study of French politics. After serving as director of the National Printing Office and general secretary of the Ministry of Economic Affairs, he assumed the management of *Ephemeridos,* which he converted into a great political newspaper. In

Constantinople he learned the Turkish language and studied the Otto-man administration of justice. His major assignment before coming to the United States was as consul general in Salonika, beginning in 1904, where he labored in behalf of Greek claims in Macedonia. The Turks, finding him too active along these lines, wanted him removed. Apparently it was in recognition of his patriotic services that he was assigned the difficult task of mobilizing the physical, spiritual, and financial resources of the immigrants in the United States.[21]

The first reaction to the news of the appointment of Coromilas was that a very competent man was coming to perform a very big mission. His subsequent trip to Italy, presumably to observe how the Italians handled the immigration problem, a visit to England, and the an-nouncement that he was to address the Panhellenic Union late in 1907 reflected the seriousness of his purpose. After his arrival, Coromilas made a cross-country tour of the United States, visiting Greek com-munities. Wherever he spoke he pleaded with his compatriots to forget their differences, to remain loyal to their families and country, to unite themselves into one mighty organization, to strive for the respect of the American people, and to realize that one fourth of the working population of Greece was now living in the United States.[22]

During the first half of 1908 the leaders of the Panhellenic Union spoke eloquently about "the national language," "the national treasury," "the national strength," and "the binding tie." They aspired to make the Union the most influential Greek organization so that it could assist the immigrants and protect "national interests" from the Bulgarians and other enemies.[23] By the latter half of 1908, however, sharp differ-ences had developed over the purposes of the Panhellenic Union. While Coromilas sought to make it the focal point of Greek nationalism, another equally determined group, headed by the *Atlantis,* wanted the Union to concentrate on helping the immigrant to adjust to his new surroundings. This group saw nothing wrong with furthering the national and religious traditions of the mother country; but it saw a more important goal in educating the Greeks to understand their obligations to the United States. Naturalization had to become the major goal, for it was only then that the Greeks would acquire rights and be able to show their respect for the country in which they labored. Nor was this all the Panhellenic Union could accomplish. It could persuade members to join labor unions and protect them from the "flesh peddlers," dishonest interpreters, and other rascals who feasted on their ignorance. It had to come to the assistance of every immigrant in need.[24]

These differences over objectives broke into the open during the second annual convention of the Panhellenic Union. In an open letter published in the *Atlantis* and addressed to all Greek communities and societies in the United States, three delegates declared that, according to the program of Minister Coromilas, it was impossible for the Panhellenic Union to serve both the needs of the immigrants in the United States and the national interests of Greece.[25] The issue, as these three saw it, was this: "The laws in a democratic society are made by the people. The people create the government. The leaders are servants [of the people] and not lawmakers, and neither the Minister nor the King should be permitted to make laws arbitrarily." It was wrong for the official representative of a foreign government to head an organization whose program conflicted with the best interests of the United States. A repudiation of the minister's recommendations might be construed as a repudiation of the government he represented.[26]

In this instance *Atlantis* came to the defense of Coromilas and the aims of the Panhellenic Union. Predicting that the organization would survive this crisis, *Atlantis,* evoking the spirit of 1821, reminded its readers that "the Greeks of Rumania who brightened the Greek name on the Danube and honored the flag exist no more; the Greeks of Bulgaria and Eastern Rumelia who waged their campaign for the good cause in these parts no longer exist . . . The Greeks of Russia are no longer what they used to be. Only the Greeks of Egypt remain but does not the nation owe them enough already . . . The only Greeks the nation can look to with hope are those in America." *Atlantis,* besides stressing the patriotic objectives that the Panhellenic Union could fulfill, reiterated the more immediate needs of the immigrants. These included ecclesiastical reforms that would make it impossible for noncanonical priests to conduct church services, the promotion of a phil-Hellenic spirit in the United States and of "Greek rights" throughout the world, the learning of the English language, the attainment of United States citizenship in order to avoid the classification of undesirable aliens. But these immigrant needs were no reason for disbanding the local societies which, if anything, had to be strengthened.[27]

The dispute between Coromilas and the disaffected members of the

Union subsided, at least temporarily, with the election of Coromilas to the presidency of the organization and the short-lived support of the *Atlantis*. Opposition to the minister also ebbed after a statement appearing in the *Detroit Journal* to the effect that "the Greek Government had no objection to the naturalization of Greeks in the United States." [28] But in December 1908 *Atlantis* unleashed a blistering attack against Coromilas that brought the honeymoon to a bitter end. How much of this was owing to a clash of personalities and how much was the product of honest differences of opinion between the publisher and the minister probably will never be known. Suffice it to say that the struggle was waged with a vindictiveness that lasted until Coromilas left the United States in 1910.

Solon Vlasto, publisher of the New York daily, was a strong-willed individual who, although lacking in journalistic training, found that being locked in battle with some adversary increased the circulation of his paper. The *Atlantis* was a hobby that flourished despite his greater interest in the brokerage business. Rarely was he lacking in opponents and arguments; the feud with Coromilas, we shall see, was merely one of a chain of journalistic encounters in which he was involved.

Vlasto's opposition to Coromilas was unmistakable and savage. He left no stone unturned. He accused him of failing to advance the interests of the Greek currant producers in the United States, of opposing the appointment of a Greek bishop, of designating a noncanonical priest for the Rhode Island community, of becoming unduly involved in community disputes, and of advocating openly the election of William Jennings Bryan as president of the United States.[29] Coromilas, said Vlasto, came to the United States convinced that in the immigrants he would find "200,000 blockheads" instead of "200,000 human beings." "Do not expect me to encourage the patriotic and religious thoughts of the Greeks in America," he supposedly informed his superiors in Athens. "I inform you that the Greeks here are so coarse, and so simple that there does not exist any danger of losing either their religion or their patriotism." But despite his contempt for them, Coromilas still wanted "to become the absolute master of the Greeks . . . the Aga, as the Turks say, the Boss as the Americans say. He wanted in effect to abolish the committees . . . to build an organization enabling him to appoint presidents, priests, and committees, that is, to govern a miniature Sultanate of which he was to become the Monarch, the Tsar of the Greeks of America. All this within the United States in the year of our Lord 1908." Even more fantastic, Vlasto charged, was his effort to levy a head tax of twelve dollars per year on every Greek living in the United States.[30]

Shortly after this, Coromilas was assailed for his portrayal of life among the immigrants in the United States as one of poverty and misery. It was this particular episode, we have seen, that forced George Horton, the head of the American legation in Athens, to reply that the Greek colonies he visited in the United States reflected a high degree of prosperity and progress.[31] Added reason for attacking Coromilas came after the anti-Greek riot in South Omaha. *Atlantis* published a dispatch from a Mobile, Alabama, newspaper, which apparently had been carried by other newspapers. It said in effect that the minister had advised the Mobile police authorities to detain all unemployed Greeks until they could give an account of their activities.[32]

The behavior of Coromilas—which Vlasto only slightly exaggerated —cannot be dismissed merely as the action of a brusk and blundering diplomat. It was this and something more. It was a manifestation of the contempt that members of the educated, professional, and government classes of Greece had for the immigrants. They despised them as a horde of crude illiterates who had to be driven like cattle, if they were going to contribute to the physical and financial support of the mother country. It is difficult to believe that Coromilas came to the United States oblivious to the fact that his wholesale solicitation of funds for the defense of Greece, and his preparations for the mobilization of Greek manpower in a friendly country, was inconsistent with the laws of this country. His actions were based on the premise that the immigrants belonged to Greece, that they had left the mother country in the prime of youth when they should have been rendering military service or expending their energies in developing its resources. As nationals who expected to return to Greece, they were obligated, he felt, to heed the advice of her official spokesman.

But Coromilas discovered that he could not stampede the immigrants into his kind of program. These people, the peasants of yesterday, were ardent patriots who loved their country with a passion that many Americans found it difficult to understand; but they also lived in the United States. Here they found opportunities, gained access to new thoughts and opinions, and felt no need to cringe before a Greek officialdom whose contempt for them was exceeded only by its arrogance. As much as they loved Greece, they preferred to show their affection for her in their own individualized fashion, instead of by the imposed and regimented methods demanded by Coromilas.

The Panhellenic Union had become a seething cauldron of troubles. The ill-will stirred up by the warring factions, the intemperate behavior of Coromilas, and the attacks of the *Atlantis* left the members of the Union and the communities bewildered and confused. Very little was accomplished by an organization from which so much had been expected.[33] Still, though, the flame of Greek patriotism was as bright as ever. News soon reached the United States that Speros Matsoukas, one of the foremost "apostles of nationalism" of the day, was coming to promote the national effort.[34] A whirlwind money-raiser, Matsoukas had stirred Greeks in Greece, Egypt, Cyprus, and other parts of the world to contribute toward the purchase of a naval vessel that was to be donated to the Greek government. To be christened "The New Generation" as a tribute to the reborn national spirit, the vessel, so the plan went, would steam into Greek waters at the time of the Olympic Games of 1910.[35]

Matsoukas was a sentimentalist, a colorful orator, and a composer of third-rate verse. His greatest stock in trade was an understanding of the immigrant mind and an ability to preach the sermon of patriotism with evangelical fervor. This itinerant patriot, upon announcing his intention to visit the United States, wrote two verses entitled "I Am Coming," which he promised would "rip the oceans" and greet his countrymen prior to his arrival. Matsoukas vowed to bring them news of the joys and sorrows of parents who were patiently awaiting their return, carry with him some of the sacred soil of Greece, and regale them with a native song that would soothe them in their loneliness. Matsoukas frequently appeared in the an *evzone* costume, as a means of dramatizing his mission. Once he told his compatriots that Greece needed "Guns and canons and ships and love and strong arms." "Praise and honor calls for nothing else. Curses and anathemas for those who ignore their duties. Forward boys, our country needs money and blood to become great!" [36]

Perhaps nothing better reflects the atmosphere in which Matsoukas worked than the Greek Independence Day program that was celebrated in Boston in 1910. As a preparatory step Matsoukas, in his customary flamboyant style, dispatched the following patriotic message to the Greek communities of Boston and the surrounding areas: "Do you believe in God? Do you believe in country? Do you believe in your blood, the pure, the Greek? Come to Boston on Sunday. There will be celebrated two great holidays, the high and holy holiday of our brave and hallowed ancestors of 1821, who liberated one small corner of our country, the other holiday the laying of the base of the warship the 'New Generation,' which the Greeks of America and Canada will donate to our country to glorify with the other Greek ships the immortal waters that will free our beloved brothers from slavery and tyranny."

About ten thousand responded to this appeal. They began congregating early in the morning of March 21 in the Greek district of Boston which was decorated with Greek and American flags. Units of volunteers that had pledged themselves to return to Greece also arrived from Peabody, Dover, Worcester, Providence, Haverhill, and Manchester to march in the parade. On this day emotions reached Olympian heights. At the proper psychological moment, Matsoukas approached the speakers' platform carrying a silver cross in one hand and the blue and white flag of Greece in the other. After the shouting subsided, a group of priests from the neighboring communities participated in the doxology. They offered prayers for departed souls, the "enslaved" provinces of Macedonia and Epirus, and fallen brothers in Crete. The national anthems of the United States and Greece were sung.

Matsoukas again proved the master of the hour. At the end of his stirring oration, he proceeded to a flower-decked platform symbolizing the hulk of the "New Generation" for which he was soliciting funds. After two hours of collecting and handshaking, the pupils of the Greek school of Boston rendered the customary patriotic recitations. The contributions totaled $25,235. As one columnist put it, "What occurred on that day cannot be put into words." [37]

For some time reports had circulated that the Greek government planned to levy an annual per-capita tax on its subjects. This levy, though in theory applicable to all Greeks living abroad, was designed especially for those in the United States. It was intended to replace the haphazard and ineffective money-raising drives of the past and to eliminate fraudulent fund-raisers. [38]

An official pronouncement regarding this tax never was released to the public, but the tax was probably proposed. Such a procedure was hardly novel: taxes were levied frequently, and money-raising drives among the immigrants had become commonplace. Certainly the political leaders of Greece would have been receptive to the idea. An Athenian newspaper account suggested that the proposed tax, presumably a fee for a certificate of Greek citizenship, would be levied on the merchant, artisan, and working classes. The big question was how this tax would be collected. Would not the payment of it depend largely on the patriotism of the individual?[39]

Stories of the proposed tax began to appear in the American press early in 1910. According to these accounts, the Greek Chamber of Deputies had legislated that all subjects in foreign countries had to pay this levy to Greek consular representatives in the cities of their residence; the names of a number of prominent community leaders in New York City and Chicago also were linked with the project. But Coromilas was credited with having fathered the plan. The reactions were varied. The American press concluded that such a levy was illegal and unjust. If we are to believe some Greek newspaper accounts, whose reports we are inclined to doubt, most immigrants accepted the proposed tax as a righteous one. Others were skeptical; they felt that it would interfere with the administration of the Greek communities in the United States. *Atlantis* opposed the tax because it was arbitrary, unjust, and constituted an invasion of the liberties of Greeks living in the United States. The paper could have added that it opposed the tax because it was the brainchild of Coromilas.

Shortly after the *New York World* and other newspapers criticized the tax in their columns, Vlasto and the *Atlantis* were bitterly attacked by many enraged Greeks for having "betrayed the sacred plans and ideals of the homeland" to the American press. Vlasto denied this and countered by saying that the accusation was part of a conspiracy to defame his character and discredit his newspaper.[40] There were also some supporters of the proposed tax, and they exhorted all Greeks who loved their country to pay a small per-capita fee of two, five, or ten dollars a year. This would be proof of their loyalty and an effective means of supplying income to the homeland.[41]

Few immigrants paid the tax. It was not a matter of ignoring their country and relatives; it was simply one of refusing to cater to the whims and caprices of the Greek government. For instead of succumbing to the exhortations of the politicians who persistently ignored the agricultural classes from which the immigrants stemmed, they chose to contribute to their native villages through their own local organizations.

Those sensitive to the national interests of the mother country also kept a close watch over the activities of the enemies of Greece in the United States. Greek-Macedonians reported that they had been approached by the Bulgarian comitadji with veiled threats that their families in Macedonia would be killed unless they contributed to the Bulgarian cause.[42] Early in 1908 the Albany chapter of the Panhellenic Union advised its members that they could start the new year on the side of "God and Country" by aiding the Greek refugees from East Rumelia, the victims of the "black Bulgarian soil and heart." [43] Bulgars in the United States were remitting money to relatives with which they were to purchase property abandoned by Greeks fleeing from Bulgaria, East Rumelia, and Macedonia.[44] Others knew of Serbs, Montenegrins, and Bulgars in California who were purchasing weapons, training, and organizing to further the ambitions of their respective countries.[45] Concern also was voiced over the activities of the New York branch of the "Young Turks' Committee" which was working zealously to win American support.[46]

Much concern was displayed over Panslavist influences, especially over a bill pending in the New York legislature during 1909, which sought an amendment to the religious-incorporation laws. This bill, after being approved by the senate, needed only the signature of Governor Charles Evans Hughes to become law. The Greeks of New York City, aroused by the *Atlantis,* demanded that Hughes veto the bill. As laymen of "the Greek Orthodox Catholic Apostolic Church," they wired the governor that passage of the bill would work irreparable harm on the Greek churches of the state and nation. The measure was inspired by tsarist Russia for the purpose of obtaining control over all the Christians of the Greek Catholic Apostolic Church in the United States; it was also part and parcel of the greater Russian effort to get "His Holiness the Ecumenical Patriarch to assign to the Holy Synod of Russia His Rights over all the Greek Orthodox Apostolic Churches outside the Turkish Empire." But the Patriarch, instead of yielding to Russian pressures, "Transferred His Rights over all Greek churches" of the diaspora to the Holy Synod of Greece, the only authority the Greek-Americans could recognize. If the bill before the governor became law, the wire continued, the Greek-Americans would be deprived of their religious freedom, and a precedent would be established for similar legislation in other states, until the 300,000 Greeks in the United States had become subservient to the tsar of Russia through the medium of the Russian church.

Reverend C. H. Demetry, who signed himself as the "pastor of ten thousand Greeks" in Lowell, Massachusetts, wired Governor Hughes that "the Russian Church is Orthodox but not Greek. The Earth's rotation is easier to be changed than the Greek church to be under Russian submission. Wishing for the liberty wic [*sic*] we are struggling." [47] These efforts had results. The bill was vetoed amidst the rejoicing of Greeks, who proclaimed this as "the great triumph of Hellenism over Panslavism." The jubilant *Atlantis,* which had borne the brunt of the campaign, carried a front-page picture of Governor Hughes, who was portrayed as the man who had saved the Greeks in the United States from falling into the clutches of the Russian tsar. [48]

Perhaps the most positive evidence of Hellenic nationalism was furnished by the volunteer units formed in the large cities of the United States. Comprised of enthusiastic young men, usually between the ages of twenty and forty—sometimes younger—their members vowed to return and defend Greece when her critical hour arrived. The first units were formed in the New England cities during 1909 as a reaction to the "burning insults" that the Young Turks had been inflicting on Greece. Many were worried lest she suffer a humiliating defeat; others "scratched Greece off their books" and wanted to forget her, believing that "she was condemned to die." Even more alarming, "Cosmopolitanism was eating its way into the fabric of Greek nationalism." The formation of these volunteer units was seen as a wrathful warning to the world that Greece meant to live. It was a challenge to the voices of national despair, the wavering loyalty of the "cosmopolitan Greeks," as well as a warning to the enemies of Greece that the country's future would be propped by the strong arms and bayonets of her devoted sons. [49]

It is generally believed that the Greeks in the New England states assumed the initiative in forming the volunteer units and in inspiring their countrymen elsewhere to follow suit. At least the youthful editor of *California,* Mountanos, was sufficiently impressed by the actions of the patriotic Greeks of Lowell to invite all interested compatriots to come to his office and discuss the formation of a similar unit in the San Francisco area.[50] The first to seek membership was a native of Thessaly who donated one hundred dollars to the effort. Others followed with smaller contributions.[51]

By late August 1909 a national committee was busying itself with organizing units in all parts of the country. About two hundred formed a "national phalanx" in Pittsburgh; three hundred and thirty-five were reported belonging to the New York City unit where former officers of the Greek army volunteered to drill them.[52] Meanwhile, Greek-Americans were advised to be prepared for the defense of Greece in the event that war was wished on her by Turkey. If the tragic news came, they were urged to head for New York, where ships would be held in readiness to take them to Greece.[53] The reactions to the volunteer units were mixed. Some joined enthusiastically with little or no prodding on the part of their more rabid friends. These young men assembled and drilled in the basements of their respective churches, in rented halls, in municipal parks, and in open fields away from the mocking of their less zealous friends. Others simply refused to join, fearing that such organized efforts would react unfavorably against the Greeks in general.[54]

Coromilas, to the consternation of some, questioned the sincerity of those who were spearheading the drive for volunteers. To him these brigades were products of momentary enthusiasm and woefully inadequate to aid the mother country in an hour of need. Such units as had been formed were more occupied in the election of officers and the distribution of high-sounding titles than with anything else. If war suddenly was declared, he doubted whether these units could be assembled in time and sent overseas for further training and service. They lacked the most elementary training, let alone leadership.[55] As far as it can be determined, the volunteers received some rudimentary training in marching, gymnastics, and tactics. Most units were urged not to buy guns, uniforms, and other supplies, and it appears that most of them abided by this advice. However, in San Francisco where the enthusiasm reached frenzied heights, a local military-supply store was preparing to outfit each member with a uniform similar to that of the American soldier.[56]

The more exuberant heralded these volunteers units as "the pride and hope of Hellenism in America." By mid-1910 the number of units was placed at about fifty, the membership at more than seven thousand;[57] and the highest praise was voiced in behalf of those patriotic sons of Hellas in New England who had the foresight to launch this noble movement: "Joy to the country which boasts of such sons living abroad. Joy to the parents who have such offspring. Joy to the communities that have such patriotic prototypes. Joy to the Greek soul of these volunteers in which such noble seed is planted, cultivated, and harvested. Joy also to the descendants who will marvel in the future." [58] The fact that war did not break out in 1910 had a demoralizing effect on the volunteers. Once the first flush of enthusiasm was spent, it became difficult to maintain spirits at a high pitch. All that could be done was to march them in patriotic parades when the occasion presented itself. Internal bickering added to the difficulties. During 1910 concern was voiced over the lack of union, the plethora of local societies, and the wavering interest in Greece. His 350,000 countrymen, wrote one Athenian correspondent, "were scattered to the four winds, unorganized, undisciplined, incompetent, unproductive, and lacking in political and spiritual leadership." [59]

By the late summer of 1912, signs of an imminent war with Turkey became clear. In mid-September leaders of the Holy Unit of Volunteers sent a cable to the Greek government inquiring about the state of Greece's foreign affairs and the preparations being made to receive the 15,000 men being held in readiness.[60] From Brindisi, Italy, came a bulletin that immigrants bound for the United States were returning to Greece upon learning that their military classes were being called to the colors. Meanwhile, the Greek government had banned the emigration of all men who were, or were about to become, of military age.[61]

The Greek colonies in the major cities became scenes of preparations and anxiety. In Chicago all compatriots were invited to the Holy Trinity Church to hear the parish priest and others talk about the needs of the hour. The Greek consul announced that the first contingent of volunteers was leaving Chicago on the following Monday; Italian-Americans were extending their sympathies to the Greek-Americans; and Americans aviators were offering their services. In New York an audience of between 4,000 and 5,000 assembled in the Amsterdam Opera House to hear speakers expound on the duties of Greek-

Americans. Similar scenes took place in San Francisco, Boston, Manchester (New Hampshire), Lowell, Denver, Louisville, and other cities. The pages of *Atlantis* had become a clearinghouse of information on the activities of the volunteer units in various parts of the United States.[62]

Reports of the expectations and decisions of the Greek government also appeared in the *Atlantis* and added to the general confusion. A cable ordered the National Steamship Lines to place the *Macedonia* at the disposal of the Greek government. It directed the company to unload all cargo and non-Greek passengers, to accept only military and volunteer personnel, to proceed to Philadelphia where it was to take on war supplies, and then to sail for Piraeus to await further instructions. By early October about 200 volunteers had made reservations on the *Macedonia*.[63] The expectations of the Greek legation in Washington were that about 75,000 of an estimated 350,000 immigrants in the United States would return to Greece.[64] The legation, in response to numerous inquiries about mobilization, first announced that the Greek government "will not accept volunteers in the army for the time being." [65] A second telegram twenty-four hours later said that the government would accept volunteers; this communication followed Montenegro's declaration of war.[66]

The months of October, November, and December of 1912 were to become memorable moments in Greek-American history. Members of volunteer units—Greeks born in Arcadia, Sparta, Epirus, Macedonia, the islands, and Asia Minor—massed together in their respective communities, paraded down the streets of their cities, listened to patriotic orators, and departed to defend their country.[67] An estimated 600 paraded in the main streets of Los Angeles carrying flags of the United States and Greece, along with placards reading "Hail Sweet Land of Liberty," "Hail Generous People of Los Angeles." [68] The newspapers carried accounts of the embarkations; on October 26 an estimated 3,000 left New York on ships of the Fabre Line, the French Line, and the National Steamship Line. Interspersed among the Greeks were Bulgarians and Serbs, who were allies in arms for the time being at least.[69]

The outbreak of the Balkan Wars and the departure of large numbers of Greek immigrants aroused sympathy among some Americans. These included youthful admirers of ancient Greek civilization who wanted to fight for the land of Plato and Homer; some sought to volunteer in the spirit of Lord Byron. Students at Harvard, Johns Hopkins, the universities of Chicago, California, Southern California, and other institutions lent vocal support to the idea; some banded together into "The Friends of Freedom." Still others were older men who had served in the Spanish-American War; a few were doctors. The Greek legation warmly thanked these men for their offers, but regretted that it was unable to accept them. In fact the Greek government, for the time being, was not even accepting Greek volunteers.[70]

Meanwhile, continued preparations, celebrations, and great excitement charged the atmosphere of most Greek-American communities. In November preparations were made for a "mass doxology" in the churches of the nation to offer thanks for the capture of Thessaloniki.[71]

Reports from Greece indicated that the volunteers were warmly received by the populace, if not always kindly by Greek customs officials. Colonel Thomas S. Hutchison, a retired United States army officer from Tennessee, writes of the reception for the volunteers on the steamship *Laura* when they alighted at Patras. The entire city appeared to be on hand. "Excitement was at fever heat," wrote Hutchison, "and the boatmen that rowed me . . . fought among themselves about who should pull me to shore. All of them wanted to take me." He finally landed; and the crowd seized his luggage "and made a wild rush for the custom house officials to examine first my baggage, and after pushing and shoving into the custom house and making the officials acquainted with the fact I was an American coming over to join the Greek army as a volunteer, the customs house officials called to the boatman to pass on through to the street . . . and that it made no difference to them what I had in my baggage; they only hoped that it would be something that would work harm or great damage to the Turk."[72] Hutchison also told of his unsuccessful efforts to pay the boatmen for bringing him to shore and for carrying his baggage. He was informed that his money was "no good in Patras" and that if he had any need for money they would give him all he wanted.

The Greek volunteers from America, however, did not fare as well as Hutchison at the hands of the customs officials. A number of them had boxes of cigars and cigarettes friends had given them before they left the United States; and they were required to pay duties on the presents. After the volunteers passed through customs, they gathered on the main street of Patras to await inspection, amidst the large crowds that had lined the streets and sidewalks. The volunteers had with them large flags of Greece and the United States. The city was wild with excitement. Then a man dressed in an American khaki uniform approached Hutchison; the crowd caught sight of him, and the cheering grew louder. This was the famed crusader for Greek patriotic causes, Speros Matsoukas. Matsoukas was delighted to learn that an American veteran of the Spanish-American War had come to Greece as a volunteer. "He embraced and kissed me repeatedly," wrote Hutchison, "offering me his purse, his watch, his clothes, in fact everything he could to show his deep appreciation of my services."[73]

In Athens, where the volunteers congregated in Constitution Square, Harmony Square, Stadium Street, and other populous sections, the scene was similar. The first units to arrive were those from New York, Lowell, and Haverhill, Massachusetts. Each had its own flag, decorations, and headgear. But only the New York unit was reported as having its own weapons; units from other cities, according to reports, were forbidden to carry them. One could hear shouts of "Long live the American volunteers," and "Long live those from abroad."[74] The return of these immigrants as volunteers from the United States gave those in Greece much to think about. One Athenian observed:

Erect, solid, well-dressed, with a physique that one senses cannot be easily affected, have come the Greeks from America. In their yellowish attire, which gives greater lightness to their darker complexion, appear vaguely the lines of well-filled muscles.

What difference, said one who was passing in front of us. Does one think that they aren't Greeks. Did you think they had become Anglo-Saxons?

I don't know whether most of the boys we have met on Constitution Square have become Anglo-Saxons. It is certain that they present something different. In their dress? In the foreign airs they have taken by living abroad? In the different diet? In the different ethics? In all these combined? . . .

Let that be, said someone who was watching this scene. Alongside these few healthy youth, the robust, the vigorous, and the muscular which America returns to us, how many of the others does it shake off and exhaust to send back to us tubercular and ready for death? Under the light of evening we see before us again the eternal mysterious problem of immigration.

In the end does immigration benefit or harm? When we see the immigrants returning courageous, robust, disciplined, so healthy that when they walk the surface beneath them cracks, we believe that immigration benefits.

When, however, we meet in Piraeus those persons who are carried into little boats because they cannot climb out themselves and bring them to Athens in time to be buried, we do not have the slightest doubt that immigration is harmful.

We imagine that immigration has depopulated Greece, that not a single man had remained behind. But mobilization yielded numbers which depopulated areas do not yield, and the mobilized came from eparchs which complained the most about immigration.[75]

The transportation of the volunteers was financed largely on a personal basis. Most volunteers probably paid their own expenses, believing they had a military obligation to discharge. Those without funds had their passage paid by the Panhellenic Union or patriotic businessmen.[76] Chapters of the Panhellenic Union in the United States received copies of a telegram from Alexander Diomedes, the Greek minister of finance, announcing the floating of a one million dollar loan. The plan of the Union was to issue noninterest-bearing bonds in denominations of five dollars. Compatriots were urged to buy more of these bonds than they could afford and to make their respective cities the leaders in the bond drives.[77]

The number of immigrants who would return to defend Greece had been a concern both of patriotic leaders in the United States and officials of the Greek government. A number naturally refused because they were citizens of the United States.[78] By early 1913, about 25,000 of an anticipated 75,000 to 100,000 Greek-Americans had reached Greece.[79] Although nationalist spokesmen considered this a miserable, if not unpatriotic, showing, a more objective evaluation must regard this as a remarkable response. These figures did not include those who were preparing to return or were en route by more circuitous routes. Later reports placed the total number between 42,000 and 45,000. More probably would have reached Greece if adequate preparations had been made for them. In the meantime, serious thought was given to measures for punishing those who failed to return, since they were obligated to according to Greek law.[80]

The Greek-Americans were trained, at least in part, in Athens, Nauplion, and other points before being sent to the war front. Most saw action in Epirus, especially around Bezani and Janina. Newspaper accounts indicated that they were functioning better than had been expected and that they exposed themselves to many hardships and dangers, despite their limited training.[81]

Press reports from some parts of the United States indicated that the departures for the Balkan Wars had created labor shortages in some of the industries in which Greeks had been employed. The *World* of Aberdeen, Washington, stated that the lumber industry was filling the places of the departed Greeks and Slavs with Scandinavian workers from Minnesota. Comparable comments were made of those employed in the iron, copper, and quicksilver mines of the western states. The *World* expected that the majority of these volunteers would remain in Greece. The war would claim some lives; opportunities would present themselves in the conquered areas; and the Greek-Americans would employ their money and worldly experience to increase production and better the social conditions in the areas freed from the Turks.[82]

When peace was temporarily restored, the director of the Panhellenic Union warmly thanked the Greek-Americans for their sacrifices. Figures on the wounded and the dead are unavailable, although the belief is that they were substantial owing to the inadequate training of the volunteers. Many left their jobs in the United States, and now they were returning to begin all over again. Still they were reminded that this was but a pause and not the end of a long journey for Greece; they should remain in readiness to resume the march under the leadership of King Constantine until the national goal had been reached.[83]

The Greek colonies in the United States made preparations to celebrate the victories. The Lowell community busied itself to receive the returning veterans at the conclusion of the First Balkan War, not realizing that a second one was about to break out.[84] *Atlantis* chose to honor Constantine "the Liberator" for his role in freeing the Greeks from their conquerors by presenting him with a sword.[85] In September 1913 the *Chicago Tribune* estimated that there were 3,000 fewer Greeks in Chicago than in the previous year, but it also observed that, now "the battle against the Crescent was over," those "brown and muscular men, with flashing black eyes and bristling mustaches ... who went through the battles unwounded are beginning to come back."[86]

In 1915 King Constantine was quoted in an interview with the Associated Press as saying that most of the 45,000 who came to Greece as volunteers returned to the United States:

But this time the emigration has been with a signal difference. At first ... the men went alone. Their idea was to make a modest fortune, return to their families in Greece, buy a little farm or a shop in one of the cities and live in comfort to the end of their days among their own people. But a good many of those who returned to America after . . . they had served their country nobly took their families with them on the second trip. For them it was no longer an experiment fraught with the risks and dangers of unknown adventure. They had been to America once. They had learned where and how to live. They knew where to go and how to get there, even when encumbered with their families and their household goods. So when they sailed for the West the second time it was with all their belongings, not so much in the spirit of the ancient Greeks, going into the world in search of fortune and adventure as had been the habit of Greeks for thirty-five centuries, but rather as prospective Americans, almost all of them quitting their mother country forever.[87]

Obviously, some never returned to the United States; they did what the *World* of Aberdeen had predicted and what Greek nationalists had hoped for. This found support from at least one Greek newspaper in the United States, the newly founded *Saloniki* of Chicago, which advised that the enthusiasm of the Greeks in the United States should not cease with a single adventure. All compatriots who had acquired skills and experience by living among the practical and enterprising people of the United States could benefit immensely by returning to the mother country. The rich territorial acquisitions in Macedonia, Epirus, Thrace, and the Aegean Islands awaited the farmer, the herdsman, the manufacturer, the sailor. "The fattened calf of the gospel has been prepared by our loving mother, Greece, and with open arms she expects us to share the rich feast . . . Let us, therefore, take the road back." The wanderer, who had yearned to see smoke rising from the chimney of his ancestral home, could find no more appropriate time than the present. An example was being set by European and American capitalists, who were buying or leasing large tracts of land in the fertile Macedonian valley. The liberal government of Venizelos promised to rid the country of usury and other injustices, so that life, property, and opportunity would be protected in every conceivable way.[88]

Accurate information on the number of volunteers returning to the United States is unavailable. Newspapers such as the *Atlantis* and the *New York Times,* which carried periodic accounts of the veterans, were vague or had little precise information on the subject. *Atlantis* in reporting the return of the unit from Brockton, Massachusetts, wrote that of the 150 volunteers who had gone to Greece, some 15 or 20 were killed and many others were wounded.[89] The *New York Times,* whose estimate of the number of volunteers was a rather high 55,000, expected all of them to return.[90]

Probably the majority of the volunteers came back to the United States to resume their old occupations or to find new ones. Immigration statistics, especially for 1914, strongly suggest that many of those who were counted as new immigrants were returning veterans of the Balkan Wars. These veterans knew that it would not be easy to live in Greece after having been in America; or they felt that they had not amassed sufficient money to enable them to lead the kind of life they wanted to lead in Greece. Others, moreover, decided to make the United States their permanent home and brought their families back with them.

6

THE GREEK

ORTHODOX CHURCH:

THE BEGINNINGS

THE KINOTITOS, or community council, was a vital and integral part of immigrant life, as we have seen. Because it was more permanent than any other form of organization, it exerted a constant influence on the affairs of Greek-Americans. It provided for the spiritual needs of the immigrants; it arranged for instructions in the Greek language; and it furnished a trustworthy barometer of the temper, mood, and opinions of the population. In the early years the influence of the kinotitos, rather than that of the parish and the priest, was second to none, and this persisted despite the innumerable imbroglios in which it became involved.

The relationship between the kinotitos and the parish church, however, should not be underestimated. We have already seen that, whenever enough Greeks settled in a city, they formed a kinotitos, which managed the affairs of the church and the school and paid the salary of the teacher and the priest. As a result, the financial affairs of the parish church were managed by laymen instead of by priests. The kinotitos in the early years looked after the welfare of the entire Greek colony, but its activities centered primarily on the church.[1]

The parish church, as a minute segment of the Eastern Orthodox Church, came to play an all-important role in the lives of the people. Composed of many autonomous churches, the Eastern Orthodox Church was a sprawling organization whose teachings were based on the dogmas and canons set forth by the Seven Ecumenical Councils. These autonomous churches included the Church of Constantinople, known to the Greeks as the Great Church or the Ecumenical Patriarchate, the Church of Antioch, the Church of Serbia, the Church of Rumania, the Church of Georgia, the Church of Russia, and the Church of Greece. The administration of this extensive network of national churches can be compared to that of a religious confederation.[2]

But to the Greeks in the United States it was the Church of Constantinople and the Church of Greece that were of greatest concern, for it was to these two branches of Orthodoxy that they owed their spiritual allegiance. Their religious lives were affected by what occurred within these two ecclesiastical jurisdictions: they furnished the first priests, shaped church policy in the Old World that in turn reacted on the churches in the New, and designated the hierarchs for the United States. Conflicts within these bodies and an inability to understand the problems of the immigrants compounded the difficulties of the local parishes.[3]

There is significance in the fact that the Eastern Orthodox faith was introduced into the New World by the Russians. And it is relevant that the Eastern Orthodox Church, considered "the Mother of Christian churches," entered the United States from the western instead of the eastern end of the continent. Russian merchants and sailors who emigrated into Alaska from Siberia during the latter part of the eighteenth century planted its seeds in North American soil. After Alaska was purchased by the United States, the Russian church extended its missionary activities southward into the San Francisco area. With the growth of immigration the Russian church shifted its headquarters eastward in an effort to minister more effectively to the needs of the newcomers. These churches in America came under the surveillance of the Church of Russia, whose political head was the tsar.[4]

These early activities of the Russians, combined with the heavy influx of Greek immigrants—who were under the jurisdiction of the Ecumenical Patriarchate and the Holy Synod of Greece—raised the specter of Panslavism in the United States. This helps to explain, at least in part, the shifting attitude of the Greeks toward the Russian churches, as well as the indecisiveness and tardiness of the Ecumenical Patriarchate and the Church of Greece in designating an American bishop.[5]

119

Prior to the formation of the Kingdom of Greece, the head of the Greek churches was the Patriarchate of Constantinople, which also served as the political representative of all Greeks within the Ottoman Empire. The Turkish provinces that became the Kingdom of Greece were a part of this immense diocese. But once the Greeks had gained their freedom, they found that reliance on the Patriarchate, which, in turn, depended on the sultan, was opposed to their best interests. After Prince Otho of Bavaria ascended the Greek throne, the clergy declared its independence from the Ecumenical Patriarchate and established the autonomous Church of Greece.[6]

At first the Patriarchate refused to recognize this separation. Then in 1850 it reluctantly acquiesced to this and to a plan of doctrinal and civil jurisdiction. According to this understanding, the Church of Greece was to preserve its dogmatic unity with the Eastern Orthodox Church and accept the Ecumenical Patriarch as the spiritual leader of the Christian world. But at the same time, the Church of Greece acknowledged the king of Greece as its supreme head in governmental affairs and the Holy Synod of Greece, composed of prelates appointed by the king, as its supreme ecclesiastical authority. There was no infringement on the spiritual jurisdiction that the Ecumenical Patriarchate wielded over the churches of "the diaspora."[7]

This was of relevance to the immigrants, for in Greece they had been under the jurisdiction of the Church of Greece; but in the United States they found themselves included in the diaspora, hence under the control of the Ecumenical Patriarchate. As immigration to the United States increased, the rivalry between the Greek and Russian churches also grew. The Russians, by virtue of their diplomatic priority and influence, had been pressing the Greek-oriented Ecumenical Patriarchate to transfer its spiritual jurisdiction over the Orthodox churches in the United States to the better-led, better-financed, and stronger Church of Russia. But, instead, the Ecumenical Patriarchate transferred its authority over the Greek churches in the New World to the Church of Greece, which exercised theoretical, if not actual, control over them from 1908 to 1922.[8]

Almost all priests ministering to the Greeks in the United States came from Greece or territories considered Greek. Clergymen were trained in ecclesiastical colleges in Corfu, Chalkis, Tripolis, and the island of Poros; but the only institutions preparing young men for the priesthood when the immigration movement was at its peak were the Rizareion in the University of Athens and another institution of more recent origin in Arta.[9] Many priests came from the Greek-inhabited districts in Epirus, Macedonia, Thrace, Asia Minor, and other former Ottoman areas, where Greek nationalism was at a feverish pitch. Some of these priests, as already indicated, emigrated to the United States where their nationalistic preaching kept their parishioners in a perpetual state of excitement.[10]

Members of the higher clergy, very few of which made their way to the United States, for the most part came from the best families (in terms of education, income, and prestige) of their communities. The long-haired, long-bearded bishops were highly respected and impressive churchmen. The subordinate clergy, on the other hand, was of mixed quality. The archmandrite, the highest-ranking of the lower clergymen, had something in common with a bishop in that he belonged to the celibate order and came from the middle classes. But the average priest was something else. Sometimes he was a pious and dedicated man who gave much of his time and sympathy to his parishioners, but more often his role as spiritual adviser was strictly a secondary one. Generally speaking, he came from the same social stratum as his parishioners and his education was very limited—only his clerical garb distinguished him from any other villager. He was unsalaried, relying on fees received at christenings, weddings, and house blessings and on "Eastern offerings" (usually paid in food and goods). He tilled his own field and garden, pruned his vines, and stored his harvest for winter use. The urban priests, fewer in number and more fortunate in their assignments, were usually better educated and in many other respects superior to their rural counterparts.[11]

Even though the immigrants became the bulwark of support for the faith, the first Greek church in the United States—the Holy Trinity of New Orleans—was founded in 1864 by nonimmigrating merchants and factors representing commercial firms owned by Greeks. The principal benefactors of the New Orleans church were agents of the Ralli Brothers and of Benaki; they also happened to be the consular representatives of the Greek government. One was the well-known Demetrios Botassi, the Greek consul general in New York City, who reached the age of one hundred and four; the other, Nicholas Benaki, was the Greek consul in New Orleans. In this church worshiped the merchants of New Orleans and their families, Greek sailors who happened to be in port, and a few Syrians and Slavs.

When Greek merchants liquidated their commercial interests in the southern states and their agents departed for other assignments, the New Orleans church passed into the hands of the remaining Greeks, Syrians, and Slavs, who used it as a common house of worship. At this time national sentiments were in a quiescent state, and the parishioners concentrated in preserving the faith. For a few years a Syrian and a Slav served as members of the board of directors; during 1886 some of the sacerdotal vestments and other religious effects were donated to the parish by the tsar of Russia through the Russian bishop who visited the church. As might be expected, the first priest was a member of the Russian Orthodox Church. The minutes of the parish were kept in English until 1906, since some of the officers and members knew little, if any, Greek.[12]

Whenever the Greeks were too few in number to support a church of their own, and at a time when rivalries between the national churches in the country were nonexistent, they accepted, though reluctantly, the spiritual guidance of the Slavic churches and clergymen. But as soon as a sufficient number of Greeks settled in a particular community, their patriotic sentiments and national pride got the better of them. Then the Greek church, ministered to by a Greek priest, inevitably made its appearance. Relying on the Russians under such conditions was humiliating, a national disgrace. It was expecting too much for a proud and confident people, reared in a nationalistic atmosphere and owing allegiance to a state church, to content themselves with the spiritual leadership of a rival national church. This became unbearable later, after the flames of Greek nationalism had risen to full height.[13]

In the United States Hellenism and Greek Orthodoxy—the one intertwined with the other—served as the cord that kept the immigrant attached to the mother country, nourished his patriotic appetites, and helped him preserve the faith and language of his parents. The receptiveness of the immigrant to this spirit cannot be underestimated. Absence from his ancestral home, the fear that he might never see it again, the thought of losing his nationality and of dying in a strange land, caused him, at least for a time, to embrace his religion with a fervor that he never had in Greece. He attended church because it reminded him of home. Neither a coercive government nor ecclesiastical decrees could have compelled these pioneers to maintain and administer their church communities with the turbulent aggressiveness that characterized them.

The immigrants in New York City established a pattern of church organization and administration that more or less set the pace for the other communities. During 1892 about five hundred Greeks met in a small hotel on Roosevelt Street where they organized the Society of Athena, which, among other things, was to secure a priest and establish a church. The president then was Solon Vlasto, the future publisher of the *Atlantis*. The enthusiasm for establishing a church was great. As soon as a sufficient number of pledges and money had been collected, the society arranged to build a church and appealed to the Holy Synod of Greece for a priest. In time an archmandrite, Paisios Ferentinos, arrived from the island of Patmos to serve as the first priest of the new parish, which was named the Holy Trinity. One can only imagine the anxiousness with which the immigrants waited to hear the holy liturgy in their native tongue.

Hardly had they gotten under way than the members decided to separate the administration of the church from that of the Society of Athena. Apparently differences had already broken out between the officers of the church and the society. The aggrieved faction, irritated by the trend of events, this time addressed a letter to the Ecumenical Patriarchate, and not the Holy Synod of Greece, to send them "an educated priest." Patriarch Neophytos, unaware of what was occurring in New York and anxious to discharge his spiritual jurisdiction over Hellenism in America, dispatched Callinicos Dilbaes, an Asia Minor Greek, educated in the theological school of Chalkis. Callinicos had served the Greek community in Marseilles before assuming his post in the new parish, the Annunciation, in New York.[14]

A similar procedure was employed by the Greeks of Chicago in establishing their first church. By 1892, if not sooner, they had formed the Lycurgus Society, whose name indicates that it was dominated by Spartans; and they, too, applied to the Holy Synod of Greece for a priest. In response the Metropolitan of Athens assigned the Reverend Panagiotis Fiampoulis, also of Ithacan lineage, who previously served as a priest and schoolteacher in one of the Danube provinces.[15] Preparations and expenses for the church and the sheltering of the priest and his large family were undertaken by the Lycurgus Society. It selected the fifth floor of a warehouse, an inappropriate place in an undesirable neighborhood, as the temporary site of the church simply because the members wanted a central location. After Reverend Fiampoulis sanctified the premises, the church was named the Annunciation. It was in these unpretentious quarters that the first mass was held for the organized Greek community of Chicago, celebrated by the Most Reverend Dionysius Lattas, the Archbishop of Zante and reputedly the first important Greek prelate to visit the country. (Archbishop Lattas had come to Chicago as a plenipotentiary of the Greek church to the World Congress of Religions in 1893, which was held in conjunction with the World Columbian Exposition in Chicago.)

Later the Annunciation church community, in cooperation with the Lycurgus Society, rented a masonic hall as a more desirable place in which to conduct services. The Russian Bishop Nicholas officiated at the first services in the new location, with the assistance of Reverend Fiampoulis and a Reverend Procopius or Ambrosios Vrettas, a Macedonian of Greek parentage who made an unsuccessful bid to bring the Greeks into the fold of the Russian church.[16] This newly located church, which offered so much promise for the future, was to become the scene of tension and discord. According to one account, a few of the influential Spartans in control of the Lycurgus Society, which for a time was the heart of the church community, wanted to place a tax on "certain Halstead Street Greeks," namely, on the "Tripolitsiotas"— Greeks from Tripolis and the surrounding area—who were rivals of the Spartans in Greece. News of this proposed levy leaked into the open and passed from person to person, until it had inflamed the passions of the Tripolitsiotas and others.

The Greco-Turkish war in 1897 brought a brief impasse in these church community affairs, but it indirectly influenced the future. Units of volunteers had pledged at this early date to return to Greece and fight for her defense when the need arose. The war with the Turks gave them this opportunity. The Chicago unit probably never exceeded three hundred volunteers, but the enthusiasm it displayed would have sufficed for several thousand. A contemporary observer recalled the frenzied oratory of the times and the cries of "Long Live the First King of the Greeks, Georgios" and "Down with Abdul Hamid, the

Sultan." For a time it appeared as though Constantinople were on the verge of being captured from Chicago.

In keeping with church tradition, special services were conducted on the evening the volunteers departed from Chicago. After the services a procession, headed by the Reverend Fiampoulis and joined by many shouting and energetic compatriots, marched to the Illinois Central Station, where the first leg of the trip to Greece was to begin. There the priest once more blessed the volunteers as they boarded the train amidst the cries of their wellwishers. The volunteers reached Greece just in time to discover that the "thirty-day war" with Turkey had come to an end. Seeing that Greece had no need for them, the leaders of the unit agreed to return to the United States as quickly as possible; but not until after one Arcadian and a few of his friends decided that they could salvage something from this abortive mission if they returned to Chicago with a priest from Arcadia. By chance they discovered in Piraeus a Gortinian named Papatheodorou, an "unlearned man," according to his critics, who was preparing to leave for Chicago to visit his two sons. Before long the volunteers and Papatheodorou found themselves in Chicago.

During the week of his arrival, Papatheodorou, according to a friendly account, believed that he could effect a reconciliation between the feuding Spartans and Arcadians, and approached the Reverend Fiampoulis and asked if he could assist him with the Sunday services. His offer was emphatically and unceremoniously rejected by Fiampoulis, the officers of the Lycurgus Society, and the executive committee of the Annunciation Church. What was presumed to have been an offer of the olive branch was more like pouring salt on an open wound. The offended Arcadians and their sympathizers immediately appointed a committee which was instructed to find suitable quarters immediately, so that Papatheodorou could hold services on his first Sunday in Chicago. Temporary quarters were found and services were conducted under the auspices of the newly formed Holy Trinity church community. Later this same group acquired an old Episcopalian church.[17] Thus we see how Old World rivalries contributed to the building of a church in the New World.

The next community to establish a church was that in Lowell, Massachusetts. In 1893 it extended an invitation to the Reverend

Callinicos Dilbaes of New York to come to Lowell and conduct services. The community leaders had been collecting pledges and memberships for a church for almost a year; and they appealed to the New York community for assistance in counteracting the activities of the evangelists who had been making inroads into the colony. Reverend Dilbaes officiated in Lowell a few times that year, and later he resigned from his New York church to serve this smaller community. However, for reasons that are not entirely clear, Dilbaes returned to New York.[18]

From 1891 to 1899, New York and Chicago were the only cities in which Greek Orthodox services were performed regularly. The priests in these cities visited nearby and distant communities officiating at weddings, christenings, funerals, and normal church services. Those from New York traveled to Providence, Boston, Lowell, and other cities in the New England area; they also journeyed to Baltimore, Philadelphia, and Pittsburgh. Those from Chicago ministered to the needs of nearby midwestern cities. The Greeks residing in the San Francisco area often were compelled to rely on the Russian clergy.[19]

Information regarding the number of Greek clergymen in the United States during the late 1890s is fragmentary. We know that there were regularly established churches in New York and Chicago, with assigned priests serving the parishes. From 1895 to 1900 it is estimated that there were about ten priests in the United States without regular assignments, some of whom probably were not ordained or recognized as canonical clergymen. Some of these traveled from city to city where small colonies of compatriots were to be found, offering their blessings and performing the rites. Others remained in New York and Chicago where they hoped to replace the regularly appointed priests or establish churches of their own. A few engaged in commercial activities.[20]

These early experiences in New York and Chicago reveal the general pattern of church organization that was to emerge in community after community. The initial stage was to organize a society, name it after some classical hero or ancestor, and solicit for members and pledges. In New York it was the Society of Athena, in Chicago the Society of Lycurgus, and in Boston it was to be the Society of Plato. After the nucleus for a church community was formed through the society, an appeal was made to the Holy Synod or the Ecumenical Patriarchate for a priest; sometimes suggestions came from a friend or relative who knew of a priest among the ranks of the unemployed in the United States or in some poverty-stricken village in Greece. Trespasses into the spiritual jurisdiction of the Ecumenical Patriarchate were common.

In the early years, the kinotitos was a miniature democracy in fact as well as in theory; it took its duties seriously. It owned the church properties, assumed control of the administration, hired and fired priests, teachers, and janitors at will, and gave ample vocal evidence of determination to govern all the community's affairs. The churches were free of doctrinal disputes, but what they were spared in this regard was more than outweighed by the ceaseless arguments over policy decisions and administration. These stormy sessions were partly products of clashing personalities and ambitions, carryovers from the Old World, and partly honest differences over the relative merits of priests, community officials, and community needs.[21]

While the Greeks were struggling to establish their churches, the Russian Orthodox Church was extending the scope of its activities in the United States. The spiritual head of the Russian church from 1891 to 1898 was the energetic Bishop Nicholas, a graduate of Moscow Theological Seminary, who arrived in the country with an active group of young men trained for service among the immigrants. By the time he had completed his assignment, he was credited with founding a missionary school in Minneapolis, the Syrian-Arabic Orthodox Church of America, several brotherhoods, an orphanage, and the first American periodical of the Russian Orthodox Church, the *Russian-American Orthodox Messenger*.

Bishop Nicholas organized churches wherever he could, having as his ultimate objective the uniting of all members of the Orthodox faith, regardless of nationality or race, under the jurisdiction of the Russian church. He worked with Greeks in New York, Chicago, San Francisco, New Orleans, Galveston, and elsewhere. Priests were brought to the United States to minister to Greek communicants; Greeks from Asia Minor were persuaded to further their studies in the "spiritual academies" of St. Petersburg, Moscow, Kazan, and Kiev; and a few Greeks served as missionaries of the Russian church in various American cities. The Greeks in San Francisco are known to have celebrated Independence Day on at least one occasion in the customary manner with the Russian bishop officiating. In Galveston Bishop Nicholas helped organize a new church with Greeks, Russians, and Syrians comprising the board of trustees and a Greek member of the Russian church serving as the parish priest. In Chicago, where Greeks attended the Russian church, along with Russians, Rumanians, Serbs, Poles, Bulgars, and others, the Slavic priest was replaced by a Macedonian Greek, the learned Ambrosios Vrettas.

This friendliness on the part of the Russian ecclesiastical authorities was suspected by many Greeks as being a part of a grand design to bring their scattered and unrepresented compatriots within the orbit of the Russian church. And they were right. Furthermore, many Greeks resented having a countryman serving as a priest for the Russian church; they denounced such a person as a tool of the Slavs and a traitor to the mother church in Constantinople.[22] Reliance on the Russians for spiritual guidance diminished after the turn of the century, as one community after another established its own church. The Greek-speaking priest officiating in a Greek-dominated church became more and more common. By 1904 the communities of Boston, Lowell, Milwaukee, Newark, Philadelphia, Birmingham, San Francisco, as well as New York and Chicago, were among those claiming community churches. The heaviest concentration was in the urban-industrial areas east of the Mississippi River.

The appearance of these churches was fitful and uncoordinated. In the New England states the mania for church-founding reached the point where churches were organized in communities that were fifteen to twenty minutes apart in travel time; this proliferation was again proof that the provincialism of the Old World was being reborn in the New. To state that this made for an uneven distribution of the available priests and was unsound from an economic standpoint is to belabor the obvious. Unemployment, or the fear of it, raised doubts regarding the abilities of communities to maintain these churches.[23]

Churches were slower in emerging in the western part of the United States. Between 1907 and 1909, churches were founded in San Francisco, Galveston, St. Louis, Pueblo, Salt Lake City, Omaha, Los Angeles, Kansas City, Portland, and Minneapolis. More Greeks lived and worked in the western states than the number of churches would suggest. But they were chiefly railroad workers, miners, and migrant workers scattered over wide areas and therefore unlikely to contribute to the support of any organization.

The increase in the number of churches continued throughout the

First World War. By 1918 what we might call the first cycle in the history of the Greek church in the United States had come to an end. Local independent churches had proliferated until, up to 1918, roughly one hundred and thirty church communities had been established. From 1914 through 1918 alone, sixty-one churches were organized, a record that was never again duplicated during any five-year period. Twenty were established during 1917 and thirteen during 1918. There is more involved here than the above-mentioned provincialism in the desire of each small community to have its own church. It was also proof of the growing need for spiritual guidance, as well as the significant fact that the immigrants were in the United States to stay.[24]

As we have seen, these churches functioned on a local and autonomous basis, without the directing force of a central authority. These units, thousands of miles away from their spiritual center, were nurtured by the same spirit of independence that influenced the churches of the Puritans and other immigrant groups. Each church community was a democracy unto itself. It was governed by a board of trustees or directors, many of whose members were small independent businessmen, marked by that commanding proprietary air so often found in the self-made man. Authority was vested in these laymen; and many a clergyman discovered, much to his astonishment, that if democracy was diverting or rewarding for his parishioners, it was not exactly so for him. Despite the shortage of qualified priests, laymen remained in unquestioned control of church administration. They displayed a zeal for detail that confounded the clerics. There was little danger of clerical domination in the Greek church communities of the United States.[25]

The capabilities of priests and their services to the community became a common subject of conversation. Priests sent to this country by the Holy Synod or the Ecumenical Patriarchate were dedicated men who served their parishes well. The unassigned clergyman often was a poorly trained one or an imposter who sold his services to desperate communities. Such a person bore credentials, sometimes of doubtful validity, from unqualified individuals in Greece, recommending him to unsuspecting members of a community.

The clergymen, qualified or unqualified, had adjustment problems of their own. The transition from a Greek rural to an American industrial environment, comprised of people of many ethnic and religious backgrounds, posed special difficulties. Greek Orthodoxy was a strange religion to the average American. This was a bewildering experience for a priest who hitherto had known only a state religion, whose compatriots had worshiped in one faith, spoken the same language, and observed the same customs.[26]

In the beginning priestly attire made for a good deal of difficulty. In Greece ecclesiastical tradition required the priest to wear long, wide, black robes and a tall hat. In the United States this seemed strange and out of place. When the first priests appeared in the city streets, they became objects of mirth and mockery. They attracted noisy attention and were often insulted, even stoned. The priests, it appears, were inclined to dismiss such incidents as the doings of mischievous youths and pranksters; but their compatriots viewed such behavior as "uncivilized, irreligious, and unjust" and thought it wrong of the municipal authorities to tolerate it.

The question of ecclesiastical garb brings to mind the visit of the Archbishop of Zante, the first ranking Greek prelate to visit the United States. The tall, dignified, and long-bearded hierarch, dressed in complete ecclesiastical accouterments, was surrounded and followed by jeering crowds whenever he walked in Chicago. He became the object of so much curiosity and ridicule that a bodyguard had to be provided for his protection. Some of his infuriated countrymen urged him to complain to the municipal authorities about this treatment. But he refused, saying that "The people are right. My apparel is wrong, and no complaint shall be made." But some indignant Greeks whose pride had been ruffled proceeded to the mayor's office where they demanded action. The mayor is quoted as having said to them: "Our American people are peaceable and would never have annoyed your bishop if he had complied with the habits and customs of our country and had attired himself accordingly."

Far more serious were the repeated complaints about the training, capabilities, and spiritual qualifications of the clergy. The criticisms were loud, persistent, and pointed. One such attack went as follows. The Holy Synod of Greece had sent to the United States as priests men who would be unable to qualify as messenger boys, coachmen, moneylenders, or gravediggers. These men, under the protection of the priestly robes, behaved in a manner that was unmeritorious in the eyes of God and Christians; some immigrants were led to fear unscrupulous clergymen more than the lack of a church. These were "deadwood," "scourges," and "invaders," who were undermining the pillars of the very religion and Hellenism they were supposed to be defending. What was needed by the communities was another Voltaire to strike down these ecclesiastical pirates.[27]

For two or three years prior to 1908, reports had been circulating that persons posing as priests were being admitted into the United States under the "exempt classes" clause. The presence of these false priests was known to the immigration authorities, but according to Oscar G. Straus, the secretary of commerce and labor, "they have . . . been molested to a very slight extent, by reason of their ecclesiastical status." The persistence of reports of fraudulent religious practices finally prompted the Immigration Service in Boston to employ Miltiades M. Constantinides, an interpreter, to investigate.[28]

Constantinides studied the cases of a few of these alleged Greek priests and learned that they "were not Greek Orthodox Priests at all and that they have no authority to perform a marriage ceremony or any other ceremony according to the Greek Orthodox Church." In most cases, he said, "their papers" (presumably the naturalization records) showed they were "inmates of a Monastery in Greece or Turkey" who came to America on the pretense of visiting relatives or, in rare cases, on annual leave. For the most part they were ordained as monks, not as priests, and had received no assignment in the United States from the church authorities. In some Greek colonies rumors were current that a few of these men were "plain outlaws" who came disguised as priests so as to enter the country without too close an examination.

Constantinides found that these monks traveled from community to community, offering their services "as fully qualified and properly ordained priests" for "half the salary the real priests of that Church demand." Marriages they performed were null and void; hence, one married by such a person was free to marry again without being subject to punishment. Constantinides also pointed out that a priest appointed for the diocese of Boston could not, according to the canons of the Greek Orthodox Church and the regulations of the Greek government, perform a lawful marriage ceremony in New York or any other state outside of Massachusetts, unless he had special authority to do so.

As a means of remedying these conditions, Constantinides recommended that every Greek Orthodox priest coming into the United States be required to have a passport signed by the Holy Synod of Greece, countersigned by the secretary of ecclesiastical affairs in Greece, and visaed by the American consul in Athens. This, he believed, would impose no hardship on the properly qualified priest and would be appreciated by the authorities in Greece, who were at a loss on how to handle these alleged priests.[29]

After the report of Constantinides was received and studied, Secretary Straus asked for the cooperation of the State Department in devising tests that could be used in detecting impostors.[30] Secretary Root accepted the recommendation of Straus and wrote Minister Coromilas for his opinion of the extent to which his government could go in certifying "the sacerdotal character of this class" of immigrants.[31] Coromilas responded that an agreement had been reached by the Holy Synod and the Patriarchates of Constantinople, Jerusalem, and Alexandria, which placed all priests emigrating to North America and belonging to these three Patriarchates under the jurisdiction of the Holy Synod of Greece.[32] Straus, however, felt that the Greek minister had not met the problem of how to detect the spurious priests who perpetrated their frauds on innocent people, and he pressed for a satisfactory explanation.[33] Root, on the other hand, felt that Coromilas' note was merely a preliminary response, that official documents would be provided the genuine ecclesiastics.[34]

Still another concern of the troubled church communities was the spread of evangelical sects among an immigrant people who did not know the language of the country, who felt neglected and alone, and suffered from unemployment. But in working among the Greeks the evangelists discovered that they were among people who were difficult to convert to another faith. In the end, the Greek church's initial concern was found to be unjustified.

The exact date that the evangelical groups made their appearance in Greek colonies is unknown, but it was probably at an early date. In 1910 an Athens newspaper noted the formation of the Greek Orthodox Reformed Church by one Meletius Golden, who described himself as a former archmandrite, guide at the Acropolis, teacher in the masonic lodge of Athens, an author of articles on the reformed faith, and a Salvation Army worker. In Chicago in 1915, a Bishop Papadopoulos and an associate issued a publication called *Hope* and distributed many tracts and leaflets in the Greek quarters of the city.[35] Evangelists did make some inroads into the Greek community of Chicago, and the resulting reaction was strong. Some blamed the chaotic conditions in their community affairs, the quarreling boards of trustees, partisan clergymen, and the failure of the priests to minister to the needy, the sick, and the distressed. Others, appealing to the patriotism of the Greeks, found little sympathy with "traitors" who embraced a strange faith. In their estimation, a man who renounced the Greek Orthodox Church was no Greek.[36]

All of these problems—dissension within the church communities, unqualified priests, evangelism—only underscored the long-recognized need for establishing a central authority over the immigrant churches. Ever since the Patriarchate of Constantinople had transferred its authority to the Holy Synod of Greece in 1908,[37] it was expected that the Church of Greece would appoint a bishop to the United States to function with a stern hand.[38] Segments of the Greek press in both Greece and the United States blamed Coromilas for the fact that no bishop was forthcoming. They believed that the minister was less concerned with the plight of the church than he was with the future role of the Panhellenic Union. Rightly or wrongly, Coromilas was accused of viewing religion as a medieval hindrance and of wanting the church to remain "headless" so that he could become the unquestioned leader of his compatriots in the United States.[39] It might be added, however, that Greece was having its own problems throughout these years. And it was not until after the Venizelos victory, the elevation of Meletios Metaxakis to the metropolitanship of Athens, and the outbreak of the Russian revolution, which undermined the position of the Russian church in the United States, that the Church of Greece felt free to act.

If conditions in Chicago from 1914 to 1917 were typical of those in communities across the country, the prestige of the clergy and local ecclesiastical administrations had fallen to an all-time low. The Greek-language press continued to attack what they called greedy, stingy, grasping priests, who, in league with conscienceless members of the boards of trustees, were trampling on the dignity of the church and the integrity of their communities. Lengthy court trials, criminal waste, and the extravagant use of church funds for litigation and lawyers' fees had become a disgrace.[40] Clerical commercialism became a favorite theme of the journalists. Even in sizable parishes, it was common to find a church without a priest on Sunday: he was in another community officiating at a baptism, wedding, or funeral, for lucrative fees.[41] There were other complaints as well, involving the unwillingness and failure of the clergy to adjust themselves to their new surroundings, to furnish education for the young, and to meet the spiritual needs of the parishioners. Too many priests thought that their only duties were to conduct routine services, often mumbled in an incorrect, parrotlike manner for a small group of inattentive worshipers.[42]

Pleas for unifying the parishes of Chicago were voiced frequently, and for a time it appeared as though they would be heeded. During the fall of 1915, the United Greek Parishes of Chicago, consisting of local priests, board presidents, and other representatives, announced an eight-plank platform designed to bring order out of confusion. The platform called for a thorough auditing of the financial records of the three parishes, the public listing of all debts, the purchase of a common burial lot, the maintenance of a consolidated school, the establishment of a high school with dormitory facilities that would be available to all Greek students in the United States, the creation of a special fund for the needy, and the building of a hospital.[43]

Others, even more ambitious in their aims, spoke out for a centralized program embracing all the parishes of the United States which, if nothing else, would regulate the priests. Listed among the more specific objectives was the regularization of priests' salaries in all parishes, the devising of ways to prevent an undesirable priest from moving from one parish to another, the rearranging of parishes so that no section of a large city would be without one, the standardization of ritual, and provision for the arbitration of disputes between the parishes. If the Holy Synod of Greece, for religious or political reasons, had not seen fit to send a bishop to the United States, it was up to the churches and their boards of trustees to provide a centralized administrative authority of their own.[44] The Chicago plans unfortunately went unfulfilled, largely because the time was not yet ripe for such concerted action.

At this point, two significant developments occurred which were to have momentous consequences for the church communities across the country. The first was the political division of Greece into the royalist

faction of King Constantine and the liberal faction of Eleutherios
Venizelos which, in turn, split the state church wide open. The second
was the decline in the influence of the Church of Russia and the
simultaneous rise of the Ecumenical Patriarchate to a role of temporary
importance in international affairs. These developments, instead of
pacifying the Greek-Americans and persuading them to bury their
differences, provided still further reason for the intensification of inter-
community quarrels.

The Eastern Orthodox Church, we have seen, consisted of a series of
independent churches and was comparable structurally to the Anglican
Church, which also was comprised of a series of independent churches
—such as the Irish, the Scottish, the Welsh, the American, and the
South African—under the primacy of the Archbishop of Canterbury.
In the past, various attempts had been made to effect a union of the two
churches. There were doctrinal differences between the two, to be sure;
but there also were structural similarities. Many continued to believe
that some kind of union would take place between them in the not
too distant future.

And for a time that moment appeared to have arrived. Prior to the
outbreak of the First World War, discussions began between the Anglican Church and the Russian Orthodox Church at the Patriarchate in
Moscow, with a view to removing doctrinal differences between the two.
This is believed to have been a factor in the secret Anglo-Russian
agreement of 1915 by which the British Foreign Office acquiesced to
Russia's design to annex Constantinople. But when tsarist Russia col-
lapsed in 1917 and the influence of the Russian church was thereby
weakened, this venue in Anglican-Orthodox interests was transferred
to the Ecumenical Patriarchate in Constantinople. Under the leadership of Venizelos, the Ecumenical Patriarchate and the Church of
Greece were to make common cause in behalf of Orthodoxy.[45]

By 1916, the royalist-liberal controversy was beginning to take its toll
in Greece. For this tragic chapter in history both church and lay leaders
were to blame. The church found itself hopelessly involved in a bitter
and bloody controversy from which it could not extricate itself. The
Church of Greece, we have seen, had been a state church from the very
beginning of the modern Greek nation, and willingly or unwillingly it
often served as the right arm of the political faction in power. It either
could not or would not steer a neutral course in the civil war raging

between the forces of Constantine and Venizelos. This partisanship was to shake the church communities of Greece, the United States, and other nations to their foundations. The first major event occurred late in 1916, when the royalist Metropolitan of Athens, surrounded by a group of bishops, excommunicated Venizelos according to an ancient ceremony.[46]

The reaction in the United States was violent. Liberal priests supporting the policies of Venizelos showed their displeasure by refusing to mention the name of the king and his family in the church services, and some priests insulted the king in public. In many communities the boards of trustees were divided into voluble royalist and Venizelist factions, with the priest often having to abide by the political preferences of the majority. Trouble was in store for any priest whose political preferences ran contrary to the sentiments of the majority of board members, or even of a vocal minority. Being neutral, something rare in the circumstances, could also get a priest into difficulty. In a large city such as New York, a determined group could, if necessary, found a parish committed to the political philosophy of its political idol. For instance, on May 2, 1918, St. Eleutherios, a liberal church named after Venizelos, opened its doors to partisan worshipers. Its priest, a native of Asia Minor, where Greek irredentism and political liberalism ran high, was a refugee from the royalist-dominated St. Constantine's Church of Brooklyn. Committed to a definite political philosophy, the church community worked toward the realization of the political ideals of its members.[47]

When the first period in the history of the Greek churches in the United States came to an end in 1918, confusion, dissension, and the lack of a centralized authority were the hallmarks. Court involvements, the spending of tens of thousands of dollars, and misspent energies paralyzed the resources of scores of communities. Each community considered itself a miniature democracy, but frequently it gave the impression of being a miniature kingdom. Each board of trustees concerned itself with its own affairs and ignored those of others. Churches were built too large or too small, often incompleted and flawed. Constitutions and bylaws confused clerical duties with lay responsibilities and clerical responsibilities with lay duties. And the priests, despite their professed belief in Christianity, displayed the same un-Christian and uncharitable spirit as their parishioners.[48]

The political civil war in Greece compounded the difficulties of the church communities in the United States. The arrival of a bishop in 1918 was welcomed, and many hoped that this would usher in an era of peace and order. But such was not to be the case. The angry clouds gathered on the horizon soon burst, thrusting the community churches into the fiercest ecclesiastical storm of their careers.

7

OLD-WORLD POLITICS
IN THE NEW: VENIZELISTS
VERSUS ROYALISTS

T HE OUTBREAK of the world war in 1914 had repercussions on the Greeks, as it had on the other nationality groups in the United States. They expressed concern over the role the mother country would play in the world struggle, and they soon aligned themselves into partisan factions. One group—Venizelist to the core—believed that the best interests of Greece would be served if she threw her lot in with France and Britain. A second group—consisting of diehard royalists— believed with equal determination that Greece should remain neutral. In these manifestations of partisanship, the Greeks unwitttingly were upholding a well-established American tradition. By displaying their preferences in European politics, they behaved no differently from the Puritans and Anglicans, the parliamentarians and royalists of seventeenth- and eighteenth-century America; from Americans of the post-Revolutionary era who divided themselves into pro-English and pro-French camps; or from the Irish-Americans, the German-Americans, or any other nationality group, new and old.

The interval between the Balkan Wars and the First World War was one of anxiety. Greek colonies in the United States tried to readjust themselves to peace and to plans for the future. As had been stated, the great majority of the 42,000 who fought for the mother country in the 1912–1913 wars are believed to have returned to America, many with their families and others with their brides.[1] The officials of the Pan-hellenic Union, we have seen, kept advising them to await the next call of their "beloved King Constantine," who would lead them farther along the road to national greatness.[2] The Greek-Americans, as a result, kept a vigilant eye on developments in Europe. Some departed for Greece as soon as their military classes were called to the colors. In cities such as Chicago, groups of fifty to one hundred grim and serious men often gathered late at night in the railroad station, to commence the first leg of their long journey overseas. They sensed that something of a far-reaching nature was soon to happen; and they departed without the fanfare of the Balkan War years.[3]

These preparations grew from the fear that the territories awarded Greece as a result of the Balkan victories were coveted by Bulgaria, Turkey, and Italy. But however apprehensive the Greeks were, they felt confident that their "national hero" King Constantine, Prime Minister Venizelos, and the Greek army would fight for the honor and integrity of the mother country. Everyone in the United States was expected to do his patriotic duty: support his family and relatives in Greece; contribute financially to the national cause; and, if necessary, return to the "sacred soil" of Greece to share in its perils.[4]

During 1914 many Greek-Americans became aroused over attacks leveled at Greece and the Greek army by segments of the American press. Particular exception was taken to "the Bulgarian propaganda" appearing in the columns of the *Chicago Examiner*.[5] George Knapp of the *Chicago Journal* was honored at a public dinner for answering "the Bulgarian press" in Chicago.[6] Concern, too, was displayed over the pending visit of Queen Eleanora of Bulgaria, lest this be used as another effort to vindicate Bulgaria and vilify Greece.[7]

The Greek-Americans also watched happenings along the Mexican border. If the United States had declared war on Mexico in 1914, the likelihood is that many Greek-Americans, for the first time in the country's history, would have enlisted in the armed forces in large numbers. But such hostilities never broke out; hence this restless and patriotic element concentrated its attention on happenings in the Old World. If Greece had declared war against its ancient enemy, Turkey, the exodus from the United States would have been large.[8]

Meanwhile the Panhellenic Union made feeble efforts to revitalize the Hellenic spirit in America. The records show that as late as October

1914 it had a paid membership of 4,931, but many thousands who never paid dues or attended its meetings subscribed to its principles.[9] The arrival in December 1914 of Demetrios Callimachos, the eloquent exponent of Hellenism, at the invitation of the Panhellenic Union, was but one sign that the campaign to advance the Greek national interest was being accelerated. Early in 1915 a speaker informed an attentive audience in New York City that King Constantine wanted a strong Panhellenic Union in the United States.[10] Its leaders repeatedly urged the establishment of more schools, churches, and other agencies capable of prepetuating Greek customs and traditions.[11]

Some people considered the Greek population of the United States a psychological and cultural, if not an organic, part of the Greek nation. Endless discussions of the impact that the war was likely to have on Greece went on, often creating the impression that the Greek-Americans were more aroused about the war and its effects than were their relatives abroad. One nationalist organ boasted: "For our people, no such thing as Bulgaria exists. We have visions of Rumania and Greece carving up the kingdom of Krummus [an ancient Bulgarian king], while with the support of the French and British fleets we can capture Constantinople, which we consider a traditionally Greek city. In the meantime we are expecting Mr. Venizelos to secure Asia Minor for Greece." [12]

There was much speculation about whether Greece would side with the Allies, the Central Powers, or neither. During the early stages those advocating neutrality seemed to be in command. But pro-Ally sentiment in the United States began to increase, especially after the appearance of the *National Herald*. This preference for the cause of the Entente is understandable. The pro-Ally sentiments of the American people naturally fed the latent pro-Ally sentiments of the Greek-Americans. Many of them knew enough modern Greek history to realize that England had contributed to the independence of modern Greece. Venizelos, who had a following in Western Europe, was pro-Entente. Consequently, when word was received late in April 1915 that the Greek government planned to pursue a course favorable to the Allies, it was no surprise that the Venizelist organ *Saloniki* of Chicago exclaimed: "We here in America and the entire Greek nation receive the pronouncement of the new government with great joy." [13]

Greece's entry into the war on the side of the Allies, according to the American Venizelists, was a necessary sacrifice. Her historic aspirations would be fulfilled through joining Servia against Bulgaria, through avenging herself for "five hundred years of slavery and torture" under "the unspeakable Turk," and through reclaiming lands such as Constantinople. Britain's offer of Cyprus, the Dodecanese Islands, and other territories was ample cause for the Greek-Americans' championing of the policy of Venizelos.[14] When it became apparent that King Constantine would not pursue a pro-Ally policy, tensions between the royalists and Venizelists increased. Spearheaded by the *National Herald,* the liberals became outspoken in their sympathies for Venizelos.[15]

This movement to mobilize forces behind Venizelos seems to have gotten under way in December 1915, when residents of New York City assembled to express their confidence and affection for the king of the Hellenes, but also to declare themselves "once and for all in favor of the Allies." [16] This was followed up by sending a copy of the resolutions to King Constantine, Venizelos, and the Greek committee in Paris that was arranging for a congress of Greek communities from all nations; the committee was under the complete control of Venizelists. After a prolonged discussion, the congress resolved that the constitutional liberties of Greece had to be safeguarded and that she had to abandon her policy of neutrality.[17]

The royalists were headed by the tall, popular, handsome King Constantine. When Constantine ascended the Greek throne, he felt that he had a divine mission to restore the grandeur of the old Byzantine Empire. He believed in the ancient prophecy popularized by the Greek clergy that, under the reign of a Constantine and Sophia, the Eastern Empire would be called back to life and the Crown would replace the Crescent on St. Sophia. Constantine had a German education, a profound admiration for German military might, and was married to Sophia, the sister of William II of Germany. Many believed that he wanted to lead Greece into the war on the side of the Central Powers, but regardless of what he did, he would offend one faction or another.[18]

Pitted against Constantine were the forces of Venizelos, the irredentist par excellence, who, we have seen, gained fame first in Crete and then as prime minister under George I and Constantine. Venizelos, unlike Constantine, believed that Greece's future was contingent upon the good will and cooperation of the Allies. He too appealed to the patriotic sentiments of the Greeks, and he pointed out the advantages of cooperating with France and Britain.[19]

The royalist and Venizelist factions in the United States were quick to assert themselves. *Atlantis* lost little time in making known its royalist preferences. Solon Vlasto was an ardent admirer of King Constantine and he made no secret of it; his sentiments were shared by many others in the United States. He and his newspaper had become so identified with royalism that it was difficult to think of Vlasto without also thinking of the king. When antiroyalist sentiment was running high, the foes of Vlasto never permitted him to forget his fanatical admiration for the king and the sword that he had presented to Constantine as a gift from the Greeks of the United States.[20]

Vlasto's editor during these years was Adamantios Polyzoides who, according to reports, once had been a Venizelist. This at least was the view of Garrett Droppers, the minister of the American legation in Athens, who informed Robert Lansing that "Polyzoides visited Greece in May, June, and July, 1916." [21] A number of years later Polyzoides stated that he had been on friendly terms with Venizelos, but that he opposed him politically.[22] In 1915, however, Polyzoides wrote that Venizelos had built a powerful organization modeled after the American party machine and the British political clubs, and that he was admired by Greeks at home.[23]

The first major Venizelist broadside in the United States was fired by the *National Herald,* which started to appear as a daily on April 2, 1915. Its publisher and editor-in-chief, as noted, were Petros Tatanis, a merchant of moderate wealth, and Demetrios Callimachos. Both came from the "unredeemed" portions of Greece. Earlier challengers of the *Atlantis* had been motivated more by a personal ambition to obtain a foothold in the Greek journalistic world of the United States. But this latest challenger of the *Atlantis* was inspired by its own set of principles and, as a result, succeeded where the others had failed.

It is difficult to state accurately how many Greek-Americans in the United States supported the royalist policies of the *Atlantis* and the Venizelist policies of the *National Herald.* Royalists claimed the support of the rank-and-file Greek-Americans; Venizelists countered with the charge that they, not the royalists, appealed to most Greek-Americans and to the most progressive elements in all communities. What ensued was a miniature Pulitzer-Hearst war. Both newspapers had followers in the form of subscribers and nonsubscribers who read their columns with the zealousness of religious converts.

Callimachos proved himself a crusader of the first order.[24] He identified himself with the new political era in Greece and helped to build effective Greek political clubs in the United States. And the magic name of Venizelos was strong enough to lend prestige to a movement in a land where sentiments were preponderantly pro-Entente.[25] Events in Greece accelerated the liberal campaign in the United States. Venizelos, after a series of unsuccessful attempts to persuade the king to abandon his policy of neutrality, in the fall of 1916 established a revolutionary government in Salonika. Greece for a time found herself under a dual role: the neutral government of Constantine and the revolutionary pro-Ally government of Venizelos. "New Greece was with Venizelos, while the old one was with the king." Both factions then reached out for the support of Greeks living abroad.[26]

The formation of the revolutionary Salonika government produced a chain reaction in America. On October 15, 1916, a tumultuous and enthusiastic crowd of more than three thousand Venizelists assembled in New York City to listen to a series of speakers espousing the cause of liberalism. An additional seven thousand held an overflowing meeting on the sidewalks, where they heard the king denounced for betraying their country and Venizelos applauded for wanting to save it. Resolutions were adopted that denounced Constantine for abandoning forts and munitions in Macedonia, allowing the Fourth Greek Regiment to be "kidnaped," and dishonoring Greece and all Hellenism in the eyes of the world. More than four thousand dollars was subscribed; several hundred, who were unable to contribute, offered themselves as volunteers in the army of Venizelos. A Committee of One Thousand also was formed to expand the work of organization.[27]

On October 21 Venizelos and his Revolutionary Committee in Salonika sent the following message to supporters in New York:

We wish to express our warmest thanks and appreciation to all organizers and collaborators who took part in the great national rally of last Sunday, and for the courageous expression of an undying patriotism. We congratulate the worthy Greeks of America and their heroic representatives who toil with honor and dignity. You are living in a great land where you enjoy individual and social freedom, feeling, however, as Greeks and as residents of the United States cognizant of your objections to a nation proud of its past and concerned over its future . . . Pursue your efforts with care . . . support our military organization . . . establish a treasury . . . for the support of the families of our soldiers.[28]

Elated by the swift response from Venizelos, the *National Herald* urged upon its readers the need for supporting his program. They would thus aid the Allies and the interests of a "Greater Greece." [29]

The royalists now began to mobilize their forces. According to Venizelist sources, thirteen hundred Greek soldiers had come to the United States, with expenses paid, to inform the Greek-Americans that they had a devoted king who was idolized by the masses.[30] Steps also had been taken by the Athens government of Constantine in 1916 to prevent the emigration of all males up to the age of fifty-one, including five hundred reservists who had residences in this country.[31]

The objectives of the revolutionary government of Venizelos were to obtain recognition and a free hand abroad in recruiting for its army. Once the Venizelist government had been recognized, the plan was to send official representatives to the United States, Egypt, Cyprus, and the other countries with substantial Greek colonies. In time George Kafantaris and Panos Aravantinos reached the United States for the express purpose of recruiting Greek and American volunteers for the army of the Salonika government.[32] The liberals knew that the royalists would react sharply to the mission of Kafantaris and Aravantinos, and one result was that Loyalist Leagues (Syndesmoi Nomotagon) sprang up in the major cities. What originally was announced as a campaign to recruit soldiers for the forces of Venizelos was now publicized as a mission for the "new Hellenism." Kafantaris and Aravantinos were here for the purpose of studying the living ways of the Greek-Americans with the hope of suggesting means of improving them. Men who were contributing with their blood and money for the regeneration of the mother country, in their opinion, deserved something more than they were receiving from the government of Constantine.[33]

Two other events worsened relations between the Venizelists and the royalists during December 1916: the first was the blockade of Greece by the Allies. A note was handed to the State Department by J. J. Jusserand, the French ambassador to the United States, announcing that the blockade of Greece would begin after December 8, 1916. Robert Lansing informed Jusserand that since Greece and the Allies were not at war, "the Unted States does not concede the right of a foreign power to interfere with the commercial rights of uninterested countries by the establishment of a blockade in the absence of war." In short, the United States refused to acquiesce to the extension of the "pacific blockade" that affected "disinterested and neutral nations." But Greek-Americans knew that the blockade would have disastrous effects on Greece, and they appealed to President Wilson to use his influence to have the Allies lift it.[34]

The second event which had a tremendous impact on the Greek-Americans was the excommunication of Venizelos. On December 26, 1916, Theoclitus, the Metropolitan of Athens and president of the Holy Synod of Greece, resolved to punish Venizelos for his revolutionary activities by performing the medieval rite. The Metropolitan, surrounded by eight bishops representing royalist Greece, chanted: " 'Cursed by Eleutherios Venizelos who imprisoned priests, who plotted against the King and his country.' Each participant cried, 'Cursed be he,' and cast a stone upon the cairn." [35]

The involvement of the Church of Greece in the politics of Greece gave Venizelist priests and laymen in the United States additional cause for stepping up their antiroyalist campaign. More priests began to omit the name of the king and his family from the services. This prompted the chargé d'affaires in Washington to dispatch a note to Greek consuls throughout the United States, asking what priests and in what communities omitted the name of the king and the members of the royal family in the services "so that the Holy Synod may adopt the necessary measures." [36]

Meanwhile, the royalists busied themselves in counteracting the activities of their liberal rivals. Branches of the Loyalist League eventually appeared in most, if not all, cities to defend Constantine from his American detractors. The royalists of New York City, under the leadership of the *Atlantis,* launched their crusade to undercut the efforts of the Venizelists "to drown Greece in blood," dethrone the king, and divide the Greeks of the United States into warring factions. Royalists in Washington, D.C., gathered in the Odd Fellows Hall of that city to hear a veteran of the Balkan Wars attack the Allies for their methods in trying to win the support of King Constantine.[37]

On the west coast the columns of the royalist *California* in San Francisco were filled with emotional letters to the editor, strongly worded resolutions, and exhortative comments that left little doubt about the preferences of the contributors. They believed they were making a last-ditch effort in behalf of faith and country. The king was no Germanophile, tyrant, or coward afraid of enemy bullets. "He is a Great Patriot," wrote one ardent admirer—"Such a King Hellenism wants and loves and admires. A King such as Constantine." [38]

In October 1916 Spiridon Lambros, a professor of history in the University of Athens, became prime minister. He was committed to a policy of "benevolent neutrality." [39] Lambros conferred with Garrett Droppers, the United States minister in Athens, on the current and future status of Greco-American relations. Droppers, in his memorandum to the Department of State, reported that during the course of the conversations Lambros used the German language "not only with fluency but with distinction." "He developed his theme with such a sureness of touch, going from point to point with such clarity and penetrating vision that at the end of the time I felt that I had listened to an intellectual display of a very high order." All the scholarly arguments at his command were laid out in support of Greek neutrality.

Lambros first touched upon the close commercial relations existing between the United States and Greece. American imports into Greece had increased because they were articles of high quality and suitable to Greek tastes. At the same time, products of Greek mines, such as emery and magnesite, and tobacco and currants had a good market in the United States. Lambros then spoke of Greece's lag in the application of science to agriculture and industry, and of how the United States could help in this regard. He mentioned the need for an intensive study of agriculture and the assistance that could be rendered in establishing schools in the practical arts. Lambros also stressed the need for a fundamental reorganization of the public utilities, harbors, docks, and telephone systems of Greece. Piraeus had to be prepared for the anticipated postwar expansion. After the war the railway from Piraeus and Athens had to be reconstructed as far north as Lamia, and materials, engineering skills, and capital would be needed. Why should not America invest some of her capital in Greece? Such investments would pay well and benefit both Americans and Greeks. A well-established American bank in Athens could serve as a medium for the introduction of such capital and the promotion of Greek business.

Nor were the immigrants in the United States forgotten. These immigrants, said Lambros, had been left to their own devices and went astray in a foreign atmosphere. He thought that this traffic could be regulated and a better class of immigrants sent to the United States. At the same time, more Americans could be persuaded to visit Greece during certain seasons of the year, if proper arrangements were made to receive them. Lambros also dwelled upon the tradition of good will that prevailed in Greece toward the United States. This went back to the days of the Greek War of Independence and the Cretan revolution of 1866. He cited the establishment of the Hill School, for many years the leading school in Athens for the education of girls; and he spoke of the need for establishing every "normal bond of law and justice" between the two countries. The need for closer intellectual ties was also discussed. The founding of the American Archaeological School, Lambros observed, was a good beginning. But there was need for more of this kind of intellectual exchange. "France and Germany had instituted the system of exchanging professors with the United States; was it not possible for Greece to establish the same practice?"

Droppers viewed this as "a refreshing discussion," which belied the actual pressure of events. But, he added, Lambros believed that "to realize these purposes, Greece is in need of peace. The war and its fatal results for Greece must come to an end, and towards this consummation he begged to bespeak my assistance and that of my Government." Lambros was a very intelligent man with a reputation extending beyond the borders of his own country. But he was at the head of a caretaker government; hence, he had no party backing.[40]

Events in the United States were proceeding at a dramatic pace. Early in February 1917, the Liberal Club of Chicago invited Kafantaris and Aravantinos to address members and sympathizers at a rally in the Coliseum Annex. The public announcement had made it clear that this mass meeting was intended solely for those who had committed themselves to the Salonika program. This meant that anyone holding a contrary position was unwelcome. The rally was called to hear speakers elaborate on an established position without the customary disorders and wrangling, to present a massive display of Venizelos strength, to clarify the differences between royalists and Venizelists, to make evident whose side the leading citizens of the city were taking, and to adopt a program of action for the liberals of Chicago.[41]

The police authorities of Chicago were familiar with what had happened on previous occasions when "Greek met Greek" to discuss politics. And in their determination to prevent the Coliseum Annex from being converted into a Greek battle front, they dispatched a force of seventy-five policemen to the scene. A committee of two hundred and twenty-five Venizelists also had been commissioned to help preserve order; above all else, the duty of this massive committee was to see to it that no royalists gained entrance. Royalists had been warned days in advance that, for the sake of the Greek name, decency, and their own safety, it would be unwise for them to attempt to attend. The notices stated that force would be employed, if necessary, to implement this warning.

But the inevitable occurred. Chicago Loyalty Leaguers disregarded the Venizelist warnings and decided in behalf of the national interest to invade the enemy camp. Their arrival was preceded by that of the Venizelists, who came in phalanxes of fifty deep. Then came some seventy royalists, headed by three leaders, who were intercepted by a group of about seventy-five Venizelists, flanked by policemen. But as the opposing forces met, the policemen were unable to tell a Venizelist from a royalist: "it was all Greek to them." But according to a sympathetic account, "the committee gently picked up the Royalists from the ground as if they had been so many dolls and set them aside . . . making room for the arriving phalanxes of Venizelists."

In time two hundred Cretans in military formation reached the scenes, followed by hundreds of other Greeks. Upon learning of the royalist attempts to disrupt the rally honoring their Cretan compatriot, Venizelos, they hurriedly relieved themselves of their flags, banners, and other paraphernalia, and "fell upon the poor Royalists like hounds." People arrived in such multitudes that the Coliseum Annex was filled to the point of suffocation. For the most part, the royalists' efforts to enter the meeting hall and prevent the revolutionary emissaries from slandering the king were frustrated; a few were arrested for carrying concealed weapons. When the meeting began, about one hundred and fifty royalists were outside and more were arriving, "uttering threats to air and cloud . . . The policemen's ears were not shocked at all. Everything was in Greek; not one word in English."

Inside, the meeting proceeded in a quiet and dignified manner until one inflamed Venizelist arose and cried: "The followers of the traitorous King are hereby requested to leave the auditorium." Pandemonium broke loose: whistling, catcalls, and angry shouts filled the air. When the fighting ceased, ten were wounded and a number of others seized by the police.

The actual meeting took its expected course. Kafantaris and Aravantinos informed their listeners that Greece had been dishonored, discredited, and disunited by the regime of the king. The resolutions adopted by the mass meeting lived up to the fondest expectations of the revolutionary committee. They endorsed the Salonika government of Venizelos, denounced the "unconstitutional and courtier government of Athens" for surrendering Greek territory, people, and forts to the Bulgars, asked for an Allied victory, and informed the President of the United States that those in attendance were prepared to serve under the American flag whenever the call came. Finally, asserting that three fourths of the Greek population in the United States was Venizelist, the President was asked to recognize the Salonika government in order to serve the interests of the Greek-Americans.[42]

The Chicago liberals waxed eloquently over the magnitude of their February rally. More than twelve thousand Greek-Americans had assembled under one roof—an achievement in itself—to denounce the king and announce their willingness to give body and soul to the Venizelos government. They obtained added moral encouragement from a telegram sent them by their "saviour."[43] "Accept my deep appreciation and thanks," said Venizelos. "Your patriotic sentiments gave tremendous moral support to the endeavors of us Greeks, united under the temporary government, who are striving to restore our national honor and prestige and fulfill Greece's obligations to our protectors, the Allies."[44]

The royalists met kind with kind, deriding and discounting the claims of their political foes. *Atlantis* branded the Chicago meeting a hoax, saying that the bulk of the participants were Hungarians and members of "other races," not Greeks.[45] They blamed Kafantaris and Aravantinos for the disorders in Chicago and other cities they visited; they warned that as long as these revolutionary emissaries remained in the United States, they would serve no purpose other than to create dissension and riots that would prove harmful to Hellenism.[46] A genuine Greek, in the opinion of the Loyalty Leaguers, could not recognize as Greeks those who planned to dethrone Constantine. The king was a Greek's Greek: "those who are Frenchifying, Anglicizing, Italianizing, or wishing to sell their country to the foreigners, let them remain outside Greece permanently. They are not Greeks. They are tools of foreigners. They are tools of the most repulsive infamies. They are slanderers. They are base. They are ungrateful. They are bloodthirsty." The finances of these revolutionaries, said the royalists, came from Anglo-French sources.[47]

Thus by March 1917 the struggle between the revolutionary government of Venizelos in Salonika and the government of King Constantine in Athens had stretched out into the United States. Each faction accused the other of disloyalty to the Greek cause, stupidity, and base motives. The liberals were ardent irredentists, sharing in the same spirit of self-determination held by the other subject peoples of Europe; they believed that the future greatness of Greece woud be insured only if she became an ally of the Western powers. The irredentist beliefs of the royalists were just as strong, except that they believed Greece should remain neutral, consolidate her gains of the Balkan Wars, and refuse to enter the war unless her security and territorial aspirations were respected.[48]

Many Greek-Americans protested the formation of both the Liberal Clubs and the Loyalty Leagues, claiming that they had no place in the United States. But since the most vocal elements were either liberals or royalists, all with their own publishing outlets, and not the uncommitted, it is impossible to state just how many Greek-Americans disassociated themselves from both factions. These nonparticipants had no newspaper of their own; they merely abstained with varying degrees of indifference or contempt. The editor of *California* agreed in part with the critics of both factions. Loyalist Leagues, he charged, probably would never have appeared had it not been for the liberals staging the first meeting and proclaiming that most of the Greeks in the United States were liberals, united in a campaign to dethrone the king. It was because of the appearance of the Liberal Clubs, and the derogatory accounts of the king and Greece in the newspapers, that Loyalty Leagues came into existence in New York, Chicago, San Francisco, and other cities.[49]

On April 8, 1917, two days after President Wilson delivered his war message to Congress, the royalists and Venizelists held mass meetings to proclaim their loyalty to the United States. Nicholas Murray Butler, the president of Columbia University, addressed the Venizelists and commended their efforts; Paxton Hibben, a newspaper correspondent and a confirmed royalist, praised the Greek nation and defended King Constantine against the charges of pro-Germanism. Both meetings were attended by veterans wearing service medals won in the Balkan Wars; men in both meetings rose en masse to offer themselves as volunteers to the United States army.[50]

The liberals had an easier time in identifying themselves with the American war effort, for all along they had been urging the entry of Greece into the war on the side of the Allies. They resolved to make any sacrifices asked of them on behalf of the United States; no request was too big; and they demanded that King Constantine be deposed. A message from Venizelos avowed that sacrifices made for the United States were sacrifices for Greece. Aravantinos, while still in America, informed his audiences that Venizelos authorized him to urge all Greek subjects to enlist under the American flag.[51] For the royalists, the entry of the United States into the war on the side of the Allies placed them in an unenviable position. Royalist newspapers had been regaling the people of Greece with stories that the United States would intervene and support the regime of Constantine. But now that the United States had declared war on Germany, their fondest hopes were shattered.[52]

The declaration of war in no way interfered with the loyalty of the Greeks to the United States. The Greek-language press, liberal and royalist alike, did its part in making the people conscious of the war and its meaning. Both factions published war dispatches, echoed and re-echoed the policies of Woodrow Wilson, and urged their readers to grow more food and purchase war bonds. Rarely, if ever, was there any overt expression of opposition to the policies of the federal government. Allegiance to Old World political favorites, royalist as well as liberal, was portrayed as being consistent with the war aims of the United States.

If the Greek-Americans were unanimous in support of American war aims, there is little evidence that they forgot their own partisan differences. These continued as if the United States had still been at peace. In Brooklyn a miniature civil war was fought in the basement of St. Constantine's Church, when the royalists sought to expel the priest for omitting "Long Live the King" from the Sunday prayer, and police had to be called to restore peace. While "the king's men" were at the police station complaining about the religious, political, and military zeal of the priest and the liberals, their adversaries hastily elected a new board of trustees, which informed the priest that he was free to omit the prayer for the king.[53]

The royalists were quite right in charging that the major aim of the Kafantaris-Aravantinos mission was to help obtain recognition for the Venizelos government. Official channels had started working in that direction before the United States entered the war. On March 30, 1917, Garrett Droppers telegraphed from Athens to Secretary of State Lansing: "Provisional Government Salonica requests recognition by Government of the United States with a view of sending accredited agent Washington."[54] A few days later, Walter Hines Page, United States ambassador in London, telegraphed to the State Department: "Gennadius long Minister here of Greece and now representative of Venizelos and an important man in the liberal faction in Greece requests me informally to present to you the great desire of the Venizelos Government for recognition by the United States. Great Britain and France had recognized the Federal [Venizelos] Government. Gennadius you will recall was formerly in Washington."[55] On April 4 Secretary Lansing telegraphed Droppers: "Cable Department full details status provisional government, both as to the extent of territory over which it exercises authority, and the character and completeness such authority. Also cable all available data relative to parliamentary elections won by Venizelist on war issues, and to action of King dissolving Parliament and calling new election while army was mobilized. Any further information which might be of use to Department in forming correct opinion on Grecian situation desired, also your opinion on matter."[56]

Informed royalists left no stone unturned in attempting to block the recognition of the Venizelos government. Demetrios J. Theophilatos, a rabid supporter of King Constantine, protested the recognition of the Salonika government and complained of the partisanship of Droppers. Venizelos, charged Theopilatos, was a dictator whose government could not stand without the active aid of American bayonets. Recognition would harm the United States more than it would the European powers. He added that thousands of Greek reservists who fought in the Balkan Wars hesitated to join the armed forces of the United States, lest they be called upon "to fight their brothers of constitutional Greece." The sensible thing for the President of the United States to do was to appoint an impartial committee to inquire into actual conditions and thus safeguard the interests of both the United States and Greece.[57]

Demosthenes T. Timayenis, a voluble participant of long standing in Greek-American affairs, and a man with a talent for inconsistency, also protested the proposed recognition of the Venizelos government. He addressed letters to various groups and individuals, attempting to influence opinion on the attitude the United States should adopt toward the rival Greek governments.[58] On May 2 Timayenis also addressed a letter to Secretary of State Lansing, identifying himself as both consul general of Greece and an American citizen. He complained that Kafantaris and Aravantinos came to the United States for the sole purpose of rallying the Greeks in America behind Venizelos: "they had no purpose to advance the interests of the United States but merely to stir up sedition against the established Greek Government."

Timayenis insisted that the majority of Greeks here and abroad believed in the king and asked that the Allied nations cease coercing Greece. If the United States viewed with displeasure the German invasion of Belgium, it must view with equal displeasure the "unlawful invasion of Greek territory and the abuse of Greek sovereignty by the Allied forces." Then, continuing in the fashion of Theophilatos, he added, "There are many Greeks in this country who are now desirous of serving their adopted land in the same way. I think I speak in the interests of the United States when I urge upon Mr. Secretary that our government be not involved in activities on Greek soil and concerning Greek politics."[59] State Department representatives took a dim view of the letter-writing activities of Timayenis. The Greek chargé in Washington had already presented the royalist side of the controversy. But since the consul was now interfering in the affair, there was a matter of protocol involved. Was he writing as the consul general of Greece or as an American citizen? If as the consul general, he was writing in violation of protocol; if as an American citizen, he had made statements that were "false and misleading."[60]

Lansing in time informed the Greek chargé d'affaires in Washington of the communication he had received from Timayenis. The Greek chargé lost little time in admonishing Timayenis "never again to resort to such a practice," to which he replied with equal dispatch. Timayenis said he had no idea that the State Department would resent his actions and insisted that he had acted as an American citizen. For that reason he had not sought the advice of the royal legation.[61]

Meanwhile, events in Greece took a course favorable to the cause of Venizelos and the Allies. Allied pressure on King Constantine continued, and on June 12, 1917, he abdicated. Crown Prince George was eliminated as a possible successor to his father because he was pro-German. As a result, the crown passed to twenty-four-year-old Prince Alexander, a Venizelist and pro-Entente in sentiments.[62] Allied troops occupied Athens to preserve order while the new government took office and a blockade was raised. Alexander then called upon Venizelos to assume the premiership of Greece, and shortly afterwards diplomatic relations between Greece and the Central Powers were broken.[63]

With Greece safely on the side of the Allies, the Greek-American liberals turned their guns on the *Atlantis,* hoping to silence its endless attacks on Venizelos. Liberal Clubs in various parts of the country drafted resolutions in denunciation of royalist critics.[64] The old consuls representing the royalist government were gone; those representing the newly formed government, even though most had come from assignments in Turkey and Bulgaria, were "thoroughly loyal to the Entente cause." [65] Only the hostile press remained.

On July 29, 1917, the Greek liberals of Marlboro, Massachusetts, initiated the move that led to an inquiry into the activities of the *Atlantis.*[66] The Marlboro liberals, after pledging their support to Venizelos, rejoicing over his return to power, and expressing gratitude to the Allies for protecting Greece, called attention to "the pro-German propaganda" being disseminated by *Atlantis.* The Office of the Attorney General of the United States, after receiving a copy of the Marlboro resolutions, called upon Francis G. Caffey, the United States attorney in New York City, to look into the columns of *Atlantis,* "to determine whether its publication and circulation constitute a violation of any Federal law." Nicholas G. Psaki, a practicing attorney of many years standing and a naturalized citizen who knew the Greek language, the activities of *Atlantis,* and the various organizations and individuals concerned, was appointed as special assistant on the case. His job was to help decide whether *Atlantis* had violated the Espionage Act of June 15, 1917.[67]

Psaki, after studying the contents of *Atlantis,* especially for the month of September 1917, submitted a series of exhibits which he believed violated the law.[68] The day after Psaki submitted his report, *Atlantis,* perhaps by coincidence, proclaimed its Americanism in unmistakable terms. In a special article it reviewed the position it had taken on the war from the day that hostilities began, in August 1914, down to the time the United States declared war against the Central Powers. From then on *Atlantis* had maintained that Greece must join the Allies; the only reservations it voiced were that the national rights of Greece had to be recognized and that Greece was to choose the proper moment for entering the war.

The *Atlantis* had proclaimed its loyalty to the United States on various occasions. It had condemned the sinking of the *Lusitania,* branded Germany "an outlaw nation," and "never compromised with German barbarity." It had hailed the war message of Wilson as "the truest gospel of liberty," urged Greeks to volunteer in the United States army, and pleaded with them for twenty-four years to become fullfledged American citizens. In fact, the article went on, *Atlantis* had persistently advocated naturalization when the same "pseudo-patriots" now slandering the paper were opposing it. Its opposition to the Allies was one of detail, not principle; its criticism of Venizelos was based on the belief that he was an obstructionist and thus of disservice to Greece and the United States.[69] This statement by *Atlantis* does seem to be a reasonably fair account of its policies.

Caffey, at any rate, differed with Psaki over the guilt of *Atlantis.* Caffey wrote: "I do not feel that the extracts in question, whatever may be the intent behind them, fairly fall within the prohibition of the statute in question. The propaganda appears to be directed against Mr. Venizelos personally as not being the best qualified leader of the Greek nation in the present crisis, and there is so much exhortation to loyalty to this nation and to the cause of the Allies in the selections submitted, that the Grand Jury, in my opinion, would never return an indictment if the matter were presented to it." [70] The reply from the Office of the Attorney General concurred with the opinion of Caffey.[71]

Rumors of a plot to take the life of Venizelos also reached the United States. In a communication to the Greek legation in Washington, dated November 26, 1917, a member of the Greek diplomatic corps in Paris said: "The French Government informs me that New York

Royalist Committee composed of Mr. Theophilatos Pandelis Sioris is reported to have organized a plot against the life of Mr. Venizelos. Fotios Doufas selected to commit criminal attempt is now in France ... Organization is said to have paid $18,000 for assassination." [72]

Complaints against the *Atlantis* did not cease here, however. After it became apparent that the paper could not be prosecuted for violating the Sedition Act, the charge arose it was being subsidized with royalist funds to wage an anti-Venizelist campaign in the United States. The State Department immediately took action to investigate the charges of the Venizelists. On November 23, 1917, it sent a telegram to the American legation in Athens, asking information and evidence that $5,000 had been sent the *Atlantis* in appreciation of its anti-Venizelos activities. [73] On December 8 Droppers telegraphed the State Department that the Greek government did appropriate $5,000 for the Greek chargé in Washington to combat Venizelism in the United States, and he singled out *Atlantis* as the logical outlet for this. "I agree with the Greek Government [that of Venizelos] that Constantinism is a form of German propaganda and supported in part by German funds. Agents of this propaganda in New York are Vlasto Theophilatos Sioris Polyzoides. Last named here in May, June, July 1916, and to my knowledge changed to royalist cause from Venizelist at that time." [74]

Droppers was convinced that the only newspaper in the United States that had the earmarks of having been subsidized by the royalists was the *Atlantis*. Vlasto had "a very unsavory reputation in Greece," according to Droppers. "In all my three years of residence in Athens, I have never heard a good word spoken of him. Former Greek consular officers in the United States all describe him as mercenary and corrupt." Members of the Kafantaris and Aravantinos mission to the United States reported that they encountered their greatest opposition from the *Atlantis*. Droppers also related that Polyzoides, the editor of the *Atlantis,* visited Greece during 1916 and returned to the United States on the same steamer that carried his own family. On his arrival in Athens, Polyzoides had been an ardent Venizelist, but on leaving, said Droppers, "I saw that he had completely reversed his position."

The *Atlantis,* it appears, had also antagonized the British authorities in Greece. On October 28, 1917, Lieutenant-Colonel Edward Grogan of the intelligence bureau of the British Salonika force addressed a letter of complaint to George Horton, the American consul general in that city. Grogan wrote: "The circulation of this paper, as you probably are aware, is prohibited in Greece, and it is thought that you might perhaps wish to call the attention of the American Press Bureau to the sentiments expressed, or even to recommend to them to take steps to suspend its publication entirely."

The indignation of official British circles was aroused by an editorial that appeared in the August 22, 1917, issue, which stated that the unfortified city of Athens had been bombarded by an Allied fleet in December and that innocent persons had been killed. Members of the American legation in Athens at the time had testified that the Allied fleet did fire about thirty shells, from which charges had been removed to prevent explosions, over the city into the hills beyond. There was no loss of life, as far as was known. "This action was taken to intimidate the Royalist troops who had been attacked and slain a number of French marines, and who at that time were engaged in maltreating and imprisoning prominent members of the Venizelist faction and looting their homes. Moreover, artillery was fired from at least two places in this so-called 'unfortified city.'" Paxton Hibben, who had written many articles in favor of the government of the ex-king and was quoted in this particular editorial, was relieved of his duties by the Associated Press. The Parliamentary Committee of Investigation, according to the Athens and Salonika newspapers, said that Hibben had received a decoration and a substantial monthly stipend from the royalist government.[75]

On February 28, 1918, another strong protest was made against *Atlantis* by George Roussos, the Greek minister in Washington. In a letter to William Phillips, the first assistant secretary of state, Roussos warned that the harm done by *Atlantis* was great and that measures had to be taken to curb it. For a time its activities had been confined to the Greeks in the United States; now it was confining its activities to Greece. It exaggerated the news by representing the internal situation in Greece as a hopeless one, writing, in one instance: "Greece forsaken by her allies and with everything to lose and nothing to gain by the war." It fabricated or exaggerated accounts of officers being jailed or shot and men not responding to the call of arms. "It is an indirect continuation of the defeatism . . . carried on in Greece by German propaganda which preaches that as a neutral Greece had Germany's guarantee of her territorial integrity while as a belligerent she had no such thing." "Why should we bear with those agents of defeatism, allow them to carry on their nefarious work?" asked Roussos. "They are not even American citizens; they are all aliens. Why let them abuse your hospitality in engaging in pursuits which at home would have landed them in jail long ago? If the newspapers cannot be suppressed, why tolerate the presence of those men who were in fact the tools of the common foe?" [76]

The sentiments of the American minister in Athens appear to have been of a very rigid nature. Droppers wrote and spoke in positive and unhesitating fashion. Compton Mackenzie of the British secret service found that he "was like an American Minister in a novel or play; and, so unerringly did he speak and behave as one expected he would, I ended by finding it hard to believe he was real." Prior to his appointment as minister, Droppers had been a professor in Williams College, where he was an authority on international law. He brought with him to Greece "every New England prejudice he possessed," Mackenzie stated. He was perpetually exasperated with the backwardness of Europe. "His credulity was excessive," said Mackenzie, "and after listening to his tirades I felt I understood a little better that astonishing business of the witch-burnings in Salem." Mackenzie found that Droppers was unable to understand many things about Europe, especially that these nations were fighting for their very existence. "He had written a book on International Law, and his attitude on Greece during those heartbreaking years remained that of an angry professor who had been compelled to watch a lot of naughty little boys deliberately tearing out page after page of his life's work." [77] There can be little doubt that Mackenzie's assessment had a good deal of truth in it. Droppers' inflexible attitude, as seen in his communications, was exceeded only by his contempt for the Greeks, whom he never understood.

The reports of George Horton, the American consul general in Salonika, were marked by a greater degree of reasonableness, charity, and understanding. On November 23, 1917, Horton submitted a report to the State Department, on the "Political Situation in Greece," in which he gave a very penetrating analysis of conditions in the country. Horton had a thorough knowledge of the Greek language and said that he spoke it almost as well as his own. His twenty-five years of experience in Greece or among Greeks had brought him many good friends in both Venizelist and royalist circles, and this gave him an unusual opportunity to hear both sides of the question.

Horton made it clear that Constantine was popular among Greeks who were also pro-Entente. He was well liked because of his role in the Balkan Wars; his expulsion by the Allies elevated him to the status of a mythical hero among those who remembered him for his personal and military successes and forgot or were unaware of his political blunders. (The influence of German propaganda was still being felt in Greece.) Horton emphasized what consular, diplomatic, and business representatives had so often said: "The Greeks are a proud sensitive people, and can be led by flattery and enthusiasm where they cannot be driven or coerced." He pointed out their insatiable patriotism and the deeply felt influence of the Great Idea of Hellenism. The Greeks also were "a keenly practical race, and must know why and for what they are fighting and expending blood and treasure." The failure or unwillingness of the Allies to understand these attributes of the Greek character contributed to the continuance of the political crisis in Greece.

This was an appropriate time, Horton went on, for the United States to send food supplies to suffering Greece. It would be a humanitarian move that the people would never forget. And it "would give the American people first place in the hearts of the country, and in the commercial and industrial awakening which is certain to take place at the conclusion of hostilities. From the military standpoint, also, it would . . . greatly add to the growing prestige of the United States in the Near East." [78]

The Greek-Americans found it quite impossible to divorce themselves from the internal politics of the mother country. This was inevitable, since they had been in the United States for only a few years and many had planned to return as soon as circumstances warranted. Being people with strong political inclinations, they organized themselves into rival factions; both sides issued propaganda, held public rallies, raised funds, passed resolutions, and denounced each other with passion. Both sides attempted to influence American foreign policy toward Greece, and the evidence shows that the Venizelists had more success than the royalists.

8

THE FIRST WORLD WAR

A s WE have seen, the heated intracommunity struggles between royalists and Venizelists over the government of Greece in no way lessened the concern of the Greeks with the American war effort. They had declared their affection and loyalty to the United States time and time again, and years before hostilities began. If there were any doubts, it was soon proved that being partisan in Old World politics in no way hampered the Greek-American's allegiance to his new country. Once Congress voted for war, the Greeks seized every opportunity to demonstrate their loyalty. They responded enthusiastically to the call for volunteers in the armed forces, purchased liberty and victory bonds, passed resolution after resolution expressing their determination to see the war fought to a victorious conclusion, pleaded with their compatriots to contribute their utmost to the war effort, and served notice that as a national group their loyalty was second to none.

There had been attacks on Greece and the bravery of her soldiers during the Balkan Wars, which had been deeply resented, and this inspired some of the more sensitive to proclaim publicly that they were prepared to defend American rights at the first call. A Captain George Petropoulos, the president of the Greek-American Athletic Club of Chicago and the leader of a Chicago regiment that fought in the Balkan Wars, announced that his six hundred veterans were prepared to go to the front lines at a moment's notice.[1] At about the same time, Colonel Thomas Hutchison, the retired army officer who had served as a volunteer in the Balkan Wars, was invited to come to Chicago to organize a regiment of evzones and lead it into battle against the Mexicans when the need arose. Compatriots in other cities also were reported as organizing to march into the Mexican trouble zone.[2]

"There is no Greek in America whose blood does not race at the prospect of war between America and Mexico," wrote *Saloniki*. "Many Greeks from all over America have made public statements of their sincere willingness to fight for the honor of the Stars and Stripes as gallantly as they would for the Blue and White of Greece." [3]

As the prospects of war between America and Germany increased, the proclamations of Greeks willing to fight for the United States multiplied. "We are, as a race, Greek, and will remain so, but America is our country, America is our home, our estate, our family, our church, our education, and everything we possess. Therefore, it is our holy duty to fight and protect our country which is our life." [4] One Constantine Paleologus of Chicago, who signed himself as a member of "the Byzantine Imperial House," cabled President Wilson: "In the name of my countrymen and as an echo of the feelings of three hundred thousand Greeks who are living in this country, I respectfully report to you that we are ready at your Excellency's order to sacrifice ourselves on the altar of our glorious and beloved country." [5] A few weeks later this same Paleologus announced: "I decided to organize a battalion composed of Greek men who will offer [their] services to the American government. Many such battalions have already been organized by various clubs and some of the other language groups of Chicago. Therefore it is fitting that the Greeks of Chicago should organize such a battalion immediately." [6] *Hellinikos Astir,* whose patriotic editorializing could match that of any Greek newspaper, observed: "Now it is no longer a question of being pro-Ally or pro-German, but it is a question of pure Americanism. And we, the Greek-Americans—loyal Americans—are here to stand by the flag—the flag that flies over 'land of the free and the home of the brave.'" [7]

When the Selective Service Act was passed in 1917, the Greeks were urged to heed Wilson's proclamation and register on June 5. [8] One sensitive, perhaps astute, editor advised all countrymen whose names had been abbreviated or Anglicized to register under their full Greek name and any Greek aliases they may have used. This, he argued, was necessary, for it added honor and distinction to "fighting for Uncle Sam." If America was fighting for liberty, democracy, and justice, "your full Greek name must be registered in the annals of Greek-American history." [9] The purchase of liberty bonds was urged upon all societies, organizations, and individuals. "Distinguish yourself; buy more than your neighbor; buy more than you can. But the best way is to buy as a group. Let us have Greek meetings and make our object known. Let us lead, so that other nationalities will follow our example. United States government bonds are our safety and our security." [10]

A representative community meeting in Hull House in Chicago passed resolutions urging members of all Greek communities to display their loyalty to the United States in the most effective manner possible, volunteer for the armed forces, buy liberty bonds, support the American Red Cross, and above all express thanks and appreciation for the sincere and humane consideration that the United States has displayed toward Greece since 1821.[11]

The Greek-Americans proved sensitive to the slightest insinuation that they were either unpatriotic or unwilling to serve with the armed forces of the United States. These charges generally stemmed from letters written by royalist propagandists and sympathizers to the press and congressmen, stating that Greek-Americans were reluctant about joining the United States army lest they be used to fight against their brothers in Greece. But community leaders insisted that their members were enlisting in the armed forces in substantial numbers, and that veterans of the Greco-Turkish War of 1897 had fought in the Spanish-American War in 1898.[12] At first Greeks were urged to join the armed forces of the United States as proof of their loyalty and love for America. Then late in December 1917 they were instructed to enlist as though they were enlisting for service in the Greek army; for enlistment in the armed forces of the United States, they were advised, was tantamount to serving with the armed forces of Greece.[13]

The Greek legation in Washington made at least two requests of the United States government for aid in mobilizing Greek nationals for military service. The first request, if successful, would have them returned to Greece. But it was disapproved on October 30, 1917, on the grounds that the United States "was not at war with Austria-Hungary, Bulgaria, or Turkey [countries] against whom the Greek forces would probably have to fight," and that ships were unavailable for the transport of such troops. Failing in this initial effort, the legation then proposed recruiting "the mobilizable classes" of Greek nationals in the United States, concentrating them in camps selected by the United States, and, if possible, forming them into separate divisions. These troops, according to the legation, could be officered by the reservists in their midst or by such men as the Greek government might furnish. Many men had seen service in the Balkan Wars and could be incorporated into the United States army and fight when ordered. The ranking officers of this command were to be Americans, unless the United States decided differently.

This time the War Department denied the request of the Greek legation on the grounds of precedent and policy. The secretary of war referred to a comparable request made by the Russians for help in forming a regiment and that he had replied that "the forming of organizations from unnaturalized residents of the United States in order that they may serve in the Allied armies is not permitted." In another instance, "the Bohemian societies were informed that Bohemians cannot be allowed to serve in separate organizations or be permitted even on the battle line to carry their flag." For these reasons, the Greek request had to be refused. Secretary of War Newton D. Baker said: "If the request of the Greek Legation be approved, similar offers from other countries could not in the future be denied." [14]

The war, it appears, gave business competitors of the Greeks an opportunity to make unjustified attacks on them. In December 1917 there were complaints that certain persons and newspapers in Chicago would stop at nothing in finding fault with the Greeks; if they were unable to find a legitimate basis for this, they fabricated a story to make news. This, they complained, was part of a systematic campaign to undermine the flourishing Greek business interests in the Chicago area by spreading prejudice: "For instance, if there is a discussion about military exemption the Greek is put on the top line of those accused; if there is a matter of slackers, the Greek is used for ridicule and humiliation; if the subject is meatless and wheatless days, the Greek is again the target of accusation on the first line; if sanitary conditions in restaurants are questioned, the poor Greek is again accused and blamed; if the elements of nature go wrong, the Greeks and their Gods are blamed for corrupting them." [15]

The butt of these particular attacks were the restaurant keepers, who encountered opposition in times of peace as well. Of an estimated four thousand Greek restaurant owners in Chicago, a few probably violated some wartime measure, as did some native Americans and representatives of other nationality groups. But many more did not, and the Greeks found it difficult to take this kind of criticism, especially in time of war. Angry compatriots asked the Greek-American Restaurant Association to honor its name and render a service to the country and its members by rooting out those delinquent countrymen who brought shame on their nationality. One could not be a good citizen by buying saving certificates and liberty bonds and then violate the laws of the country.[16]

At about the same time that business rivals and others were questioning the loyalty of the Greek-Americans, Nicholas Politis, the minister of foreign affairs in Greece, expressed the concern of his government over the misunderstanding created by Solon Vlasto and *Atlantis* regarding the enlistment of Greek citizens in the United States army: "Greece has never thought of hindering Greek citizens from serving as volunteers in the American army." Politis instructed George Roussos, the Greek minister in Washington,

to complete his declaration to the American Government by adding that on the contrary the Royal Government, keenly alive to the common interest, desires to favour such voluntary enlistments on the part of the Greeks in the American army; and to this end I have authorized him to make it known publicly that all such enlistments past or future, being approved by the Hellenic Government, will not entail the loss of Greek nationality nor any other penalty against the interested parties, but on the contrary the Greek Government will recognize and reward all acts of bravery performed by Greeks in the American army, just as if these acts had been performed in the Greek army.

Politis also seized this opportunity to inform Droppers of "the lively indignation" arising from the "monstrous act of treason" performed by Vlasto, and to add that "we would be glad to see the American Government treat Vlasto as an enemy to the common cause and his paper as organ of treason in the service of Germany." [17]

In a telegram to the State Department, Droppers restated that the Greek government approved of the volunteering of Greek subjects in the armed forces of the United States, and that it approved of "forming Greek regiments under Greek flag but under American officers in France of all Greek subjects who are now or in the near future ought to join the army in Greece but are prevented by difficulties or transportation." [18]

As a further means of publicly demonstrating the dedication of the Greeks to the Allied war effort, the Greek government instructed its diplomatic and consular authorities in the United States to organize a

national celebration on June 27, 1918, the first anniversary of the entry
of Greece into the war. *Te Deums* were to be offered in the Greek
churches of the country. This was viewed as necessary, from a national
standpoint, to demonstrate to the American public in a convincing
manner that the Greeks were inspired by unquestioned sentiments of
enthusiasm for the Allied cause.[19] In Chicago the celebration was held
with much pomp and ceremony. The first portion of the festivities
was held at Hull House, whence a throng headed by youths wearing
the national costume of Greece, and bearing the flags and banners of
their different organizations, marched to the Blackstone Hotel and
filled its theater to capacity. Samuel Insull, the utility magnate, served
as chairman for the evening.[20]

Meanwhile, the Greek-language press kept urging its readers to buy
more and more bonds.[21] By May 1918 the Greeks in the country were
said to have purchased an estimated $10 million in liberty bonds, the
purchase of those in Chicago alone exceeding $2 million. According
to local press releases, the Greek residents of Chicago subscribed on the
average of $167.83 per capita, which was said to be the highest of any
national group. These high purchases were attributed to the intense
patriotism of the people, their desire to demonstrate their loyalty to the
country, and the fact that the purchasers were preponderantly unmarried males and prosperous businessmen.[22]

This breakdown of bond purchases in terms of nationalities was the
product of American efforts as well as a manifestation of pride on the
part of the various ethnic groups. Efforts were made quite early to
determine to what extent the foreign-born purchased liberty bonds. All
indications are that the various Liberty Loan committees made strong
appeals to foreign-language groups in the country, and that these
groups responded by purchasing bonds. In Massachusetts the Greeks
cooperated with the Liberty Loan Committee of New England and the
Massachusetts Committee on Citizens of Foreign Birth or Descent.
According to George Creel, the head of the Committee on Public
Information during the war, the Greeks purchased $30 million worth
of bonds during the first four drives, and all these came in small
amounts that represented sacrifices.[23]

The energetic and patriotic head of the Pan-Epirotic Union of
America, Nicholas J. Cassavetes, urged the Greek communities in the
New England states to buy bonds out of duty to the country in which

they lived and prospered, to help defend it from attack, to enable the United States to lend money to Greece, and because they, more than any other nationality group, were obligated to buy and thus help the United States free their "brothers" in northern Epirus, Thrace, Constantinople, Asia Minor, and the islands.[24]

The Greeks continued to enlist in the armed forces of the United States, and their leaders kept encouraging them to do so. Even Meletios Metaxakis, the Metropolitan of Athens, who came to the United States during the summer of 1918, urged his compatriots to enlist for military service.[25] Venizelists even conceded that their hated political rivals were responding to the war effort, despite the foolish clinging in devotion to their dethroned King. The fact that they were not imprisoned was proof that the United States government had nothing definite against them, other than their professed allegiance to the king.[26]

During the summer of 1918 reports circulated of an approaching understanding between the United States and Greece regarding military service to be rendered by the nationals of the two countries. According to advance accounts, every Greek between the ages of twenty and forty-four, whether a citizen of the United States or not, was to be drafted for military service. The draftees were to be trained in the United States and France by officers of the French and American armies. The more nationalistic-minded among the Greeks were hopeful that this would mean the eventual formation of a Greek army of some seventy-five thousand that would be sent to the Macedonian front in southeastern Europe.[27]

On August 29, 1918, Droppers telegraphed to Washington that the Greek government had given full power to its minister plenipotentiary in the United States, George Roussos, to sign a military convention between the two governments, "with the view of insuring the military service in the Army, respectively of the country of their residence, of the citizens liable to military service of the United States residing in Greece and of Greek subjects residing in the United States." [28] This military convention was signed in Washington in August by representatives of the two governments and ratified by Greece on November 12.[29] Obviously by this time the armistice had been declared and the war had come to an end for the United States. Greece was to remain on a war footing for a number of years. The military convention had no significance for the Greek-Americans remaining in the United States, but it was to become the source of extended controversy for those who subsequently returned to Greece and were drafted, under protest, into the Greek armed forces.

This military agreement was but one of many signed by the United States and the European nations fighting on the Allied side. America entered into comparable treaties with Italy and France, calling for a reciprocal drafting of their citizens and its own in the respective armies. After being ratified by the United States Senate, these treaties were to go into effect as soon as ratification was completed abroad. Once ratified, it would have made no difference whether Greeks, Italians, or Frenchmen had taken out their first American papers insofar as liability for military service was concerned. Hitherto, except for the treaties with England and Canada, only declared aliens were inducted into the service.[30]

It is impossible to give an accurate figure of the number of Greeks who served with the armed forces of the United States. Nicholas Culolias, who had been active in the Greek Republican Club of Massachusetts, upon inquiry in 1920 was advised by the adjutant general of the War Department that it was impossible to furnish this information. Said the adjutant general: "This office has not compiled lists of names and addresses of the soldiers who served in the World War according to their nationalities and the districts in which they resided at the time of their entry into the service."[31] Nicholas Cassavetes, long active in Greek community affairs in the United States, estimated that sixty thousand Greeks served with the armed forces. He cited as his source for this figure an article written by George Creel that had originally appeared in *Everybody's Magazine* and then in the *Literary Digest* for March 8, 1919.

Cassavetes buttressed his claim by stating that eight of every ten Greeks in the United States in 1917 were of military age, and that Creel counted as Greeks those coming from Turkish-occupied areas in Asia Minor, Thrace, Macedonia, Epirus, and the Aegean Islands (in the census for 1910, these had been counted as Turks). "George Creel did not do the injustice to credit the Turks with tens of thousands of soldiers of Greek descent simply because these men . . . happened technically to have been registered as Turkish subjects." Thousands of

Greeks volunteered even though they had been so classified. Thousands were inducted into the service despite the fact they were aliens and had not declared their intentions of becoming citizens.[32]

Seraphim G. Canoutas, the well-known Greek-American publicist and exponent of the legend that Christopher Columbus was a Greek, took issue with the figure of 60,000 cited by Cassavetes. Canoutas gave no definite numbers, except to state that he received a letter from the adjutant general's office stating that from June 5, 1917, to September 11, 1918, only 22,090 Greeks were listed in Class I, meaning they were liable for military service. In the opinion of Canoutas, it was difficult to state how many actually were inducted into the armed forces.[33] It would appear that, on the basis of the patriotic exuberance of the Greek-Americans and their preponderantly male members, the figure of 60,000 or even 70,000 would be a reasonable estimate. This, of course, does not include the many thousands of others who worked in essential war industries and in various other ways served the civilian needs of a nation at war.

All evidence shows that the Greek-Americans supported the war effort with undiminished energy and devotion. Differences between royalists and Venizelists over the foreign and domestic policies of Greece in no way detracted from their loyalty to the United States. If anything, these differences inspired them to outdo each other in displaying their loyalty to the country. The Venizelists had an easier time of this than the royalists, but no royalist was ever found to be disloyal to the United States. This chapter in Greek-American history, we shall see, was the turning point in the lives of many. For the majority the die was cast: they were now Americans and in the United States to stay.

GREEK-AMERICANS AND
THE GREAT IDEA

F OR years Greeks had dreamed of a Greater Greece in which all
Greeks, especially those living under foreign governments, would
be united under one flag. No Greek thought of bringing his compatriots in Egypt, the United States, or England into this Hellenic fold,
but nearly every Greek thought and hoped in terms of rescuing his
"enslaved brothers" from Turkish rule. The most concern was shown
for those in the Smyrna district, the Bulgarian littoral, Macedonia,
Epirus, the Dodecanese Islands, and Cyprus (which was offered to
Greece in 1915 as an inducement to enter the war on the side of the
Allies). This Great Idea, the hope for a Greater Greece, was a national
ideal that transcended party lines. The American Venizelists supported
it with as much passion as the American royalists.[1]

These aspirations were aptly fed by Woodrow Wilson's plea for
government by the consent of the governed, and all subject peoples
took new hope. In the United States, the Irish-Americans were agitating
for an Irish republic; the Polish-Americans were living in expectation
of a free Poland; Czech-Americans and Slovak-Americans patiently
awaited the formation of the Czechoslovak state; the southern Slavs
in America wanted justice for their countrymen; so did the Italian-
Americans.[2]

For the Greek-Americans to support the territorial claims of the
mother country was a logical aftermath of the war. Had they not
struggled to bring Greece into the war on the side of the Allies? Had
they not as Venizelists and royalists stood solidly behind President

Wilson? Was not Wilson the friend and champion of all subject peoples, including the Greeks? Agitation for territories considered Greek was waged in the United States prior to the First World War, but by no means as persistently and methodically as when Greece became an Ally.[3] George Roussos, the first minister of the Venizelos government, expressed hope that the influence of the United States would become a positive force in uniting the Greeks of Asia Minor with those of Greece.[4]

The next phase of this campaign was the formation in November 1917 of the American Hellenic Society, which was officered by an imposing array of American scholars and educators. Nicholas Murray Butler, president of Columbia University and a friend of the Greek liberals, became president; Charles W. Eliot, president emeritus of Harvard University, and Jacob Schurman, president emeritus of Cornell University, were chosen vice-presidents.[5] The Greek-Americans had little difficulty, at least in the early stages, in arousing the sympathies of influential American educators.

Basically, the American Hellenic Society was a propaganda organization dedicated to publicizing the territorial claims of Greece. Stated more specifically, its aims were to defend the just claims of Hellenism; to further the educational and political relations between the United States and Greece; to promote the establishment of exchange professorships between the universities of the two countries; to spread a knowledge of the literature and political institutions of the United States throughout Hellas; and to encourage the study of ancient and modern Greek language and literature in America.[6] A number of publications were issued by the American Hellenic Society, many of which found their way into the libraries of the leading colleges and universities of the country. Butler, in a glowing prefatory statement in one of the publications, wrote: "It appears that a happier day for Greece is about to dawn. Under the inspiring leadership of M. Venizelos, whose statesmanlike qualities are one of the ornaments of our generation, Greece has taken its place with the friends and defenders of liberty in opposition to the forces of autocratic power and the rule of military might."[7] Perhaps nothing could boost the egos of Greek-American irredentists as much as these remarks from the pen of a world-renowned educator.

Among the first and best-organized Greek-American groups to launch a crusade in behalf of the territorial aspirations of Greece were the Epirotes. Most of them came from northern Epirus, the contested area, in which their families lived and for whom they wanted protection. In 1914 many Epirotes returned to Greece "to help their brothers . . . beat off the Albanian invasion of their liberated homes." But after the Northern Epirotic Autonomy was recognized by the Conference of Corfu, the American Epirotes returned to the United States. The Italian invasion of northern Epirus revived complaints of persecution, however, and Epirotes in the United States, as well as in Egypt, Greece, England, France, and South Africa, came together to form the Pan-Epirotic Union.[8]

During 1919 American branches of the Pan-Epirotic Union appeared in twenty-six cities, chiefly east of the Mississippi River. The stated purpose of the Union was the unification of all northern Epirus with Greece, informing American public opinion regarding the Hellenic character of the province and resisting efforts to detach any portion of Epirus from the mother country. The American Epirotes placed stress on the proportionately large number of their compatriots who contributed to the political, economic, educational, and humanitarian phases of Hellenic life. One writer claimed that "The Epirotes are more Greek than the other Greeks," and it is quite true that many of those who contributed a good deal to contemporary Greek culture were Epirotes. Arsakis left his fortune for the education of Greek girls. Zappas founded many schools in Greece and Turkey and the Museum of Art in Athens. Zographos established a college and hospital bearing his name in Constantinople, and his son became a minister of foreign affairs in Greece. George Averoff donated a cruiser, bearing his name, that helped defeat the Turkish fleet in 1912, financed schools in Epirus and in other parts of Greece and Egypt. Stournaras founded and endowed the famed Polytechnic Institute in Athens.[9] Rhizos founded the theological seminary bearing his name at the University of Athens. Epirus, claimed its proud and outspoken sons, performed the same role in the history of Greece that Massachusetts and the New England states had performed in the history of the United States.[10]

These natives of Epirus, through the offices of the Pan-Epirotic Union of Boston, informed the American public that they were pleading for the Epirotes and the four million Greeks of Thrace and Asia Minor who were exposed to the dangers of "extermination and Turkification." "Greek girls are being sold to harems for a para a piece. Greek children are being reared in mosques. The older people are being abandoned to die. The young, tortured and refusing to abandon Christianity, are submitting to an agonizing death." These Greeks in Asia Minor and Thrace had to be made to understand that Greeks elsewhere would not forget them.

On July 1, 1918, a nationwide campaign was launched to aid the Greeks in Asia Minor and Thrace. Each Greek in the United States was asked to contribute one day's wages to redeem Smyrna and Constantinople, to aid the Cross in conquering the Crescent, and to make Greece a united nation numbering nine million.[11] Impetus was given the crusade by the arrival of Nicholas Kyriakides, the president of the Central Committee of Unredeemed Greeks, Christos Vassilakakis, and Meletios Metaxakis, the Metropolitan of Athens, with his ecclesiastical mission.[12] Kyriakides, a native of Marmora, a graduate of Robert College, Constantinople, and a wealthy shipowner, and Vassilakakis, a member of the Greek Chamber of Deputies, had taken an active part in promoting the cause of "the unredeemed." [13]

The aim of the Kyriakides mission was to enlighten the American public and the United States government on the just claims of Greece. "We rely upon this great American Republic and our Allies," said Kyriakides, "for help and support in shaking off this hateful yoke." [14] And he and his associate quickly set out on a tour of the United States to preach the gospel of redemption. Kyriakides at one time expressed hope that the United States government would permit Greek nationals to depart as a group to fight for the claims of the mother country. But when he realized that this was not feasible, his next aim was to induce Greeks who were Turkish subjects not to claim exemption from military duty on the ground that they were aliens.[15] At South Bethlehem, Pennsylvania, Kyriakides was greeted by hundreds of compatriots at the railroad station; at Hungarian Hall he addressed a crowd of about fifteen hundred, many of whom were natives of liberated Greece. Enthusiasm was great, and after his patriotic address, many took an oath to enlist in the armed forces of the United States as a means of implementing the claim of Greece.[16]

While Kyriakides was conferring with Greek and American leaders and making public appearances the *New York Times* published a letter by N. Manousis, the secretary of the National Union of Dodecanesians, which was addressed to Prime Minister Vittorio Orlando of Italy. The letter said in effect that the inhabitants of the Dodecanesian Islands were entirely Greek, having preserved their Greek character when the islands were in the possession of the Venetians, the Genoese, and the Turks. "If they received the Italians as their liberators, they did this because the Greek nation has always looked to Italy as a sister nation, and consequently they, at that time, regarded the Italian armies as new crusaders, who had come to pursue the hated crescent, and looked upon the temporary Italian occupation as a foretoken of their national restoration." [17] Late in October 1918 the *New York Times* also published a letter from President Wilson to the Committee of the Unredeemed Greeks, which the committee members felt was tantamount to a recognition of Greek claims in Asia Minor. This letter was considered as the first official step toward the attainment of justice.[18]

Meanwhile, Christos Vassilakakis journeyed to Washington where he met and discussed the claims of Greece with Thomas Marshall, the vice-president of the United States. Marshall, as chairman of the Senate, was in a strategic position to aid the Greek cause. Marshall introduced him to Senator Henry Cabot Lodge, the republican leader, and Gilbert Hitchcock, the Democratic spokesman, who assured him that the senators would be happy to hear the case for Greece at some prearranged time and place. But on the next day, October 24, word came that Venizelos planned to visit the United States; out of deference to his superior, Vassilakakis chose to speak only with members of the Foreign Relations Committee, expecting that the prime minister would confer with the higher authorities when he reached the country. Unfortunately, Venizelos did not arrive.

Vassilakakis also met the president of the Mid-European Union, Thomas Masaryk, who had been laboring in behalf of an independent Czecho-Slovak nation. Masaryk had enlisted the cooperation of the Poles, Transylvanians, Ukranians, and other peoples, and also had the personal support of President Wilson. Realizing that the efforts of Masaryk had much public sympathy in the United States, Vassilakakis believed that the cause of Greece woud be aided if it was identified with that of the Czecho-Slovaks.[19]

Perhaps one of the most dramatic pronouncements of the period was made by Metaxakis, the primate of Greece, at a dinner given in his honor a few days before his departure for Greece. The metropolitan expressed the conviction that the people of the United States wanted

Hellenic territories restored to Greece as a means of helping her achieve national unity. He also assured his listeners that Greece was better prepared to govern and care for Constantinople than the original thirteen colonies were to govern themselves when they gained their freedom. "I am eagerly waiting for the time," he continued, "when the children of Greece will be able to enter their historic temple of St. Sophia and complete their long unfinished prayer." [20]

Once the armistice was declared, the Greek-Americans intensified the drive in behalf of Greek territorial claims. Early in December 1918, Greek-Americans assembled in Faneuil Hall, Boston, and asked that the Paris Peace Conference reunite "districts normally Greek in population" with Greece. On the same day four thousand Irish-Americans gathered on the Boston Common to demand a free Ireland. The New York Committee of Unredeemed Greeks declared that the return of Constantinople, "our eternal city," would fulfill a dream of five hundred years.[21] On December 20 John Metaxa, the former governor of Salonika, informed the Harvard Club of Boston that the Greeks in Thrace, Asia Minor, and the Dodecanese must be freed from foreign rule.[22]

These demonstrations occasionally precipitated disturbances. On December 29 a minor riot broke out in the Copley Theater of Boston that brought five policemen to the scene. The meeting was sponsored by the Pan-Epirotic Union to further Greek claims. Sixty Albanians who were in the audience cheered the mention of the name of Woodrow Wilson and his Fourteen points, especially the principle of self-determination, but they opposed the Greek demands for Epirus and a wild uproar followed. The Greek-American Epirotes felt that if the Albanians differed with them, they were free to rent their own meeting hall and protest, but not to disrupt their meeting.[23]

Among others who came to the United States was Platon Drakoules, the founder of the Greek socialist and labor movements. His task was to present the war aims of Greek labor to Greek wage-earners and labor leaders in the United States. Greek labor, too, wanted the liberation of all Greek communities in the Balkans, Asia Minor, and the Aegean Islands; but Drakoules spoke of the establishment of a federation of Balkan republics, the internationalization of Constantinople, and the conversion of the city into the seat of the Greek government under a mandate from the League of Nations.[24]

Early in 1919 Michael Tsamados, the consul general of Greece in San Francisco, invited the presidents of all Greek societies and journalists in the Bay area to attend a rally for Greek rights. At least on this occasion, every Greek was asked to rid himself of partisan thoughts and devote himself unreservedly to furthering the national goals. Among the scheduled speakers was Benjamin Ide Wheeler, the president of the University of California. A copy of the resolutions was wired to President Wilson in Paris and given wide publicity in the newspapers of the country. The theory was that if Greek communities across the country raised a consolidated appeal, the Paris Peace Conference would be influenced when the claims of Greece came up for consideration.[25]

Greek-American spokesmen continued to identify themselves with other national groups having irredentist claims. On February 16, 1919, representatives of the Armenians, Greeks, and Jews who shared common experiences under Turkish rule met in New York City, where they pledged support to each other in their national aspirations. The Greeks wanted union with Greeks living under Turkish rule; the Armenians sought the independence of their countrymen; and the Jews wanted Palestine for a Jewish homeland under the trusteeship of Great Britain.[26]

Despite all of this activity, the claims of Greece at the Peace Conference were resisted. This brought charges and countercharges of intrigue carried on by American missionaries and their allies. The American press carried accounts of "a missionary lobby" in Paris, which was attempting to advance the case of the Turks and the Bulgars at the expense of the Greeks and the Armenians. This missionary lobby was accused of opposing the territorial aspirations of Greece in Thrace and the Aegean Sea and of striving to salvage some of the Bulgarian and Ottoman power in the Bosporus. It was working with some degree of success; and it was described as the only group which objected to the assignment of Smyrna and its strip off the coast of Asia Minor to the Greek kingdom on the grounds that Turkey should have a Mediterranean port.

According to reports, Robert College, the famous missionary institution in Constantinople which had many friends and graduates in official Bulgaria, was inspiring the lobby. Furthermore, it was known that some of the American missionaries distrusted the "formalism" of the Greek and Armenian churches and preferred that these ancient churches remain under Ottoman tutelage in Asia Minor rather than pass under the control of the Greeks and Armenians. The American missionaries, according to this line of reasoning, believed that opportunities for proselytizing would be far better under Ottoman than Greek and Armenian control. "But is not this," queried a correspondent, "from the broad point of view, a dog-in-the-manger policy? For the sake of missionary opportunity, is America to be committed to an obstructive policy toward the two most helpful Christian peoples in all the East?" [27]

The Greek-Americans naturally were concerned over the purported position that the American Board of Commissioners for Foreign Missions had taken in the matter of Greek claims at the Peace Conference. On March 29, 1919, William E. Strong of the American Board headquarters in Boston prepared a statement which he sent to Nicholas Culolias, long active in Greek liberal circles and a spokesman of Greek irredentism in the Boston area. The statement sought to emphasize that "the American Board does not mean to interfere in questions of national or international politics." Elaborating, Strong stated that missionaries had been "uniformly instructed to regard themselves as guests of the government by whose permission and under whose protection they labor" and to remain "aloof from political entanglements." In times of peace this course was comparatively simple and easy to follow; but in periods of war and readjustment when claims and ambitions clashed, this neutral position was difficult to maintain.

Missionaries grow attached to people for whom they are giving their lives. They are sensitive to the criticisms and the policies which affect them. The impulse is strong to champion their cause. It is not possible for the Board to guard every utterance of all its missionaries, at home or abroad, or to prevent them altogether from defending those for whom they speak and the cause for which they would plead. It was inevitable that the prospect of friendly or unfriendly treatment of the work to which they have given themselves should influence the sentiments of those who watched the struggle for the land in which they were located. Some missionary might have spoken inadvisedly and permitted his influence to be felt in a manner that had political bearing.

Strong said the rumor that the American Board was opposed to Greek claims in the Balkans and the Levant was unwarranted. This question had never been discussed by the Board or its executive committee. The officials kept aloof from the movement and gave no authority to any missionary to ally himself with one group or another. The Board agreed that race, language, religion, and other factors binding people should be duly regarded in assigning territories. It was prepared "to accept loyally and cheerfully whatever settlement of disputed claims shall be made and asks only that a real religious liberty be assured under whatever flag its work shall be continued. In its hundred and nine years of activity in many lands, the American Board has never been involved in political intrigue. It has kept to its own moral and spiritual task." [28]

Strong's letter of March 29 was satisfactory to Culolias, with the exception that it failed to make reference to its relations with individual missionaries. Strong replied that the Board refrained from making public utterances "concerning its dealings with individual missionaries." But it did "take cognizance of such individual cases as may be reported to have broken over the rules of the Board and that we take up the matter at once with them. But these matters of administration we are not accustomed to publish specifically and by name." [29]

Culolias informed Strong that he wanted a summary of the March 29 statement prepared for publication, but he did not state where he would publish it and what purpose it would serve. Without this knowledge, replied Strong, "I hesitate to assent to its publication." If it was to be cabled abroad for publication in the papers there or for presentation in Paris, he objected: "It might seem pretentious for the American Board to make so extended an announcement in foreign press or before foreign bodies." The statement in full, Strong continued, "might be used in your Greek papers in this country or for the information of your Greek constituency," for it went into the matter in some detail and gave them information they did not have. A cabled dispatch, on the other hand, would "imply an importance and prominence that this Board does not wish to assume in the matter." He ventured to enclose "a much shorter, but . . . sufficient statement for any cable use that might be needed or properly desired in this matter. Even so I should be glad to know what use is proposed to be made of it since, as I have informed you in my letter, this Board does not wish to be involved in political discussions or plans on one side or the other." [30]

Culolias replied to Strong that the extended statement of March 29 had already been published in Greek papers of New York and that the condensed statement, which he had read to "your Dr. Case" over the telephone," was cabled to one of the Greek leaders in Paris on about April 6. He expressed no knowledge of the use that would be made of the condensed statement. Culolias denied any intent on his part to abuse the courtesy Strong had shown in discussing the Board's policy in matters of national and international questions. However, he did assume that "when a statement is given out for publication, it includes transmission from one place to another by wire." Culolias said he had guarded against "extracting statements which would not represent the spirit and intent of the longer statement." [31]

Subsequent correspondence indicates that Strong objected to Culolias' not awaiting his approval before issuing the statement. He added that: "one reason why the American Board is disinclined to grant interviews or make statements is because those who secure them sometimes use them quite as they please and without regard to the wishes of those who give them." [32] Strong's displeasure in what Culolias did, however, shows some flaws in reasoning. Why should Strong consent to the publication of the longer statement in the Greek-American newspapers and object to the release of the same statement abroad? Certainly the statement appearing in the Greek newspapers could be republished in full by the foreign newspapers.[33]

To turn back to the Paris Peace Conference, new events were developing which were to have an even greater effect on Greek-Americans. Venizelos presented a concise statement of Greek claims to the conference on February 3 and 4, 1919. Most commissioners favored giving Smyrna to Greece, but the American members objected on the grounds that Smyrna was a port of entry. As for the Dodecanese Islands, the commission was unanimous in recognizing the justice of Greek claims and favored incorporating them into Greece; but the French, British, and Italian delegates, in view of the secret Treaty of London, withheld their approval until this could be adjusted diplomatically with Italy.[34]

In due course others began protesting about the "brutal and barbarous" treatment that the Dodecanesians were receiving at the hands of the Italians. In a meeting in New York at the Amsterdam Opera House, an estimated two thousand Greeks rose and took the following oath: "As long as the sun keeps its course in the heavens we shall never make peace with those who menace Greek liberties or tread upon Greek rights." On the stage appeared a large banner bearing the inscription: "We demand unity with our motherland Greece."[35]

Late in May word came from the Peace Conference that the United States had refused to accept a mandate over Constantinople. Greek-Americans immediately seized the opportunity to wire President Wilson and urge him to use his influence to persuade the conference to give the mandate to Greece. Hitherto all Greek appeals to Wilson had received careful consideration, and the hope was that this one would be also well received. Greek-Americans were urged to bombard Wilson with telegrams.[36]

At about this time, Wilson dispatched an American commission headed by Henry C. King, the president of Oberlin College, and C. R. Crane, the treasurer of the American Committee for Armenian and Syrian Relief, to conduct an investigation into the questions of Syria, Palestine, Armenia, Turkey, and the Greek claims. By this time the Greeks had landed in Smyrna with the permission of the Big Three powers.[37] The report of the King-Crane commission was not immediately available, but the general tone of its contents were known. It recommended that an area in western Asia Minor should not be set off as a special Greek region and placed under a separate mandate. The report stated that "in the long run the better good both of the Greeks and of the Turks is to be found in their union in one cosmopolitan state."[38]

Meanwhile, the Greek-Americans accelerated the tempo of their campaign to win, if nothing else, the support of the American people. On August 10, 1919, a giant rally, attended by twelve to fifteen thousand and representing one hundred and twenty-six societies, mostly from New England, assembled in Mechanics Hall, Boston, to open a nation-wide campaign for Greek territorial claims. A parade of Greek-Americans attired in United States army uniforms and ten bands preceded the meeting, which was opened by a religious service. The greatest disappointment of the day was the inability of Sergeant Hercules Korgis, the captor of over two hundred Germans—variously described as "the Sergeant York of New England" and "the one-man army"—to appear because of a railroad strike.

The meeting was presided over by Albert P. Langtry, the secretary of state for Massachusetts; it adopted a long series of resolutions and paid tribute to the many friends of Greece. Votes of thanks were extended to Senators Brandege, King, Moses, and Lodge for their defense of Greek claims, and a protest was stated against Senator Thomas of Colorado for his "unwarranted statements" to deliver Thrace to Bulgaria on economic grounds. Gratitude was expressed to the entire press of the United States for the warm support given to Greek claims. A novel feature of the rally was the memorial services chanted by Bishop Alexander of New York and a score of accompanying priests. Attired in glittering robes, the bishop wore the tall black headdress characteristic of the Greek prelate. A solemn effect was created by the long line of bearded chanting clergymen.[39]

The next step was to carry the claims of the Greeks closer to official Washington. On August 19 more than one hundred and fifty delegates, representing communities from different parts of the country, gathered in Washington. These "Friends of Greece," composed of both Greeks and non-Greeks, wanted to solicit the aid of Wilson in keeping Thrace from being apportioned to Bulgaria. Present at the meetings of this group were fifty Greek-American soldiers who had fought with the armed forces of the United States and Sergeant Hercules Korgis (who had disappointed those in attendance in Boston). A committee of seven was designated to lay the facts before the President and the leaders of the Senate. On the following day a full-page advertisement appeared in the *Washington Post,* entitled, "Will America Deny Justice to Greece?" Senator George Moses of New Hampshire stirred the delegates with his endorsement of Greek claims: "We ask for the Greek people only those lands where Greek blood has been shed and where Greek blood is still preponderant. We ask only for those lands where Greek ingenuity and Greek enterprise have made the Greek name famous; and we rebel at every suggestion that that beastly nation of Slavic origin shall take from the Greeks that which is rightfully theirs." [40]

President Wilson was bombarded with telegrams, resolutions, and letters outlining the claims of Greece. On the day that the President reached Oakland, California, in his tour of the country to win public support for the ratification of the Treaty of Versailles and the League of Nations, a letter publicly addressed to him was printed in the *Oakland Tribune* making a special plea for Thrace.[41]

Support for Greek claims also came from a group of American college and university professors. Professors A. D. Hamlin and K. D.

Miller of Columbia University, Edward Capps of Princeton University, Carroll Brown of City College of New York, and William Bates of Pennsylvania went to Washington as representatives of two hundred and twenty-five academicians and presented to President Wilson, through his secretary, a statement in behalf of Greece's claims.[42] While the Greek-Americans, who for the most part were Venizelists, were pressing their claims for Greek territories, the American royalists noted that the optimism of the earlier days had weakened.[43] They continued to denounce Venizelos as a tyrant, a French agent, a dictator; and now that the war was over, they revived the charges that Greece had been mistreated by the English and the French.[44] In time the royalists began to send telegrams to Wilson in Paris, urging him to intervene in Greece and prevent bloodshed "by ordering that General and King Constantine shall immediately resume his command of the Greek Army and his place on the Greek Throne." [45]

Most of the year 1920 was concentrated on lobbying in the United States Senate. A resolution supporting Greek claims in Thrace was reported out of committee in January 1920 as a substitute for one introduced by Senator King of Utah. The resolution declared that all territory in Thrace surrendered to the Allies by Turkey and Bulgaria should be awarded to Greece, provided that an outlet to the Aegean Sea was given Bulgaria. It was adopted by the Senate in a standing vote. A few senators rose in opposition, and Senator William Borah remarked that it was "none of our business." [46]

The future of Constantinople, as might be expected, elicited more than casual concern. "Constantinople is not and never has been a Mohammedan or Turkish city, and it is high time, in the interests both of Christianity and Mohammedanism that every vestige of Ottoman rule should disappear from that famous center of Hellenic culture and civilization," observed Theodore Ion.[47] "Must the Turk remain in Constantinople?" queried a front-page editorial in *California*.[48] The Holy Synod of Greece addressed a letter of gratitude to Bishop James H. Darlington of the Episcopalian Church for the efforts of American churches in helping to liberate the non-Turkish people of Asia Minor.[49]

More moral support, ineffective as it turned out to be, came from the United States Senate. Early in May Senator Lodge introduced a resolution favoring the award to Greece of northern Epirus, including Koritsa, the Dodecanese Islands, and the Greek portion of the west coast of Asia Minor. A few weeks later the Senate passed the resolution without dissent.[50] Thus the Greek-Americans at least had the satisfaction of knowing that the United States Senate, if not the Peace Conference and the major European powers, considered the Greek claims just.

With a presidential election coming up in 1920, it was hardly surprising that the more politically minded Greek-Americans examined the position of the candidates of both the Republican and Democratic parties with respect to Greek territorial aspirations. They believed that the outcome of the election would have some bearing on the attitude of the United States toward Greece. Efforts were made to examine the records of the candidates to discover what position, if any, they had adopted in the Turkish-Bulgarian-Albanian crisis and to determine their religious affiliations in order to judge how these would affect their attitudes toward Greece. "We know the instigators of antipathy toward the Greeks," protested *Saloniki*. "They are the missionaries and professors of the American schools in the east. Despite all efforts, they remain our enemies and fight us at every opportunity. They are responsible for the change of heart of the American representative in Paris, who changed from a Philhellene to a 'Bulgarophile' or even a 'Turkophile.' It is known that our enemies in the White House are Cleveland Dodge, treasurer of Robert College, and Charles Crane, treasurer of the American school at Koritsa." [51]

President Wilson, according to these arguments, believed everything told him by the missionaries of the Baptist, Presbyterian, Congregational, and Methodist churches, and discounted everything reported by the representatives of Greece. This receptivity to the recommendations of American missionaries was believed to have done more harm to the Greek cause in Paris than anything else. For this reason *Saloniki* believed that the religious affiliations of the next president would have a crucial effect on the future of Greek interests. The choice, as the writer saw it, was narrowed down to Harding the Baptist and Cox the Episcopalian. The Baptists, it followed, agreed with the friends of President Wilson, the Presbyterians; they were anxious to protect the interests of their schools and missions in the Near East; they worked "hand in glove" with Crane. Hence efforts had to be made to prevent them from gaining a foothold in the White House. Cox, an Episcopalian, would be free of this kind of religious pressure. The Episcopalian

Church was recognized as a friend and co-worker of the Greek Orthodox Church. During and after the war, the highest officials of the
Episcopalian Church fought unceasingly for Greek rights and proclaimed the justice of Greek claims to Constantinople. They circulated
and signed petitions by the thousands demanding that Thrace, Epirus,
and Asia Minor be given to Greece. If Cox was elected president, even
their bitterest enemy would have difficulty in doing much against the
Greeks from within the White House.

A friend in the White House was also needed in view of the anticipated trouble between Greece and Italy over the Dodecanese Islands.
Harding, it was assumed, would not wish to incur the wrath of the
missionaries in whom he and the incumbent president had so much
faith. Even if he did, he would be hesitant about angering the Italian-
Americans. The Italians were not only more numerous than the Greeks,
but they were politically and socially better organized. "Don't forget,"
warned *Saloniki,* "that all Italians will go to the polls with the purpose
in mind of overthrowing the Democratic Party. They believe that the
Republican Party will help Italy hold Rhodes." [52]

This singular religious analysis of the issues in the election was not
subscribed to by the majority of Greek-Americans. At most, it represented the views of a vocal element obsessed by the Greek imperial
dream. The other Greek-language newspapers, because of their almost
exclusive emphasis on Greek themes, had not acquired a reputation
for Republicanism as had *Atlantis* and the weekly *Hellinikos Astir,*
whose editor became preoccupied with drawing parallels between Lincoln and Pericles (despite the changes in the Republican Party since
Lincoln's time).

Still the Greek-Americans were unhappy over the failure of Greece
to obtain a fulfillment of her territorial ambitions. And the Greek-
language press, as we have seen, gave full vent to these frustrations.
But as of this early date few Greek newspapers had acquired a partisan
reputation in American politics. The absorption of the overwhelming
majority of Greek-Americans with the politics of the old country, their
comparative short residence in this country, and the failure of most of
them to become citizens meant that American problems had less appeal
than strictly Greek problems. Consequently, the Greek-language press
was little inclined to dwell on American issues. It sought to capitalize
on the partisan Old World preferences of its readers.

The Greek-Americans waged a strenuous campaign in attempting to mobilize American public opinion behind Greek territorial claims. They organized as Epirotes, Thracians, Dodecanesians; they enlisted the support of American educators and Philhellenes; they staged public rallies, passed resolutions, collected money, circulated petitions, conferred with United States senators, leveled blasts at American missionaries, and directly appealed to President Wilson. Never before had Greek-Americans taken such a vigorous stand over the claims of the mother country. They had learned the value of the lobby in the political arena, the wisdom of winning the cooperation of influential segments of the American population, and in part the need for becoming United States citizens. They were beginning to realize the power of the vote and the value of taking a more direct hand in the political affairs of their communities.

10

ROYALISTS VERSUS VENIZELISTS: SECOND PHASE

WHILE Greeks everywhere were waging relentless campaigns over Greek territorial aspirations, events in the United States were leading up to a second and even bloodier struggle between royalists and Venizelists. The royalists, now that the war was over, found themselves free to renew their attacks against the English and French for forcing the abdication of Constantine in 1917 and for making possible the return of Venizelos. Their strategy was to undermine the confidence of all Greek-Americans in Venizelos in order to bring about his downfall. They made much of his failure at the Peace Conference, the new burdens Greece assumed by her occupation of the Smyrna district and Thrace, and the merciless treatment she received at the hands of England and France, in whom Venizelos had placed so much confidence. A new weekly publication, *Nomotagis* (The Loyalist), was also launched in New York City during the spring of 1919 to strengthen the royalist campaign.[1]

As the royalists were stepping up their anti-Venizelos campaign, they were also urging their adherents and sympathizers to become citizens of the United States. As we shall see, fewer than 20 percent of the Greeks were naturalized, and they did not wish their affection for the mother country to be misinterpreted as an act of disloyalty toward the United States. They chose May 1, 1919, as an appropriate day for

proclaiming their loyalty. At the conclusion of services in the Evangel-
ismos Church of New York, some two hundred filed into automobiles
that had been waiting to take them to City Hall, where they were to
declare their intentions of becoming citizens. Amidst the waving of
American and Greek flags and honking of horns, they headed for
their destination, where they heard a battery of patriotic speakers.
Demetrios Theophilatos said that citizenship, apart from reflecting
loyalty to the United States, would also make it possible to aid the
motherland. Theophilatos claimed that the Greek cause at the Paris
Peace Conference could have been served better if more immigrants
had been American citizens and voted for those candidates for public
office who had supported Greek claims.[2]

Besides urging all Greek-Americans to become citizens and publicizing the names of all who became naturalized in the pages of *Nomotagis*
the royalists renewed their bond-purchasing activities, spoke passionately
about Wilson as a "Philhellene," and voiced common American and
Greek ideals.[3] At no time did the royalists fail to proclaim their
allegiance to the United States. Now, as in the past, the opposition to
Venizelos was vitriolic and ceaseless. The royalists stressed the incompetence and duplicity of Venizelos and his agents in the United States.[4]
They pleaded with "their American-born brethren" to urge President
Wilson, "the only sincere and true friend of Hellenism," to force the
removal of Venizelos from the Peace Conference. For Wilson was "the
one and only man at the table" who condemned the secret treaties that
were calculated to divide the territories claimed by the small nationalities among the major powers.[5] The secret treaties involving England,
France, Russia, and Italy, if invoked, would have been at the expense
of a Greater Greece. Fortunately, for Greece, the collapse of Russia in
1917 mean the abrogation of the treaty with Britain and France which
would have given her the right to annex Constantinople. But even
more menacing was the later Treaty of London, which promised Italy
major concessions in Asia Minor, at the expense of Hellenism.[6]

The royalist strategy in America was to emphasize that because the
the British and the French had been used to elevate Venizelos to
power, the Greek people had been deprived of their constitutional
rights in electing their own rulers; American Greeks were obliged
to raise their voices in protest against such undemocratic practices. The
royalists also demanded that an election be held in Greece as soon as

possible.[7] The royalists circulated an article published in the June 14, 1917, issue of the *New York Evening Sun,* which to them appeared to be a fair presentation of the facts at the time King Constantine was dethroned:

the State Department declared that thus far the United States has taken nothing more than an academic interest in the Grecian situation and has not participated in any of the conferences, which the other Allies have respecting it. It was specifically denied that this Government had been consulted by the other Powers as to the alternative put up to Constantine— that he abdicate in favor of his second son, Alexander, or the Entente would recognize the Venizelos provisional government. It was admitted that Venizelists had besought recognition from the United States, but it was intimated that this Government, acting independently, had merely determined that the time was not ripe for such recognition.

At the same time, it was stated, this Government, while favoring the maintenance of free and independent forms of Government where ever they are set up, is not concerned as to whether these Governments shall be Republican in form or not, providing the popular will controls.[8]

Additional royalist support was found in the report of William T. Ellis printed in the *New York Herald.* On April 13, 1919, he wrote that the French had control of the Greek army, the British of the Greek navy and air force, and that "Greece is now a one-man country and Venizelos is that man." Ellis, according to royalist sources, had to remain in Greece briefly, owing to difficulties with the British and the hostility of the American minister, Garrett Droppers.[9]

The American royalists viewed Droppers as a highly partisan individual and an arch accomplice in the overthrow of the king:

We accuse Mr. Droppers of being a party in the Venizelos movement from start to finish. His embassy became the den of the Venizelos conspiracy and instrumental in bringing about the dethronement of King Constantine . . . Garrett Droppers was constantly working in the closest touch with Venizelos while he was plotting the overthrow of the Constitutional Government of Greece under King Constantine. Mr. Droppers knew that Venizelos was going to leave Athens for Crete to get up a revolution against the Government to which Droppers was accredited before Venizelos took the step . . . Droppers hid in the American Legation men who were wanted by the police for complicity in the revolutionary plot.[10]

More ammunition was provided the royalist cause with the publication of Paxton Hibben's *King Constantine I and the Greek People,* in the spring of 1920. Written three years earlier, the release of the book was held up at the request of the American authorities. Hibben, a journalist of some note, wrote what he considered to be the truth. He told of the activities of the French and the English in a manner that was unlikely to win them friends in the United States; he also mentioned, in moderate fashion, the behavior of Droppers, which was inconsistent with the behavior of a neutral diplomat of a neutral nation.[11] Droppers had acquired an advance copy of Hibben's book as early as 1917, almost three years before it was released, and proceeded to outline to his superiors in the State Department his experiences with Hibben. Droppers referred to Hibben as a Francophile in the beginning, and though "an excellent newspaper correspondent," for reasons other than becoming pro-royalist he was not to be trusted.[12]

Nomotagis, of course, welcomed Hibben's volume as the work of "a neutral, disinterested, impartial American—an American citizen, born of American parents and American grandparents, whose ancestors had fought in the American Revolutionary War."[13] The royalists also found it appropriate to reprint Hibben's observations in Smyrna during 1920. Intended as a friendly warning against the overoptimism of the Greeks, Hibben concluded that the Greek army in 1920 was not "the glorious army of 1912–1913"; it had neither staff nor officers; the soldiers had been under arms continuously since 1912, and they were sick of war. Greece was also faced with economic disaster. She was mortgaged, her treasury was bare, and, even if victorious in Asia Minor, there was no assurance that she would benefit from this. The army of Mustapha Kemal Pasha was more formidable than believed; and unless the Kemalists were defeated immediately and overwhelmingly, the massacre of the Christians was inevitable.[14]

The royalists could always hold their own with the Venizelists in the battle of words and name calling. On one occasion, they published a lengthy list of Anglo-French agents in the Athens-Piraeus area, which the uninformed Greek-American might accept as a "Who's Who in the Greek Underworld." Each agent, according to *Nomotagis,* had a police record of one kind or another, ranging from gambling and opium smoking to the white-slave trade. If the Anglo-French agent fell into none of the above categories, he was classified as a vagabond.[15]

Meanwhile, many things had happened in Greece and Asia Minor since the armistice in November 1918. Venizelos still had his armies in readiness on the Thracian frontier and in the Smyrna district, waiting to move against the Turks should the Allies so order him. Early in July 1920 Venizelos asked for and received a mandate from the Allies' Supreme Council to restore order in Thrace and western Anatolia; and in the face of British doubts and French opposition, he proceeded to carry out his mandate.[16] The startling initial success of the Greeks in the east and the diplomacy of Venizelos culminated in the signing of the Treaty of Sèvres in August, the crowning point of his career. All of Thrace up to Chatalja, the Gallipoli Peninsula, and the northern shore of the Sea of Marmora—the two areas being subject to an international commission which was to control the Straits—were given to Greece. Smyrna was to be administered by Greece, and she was given the right to incorporate it into her own state. This was very gratifying to Venizelos, for, after ten years of hardship, Greece emerged with enlarged territory and several million liberated inhabitants. Greece was on the threshold of becoming a Mediterranean power.

Meanwhile, the Greek-Americans were elated by these events. The successes of Greek armies became the subject of coffeehouse conversations, social gatherings, and school sessions. The hopes and aspirations of the Greek-Americans were echoed in the Greek-language press, the entreaties of community leaders, the poetry and dramatic recitations to which pupils and parents were subjected. Anyone attending a Greek school in those days can relate the stirring chapters in the history of the Greek War of Independence that were retold in the classroom.

But partisanship was working away at the foundations of Greek patriotism. During the two years Venizelos had been away from Greece negotiating in her behalf, momentous changes had occurred within the country. Wartime restrictions had been relaxed and royalist propaganda had re-emerged; the people were reminded of the privations of blockade and the war.[17] Venizelos, after hearing the Chamber of Deputies approve his policies unanimously and proclaim him "the savior of Greece," took the next step that contributed to his undoing: he ordered the lifting of all restrictions so that Greece might hold elections under constitutional conditions. He believed the success of his policies depended upon a vote of confidence from the electorate, and he thought he would get it. He could have prolonged his tenure as prime minister had he so desired; but after the signing of the Treaty of Sèvres, he had given a pledge that he would no longer postpone the elections. He also asked that the return of Constantine not become a campaign issue.[18]

Meanwhile, Greek-American liberals prepared to exploit the accomplishments of Venizelos to full advantage. They expressed satisfaction with the progress of the Greek armies in Asia Minor and Thrace.[19] A meeting in New York City loudly protested the new attempt to assassinate Venizelos, applauded each mention of his name, and interrupted speakers with cries of "Death to the Traitors" and "Down with the King."[20] Chicago liberals also assembled early in October 1920 to celebrate the deeds of the victorious Greek armies. Bishop Alexander praised Venizelos; Bishop Anderson of the Episcopalian Church voiced the hope that Constantinople would become the metropolis of the Greek Orthodox faith; and Archmandrite Mandeleris claimed that the two bulwarks of Greece were the army and Venizelos. The editor of the *Chicago Journal* believed that Constantinople would become a Greek city, while the consuls of France and Poland spoke of Greek friendship, courage, and patriotism.[21]

The forthcoming election in Greece prompted the *National Herald* to launch a vigorous campaign asking all its readers and sympathizers to write immediately to their parents, relatives, and friends in Greece, to urge them to cast their votes for the candidates pledged to Venizelos —"And to blacken ruthlessly all the infamous, all the traitors, all the conspirators, and all the assassins." This marked the inauguration of a novel crusade that continued without let-up for weeks prior to the November elections.[22] This campaign was reinforced by liberal rallies in all major cities of the United States. A large gathering in New York dispatched a telegram with two thousand signatures to Greece.[23] A giant rally in Akron, Ohio, could easily have created the impression that Venizelos had been running for office in the United States instead of a foreign country.[24] A similar atmosphere prevailed elsewhere.[25]

American royalists were not to be outdone in their efforts. At a mass meeting in the Central Park Opera House in New York City they prayed for the speedy recovery of the stricken King Alexander—he had been recently bitten by a monkey—and condemned as "inhuman" the refusal of Premier Venizelos to permit the exiled father and mother to visit their dying son. Another resolution appealed to the United States government to "prevent the stealing of the forthcoming elections" by Venizelos.[26] This latter appeal brought an immediate response from the Venizelist Greek legation in Washington: it said Venizelos exercised "the utmost liberality toward his political opponents by demanding not only a general amnesty to those exiled for political offenses, but also in inviting political refugees to return to Greece and take part in the elections." [27]

Then tragedy struck again: on October 25 King Alexander died and the Greek government faced another crisis. The elections scheduled originally for November 1 were postponed as a matter of necessity.[28] Rumors that Greece would be converted into a republic were rampant but ill founded; for if Venizelos seriously considered this, he would not dare propose it for fear of offending Britain, his only ally.[29] In an hour of desperation, a regency was set up under Admiral Coundouriotis, and the throne formally was offered to Prince Paul, the third son of Constantine. Paul refused it; he said he would ascend the throne only if the Greek people decided that they did not want his father and would exclude his brother, George.

The rebuffed Venizelos then proceeded to make arrangements for the elections, which he still believed would bring him an unquestioned victory. Had not his foreign diplomacy brought Greece territory, more people, and prestige, and were not the Greek armies triumphant in the east? In fact, his confidence of victory was so great, and his program of such a patriotic and idealistic character, that he finally conceded to make the restoration of the exiled king an issue in the elections on November 14.[30] He, of course, continued to oppose the restoration.

D. J. Theophilatos, upon hearing of the offer of the throne to Prince Paul, cabled Constantine at Lucerne, in behalf of 105 Greek-American organizations: "American Greeks sternly oppose any concessions to any foreign influences calculated to deprive the Greek people of their inalienable constitutional rights to demand Your Majesty's return to the throne of Greece, which by inheritance and tradition belongs to you." [31]

The liberals and the *National Herald* accelerated the tempo of their electioneering. At Hull House in Chicago, their meeting room was decorated with American and Greek flags; beneath a large map of Greater Greece was a picture of Venizelos garlanded by a wreath of flowers from the mountains of Epirus. After the rally "thousands of telegrams" were sent to Greece, urging relatives and friends to vote for Venizelos.[32] Greek-Americans had become so inflamed over the Greek elections that the 1920 presidential election of the United States seemed of little import. The first serious mention of the American election was made by the *National Herald* in the November 2 issue.[33] The story of the victory of Harding over Cox filled less than one third of the front page of the *Herald;* the bulk of it was devoted to Venizelos, the king, and the forthcoming elections in Greece.[34]

Feelings ran high, more so than many Americans, who took their politics lightly, could realize. In one instance Venizelist printers working for a royalist publication went on strike because of the appearance of a picture of the king on the front page. This was unusual— Greeks rarely joined a strike and few had connections with labor unions. But a political issue could arouse them to a point of frenzy.[35] One may ask the reason for such a fanatical interest in the politics of the old country, and such a lack of enthusiasm for the politics of the United States. Why would a Greek-American make constant telephone calls to the offices of a metropolitan newspaper on a Sunday afternoon to learn the outcome of a Greek election, or wait for the latest edition of the local newspaper with the nervous restlessness of an expectant father?

There is no single explanation for this. It may be attributed to natural youthful energies, an affection for the mother country that had been whetted by years of absence, or, as someone put it, "because we didn't know any better." But there probably were deeper reasons. To many, especially after the war, Greece appeared to be on the threshhold of that greatness its poets, politicians, and priests had for so long written and spoken about. Some naturally had thought of returning to Greece, and what could be more satisfying than to return to a Greater Greece? Nor must one forget the passion of the Greeks for politics; this was a favorite pastime of which emigration to the United States could not purge them. American politics were too foreign or stale for them. The political candidates and the issues lacked the luster, drama, and tradition of the candidates and issues of the Old World. Most of them were not citizens of the United States. Finally, the Greek-language press, letters from home, and the rival political factions made it difficult for them to forget Greek politics, even if they had wanted to.

Greek-American liberals were so confident of victory in the elections of November 14 that the *National Herald* predicted Venizelos would control 313 votes in the Chamber of Deputies, and the opposition only 55.[36] Needless to say, they were shocked beyond belief when only 126 of the 313 anticipated liberals were elected. Sixteen political factions had united to oppose Venizelos. His defeat was decisive; the people had voted against him. The liberals still comprised the largest single political bloc in Greece, but the royalists had become the masters.

Venizelos was wrong in assuming that success in foreign policy would bring him victory in the election—the ordinary people were influenced by domestic and not foreign issues. And as we have seen, there were other causes at work against him. The Greeks had grown weary of mobilization and war and the promise of greatness; they disliked being dominated by one person too long; they could not forget the privations suffered during the blockade. Moreover, the death of King Alexander hurt Venizelos' position; royalist propagandists proved effective; and the Venizelists were too relaxed and overconfident. All these forces contributed to the downfall of the prime minister. By voting against Venizelos, the Greeks expected to obtain relief from the factional strife that had eaten its way into the body politic of an exhausted nation.[37]

The smashing defeat of Venizelos and the anticipated return of Constantine brought rejoicing to American royalist quarters. Four thousand turned out in New York City to celebrate his triumph amidst reports that Venizelos, the most prominent members of his cabinet, and the leading editors of his faction had fled the country.[38] American liberals were stunned by what had happened; many found it difficult to accept the fact. But after regaining their composure, they girded themselves for the next round of battle. One of their prime targets became the former Mrs. William B. Leeds, the wife of Prince Christopher of Greece, who was accused of subsidizing the royalist propaganda campaign with American dollars. A New York meeting of liberals angrily asserted that Mrs. Leeds' dollars and a German slush fund had furnished the foundations for the return of Constantine.[39]

A nation-wide campaign was then inaugurated to protest the return of Constantine. The liberals of Chicago became very active in this and urged England and France to intervene once more. A message addressed to the prime ministers of both countries read in part: "The Greek people, bred and misled by organized Germanophile leadership, voted against its savior Eleutherios Venizelos . . . your Government, as the protector of Greece, [should] save her from the iron heel of Germanism and bar the return of the traitor Constantine, to the Greek throne." England and France, however, had made it known that they would accept the decision of the Greek voters in the plebiscite for the king.[40]

The Chicago liberals gave evidence of their intentions to reorganize their ranks and fight to the finish to rid Greece of "the German clique." Their stated purpose was to build a new organization, clarify the issues for the Greek-Americans of Chicago and other cities, and launch a campaign for the establishment of a democracy in Greece.[41]

A news story reported that Mrs. Leeds, now Constantine's daughter-in-law, was preparing to assume her place as the head of Greek society and revitalize the Greek economy with American money. Mrs. Leeds, according to an Athens account, contemplated converting Greece into a Monte Carlo, with hotels and casinos on a grand scale. Her influence in the United States and the climate of Greece were viewed as adequate to persuade millionaires who normally wintered on the Riviera to come to Greece.[42]

Fears had begun to emanate from the Ecumenical Patriarchate in Constantinople that Greece would be stripped of her victories if Constantine were restored. These fears, a spokesman of the Patriarchate said, were voiced chiefly in behalf of "the sacred interests of Greece."[43] Now France, Britain, and Italy reacted, even though the restoration of Constantine was a Greek affair. One interpretation goes as follows:

Italy, indeed, rejoiced openly and loudly at the change, not, however, from love for Greece or her King, but from satisfaction at the defeat of the dreaded statesman [Venizelos] whose policy was considered to be an obstacle to Italian Imperialism. France was specially hostile to Constantine and began to veer round to that Turkophil policy which for centuries has alternated with her traditional Philhellenism . . . In Great Britain many people had been friends of Greece because they admired the genius of Mr. Venizelos, and when he fell they unfairly vented their disgust upon his whole country; moreover, the British public was weary of war and disinclined, as it usually is, to occupy itself with foreign affairs. On the eve of the plebiscite these three Powers had declared that they would consider Constantine's restoration "as the ratification by Greece" of his "acts of hostility" during the war, and as creating "a new situation unfavourable to the relations between her and her allies."[44]

The United States was influenced by these developments, as we shall see. On December 12, 1920, Edward Capps, the United States minister in Athens, cabled the State Department that Great Britain and France had informed the Greek government that they would not honor any further drafts on the unused balances of the tripartite loan being held for Greece in Paris and London banks.[45] The background of this loan appears to have been as follows. In February 1918 England, France, and the United States had agreed to underwrite a Greek loan of 750 million francs. Greece, in turn, promised to keep a certain number of men in the field during 1918, engage in other military and naval operations, and abide by certain other conditions regarding the use of this money. As a result, the United States established a credit of $48,236,629 for Greece to draw on. Of this, a total of $15 million had been advanced by November 15, 1920, and $33,236,629 remained on the books in Greece's favor. Correspondence showed that Great Britain and France had established book credit, but that neither one had advanced any part of its share. The correspondence of Minister Capps also indicated that neither of these countries was likely to change its mind in the immediate future.[46]

This assistance, it appears, was for the rehabilitation and relief of Greece and not for the furthering of her postwar military aims. The Treasury Department also had agreed to make these advances only when it received assurances that the money would be spent in the United States. But as late as November 1920, only the names of the parties receiving the money was shown; no statement was on record of how the money had been spent. Finally, this loan had been made to the Venizelos government, which had been defeated in the election of November 1920.[47]

Capps reported that the royalist-controlled press in Greece spoke in confidence of future financial support from the United States. If the United States advanced further funds at this particular time, it would be accepted as a rebuke to Venizelos and an endorsement of the incoming administration. Capps further suggested: "If the United States does not consider making any such advances, I think it would be very desirable to clearly indicate this to the Greek government. The French and British ministers are expecting to receive notifications that they are recalled. Have you any instructions for me in the premises?"[48] Senator John Sharp Williams took the view that any future request for advances should be refused in view of the return of Constantine. "This refusal can well be based upon the fact that we were helping a friend, or a friendly government and people, and that when an enemy has been substituted for the friend, we do not consider ourselves compelled to extend any gratuity. It is a gratuity, although the gratuity is expected to be paid back." [49]

An exchange of correspondence between State and Treasury Department offiicals failed to clear up this controversy. Suffice it to say that, upon the failure of the Treasury Department to release all or a large part of the credit established for Greece, the government of Constantine retaliated by raising the tariff on certain American goods sold in Greece. The tariff on oleomargarine, for instance, was raised 300 percent.[50]

The year 1921 saw no change in relations between the royalists and liberals or in their demands for a Greater Greece. Venizelos went to Paris as a private citizen to oppose any attempt to revise the Treaty of Sèvres at the London conference on February 21. In Town Hall, New York, two thousand supporters gave proof that they maintained a close watch on the course of events, hailed Venizelos as "the Lincoln of Greece," hissed the king, and burned a copy of the royalist *Atlantis*.[51]

A few American newspapers were favorably disposed toward the claims of Greece to northern Epirus, Thrace, the Dodecanese Islands, and portions of Turkey, and their positions seemed to re-echo the demands of the Greek-American liberals. The *Christian Science Monitor,* in an editorial entitled "The Lion Resumes His Skin," expressed such sympathies.[52] Liberals in Dover, New Hampshire, affirmed that Venizelos represented the sentiments of 45 percent of those who had voted for him recently in Greece, and most of the Greeks in the United States and the Turkish territories. They feared that the Allies would sanction a revision of the Treaty of Sèvres as a reprisal for the return of Constantine, and that another Armenian tragedy would occur if Thrace and Smyrna were returned to Turkey under the revision. Predicting that the Greeks would force the abdication of Constantine for a second time, the Allies were asked to refuse recognition of his regime for a short time longer and refrain from altering the treaty: "European diplomacy will be spared the opprobrium of having scrapped just another treaty, and of having violated a traditional policy of never surrendering liberated Christian peoples to Mohammedan ruthlessness." [53]

On February 22, 1921, a committee of liberals appeared before Secretary of State Bainbridge Colby and the ambassadors of Great Britain, France, Japan, and Belgium to submit a memorandum protesting the proposed revision of the Treaty of Sèvres. The protest set forth that "the award of Thrace and Smyrna to Greece was not made as a reward of the merit of one person, but as a matter of plain justice . . . We need not speak of the folly which has recalled Constantine. This is visible to all the world and the Greek victims themselves are fast awakening to it. But the folly of a part of the Greek people ought not be made an excuse for inflicting a fresh outrage upon the Hellenic race as a whole outside the old kingdom of the Hellenes." This same committee appeared before the ambassador of Brazil and submitted a protest on behalf of thirty thousand northern Epirotes against Albanian outrages. The committee asked the Brazilian ambassador to transmit the protest to the representative of the council of the League of Nations that was then in session.[54] The *Boston Herald,* in an editorial entitled "Must Greece Lose Smyrna?" echoed the sentiments of the liberals who kept insisting that the revision of the Treaty of Sèvres was the price the Greek people were being asked to pay for the return of Constantine.

A new phase in the dramatic struggle between royalists and liberals began when reports filtered into the country of the proposed visit of Eleutherios Venizelos. This was good news to his many admirers and well-wishers, but caused apprehension and doubts in official Washington circles. On September 2, 1921, Charles Evans Hughes wired the United States embassy in London as follows: "Understand that Venizelos is to be married in London on September ninth and contemplates visiting the United States at the time of the Conference on Limitation of Armaments. It is believed that this visit would be unfortunate, not because of any lack of esteem but because of speculations and misunderstandings to which it might give rise. Suggest that you advise informally against visit at that time, if you have opportunity to do so without giving offense." [55] This effort failed. Three weeks later the State Department informed the United States embassy in London that Kyriakos P. Tsolianos, the secretary of Venizelos who was to precede his superior by a fortnight, was to be given a visa but not a diplomatic passport.[56]

At about the same time the State Department was informed that officers of the Greek army were coming to the United States on a special mission. Rumors were that these men were coming for the express purpose of waging an anti-Venizelos campaign. When the

Greek foreign minister was pressed for an explanation of the proposed mission, he explained that it was to compile statistics on the Greeks in the United States and gather other related information. Upon the receipt of this response, the requested diplomatic visas were issued by the American legation in Athens.[57]

Then on October 12 Hughes received the following telegram from Ambassador Harvey in London: "Have just had talk with Venizelos. He sails with bride Saturday remains in New York two or three days then direct to Santa Barbara, California for winter. I suggested that President and yourself [Hughes] would be pleased to receive him on his return in the spring. He was greatly gratified and will so arrange." [58]

If efforts at first were made in the east to veil the arrival of Venizelos so as to prevent any embarrassment to official Washington and others, there is no evidence that this was attempted in the other parts of the country. Admirers turned out in throngs to greet him upon his arrival in Chicago. An estimated ten thousand were on hand at the La Salle Street Station when he and the Metropolitan of Athens alighted from their car. The crowd had massed so tightly in an effort to get a closer glimpse of him that the former premier had to be escorted by a squadron of policemen to a freight elevator and leave by a rear exit. After being safely settled in his suite at the Blackstone Hotel, a crowd that swelled to some 20,000 gathered outside waving their hats and shouting, "Venizelos our hero! Long live Venizelos our saint." When a committee of Chicago liberals pressed him for permission to give a banquet in his honor, he requested that he be given a minimum of attention and be treated as an ordinary traveler. Venizelos refused to give a press interview and made known his intentions of leaving for California.[59]

On January 3, 1922, Rear-Admiral Mark S. Bristol, the United States high commissioner in Constantinople, informed the State Department of a plot to assassinate Venizelos in the United States. Bristol said this information had been relayed to him on December 21 by Vice-Admiral Pierre Ghinis of the Greek navy. Bristol added that this was not the first time he had been informed by Greek sources of Turkish plots to assassinate Venizelos and that he discounted the story.[60] Venizelos, far from being assassinated, appears to have enjoyed his visit. In California he was received enthusiastically by the Greek colonies. He went to Panama, South America, and Cuba. He was welcomed by the Greek communities of New Orleans and Tarpon Springs, Florida, visited with Secretary of State Hughes, and was a guest in the New York area. His stay in the United States ended on May 2, 1922, when he sailed for Europe.[61]

The attitude of the United States toward the government of King Constantine had become a topic of consequence. After the monarch had been restored, Alexander Vouros, the representative of Greece, tendered his letters of credence; acceptance of them would have constituted a formal recognition of the new government. The State Department, in view of the special circumstances attending the Constantinian restoration, deemed it necessary to take into account the part the monarch had played in the war, the attitude of his regime toward the acts and obligations of his predecessor Alexander, and the position of its wartime associates, England and France. If the United States extended recognition, it might place itself in the position of acquiescing in a possible review of the acts of King Alexander's government, which had borrowed money from the United States. Furthermore, none of the Allied Powers had recognized Constantine subsequent to his return to power.[62]

The American royalists reacted to this state of affairs by launching a campaign to obtain recognition for the monarchy. On January 16, 1922, D. J. Vlasto, the brother of Solon, and Polyzoides, the editor of *Atlantis*, telegraphed Charles Evans Hughes the following urgent appeal: "Many and persistent demands made on us by our readers all over the country and by many businessmen of Greece for a speedy resumption of closer official relations between us and Greece . . . have addressed to the President an appeal soliciting his kind attention to this matter remembering always with gratitude your kind feelings toward our citizens of Greek origin . . . appeal to your sentiment of fair play and justice and we sincerely trust that the issue . . . will meet your cordial support." [63]

On January 18 Senator Lodge, the chairman of the Senate Foreign Relations Committee, received a comparable plea from the Greek American National Union of Massachusetts.[64] Lodge, after forwarding this wire to the Secretary of State, was informed by Hughes that this matter was receiving "the earnest consideration" of the State Department. Hughes added that a chargé d'affaires had been assigned recently to the staff of the American legation in Athens and that this would help keep the Department more fully informed on the Greek situation.[65]

On January 19 and 20, 1922, President Harding received telegrams from various parts of the country asking that the advice of *Atlantis* be heeded in establishing closer working relations between the United States and Greece. The phraseology in the telegrams was so similar that one must conclude that individuals working in close cooperation with *Atlantis* spearheaded the drive.[66]

Following quickly on the heels of the royalist activities came a sharp protest from Petros Tatanis of the *National Herald*. Tatanis, in a telegram to President Harding, charged that the *Atlantis* represented neither the educated nor the enlightened members of the Greek population of the United States. Most Greeks, he argued, were anti-royalist and deeply appreciative of the democratic institutions under which they lived. Royalist propaganda in this country stemmed from the same "shaking throne" of King Constantine as that which tried to stifle the seeds of democracy in Greece. A better barometer of Greek-American sentiment, he believed, was the cordial and spontaneous reception that Venizelos was given in this country. Simultaneously Tatanis made a passionate plea for help to Greece in fighting a common enemy, "the un-Christian Turk." Failure to furnish this assistance would be seized upon by the Turks as proof that the war waged by Greece was unjustifiable.[67]

In another communication to Secretary Hughes, Vlasto and Polyzoides again asked for the resumption of diplomatic relations between Greece and the United States. This request, they assured the secretary, was the genuine product of hundreds of telegrams and thousands of signatures to petitions by citizens who eagerly awaited a decision. "We [of *Atlantis*] are too deeply inculcated with GOP Republicanism ever [*sic*] we first cast our ballot, to be safely immune from Royalism, Imperialism, Despotism, and Bolshevism. We, and our fellow citizens, have undertaken this campaign single-handed and independently." [68]

Efforts to obtain recognition also were put through more official channels. On November 12, 1921, Gennadius, former Greek minister to the Court of St. James, left London for the United States on a special mission for the Greek government. He came to be on hand in the event that the Near Eastern question arose at the Conference on the Limitation of Armaments.[69] However, it appears that several months were to elapse before Gennadius broached the question of recognition. On

April 16, 1922, Gennadius requested Secretary Hughes "to be so good as to allow me to call on you unofficially, when in the course of a few minutes, I may have the honour of placing before you some considerations conducive, as I trust, to the resumption of normal relations between the United States Government and Greece." [70] A. W. Dulles replied to Gennadius that the secretary would be pleased to see him informally at his house on April 25 and that he would accompany him. [71] At a later date, when asked for his opinion of the attitude of the Greek government toward the United States, Gennadius replied that "they would do anything to secure our [American] recognition, that he was prepared to discuss not only political but also financial questions and that he was confident that no difficulty would be met on either score." [72]

These efforts come to nothing. The Harding administration saw no reason for reversing the nonrecognition policy of the preceding administration. More light on this policy was cast a few years later when Secretary Hughes issued a press release specifically outlining the position of the United States from about December 26, 1920, when it broke diplomatic relations with Greece, until January 29, 1924, when it resumed them. Recognition of the Constantine government had been adjudged undesirable at the time for several reasons. Constantine had encouraged a militaristic policy in Asia Minor as a means of strengthening his hold upon the throne. Recognition by the United States would have been tantamount to separate action, for the Allied Powers had not recognized Constantine. This would have been an indirect expression of sympathy for his regime and an indirect participation in the politics of the Near East, which the United States was anxious to avoid.

Furthermore, said Hughes, the wisdom of refusing recognition was justified by the overthrow of Constantine after the military plans in Asia Minor had failed and a revolution ensued. But once negotiations between Greece and Turkey were concluded at Lausanne in July 1923, the peace ratified by both countries, and elections held in Greece on December 13, 1923, with the resulting Venizelist victory, the situation had changed so as to justify a reversal in policy. The establishment of a "stable government" helped pave the way for the formal recognition that was finally extended on January 29, 1924. [73] The political situation in Greece had changed without a doubt, but Hughes's knowledge of

Greek political history was too limited to allow the statement that a stable government had been established. The most cursory examination of Greek history would prove that it had not.[74]

The sequence of events before 1924 had foretold of a national tragedy: a humiliation such as had never before been known and the loss of all that Greece had fought for and acquired through diplomacy during the previous three years—resulting from Constantine's continuation of war with Turkey. Greek-American societies representing the Thrace and Asia Minor communities protested the plans of the Allied Powers to return Greek populations to the Turks. They protested, among other things, because a good many of them had fought on the side of the Allies in France during the war.[75] For the time being at least, the disaster hanging over Greece was tending to bury partisan differences and to promote unity in the face of the ancient common enemy. Patriarch Metaxakis even started a tour preaching the need for unity among all Greeks and urging all Greeks of military age to join the army regardless of political preferences.[76]

In the face of Turkish advances and Greek casualties, last-ditch efforts were made to forge a united front among the Greek-Americans and contribute to a common fund for the defense of the mother country. Late in May 1922 the *National Herald,* the inveterate foe of Constantine, sponsored a national defense fund for Greece. During the critical month of August 1922, when Greece was fighting with her back to the wall, horror-stricken partisans began sensing more than ever the folly of Greek factionalism. At a rally in Washington members of the audience were in tears as speakers representing the armies of Asia Minor told of the struggles and aims of Greece. Many wept with joy over the thought that the two feuding communities of St. Sophia (Venizelists) and St. Constantine (royalists) would unite during this tragic hour.[77]

News of the possible formation of a revolutionary committee for the purpose of overthrowing the king and defending the frontier of Thrace brought eloquent promises of support from Greek-Americans. In an emotional editorial, the *National Herald* demanded "the burning out of the roots of a traitorous dynasty."[78] The Hellenic Liberal Democratic Club of Chicago lost little time in asking for the establishment of a democracy in Greece, the immediate dethronement of Constantine who was blamed for the destruction of the Greek armies in Asia Minor,

and the exile of his entire family.[79] Greek churches in Chicago, Philadelphia, New York, and other metropolitan areas set aside Sunday,
September 17, as the day when all the faithful were asked to attend
church and pray for the salvation of Greece.[80]

Opinion in the United States was divided over whether Greece was
ready for a republican form of government. Royalist sympathizers were
of the belief that Greece was unprepared for any such experiment.[81]
Despite the limitations of the monarchical form of government, the
royal family of Greece was viewed as being more capable of ruling the
country and providing stability than were the Greek politicians. Certainly it was more capable of furnishing the transitional leadership that
was so sorely needed.[82]

The Chicago liberals were most emphatic in their determination to
establish a republic in Greece. They believed that the country was ripe
for it. As upholders of the Constitution of the United States, they
promised to employ all legal means of aiding their countrymen rid
themselves of the Constantinian dynasty.[83] Word of the abdication of
Constantine in late September was greeted by the Greek-American
liberals with delirious joy. "The Traitor Falls" was the front-page
headline of the *National Herald* on the day this news was received. In
a succeeding issue the deposed Constantine was portrayed in a cartoon
as a tramp with a knapsack in one hand, a pole in the other, puffing on
a cigarette, and heading up some unknown trail.[84]

Greek-American liberals coupled their satisfaction over the dethronement of Constantine with pleas for the support of the revolutionary
government and the establishment of a democracy in Greece.[85] All
were urged to wire their support of the revolutionary government—and
many did—and thus help spare Greece from "the nails of every
Glücksburg." "Kings have no place in the land which established
democracy." [86]

The last three months of 1922 found Greek-Americans proclaiming
their support of the new government by collecting money for its relief
and defense, scheduling days of prayer in the churches of the country,
and discussing the raising of an army of forty thousand Greek-Americans to rush to the protection of Thrace. Meetings were held to protest
the slaughtering of Christians, the butchering of the Bishop of Smyrna
by the Turks, and the "misconduct" of the French.[87] Macedonians in
the United States and Canada also assembled in New York, where they

agreed to form an association embracing all Macedonian societies to counteract the campaign to detach Macedonia from Greece and convert it into an independent state.[88]

By early November a wholesale campaign was under way to have Greek-Americans write or telegraph their families and friends in Greece and urge them to discard the old political factions and vote into office fresh men with fresh ideas. An Athenian correspondent, writing especially for the American audience, advised his readers in most emphatic terms that they had influence in Greece and that they should exercise it in favor of a democratic government. His theme was that the old political factions had to go—it was not enough to be either a liberal or a democrat.[89]

Greek-Americans were told that they not only had a right but a sacred duty to perform by taking an active interest in the forthcoming Greek elections. To hasten matters, the *National Herald* published a sample letter which its readers were asked to cut out, sign, and mail to their relatives and friends until the villages of Greece were swamped with letters from the United States.[90] Knowledge of the receipt of many of these letters in the province of Laconia is what apparently inspired the editor of the *Herald* to urge the Peloponnesians in the United States to take a prominent part in this letter-writing crusade. He felt that the provinces of Arcadia and Messinia, as well as Laconia, should become the focal points, for they were considered royalist strongholds. The Laconians, in particular, were appealed to and asked to maintain the pioneering tradition for which they had become famous. Being the first Greeks to reach the United States, they were to the succeeding Greeks what the Pilgrims had been to the early American colonists.[91]

But new events were shaping up in Greece that were to have a resounding and sobering effect on many. Late in September 1922, a group of Constantine's former ministers and the commander-in-chief of the Asia Minor expedition were arrested, and a special commission of inquiry was appointed by the revolutionary committee to determine the responsibility of these men for the military catastrophe. The details of this dramatic sequence of events and the quality of the justice that was meted out is a subject worthy of special study and need not detain us at this point. Suffice it to say that six men— five ex-ministers and

Commander-in-Chief Hadjianestis—were found guilty of negligence and treason and ordered shot.[92]

The reactions to this display of revolutionary justice varied. The pleas of the outside world not to proceed with the executions were ignored and the six were executed in November. The world was horrified. Critics of Venizelos charged him with acquiescing to this sordid state of affairs as a means of liquidating his political opponents. Some actually were of the opinion that the revolutionary government of Greece had fallen into hands of gangsters.[93] Many Greeks, who hitherto had taken Greek politics very seriously, reconsidered their actions and decided to withdraw completely from the affairs of the mother country. The *National Herald,* on the other hand, defended the actions of the revolutionary committee: "Yesterdays shootings of the traitors not only redeems the honor of Greece but also insures its safety and life. The fate of these traitors will serve as a lesson and will prevent a repetition of these atrocities against the nation." [94] Letters from the United States endorsing the revolutionary movement brought forth expressions of appreciation from its leaders and supporters. Plastiras, the head of the revolutionary government, expressed his appreciation, through the columns of the *National Herald,* to those patriotic Greek-Americans who supported the endeavors of the mother country.[95]

The year 1923 saw an unequaled number and variety of appeals made to Greek-Americans. They were told that it was their duty to help in the reconstruction of Greece by investing in its various enterprises, obtaining representation in the Chamber of Deputies, lending money to the Greek government in this hour of national mourning, and even assuming posts as ministers and consuls. Sending remittances to the villages was not enough, for much of this money was hoarded instead of being converted into drachmas.[96]

Greek-Americans, as well as the wealthier Greeks in Greece, were advised that the recovery of their country could be accelerated if they lent money to the Greek government. If half a million Greek-Americans lent on the average of $20 per person, a working capital of $10 million would become available, suggested Thalis Koutoupis in an article prepared for American readers. Capital was needed to increase the money circulation of the country and to put the Asia Minor refugees to work. That funds were forthcoming from the United States, but perhaps not in the volume hoped for, was evidenced in part by an article entitled "Long Live Our Greek-American Brothers in America." [97]

The death of King Constantine in Palermo on January 11, 1923, and an earlier pronouncement from Venizelos that he no longer intended to head a political faction in Greece revived hopes that the factionalism of the past would be buried. But this was difficult to achieve, for partisan feeling continued to run high. Liberals continued to assail the king even in death for the disastrous course in Asia Minor that had set Greece back four centuries in her hopes and efforts.[98] Vitriolic attacks, however, did not deter others from seeking an end to the old factionalism and the ushering in of new leaders and a new political order.[99]

Pleas for peace and support of a new order also emerged from American royalist quarters, at least for a while. The *Atlantis,* on seeing that monarchism had come to an end, endorsed democratic goals for Greece. Royalists no longer supported Constantine, for he was dead; and liberals were not supporting Venizelos, for he had reportedly retired from politics. Along with the others, it echoed: "Long live, then, popular rule and down with the King, Venizelos, and their subservient factions." [100]

During this era a startling suggestion was made for promoting the Panhellenic ideal among Greek-Americans. The principal exponents of this proposal were Thalis Koutoupis, a feature writer for the *National Herald* in Athens; Speros Kotakis, editor of *Kathemerini* in Chicago; and Andrew Vlachos, a prominent attorney, also of Chicago.[101] According to Koutoupis, perhaps the most active publicist of the proposal, Hellenism had been divided into two parts: the Hellenism of Greece and the Hellenism of "the unredeemed parts." Irredentist Hellenism, if not vanquished, at least had been temporarily subdued, creating a vacuum. That could best be filled by the Hellenism of America, which was obligated to assume a primary role in the national affairs of Greece.

Greek-Americans were urged to become active in the political affairs of Greece. This was deemed necessary on the theory that the Greek-Americans were better qualified than Greeks in Greece to advise. Their counsel would be useful in determining the most effective means of studying the mother tongue, perpetuating religious customs and dogmas, aiding those in need, and helping immigrants to reach the United States. No longer would contacts be restricted to an individual or family basis, as had been done in the past—they would be extended on a national scale. Constructive criticism from democratic sources would refurbish the political life of Greece and reform the social administration of the country. In this manner the Greek nation would have pumped into it all the benefits of the ideas of a free people living in a free country. The best way of accomplishing this would be by granting the Greek-Americans representation in the Greek Chamber of Deputies.

In unfolding this novel plan Koutoupis claimed, in perhaps exaggerated fashion, that Greek-Americans pursued developments in philology, poetry, music, the professions, and commerce in Greece with considerable interest, while the Greeks themselves showed no comparable interest in developments among their compatriots in the United States. Worse still, the image of the Greek-American was an unrealistic one. In Greece the belief was that the sole motivating factor in the life of the Greek-American was in making the dollar. This, he insisted, was misleading, as was recognized by those who came into daily contact with Greek-Americans.[102]

Such a plan for Greek-Amercan representation was the product of a romantic and patriotic, if not a practical, mind. Greek precedent was on its side, but not American. In 1831 Greeks from outside Greece had taken part in the affairs of the new government. Koutoupis and others were thinking in outdated terms: the Greek-Americans of 1923 were being urged to follow in the footsteps of their Egyptian, European, and Ottoman compatriots of the 1830s. The proposal became the subject of discussion in a number of metropolitan communities, including that of Chicago, where one meeting in Hull House ended in a general uproar. It was a project more likely to be supported by liberals than royalists, but a few of the latter were also attracted to it. The evidence is that the proposal never got beyond the discussion stage. If put into operation, the plan would have resulted in the creation of a state within a state. It would have encountered a hostile American public for its promotion of a divided loyalty. The United States recognized the territorial concept of citizenship, not the blood-tie concept that prevailed in most European countries. Greece recognized dual citizenship, which the United States did not, even though Greece respected the claims of a nation within its territorial limits.[103]

The unfolding of this unusual plan for Greek-American representation was accompanied with the customary exhortations to the Greek to pool their resources as the best means of resisting the dangers that continued to haunt the Greek nation.[104] After the Asia Minor disaster, American Hellenism was viewed as the only power capable of perpetuating "the national ideal" with the necessary zeal. From the United States had to come the spirit of brotherhood and love that would unite Greece and successfully transplant the hundreds of thousands of refugees and their families to Greek soil.[105]

The articulate Chicagoans made it clear that Greek-Americans had grown accustomed to assuming many of the burdens of the mother country, and for this reason their voices had to be respected when it came to selecting official representatives of the Greek government in the United States. There were enough competent and progressive men in the United States from whose ranks the future consuls and ministers from Greece to this country could be selected.[106] Animated by the belief that the Greek-Americans should take a hand in furthering the democratic movement in Greece, proponents of the idea called a convention of the democratic liberals in the United States and Canada to assemble in Chicago on May 11 and 12, 1923. A purpose of the meeting was to further plans for cooperating with the Democratic Association of Athens. Among the topics on the agendum were how the clubs in the United States and Canada could combine to ensure the election of the democratic candidates in the forthcoming elections of Greece; how best to combat the efforts of the supporters of "the depraved Royalist system"; and how most effectively to counteract the Turkish propaganda that was finding its way into the United States.[107]

The long-range aspirations of the most zealous proponents of Greek-American cooperation were not realized, and representation in the Chamber of Deputies of Greece never was achieved, but some degree of satisfaction was derived from the formation of the ill-fated Greek republic in 1924. The subsequent turn of events, leading to a military coup d'état a year later, did not dampen the enthusiasm of Greek-American patriots for some time to come. On May 25, 1924, Greek-Americans in Chicago assembled to express their happiness over the democratic turn of events in Greece and hear Rufus Dawes and Senator James Hamilton Fish address the meeting.[108]

The second phase of the royalist-liberal struggle was fought in the United States with the same degree of partisanship and vehemence that it was fought in Greece. Both sides attempted to influence American policy toward Greece. Both factions urged the United States to intervene in Greece at one time or another: the royalists wanted the United States to help restore King Constantine and recognize his government; the liberals wanted to prevent the revision of the Treaty of Sèvres, which was so favorable to Greek interests. Most unusual were the letter-writing campaigns of the Greek-Americans to influence the Greek elections in 1920 and in subsequent years. Some of their articulate spokesmen, if given their way, would have delegated men to represent the Greek-Americans in the Greek Chamber of Deputies. Royalists forever proclaimed their loyalty to the American government and its institutions, but they felt that the form of government Greece had was her own affair. The Greek-American liberals felt differently: their years of residence in the United States and aquaintance with democratic institutions had convinced them that the monarchy was obsolete and had to be discarded. They wanted to export an American brand of democracy and plant it on Greek soil as a part of their contribution to the homeland.

11

MILITARY OBLIGATIONS

AND THE

MOTHER COUNTRY

REEK-AMERICANS, as we have observed, often displayed a passionate desire to return to Greece for visits with relatives and friends, for the purpose of discharging their military duties, or to become repatriated.[1] Those who returned to discharge their military duties obviously had reconciled themselves to the inevitable and felt no ill will or remorse. But those who returned for visits or to stay, and were then drafted into military service, underwent a series of hard and unforgettable experiences. This was especially true of those reaching Greece between 1919 and 1922, men who had already seen service with the armed forces of the United States.[2]

The importance of this chapter in Greek-American history cannot be overestimated. American diplomatic and consular records show that neither the Greek nor the American authorities took these forced inductions lightly. The same sources indicate that the decisions of Greek military authorities often were contradictory and unpredictable, while the behavior of some American officials oscillated between disbelief and superciliousness. Matters were complicated by Greek-Americans who refused to take the advice of the American legation and often were caught in traps of their own making. Regardless of who was at fault, many painfully discovered that the possession of United States citizenship did not automatically divest one of military obligations to the mother country. Such experiences, coupled with financial reverses, left bitter memories that took years to erase.

As indicated, the most immediate problem facing the Greek-American in Greece was military service. If he returned without having acquired United States citizenship, obviously he was left to his own resources in dealing with the Greek authorities. Even if he had United States citizenship, he soon discovered that he still had something to contend with. The United States and Greece had never entered into a naturalization treaty. The Greek government refused to recognize a change of nationality on the part of one of its nationals, if this change occurred after January 15, 1914, without its consent. Consequently, one who became a citizen of the United States without obtaining this permission was subject to seizure and induction into the armed forces. And the Greek authorities were dead serious.[3] Their policy was to seize likely candidates for military service first and, if the pressure was sufficient, to negotiate later.

One of the cases brought to the attention of the American authorities was that of "P. B.," a native of the island of Mytilene (Lesbos), who became a United States citizen in 1911. After the Second Balkan War in May 1913, P. B. returned to Mytilene to visit his parents; within five or six months he was mustered into the Greek army. After eight months of service he was discharged; but when difficulties broke out again late in 1915, P. B. was forced back into the Greek service despite his insistence that he had become a citizen of the United States. The case of P. B. became more complicated because he remained in Mytilene after he served in the Greek army, and thus faced the prospect of being compelled to serve again at some future date. This action, in the eyes of Americans, appeared all the more arbitrary in that Mytilene was a part of the Ottoman Empire at the time P. B. was born; technically he never had been a Greek subject.[4]

Frequent inquiries were made of the State Department about the prospects of being allowed to travel freely in Greece without danger of being seized by the authorities; for a time, if not always, this brought warnings in the form of a "Notice to American Citizens Formerly Subjects of Greece Who Contemplate Returning to that Country." This simply advised the recipient that no treaty had been signed by the United States and Greece which regulated the status of naturalized United States citizens in Greece. By late 1915 the Greek government, then under pressure from the Central Powers and the Entente nations, not only prohibited the departure of anyone of military age but reacted unfavorably toward anyone making representations in behalf of American citizens subject to military duty.[5]

"American citizens of Greek origin" were advised by naive American officials "to find out before returning to Greece what status they may expect to enjoy" from a diplomatic or consular officer of the Greek government; the State Department refused to act as an intermediary in seeking such information. At the same time, the State Department called attention to the Expatriation Act of March 2, 1907:

> That any American citizen shall be deemed to have expatriated himself when he has been naturalized in any foreign State in conformity with its laws, or when he has taken an oath of allegiance to any foreign State.
>
> When any naturalized citizen shall have resided for two years in the foreign State from which he came, or for five years in any other foreign State, it shall be presumed that he had ceased to be an American citizen, and the place of his general abode shall be deemed his place of residence during said years: Provided, however, that such presumption may be overcome on the presentation of satisfactory evidence to a diplomatic or consular officer of the United States, under such rules and regulations as the Department of State may prescribe: And provided also, that no American citizen shall be allowed to expatriate himself when this country is at war.

Simultaneously, all United States citizens in Greece were urged to apply for registration at the nearest American consulate.[6]

A related problem involved the Greek-American who, while serving with the armed forces of the United States, claimed that his relatives were taxed by the Greek authorities because he did not return and join the Greek army.[7] The State Department, inquiring about such practices, was informed that "military service in Greece is a personal obligation, which, if not fulfilled brings punishment upon the delinquent himself, but not upon the parent, who, in the eye of the law, can only be held responsible for their own personal deeds." The pertinent point raised by this case is that every Greek-American serving with the United States army had to report his service to the proper Greek military authorities so as not to be classified as a delinquent. Anyone liable for duty was deemed a delinquent and liable for punishment, unless he answered the call within a prescribed time. The complainant, it appears, failed to inform the military authorities of his service with the United States army; perhaps for this reason he was being held a delinquent and his parents "molested" by the authorities. Since the Venizelos government during the war considered service with the United States army the equivalent of joining the Greek army, the forwarding of a certificate from the American regiment to the proper authorities in Greece would clarify his status and remove him from the delinquent list. This precaution was urged upon others to save themselves from embarrassment and hardship.[8]

More complex and exasperating were the problems of the years after World War One. The difficulties were more or less inevitable, owing to the ill-fated determination of Greece to fulfill her national aspirations in the Near East, thus compelling her to remain on a war footing for about four years after the armistice in 1918, and the refusal of the United States to recognize the government of King Constantine. This created a crisis for almost all Greek-Americans, naturalized and non-naturalized, who returned to Greece permanently or for brief periods.

On April 16, 1919, the office of the solicitor in the State Department concluded, after a conversation with a representative of the Greek legation in Washington,

that, in view of the recently concluded Military Service Convention between the United States and Greece, naturalized Americans of Greek origin who return to Greece for a temporary purpose, and who have fully complied with the Selective Service Act and the regulations thereunder, will not be liable to punishment as military service delinquents, although the delinquency might have occurred prior to the present war. I gathered from the conversation that this assurance was not to be extended to Greek subjects who had served in the United States Army or had complied with the Selective Service Act, but only to persons who are now naturalized American citizens.[9]

In the summer of 1919 Greek-Americans arrived in droves from the United States and France, those from France being members of the AEF who hoped to obtain their final release from the American armed forces in Greece. Meanwhile, the Greek Ministry of War had informed the American legation in Athens that Greek-Americans would be liable for military service in Greece, and that the amount of time spent with the armed forces of the United States would be credited to them as though they had served with the Greek army. The only ones exempt from duty were those who became naturalized citizens prior to January 15, 1914. Because of the confusion, Garrett Droppers, the United States minister in Athens, asked the State Department to refuse passports to all Greek-Americans, naturalized or nonnaturalized, until there was a clearer picture of actual conditions.[10]

Upon receiving this information from Athens, the State Department informed the United States embassies in London and Paris that naturalized American citizens of Greek birth were likely to be impressed into the army if they visited Greece. Applicants for emergency passports also had to be warned of the impending difficulties.[11] Shortly afterward, Droppers, in another communication, informed the State Department that his previous dispatch of August 15 gave only "a faint notion of the situation." Elaborating, he stated:

Those who came to Greece early in the year and were in uniform, were allowed to return to America without too much difficulty. I suppose it was thought by the Greek military authorities that they were exceptional cases and besides there was then the enthusiasm for the American uniform. But later these men came to Greece in civilian clothes. They were immediately seized by the police and as they had no proper exemption papers they were ordered to join the army. A good many of them, on one plea or another, I saved from further military service and the experiences of these men with the police of Greece will, I am sure, never be forgotten. They all, whether coming from France or from the United States, state that they were assured by both the American military authorities and by the Greek consuls that they could travel freely in Greece. Those who were naturalized citizens I was able to rescue with more success than the others, although on this point Greek law does not recognize American citizenship.

Droppers, hoping to obtain a definite ruling on the status of persons of Greek birth coming to Greece, addressed a note to Alexander Grivas, the under-secretary of state for war, asking whether service in the United States army, with an honorable discharge, exempted one from further service in Greece.[12] Grivas informed Droppers that the military convention between the United States and Greece had been suspended by mutual agreement and that the time spent in the United States army would be counted as time served in the Greek army. If the men were recruits belonging to the two annual classes serving their first two years under Greek law, they would, upon their return to Greece, be required to serve the difference between these two years and the time spent in the American army. On the other hand, if they belonged to the reserve forces, they would serve only if their class was under mobilization and then be discharged with their class.

Grivas concluded that this was justifiable, for a short service in the

American army could not entirely absolve Greek nationals from military service in Greece. If it did absolve them, this would constitute an inequality in the distribution of the military burden and a violation of the express intent of the Constitution and the Military Service Law which made military service obligatory for all citizens on an equal basis.[13] Droppers, in view of this definition of Greek military law, expressed the opinion that the American military authorities were obligated to notify men of Greek birth who fought with the United States army what they should expect if they returned to Greece for a visit. Every individual of Greek birth, naturalized or not, ran the risk of being held for military service if he had not completed two years' service with the United States Army. Some who came to Greece for commercial reasons "made their escape back to America by ways that are dark and devious," added Droppers, "and I am sure will never again run the risk of coming into the land of their birth."[14]

As of August 21, 1919, the American legation in Athens reported that United States citizens "having their papers in order" were not compelled to join the Greek army, but this hardly meant that such persons were automatically exempt. Droppers also stated that "Greeks with only first papers who served in the American Army are in many instances treated with extreme harshness by the military police, some of these are entirely American in their sentiments and were assured they could safely visit Greece."[15] A telegram from Washington instructed the American legation to "Make every effort obtain release naturalized American citizen of Greek origin from performance of military service in Greece."[16]

The State Department viewed the treatment of United States citizens in Greece as a grave matter. On October 11, 1919, it advised the American legation in Athens that the Italian government, whose military-service laws appeared to be as severe as those of Greece, "has given this Government formal assurances that American citizens of Italian extraction as well as persons who have retained their Italian nationality, who were under obligation of military service in the Kingdom of Italy . . . may freely visit Italy without molestation, provided they carry with them their discharge from the records showing that they had served with the American forces or were exempted from such service under the laws and regulations in force in the United States." This same question was being taken up with the French embassy in

Washington in order to obtain comparable assurances from the French government.

The trouble with this line of reasoning was that the needs and positions of Italy and France were totally different from those of Greece. The similarity of their military laws was a matter of coincidence, nothing else. Neither country remained on a full-time military footing for four years after the armistice, as Greece had. American officialdom lacked imagination and foresight; it seemed to suffer from a lack of realism and perhaps misjudged the determination of the Greeks to fulfill the dream of centuries. Certainly the difficulties that faced the Wilson administration after the congressional elections of 1918, not to mention the deprivations endured by the Greek people during the absence of Venizelos, did not help matters. Later we shall see that the problems of the Greek-Americans became progressively worse after Constantine was restored to the throne and the United States refused to recognize his government.

The State Department continued to be besieged with inquiries from United States citizens asking whether they were likely to be seized for compulsory military service or treated as delinquents if they went to Greece on business or visits. All that the State Department could do was to consult with the Greek authorities and advise. On April 16, 1919, a representative of the State Department discussed this subject informally with a member of the Greek legation in Washington; he was informed that naturalized American citizens in Greece for a temporary purpose, who had fully complied with the provisions of the Selective Service Act, would not be liable for punishment as military delinquents. The department then relayed this information from the Greek legation to all inquirers; many acted on the basis of these assurances and left or made preparations to leave for Greece. At the same time, the hope was expressed that the ending of the wartime military conventions among Greece, the United States, Great Britain, France, and Italy would not preclude a liberal consideration of the broad principles of comity and individual justice that were involved. It was for this reason that Garrett Droppers was asked to "take up the matter with the Greek government . . . and endeavor to obtain assurances along the lines of those given by the Italian Government or the confirmation of those already given by the Greek Legation here." [17]

Obviously the State Department was in no position to anticipate what was about to happen in Greece and Asia Minor. At the Peace Conference, Venizelos had been pressing for the recognition of Greek claims in the Smyrna district, and Greek hopes ran high. The informal discussions just alluded to, those between representatives of the State Department and the Greek legation on April 16, 1919, took place about a month prior to the Greek landings in Smyrna. In view of these events, the incongruity between the assurances from the Greek legation in Washington and the course pursued by the office of the under-secretary of war in Athens becomes understandable.[18]

Meanwhile, Greek-Americans continued to press congressmen, senators, officials in the State Department, and other branches of the United States government for the latest information and advice relative to their safety. The reasons they gave for wanting to go to Greece were personal business, such as the sale of family property and exploring the prospects of investing, the visiting of parents and other close relatives, and the making of arrangements to bring members of their families to the United States. Many of these people left for Greece believing that they were safe and would be free to return to the United States.

American legation officials placed much of the blame for the difficulties in Greece on the Greek consular officials in the United States. "If these visitors are to be believed, the Greek Consular authorities are operating their passport departments under false pretenses. These people are assured, so they say, that if they travel to Greece on Consular passports, they will have no difficulty in returning to the United States." [19] Several weeks after the receipt of this communication, the American legation in Athens was directed "to request definite statements, if possible in the form of affidavits, from American citizens who have been misled by the Greek Government authorities, and to submit such statements to the Department for its consideration and appropriate action." [20] About three weeks later Droppers advised the State Department: "An official from the Greek Ministry of Foreign Affairs has notified me formally that American citizens of Greek origin and all other Greeks who have served in the American army will be exempted from further service in the Greek Army." [21] Apparently a good deal of the misunderstanding stemmed from the interpretation of the Military Convention between the United States and Greece, and from the disorganized state of communications between the Greek legation in Washington and the Greek authorities in Athens.

Now the Division of Passport Control in Washington advised United States citizens of Greek origin who had served with the United States army that they would not be "molested" upon their return to Greece, provided they carried with them the certificates of discharge issued by the War Department.[22] One thing State Department officials overlooked was that the military manpower needs of the Greek army fluctuated suddenly. When relative calm appeared on the Asia Minor front, the Greek authorities could afford to give a liberal interpretation to military service. But when the Greek army expanded its operations, and this could be done swiftly and without notice, the authorities could insist on this military service with Draconian severity.

After prolonged discussions, the American legation in Athens believed that it had finally clarified and solved the misunderstanding over military service. On March 31, 1920, Droppers telegraphed the State Department that, according to the latest information from the Greek Foreign Office, all who served with the United States army were exempt from military service upon their return to Greece. Every Greek citizen belonging to the active army was required to present a certificate, within a month after his arrival in Greece, to prove his residence in the United States. This would exempt him from the penalties of the Greek military law for failing to present himself for service at the proper time.[23] At least this was the situation in March.

By May 1920 the picture had changed drastically; the preliminary draft of the Treaty of Sèvres had been agreed upon and the Greek military campaign had been accelerated. A telegram from Athens dated May 26, 1920, warned that all Greek-Americans who had not served with the United States army were liable for military service upon return to Greece. The British legation in Athens dispatched a similar cable to Greeks living in England or her colonies, advising them to keep away from Greece unless they were prepared to serve in the Greek army.[24] The British warning sounded more realistic, based as it was on a more thorough understanding of the problems at hand and the temper of the times.

But what had appeared to the Americans as having been the unraveling of a hopelessly tangled skein was now worsened by the seizure of naturalized citizens for military duty. Discussions once more were opened with the Greek Foreign Office, but without results.[25] A critical hour in the history of Greece had arrived and her officials were painfully aware of it. United States citizenship to them was a technical matter that for the time being had to take a subordinate place in the greater scheme of things. The authorities were little inclined to scrutinize carefully the papers of able-bodied men in Greek territory who spoke Greek.

It also appears that others besides the Greeks were to blame for this state of affairs. The passport officials of the United States could have issued sterner warnings to naturalized citizens, even to those who had served with the United States army, of what was in store for them. They could also have told the Greek-Americans in blunt language that the legation in Athens was powerless to help them until the United States and Greece entered into a naturalization treaty.

For a time it appeared as though the United States officials were more confused and disorganized than the Greeks. On August 2, 1920, the State Department informed the American legation in Athens that appropriate warning was now being sent with each passport issued to naturalized citizens of Greek origin.[26] But in mid-October 1920 the American legation advised the State Department that "naturalized Greeks arriving here report they have received no advance warning from Department." [27]

The two groups experiencing the most difficulty in Greece were the children of naturalized parents and adults who acquired their citizenship after the passage of Law 120 of January 15, 1914. Greece claimed as her subjects children, born in the United States or elsewhere, of parents who became citizens without the permission required by the 1914 law. In such cases, the Greek authorities simply refused to recognize passports issued by the United States government and impressed the holders of such passports into military service. This created a dilemma for those wanting to return to the United States. Those who had failed to comply with the provisions of Law 120 but who were permitted to leave Greece had to surrender their American passports in exchange for Greek ones. This, when complied with, caused bona fide United States citizens to lose their citizenship.[28]

The American consulate, after inquiring whether it should visa "without extra charge" the Greek passports issued to naturalized United States citizens whose American passports had been seized, was advised by the State Department: "Under no circumstances should Consuls visa Greek passports held by the Americans describing them as Greek." The State Department made its position clear. The holders of these American passports had been required to renounce their allegiance to Greece when they were naturalized. The United States government refused to concede to the Greek authorities the right "to take up American passports held by naturalized Americans," and advised the American legation to request that the seized passports be surrendered to their rightful owners so that they could return to the United States.

Edward Capps, the United States minister in Athens, to facilitate the departure of those unfortunate Americans, issued a form letter to each, addressed to the commissioner of the port of New York. This, Capps hoped, would ease their re-entry into the United States. The form letter stated that the bearer, an American citizen, carried Departmental Passport No. 000, which had been issued at a particular date. Because his passport had been seized by the Greek authorities, he was given Emergency Passport No. 000 by the American legation in Athens. Finally, the form letter indicated that since Greek law refused to recognize American citizenship of persons of Greek origin if this citizenship was obtained after January 15, 1914, Mr. X had been compelled to procure a Greek passport for his return to the United States.[29] These bewildered Greek-Americans found themselves in this predicament at a time when Venizelos had fled the country and when Greece was preparing for the return of Constantine. This, in part, may explain the unpredictable series of events that gave evidence of becoming worse before they became better.

The American minister informed the Greek Ministry of Foreign Affairs of the demoralized state of the naturalized citizens of the United States in Greece, and asked that they be permitted to return to America. The Minister of Foreign Affairs replied that instructions had been issued to the proper authorities to discontinue the seizure of American passports and to return those that had been seized to their rightful owners. But at the same time he reiterated that the Greek government could not concede American citizenship to Greek subjects who were naturalized in violation of Law 120 of 1914.[30]

Once again it appeared that this state of affairs would be untangled. The return of Constantine, we have seen, posed the problem of recognition by the United States, England, and France. And the government of Constantine desperately wanted the good will and recognition from the United States. Even though this was not discussed in the correspondence between legation and State Department officials at this time, these thoughts weighed on the minds of the royalists.

The Greek Minister expressed the willingness of his government to waive the strict application of the provision in Law 120 on Greek-Americans. Capps suggested that since the Constantine government was very anxious to obtain the good will of the United States, this was a favorable moment to obtain a mutually satisfactory agreement.[31] The State Department expressed pleasure over the favorable reaction of the Greek government. In fact the Greek government sometime ago had submitted a draft of a proposed naturalization treaty, and the State Department submitted a counterdraft.[32] This news, coupled with the information that naturalized Greeks were having less difficulty in obtaining visas from the Greek authorities, was welcomed as proof that the worst was over.[33]

But hardly had these encouraging reports been received when fresh word arrived of a new mobilization affecting all naturalized citizens in Greece. The altered conditions on the military front necessitated a reappraisal of conscription and the role the Greek-Americans were to assume. Now the contention was that exemption from military service had been a courtesy extended only to men who had served with the armed forces of the United States. The previous exemptions were a thing of the past. The Greek government exercised the right to consider a fresh mobilization for a new war. This was a war in which Greece had no allies, and one in which prior service in the army of an Allied nation could not serve as the basis for exemption from service in the Greek army.[34]

The predicament in which all Greek-Americans, citizens of the United States and noncitizens, found themselves probably will never be chronicled. Many were the victims of circumstances. A frantic appeal from fifteen former American soldiers to the American Legion in Dayton, Ohio, reflects the plight of other entrapped men. They claimed that they had come to Greece as representatives of different American firms for the purpose of finding markets for their principals. They considered themselves as "full Americans" who had complied with the passport regulations of the United States and had intentions of remaining in Greece from six to nine months. But when Greece ordered a new mobilization, these "native sons" were forced into the Greek army. After making several unsuccessful attempts to obtain relief from the American legation in Athens, they were appealing to the American Legion as a last resort: "It is a matter of honor for us to see that the United States ex-service men . . . be treated right at every corner of the earth and request you Gentlemen the Officers of the American Legion, to kindly do your utmost to relieve us from such distress . . . We are ready to serve and fight for the United States any time we are called, but no other army . . . It is ridiculous to think that while we are Americans, ex-service men of the United States Army and several of us Legionnaires, we have to serve in another army." [35] Precisely what happened to these men and others in similar circumstances cannot be determined. The representative of the national legislative committee of the American Legion wrote to Secretary of State Hughes in their behalf, but nothing seems to have resulted from the action.[36]

After considerable effort Barton Hall, the American chargé, succeeded in obtaining a written statement from the Greek Ministry of Foreign Affairs, which stated that men belonging to the military classes of 1916 through 1921 would continue to be exempt if they had served with the United States Army during World War I. These classes had never been demobilized, but other classes, called or about to be called into the service, were considered a part of the new demobilization to which exemption would not apply.[37]

Meanwhile, relations between the American legation and the Greek government took a turn for the worse. On February 18, 1921, the Minister of Foreign Affairs issued instructions that all papers presented by Greek-Americans in explanation of their failure to report for military service would be returned when applications were filed for the return of these papers. However, as late as May 1921 no such documents had been returned. Hall, in exasperation, telegraphed the State Department:

I consider this attitude of Minister of War insolent especially in view of the fact that in many cases persons interested are so obviously exempt from military service that there is no occasion to take papers at all. In view of the fact that Legation has requested return of these documents I consider it added impertinence to require these people to file claims for same. It is merely usual Greek trick to delay and arrange matters so that responsibility can be shifted if necessary.[38]

Despite assurances and reassurances that former Greek subjects naturalized prior to January 15, 1914, and that men belonging to the classes of 1916 and 1921 would be exempt if they had served with the armed forces of the United States, the Greek authorities continued to impress such persons into service. The usual procedure, according to the American legation, was to seize the papers of the victim and after several days force him into service. If such a person was able to communicate with the American legation, his case was taken up with the Foreign Office; after a delay of several weeks he might be released.

The Greek authorities also seized for military service several Ottoman subjects who had become United States citizens. Hall notified the State Department that "this action is based on their not having obtained consent of Turkish Government to change nationality." The Minister of Foreign Affairs was asked why the Greek government saw fit to pass judgment on whether citizens of another country had fulfilled their obligations to that country before becoming citizens of the United States.

Early in June 1921, Hall reported that not more than a dozen requests had come for assistance from naturalized American citizens. But the fact that the legation lost track of these people before all the facts could be obtained, coupled with rumors that many more were in trouble, suggests that the letters of others who attempted to report their cases probably never got beyond the censors.

Since Greece was preparing to launch a new offensive in Asia Minor almost any day, Hall believed it was imperative for the United States to issue strong warnings to the Greek Government, specifying that it would be held responsible for the injury or death of naturalized citizens illegally forced into military service. A fresh demand for the return of passports and other documents seized from naturalized American citizens should also be presented. Hall, however, believed it advisable for the United States to insist upon exemptions only for men naturalized before January 15, 1914, or for ex-servicemen belonging to the classes of 1916 to 1921. If the United States insisted upon exemptions for those naturalized after 1914, the question of dual nationality would be injected into the discussions, thereby causing endless delays.[39]

State Department advisers took the impressment of naturalized citizens of the United States very seriously. The office of the solicitor recommended that the United States government refuse to content itself with the assurances of the Greek government, and to "make it clear that the Government of the United States does not admit the right of the Greek Government to impress any American citizen into the Greek Army, whatever may have been their origins or the dates of their naturalization." Hall also was to be instructed that this matter had received extensive attention in the American press and that a continuation of the present course of events by the Greek authorities would strain the relations between the two countries.[40] Such a statement betrayed a complete ignorance of the facts. After all, the United States had refused to recognize the government of Constantine, as had England and France; for all practical purposes, it had broken off diplomatic relations with Greece late in 1920.[41]

Complaints of impressment were coming from other quarters as well. The United States consul general in Constantinople informed the State Department that "since the Greek offensive in Asia Minor began, many complaints have reached his Consulate General from naturalized American citizens with bona fide passports and citizenship papers, stating they are being forced into the Greek Army." [42] High Commissioner Mark Bristol in Constantinople repeated the same thing about a month later. The Greek high commissioner in Constantinople made no attempt to justify the actions of the Greek authorities in holding naturalized Americans of Turkish origin; he stated that for technical reasons it had been difficult to get prompt releases for Americans wrongly impressed into military service. George Horton, the United States consul general and delegate in Smyrna, also reported cases of illegal impressment, whch he took up in energetic fashion with the local authorities.[43]

Mounting pressure on the Ministry of Foreign Affairs this time brought the promise that in the future all men arrested in Greece for evading military service would, when they claimed foreign naturalization, be taken to the nearest consulate of their adopted country instead of to the prefecture of the police. This inspired Hall to cable Washington: "If this order is followed by authorities generally which I very much doubt it will tend to improve present highly unsatisfactory situation." [44] Hall in turn was instructed to request that holders of American passports in the custody of the Greek authorities, and those arrested in the future, be taken to the nearest American consulate for an examination of their papers: "make it clear that this Government does not admit the right of the Greek authorities to impress into the

Greek Army, naturalized American citizens, whether of Greek, Turkish or other origin, who have not taken up permanent residence in Greece or otherwise forfeited their right to their Government's intervention." Again the Greek authorities were asked to refrain from taking up the passports of American citizens and to return, in accordance with previous assurances, those which already had been seized.[45]

Hall believed that the recent decision of the Greek government to designate the campaign in Asia Minor as a "continuation of the old war," instead of the beginning of a new war as it had once proclaimed, furnished more reason for demanding the immediate release of all classes of citizens who served with the United States army.[46] In a communication to George Baltazzi, the minister of foreign affairs (and one of the six executed by the revolutionary committee when it took over the government late in 1922), Hall wrote:

I find untenable . . . the stand of the Greek Government that the present military activities have the character of a new war while at the same time they are a continuation of an old war. Such a thing is impossible. Either the war is a new one or an old one and the Greek Government has very definitely stated both in its reply to the joint note of England, France, and Italy, and now in a note to me of 27/9 August, that the war is a continuation of an old one. Moreover the Greek Government has gone farther in characterizing the war as an effort to obtain the results of the recent World War.

The heavy responsibilities that Greece had undertaken recently, in the opinion of Hall, was extraneous to the question at issue. Furthermore, the release of several hundred Americans could not have had an adverse effect on the Greek army.[47]

Minister Baltazzi saw nothing "inexact" in the reference to the Asia Minor campaign "as a continuation of the world conflict." "From the political point of view it could not be known otherwise: the reasons which have made this war inevitable have reference to the work . . . of the Allied Powers and guaranteed by the treaties concluded; the end in view is to consolidate this work by crushing a resistance springing up at the last moment which offers the greatest dangers for world peace." But at the same time, this was a new or "separate effort for which Greece has assumed the responsibility and which she does for the future conclusion of peace without any help on the part of the Powers . . . She bears exclusively the burden of it, which include among others the calling to the colors of a number of new classes."[48]

As of September 1921 the American legation in Athens had on file "about seventy-five requests" for assistance, but this number did not include the many who were arrested and failed to notify the legation. The Office of the Solicitor in the State Department pointed out that cases involving a conflict of nationality were among the most disagreeable to handle. "When the person concerned is within the jurisdiction of the other country claiming his allegiance it is difficult to go any further than making a protest, and it is, of course, always unfortunate to have to make protests which are not effective." [49] Still the United States could hardly ignore the repeated arrests of its naturalized citizens; unless it found itself in a position to make an effective protest against the Greek government, it should cease to issue passports to naturalized citizens seeking to go to Greece. At the time this memorandum was prepared, the passport office was issuing about twenty passports a week to naturalized Greeks.

On November 7 Hall informed the State Department that the acting foreign minister finally consented to exempt all classes of naturalized Greeks, if they had served with the United States army. This, he made plain, was being done "as a special favor," despite the Greek law on naturalization. Hall this time had special reason to believe that this arrangement would succeed, for the Foreign Office had assigned a special man to whom such cases were to be reported. A circular of instructions on these exemptions, however, was not released lest the English, the French, and the Italians demand the same privilege. For this reason Hall considered it inadvisable to give general publicity to the arrangement.[50]

About a month later Hall cabled the State Department that the men in question could not be exempt under the provisions of the law, but that this law could be circumvented by granting these men temporary leaves to apply to the Greek government for permission to change their nationality. "Men will then have fulfilled requirement Greek law and will be recognized as American citizens by Greek Government. This will remove possibility of being molested by Greek military authorities in future." This, in the opinion of Hall, was a very generous offer in view of the general unwillingness of the Greek government to grant such permission. Hall further suggested that naturalized Americans who refused to apply for this permission should be denied further protection by the legation or the consulates. The refusal to seek this permission "can only be for the purpose of guarding loophole escape in order to avoid some future obligation to the United States by claiming Greek citizenship."[51]

The State Department cautiously advised Hall to bring the offer of the Greek authorities informally to the attention of those interested American citizens, but to avoid advising them officially to apply for a release from Greek allegiance. However, the failure of naturalized Americans to file for the suggested permission should not be considered sufficient cause for withdrawing the protection of the United States government.[52]

Jefferson Caffrey, the *ad interim* chargé d'affaires in Athens, wrote his superiors in Washington, "since my arrival here, I have been able to secure the release of a number of these men from the Greek Army." He mentioned that he had advised the Greek government that he saw no justice in its "pretensions" that a Greek subject had to obtain the consent of his government before he could become a naturalized citizen of another country, and continued to insist that persons holding American passports could not be forced into the Greek army.[53] On June 20, 1922, Caffrey wrote that, in the great majority of cases in which he made representations, he had reason to believe that the Greek authorities complied by releasing the American citizens in question. "However, in many instances the actions of the naturalized citizens make the task of the Legation very difficult. Many of these men, instead of proceeding to the United States when released, prefer to remain in Greece and engage in some sort of business. Therefore it happens frequently that after a delay, a man who has been discharged from the army as a result of the Legation's efforts, is again apprehended by the military authorities."[54]

From Smyrna came reports of proposed action that tended to make the accounts from Athens seem mild by comparison. George Horton, the consul general in Smyrna, cabled Washington: "Naturalized American citizens impressed in Greek Army frequently take refuge in consulate. Many have been sent out of country clandestinely at expense of consular officers here. Respectfully request destroyer be sent to cooperate with me and that funds be provided for food, civilian clothing and repatriation Americans rendered destitute by enforced enlistment . . . Have exhausted every means possible of reaching agreement with local authorities."[55] The State Department bluntly informed Horton that it had no funds at its disposal for the assistance or repatriation of refugees from the Greek army who claimed American citizenship, and that it "does not desire to have destroyer ordered to Smyrna for particular purpose mentioned." Horton was instructed to determine whether the naturalized citizens involved were former Greek or Ottoman subjects and to learn the dates of their naturalization and return to Greece or Turkey.[56]

The American consulate in Smyrna, still convinced of the urgency and justice of dispatching an American man-of-war to the scene, advised the State Department that "the presence of a destroyer at Smyrna is desirable for two reasons, namely, to increase the prestige of this office with the local authorities, and to facilitate the departure of American citizens escaping from service in Greek Army by affording harbor transportation, and if necessary a place of asylum." Consulate officials added, "the British, French and Italians have either destroyers or cruisers stationed here, all of which have been used at one time or another, particularly the French and Italian, for purposes similar to those herein suggested."

The impressment of American citizens into the Greek army in Smyrna and Asia Minor involved more than a contravention of the theory of nationality as interpreted by the United States government. Inasmuch as this area formally was a part of Turkey, existing treaties between the United States and Greece could hardly be invoked in territory over which Greek sovereignty had not been established. Nor could the absence of an understanding on the subject of military service be taken advantage of in Asia Minor. Apparently influenced by this line of reasoning, the Greek high commissioner in Smyrna on several occasions ordered the release of American citizens who had been inducted into the Greek army in Asia Minor. The number of naturalized Americans forced into the armies of Greece is unknown, but the assumption is that the majority of those impressed were serving in Asia Minor.[57]

In the opinion of the Office of the Solicitor in the State Department, the zeal of the American consular officials in protecting naturalized citizens in the Smyrna district was likely to involve the United States in serious difficulties unless their actions were tempered with discretion. An American citizen in the Greek army of occupation in Smyrna and under its physical control was outside the jurisdiction of the American consulate general, despite the capitulary rights the United States had in the Ottoman Empire. An American citizen of Greek descent who escaped from the army and appealed to the American consulate general for protection was not entitled to asylum in the face of a demand by the Greek military authorities for his surrender. The actions of the consulate in helping naturalized citizens to evade the passport regulations at Smyrna made him a party to violations that generally were binding upon American citizens even in a capitulary country.[58]

In 1922 Jefferson Caffrey pointed out that practically every naturalized American in Greece was having difficulties of one kind or another. If it was not with the military authorities, it was over violations of the consortium law or laws forbidding the import of certain kinds of articles, attempting to export foreign currency, becoming involved in requisition cases, seeking exemptions from the Forced Loan of 1922, or participating in Greek politics. Caffrey cited the case of one "C. V. M.," who attempted to avoid paying duty on twenty-four pairs of shoes by declaring they were not new. However, when confronted with the fact that there was a regulation forbidding the importation of old shoes into the country without a special permit from the Public Health Office, he declared that the shoes had all been worn once or twice by members of his family in order that they might be classified as old shoes and thus not be subject to duty.[59]

The punishing or taxing of parents or close relatives for the failure of American citizens to return for military service again became a concern of the Department of State. During 1923 the Greek government was accused of having confiscated the property of the parents of naturalized United States citizens who failed to fulfill their military obligations in Greece. A comparable charge was made against the Turkish government for imposing taxes on the relatives of those who became citizens of the United States.

The office of the solicitor reminded the State Department of protests to foreign governments for cruel treatment inflicted upon their own nationals. Humanitarian considerations had formed the basis of the protests of Secretaries of State Blaine, Fish, and Hay against the Russians and Rumanians for inhumane treatment of Jews. In the opinion of the solicitor, "the soundest basis for such protests, from the standpoint of international law, seems to exist when the actions of the foreign countries [has] an injurious effect upon this country, directly or through injury to its citizens." The actions of Greece and Turkey fell into this category, for they affected the United States more directly than the actions of the Russian and Rumanian governments in maltreating their nationals.[60]

Legation officials also faced the special problem created by "two kinds of Americans." There were the Americans naturalized after January 15, 1914, and the "technical Americans" born of naturalized parents in Greece. These technical Americans constituted a special group. They were the children of men who had migrated to the United States, acquired citizenship, returned to Greece, married Greek women, remained in their native land a few months or perhaps a year or two, and returned to the United States with the idea of eventually sending for their families. These fathers made repeated visits to Greece, and in the meantime their sons had often achieved manhood. As was reported by an American legation official in Athens:

the children often reach man's Estate as Greeks of unmixed Greek blood, born in Greece, speaking only Greek without the slightest knowledge of anything American other than a vague geographical notion, and with practically no prospect or desire of ever going to the United States. Then one day or another a son discovers that there is some advantage to be gained by claiming the American citizenship to which he is technically entitled and consequent exemption from fulfilling the duties of Greek citizenship, though at the same time he had no idea of discharging those of the country whose protection he claims.[61]

The problem of military delinquency finally was resolved in 1923 by a decree stipulating that a person of Greek birth, who would be held as a military delinquent if he returned to Greece, would be absolved of the offense if he paid a fine of two hundred dollars.[62]

The endless train of difficulties facing the Greek-Americans—the harsh treatment meted out by the authorities, financial reverses, the unbearable strains and tensions resulting from such visits, plus the imposition of the fine on military delinquents—resulted in a sharp decline in travel between Greece and the United States. This tended to widen the breach between Greek-Americans and the mother country. As a means of improving these relations, the Greek government in 1929 adopted special measures. The Ministry of Foreign Affairs in a letter to the American legation stated that the government of the Republic of Greece, in order to facilitate the travels of excursionists of Hellenic origin from the United States, had decided to postpone all proceedings against those who could be classified as military delinquents during their visits in Greece. This "amnesty" originally was to run from March 1 to October 1, 1929, but it was extended to December 31, 1930.[63] Meanwhile, the American legation worked deligently to conclude a naturalization treaty with Greece, hoping to come to a definite understanding on the questions of dual nationality and military obligations.[64]

These experiences of the years from 1918 to 1923 had a lasting effect on Greek-Americans. Those who returned to the United States brought back accounts that depicted Greek officialdom as ruthless and Greece as ungrateful to her loyal sons. Greek-Americans discovered that it was unwise to visit the mother country in times of military crisis, especially if there was some question regarding their military obligations. The dream of returning to a peaceful and prosperous Greece was vanishing. Prosperous Greek-Americans who once thought of investing money in Greece were frightened off. All of this hastened the process of Americanization because it virtually eliminated all thoughts of repatriation, even on the part of some of the most ardent nationalists.

12

THE EROSION OF
HELLENIC SENTIMENT

D URING and after the First World War, Greek nationalism began
to give way to a demonstrative, flag-waving brand of Americanism that was highly reflective of the conformist spirit of the
times. For the first time, thousands made known their intentions of
remaining in the United States. Many had acquired wives—mostly
Greek but some of non-Greek background—and were raising families;
their children were attending the public schools in their communities.
Success in the business world, steady employment, and service with
the armed forces of the United States gave the immigrants a feeling of
permanence and security. And as if this were not enough, patriotic
organizations, community leaders, the press—both Greek and American—kept telling them to become American citizens and discard their
foreign ways.

The Americanization drives of the war and postwar years fostered
a new spirit of conformity. Such efforts of course antedated this era;
but a specific Americanization drive got under way in Philadelphia on
May 10, 1915, where a public reception, addressed by President Wilson,
was held for some twenty thousand newly naturalized and earlier
citizens. This ceremony was followed by the formation of committees
and the staging of gatherings in every community of the country.
Within three months after the Philadelphia meeting, the public schools
began sponsoring classes in citizenship for the foreign-born. The press
devoted column after column in lavish praise of the program; chambers
of commerce and church and civic groups gave their unstinted support.

The Bureau of Naturalization, in its report of 1918, spoke confidently of the effective hold that Americanism was coming to have. "As one great family the people of America have suddenly been cemented. People of all nationalities and of all races have voluntarily welded themselves into a single gigantic potential force for the maintenance of those principles upon which this Nation has been built." [1]

Naturalization came slowly for plausible reasons. The Greeks, as we have noted, arrived in sizable numbers after 1900 and accordingly were among the last of the newer immigrants to acquire citizenship. And naturalization, for them at least, involved more than a routine acquiescence to questions posed by federal examiners. It meant exchanging one set of loyalties for another, all of which involved a delicate readjustment of mental and social attitudes.

Prior to the First World War, nationalists had opposed naturalization on the grounds that it was detrimental to the best interests of Greece. Emigration had depopulated entire villages and eparchias; from a social, economic, and military standpoint, this was draining Greece dry. Naturalization invited permanent residence in this country and absorption into its culture. A naturalized citizen became involved in the politics of his adopted country and disinterested in those of his birthplace. The immigrants undeniably were indebted to the United States for all it had made possible, and they were obligated to respect its laws and show their devotion. But such respect and devotion had to stop short of Americanization and de-Hellenization.[2]

These nationalists comprised a determined and vocal minority, which was outshouted and outnumbered by those who either favored citizenship or preferred to remain discreetly silent about it. Among the most persistent advocates was the *Atlantis,* whose royalist activities in no way blunted its interest in naturalization. Its editorial pages counseled that one could better serve the interests of the mother country by respecting the laws of America and becoming a United States citizen.[3] Cognizance was taken of the unemployment among the foreign-born and the dangers confronting those in an alien status.[4] But as early as 1908, the formation of political clubs headed by citizens and membership in trade unions were recognized as effective means of winning the good will and cooperation of the American public. Some political groups already had made their appearance in the eastern and western states, but many more were needed. Such bodies had to be inspired by the same zeal inspiring the societies that aided the Greek villages.[5] Membership had to be sought in trade unions, even though they tended to discriminate against the newer arrivals.[6] Such action, *Atlantis* believed, would overcome the impression that all Greeks congregated in colonies of their compatriots, that they had come here for the sole purpose of making money and returning to Greece.[7]

Citizenship was gained relatively easily by those serving with the armed forces of the United States during 1917–1918. As aliens they could have claimed exemption from military service, but many waived this and volunteered. An act of May 10, 1918, made it possible for an alien who enlisted or had been drafted into the service to change his status to that of a full citizen. Group commanders under the direction of the adjutant general of the army took advantage of this law and encouraged large-scale naturalization.[8] Statistics on the number of aliens in the armed forces of the United States are unavailable, but we may assume that the majority of the Greeks in the armed services acquired citizenship in this manner.

After the war, the Americanization crusade was implemented by the activities of various Greek-American organizations, which vied with each other for honors and recognition. They publicized the Greek-American Boy Scouts, victory bond sales, campaigns for citizenship, public rallies, and other patriotic activities of the Greek-Americans.[9] A naturalization program launched by a rally of the Loyalty Leagues of New York on May 1, 1919, was designed to counteract the notion that Greek-Americans were among the aliens who espoused revolutionary doctrines. If members of other nationality groups were thus inspired, the Greeks were not; they were loyal to the United States, proud of it, and wanted others to know it. May 1, the day when others were participating in Bolshevik rallies and wild disorders, was considered an appropriate time for Greek-Americans to publicize their loyalty.[10]

The pleas for citizenship sounded a bit more realistic after the war than they had before. They now generally followed some such course: it was contrary to the character and ideals of a hopeful Greek immigrant to remain an alien. His happy and progressive compatriots in the United States understood the meaning of citizenship; the failure to acquire it displayed irreverence and ingratitude. He, as a newcomer, could not ignore the country which, from the moment of his arrival at Ellis Island, accepted him as one of her own sons.

Nationalistic arguments which showed the close parallels between Greek and American ideals were also advanced. All patriotic Greeks believed that the link between ancient and modern Greece was unbroken. Or as the loyalist stated: "The American ideals deep down in their foundations are the ideals of ancient Greece; we Greeks must realize that Americanism is but the offspring of Hellenism. The Greek who becomes a true and ardent American promotes Hellenic ideals." [11] Nor were economic arguments ignored. Citizenship, it was held, promised to foster commercial relations between the United States and Greece. This would aid the Greek economy. Citizenship would help them to win the confidence of the American government and perhaps enable them to control the Greek foreign market, which was dominated by the British.[12]

Parents were exhorted to improve their social, political, and economic status, and make their children happier, by becoming citizens of the United States. Some compatriots directed their vengeance at "the exclusive Greek school," which for all practical purposes was the exception rather than the rule. This kind of school, they argued, furnished instructions to the children exclusively in the Greek language on an all-day basis. It was singled out for criticism on the theory that it kept children in ignorance of the American language, American customs, and the American character. Sending children to such a school instead of to a public school showed gross disrespect for this country.[13]

It is difficult to state accurately how many children born of Greek parents attended the public schools. Here the census is more suggestive than accurate. For one thing, the 221,768 it lists as constituting the Greek population of the country in 1920 is too conservative a figure. The census takers probably never contacted many Greeks; if they did, they undoubtedly could not communicate with them or overcome enough of their suspicion to elicit responses.[14]

Statistics for the "native whites" born of foreign or mixed parentage indicate that an increasing number of children were born in the United States and presumably attending the public schools of the country. In 1910, of the 10,322 "native whites" having Greek parents, 7,293 had both a Greek father and mother; 2,548 a Greek father; and 481 a Greek mother. In 1920, of the 47,110 of Greek parentage, the parents of 38,465 were both Greek; 8,368 had a Greek father; and 277 a Greek mother.[15] These figures suggest that the second generation was increasing in size, and this by nature exercises an acculturizing influence. This form of naturalization had a far greater effect on foreign-born parents than all the exhortations of the professional American patriots. Those without families in some cases were influenced by the Americanization work of the Young Men's Christian Association. One such man advised his compatriots to enroll in the YMCA, for "you enter it blind and emerge with four eyes." [16]

The First World War was the great transition period. It gave many a feeling of belonging that the earlier years had not. Greece had been an ally of the United States; a feeling of kinship had blossomed; and American influences were being felt in Greece itself.[17] Thousands fought with the American Expeditionary Forces. Still more contributed to the common war effort by investing their savings in government bonds and working in war industries. Many businessmen emerged financially stronger and securer as a result of the lush years.[18]

Greek-American veterans returned from France with a healthier and more confident outlook toward life in the United States. In the past they had been unable to boast of ancestors or parents who had fought for the United States, as could the descendants of native Americans and older immigrant groups who traced their lineage to the Revolutionary War, the Civil War, or the Spanish-American War. This lack of roots had given them a feeling of insecurity and impermanence. But the First World War changed all this. As one spokesman emphasized: "We have given our all for this country. We feel that we are a part and parcel of it, and we are here to stay, standing for the ideals and honor wrapped in the American flag, the emblem of our adopted land." [19]

Professional patrioteering was engaged in by some Greek-American leaders. The editor of *Hellinikos Astir,* in an article entitled "What America Has Done for Me," advised his readers that even after the army was demobilized, "Americanism and patriotism will never be demobilized . . . [We] will never permit the 'Reds' to interfere with the principles of American democracy." [20] But more than flag waving was needed to persuade many to become citizens of the United States. There were, of course, difficulties with the English language; this, coupled with inertia and a feeling of frustration, hindered naturalization. But for some there was a high psychological hurdle. Naturalization meant compromising certain principles of nationality. It was precisely for this reason that one newspaper editor exhorted his readers:

Americanization corresponds neither to Turkification, Bulgarization, nor to becoming a Frenchman, although many of our compatriots consider it a big honor, and not a dishonor, to imitate the French until it becomes disgusting. For one to give up his Greek citizenship and accept a European one represents clear and undisguised treason; it means betrayal of everything sacred and holy; it implies base judgment and, in addition, assumes a servile character, contemptible and faithless.

America does not seek your head on a platter like another Herod, or as a newer Mephistopheles—your soul for the Devil.

America views your Americanism as the discharge of the duties of which Divine Providence entrusted you. In this endeavor it is not driven by an impressive chauvinism or an impious fanaticism.[21]

The inroads that naturalization and Americanization were making on the immigrants ran counter to all that the frenzied nationalists had prophesied. For years they had boasted that their compatriots would not be absorbed by a foreign culture because they, more than any other nationality, adhered tenaciously to their language, customs, and traditions. The Greek-Americans, they claimed, possessed many of the admirable qualities of their ancient ancestors and the pioneers of America, but they differed in their determination that "the fire of the Mother Country should never be extinguished in their Hellenic souls."[22]

This admonition was taken very seriously by some, ignored by many, and strongly opposed by others who found it impossible to reconcile such a philosophy with living in the United States. The reactions of some Greek-Americans were precisely what one would have expected in a society so strongly imbued with "America first" notions. "The Greek should feel American through and through," cautioned one overzealous countryman. "The welfare of this country should be . . . above the welfare of every other country in the world. We should love America with all our might and with all our soul. It matters little whether we can speak very well or very little the English language. We can love America with as much passion as those who were born here."[23] One superpatriot even emphasized the Hellenic origins of the Anglo-Saxons. The Anglo-Saxons, he claimed, came closer to the ancient Greek ideal than the representatives of any other living group; and all patriotic Greeks knew, he added, that the history of ancient and modern Greece was long and unbroken. The qualities of "true Americanism," according to him, were found neither in naturalized citizens nor in those born in the United States; but in "those in whose veins runs the blood of the Pilgrims." These people had the same qualities that made the ancient Greeks great.[24]

Apart from the social climate, practical and personal reasons expedited naturalization. The failure to acquire citizenship, especially after immigrant bars had been raised, brought self-imposed hardships on those who wanted to bring relatives and families to the United States. Wives separated from their husbands for many years were often compelled to return to Greece, owing to the failure of their spouses to become citizens. In such instances neither the transportation companies nor the United States government was to blame—it was the relatives who encouraged these women to come. In extreme cases a husband or a prospective bridegroom was so completely uninformed about the naturalization and entry laws of this country that he even failed to file a declaration of intention to become a citizen.[25]

These immigration restrictions became targets of criticism for those having relatives in Greece and for others who believed that they represented discrimination of the basest sort. An Athens newspaper claimed that, in 1924, one hundred thousand immigrants in Cuba were waiting to enter the United States illegally, that American border patrols were on a constant vigil, and that thirty Greeks had been killed attempting to make illegal entries into the country.[26] One Greek-American, undoubtedly speaking for many, protested the passage of the Immigration Bill of 1924 on the grounds that this threatened to convert the United States into a British nation. He appealed to the non-British elements to reconsider the discriminatory features of this measure and ask themselves whether they could tolerate such a stigma of inferiority.[27]

Naturalization, however, was hastened by the passage of the Immigration Acts of 1921 and 1924, even though the Greeks were among those nationality groups that denounced these measures as discriminatory. Most realized that the doors of opportunity were closing on their kin in Greece, perhaps even on themselves if they left the country; hereafter the naturalized citizen had a much better chance of bringing his relatives to the United States. All of this produced a mad scramble for citizenship, and the more frantic hired lawyers to facilitate matters. Unfortunately, some fell prey to professional exploiters who boasted that, because of their presumed associations with a judge, senator, or

An immigrant couple, about 1910

Eleutherios Venizelos

King Constantine of Greece

Meletios Metaxakis, Metropolitan of Athens
(later Patriarch of Constantinople)

Demetrios Callimachos, in the garden of the
Ecumenical Patriarchate, Constantinople

Solon Vlasto

A Greek wedding party, Newark, New Jersey

Students of a Greek school, Milwaukee, Wisconsin, 1919

Volunteer Greek unit of Haverhill, Massachusetts

Arrival of Philadelphia volunteer unit to fight in the Balkan Wars, Piraeus

Parade commemorating the freeing of Salonika (1912), 1952

Old Greek Church of the Annunciation, Milwaukee

New Church of the Annunciation, Milwaukee, designed by Frank Lloyd Wright

some other person of influence, they could for a price make them citizens within a matter of weeks. Every major city had at least one "interpreter" or pseudo-lawyer who posed as a "man about town" or a "real American." The exploits of these unscrupulous compatriots—who were found among all immigrant groups and who reaped bonanzas from the great naturalization and Americanization drives of the 1920s—probably will remain an untold chapter. The Greek press, community leaders, and the naturalization authorities warned those seeking citizenship to be on guard against these dishonest persons.

Many knew of the power of *meso,* or "special pull," in the old country, and they had reason to believe that it would apply here. Immigrants also heard it said in the United States that "money talks" and that "nobody asks you how you get it as long as you have it." In an era when officials of the United States government went to jail for fraud or sold pardons and liquor licenses, and when one read of crooked politicians, bootleggers, crimes, rackets, and dishonest judges, it was easy for an untutored immigrant to believe that citizenship could be purchased for a price. Better-informed compatriots pleaded with potential victims to turn deaf ears to overtures of easy citizenship. They were advised to keep a tight grip on their savings, to take heed of the prospect of serving a prison term if caught in illicit actions, to realize that they faced loss of privilege of citizenship and ultimate deportation. "There is only one way, the right way, the safe and honorable way. Wait and work and learn and in a few years you will be proud that through your own efforts you have won admission into this great family of Americans." [28]

Census statistics bear out the premise that naturalization was acquired slowly. In 1910, less than 5,000 of the 74,975 persons twenty-one years of age or older had acquired citizenship, and only a slightly smaller number had filed their first papers. After the First World War, naturalization proceeded at a more rapid pace, as the following figures indicate (for Greeks aged twenty-one or more).[29]

The accuracy of these figures is subject to question. It appears

		Males naturalized			Females naturalized		
Year	Total	Number	%	First papers	Number	%	First papers
1910	74,975	4,946	6.6	4,550	5	—	—
1920	175,972	23,786	16.6	21,080	5,693	17.6	371
1930	174,526	62,649	49.9	22,701	12,825	30.7	2,158

unlikely that there were fewer Greeks in 1930 in the United States than in 1920, even if one took into account the dead, those returning to the Mother Country, and those who were born in Turkish occupied lands but considered themselves Greeks. Still these figures, incomplete as they appear, show a definite trend toward naturalization.

An annual tabulation of Greek aliens admitted to United States citizenship, beginning with 1923, shows that the peak in naturalization was reached during the late 1920s, that it tapered off after that date, and then began rising again during the late 1930s and the first half of the 1940s.[30]

1923	2,920	1942	5,873
1924	3,837	1943	6,963
1925	4,852	1944	7,549
1926	5,668	1945	4,305
1927	9,518	1946	3,313
1928	9,005	1947	1,847
1929	6,253	1948	1,683
1930	4,011	1949	1,638
1931	3,172	1950	1,667
1932	2,335	1951	1,313
1933	1,704	1952	1,707
1934	1,727	1953	1,830
1935	1,741	1954	2,594
1936	2,015	1955	3,785
1937	2,639	1956	2,550
1938	2,625	1957	4,791
1939	3,540	1958	3,370
1940	4,378	1959	2,457
1941	4,913	1960	3,413

The naturalization drives of the 1920s hastened the participation of Greek-Americans in local politics. But this can hardly be interpreted to mean that they had been completely unconcerned with municipal politics prior to this time. Politics was part of the Greek make-up. Few compatriots failed to emphasize that Lucas Miller, who was brought to the United States as an orphan during the Greek War of Independence, had served one term as a congressman from Wisconsin.[31] In 1895 *Atlantis* proclaimed that Antonios Protos of Nogales, Arizona, was the first Greek to have been elected the mayor of an American community.[32] The oldest Greek newspaper in the United States repeatedly professed its Republican Party sympathies in politics.[33] *Hellinikos Astir* and the shorter-lived *Loxias* of Chicago frequently urged their readers to vote the straight Republican ticket.[34]

Among the first groups showing an interest in municipal politics, and for which there is some record, was the Achaian League of Chicago. This league was organized in 1910; in the following year it endorsed Carter M. Harrison for mayor of Chicago. But its members soon became disenchanted with the attitude of Harrison toward the Greeks and they asked for his defeat.[35] It appears that the Achaian League had also been active in urging and assisting members and nonmembers to become naturalized citizens and take a part in community affairs. Candidates for public office were invited to its meetings to state their positions on public issues. The all-important consideration was to get Greek-Americans to become active in community affairs.[36]

The war produced many veterans who believed they should assume a greater responsibility in government. Some of these naturalized citizens naturally felt that they, instead of their healthy and able-bodied compatriots who remained at home during the war, had earned the right to become the political leaders of their people. The professional politicians who formed organizations immediately prior to elections to corral the votes of citizens had to yield ground to the veterans. In Chicago the Achaian League claimed that it was the only substantial political organization comprised of citizens of Hellenic descent.[37] The time had come for all to take part in politics, instead of the voters' relying on a few self-styled "kings of the Greeks." [38]

Politics in the United States were organized on a different basis from what was known in Greece. Political parties in Greece were founded by individuals of special prominence, men who controlled the party and courted members only so long as they followed him, turning against them as soon as they started to oppose him. In the United States, by contrast the party made the leader, and in theory he was abandoned when his obligations to the party were unfulfilled. This was a phase in party politics that could be studied with profit by the rising new generation of politicians in both America and Greece.[39]

One of the first concerted efforts that was made to branch out beyond the municipal arena took place in Massachusetts. A political club, formed in Boston prior to the gubernatorial campaign of 1919, converted itself into a Republican organization and campaigned for the re-election of Governor Calvin Coolidge. A letter printed in Greek was sent to about a thousand residents in the state, urging them to organize in support of Coolidge. Articles also appeared in the Greek-language newspapers of New York, which had sizable circulations in New England, urging the voters of Massachusetts to organize themselves into Republican clubs.

The fact that there was so much factionalism within the Greek community makes it difficult to estimate the relative political strength of the Greeks in the United States. Differences over the internal politics of Greece did not have any appreciable effect on domestic issues in the United States. But concern was expressed, as we have seen, over the position that the Republican Party had taken on the claims of Greece in Asia Minor, the Aegean Islands, and other unredeemed lands.[40] The campaign of 1920 was the first national election in which Greek-Americans became visibly active. Some, we have noted, were resentful over the treatment Greece had received at the Peace Conference and assailed the back-door influence of the "missionary lobby" in Paris. Others, though equally irked, chose to underplay the lobby issue and urged support for the Republican Party.

This growing interest in politics inevitably accelerated the Greek-Americans' efforts to extend their political influence. Protests against restrictive immigration mounted. Agitation to learn English and to obtain the right to vote increased. And new organizations emerged which urged Americanization as a means of protecting and advancing the best interests of their members.

The importance of the right to vote began to be better understood. This brought endless pleas from the Greek-language press, the Loyalist Leagues, the Greek-American National Union, the Panhellenic Union, the Achaian League of Chicago, as well as from lesser known groups and from influential segments in all walks of American life. Frequent notices in the Greek press urged readers to enroll in night classes or in those organized by the YMCA.[41] These pleas actually recapitulated the earlier ones that had been made to small merchants who had wished to retain the respect of their patrons and to those who had wanted better jobs, higher wages, and more suitable surroundings.[42] With more American-born children graduating from public schools and increasing numbers making use of the public libraries, it became necessary for the parents to learn English and live lives more in keeping with those their children were living.[43]

This eagerness to learn English, to become a citizen, and to acquire American friends is well illustrated by the following piece of advice that was circulated widely among those who had decided to remain in the United States:

No true American will force you to learn his language, but do so in order to facilitate assimilation.

Become a voter quickly in order that you may help preserve a just and decent goverment.

Insist that your children attend school as long as possible.

Help your wife to get acquainted with American families, so that she won't feel lonesome.

Tell your friends to stay in America. They are needed here and will be given more opportunities in this country than in any other.

If you go to Europe, please tell the truth about America.

Lastly, but most important, tell about freedom and individual security people enjoy in America.[44]

Political clubs eventually emerged in all the major Greek communities. They existed in New York, New Jersey, and Massachusetts in the east; in the Chicago area of the middle west; and in the San Francisco area of California. Fragmentary information suggests that sizable segments of the politically active in New York and New Jersey worked in behalf of the Democratic Party, while the *Atlantis* labored in behalf of the Republican Party. In Massachusetts the most energetic and conspicuous were committed to the Republicans. In Illinois the voters appeared divided between the two major parties.[45]

Political activity, in addition to warding off the attacks of business competitors and America-firsters, was also seen as a check against restrictionist legislation that aimed to reduce the number of immigrants entering the country from southern and eastern Europe. It was clear the immigrant-quota law of May 1921, which limited the size of a nationality group to 3 percent of the number residing in the United States in 1910, was a stopgap measure. This act, with the amendments of 1922, was effective through June 30, 1924. When Congress convened in December 1923, a new and revised immigration law was expected to be passed.[46]

By early 1924 it was evident that the new bill, based on the numbers of the nationality residing in this country in 1890, would, if passed, almost bar the entry of Greeks into the United States. Naturally this aroused resentment and opposition among all southern and eastern

European peoples. The American Association of the Greek Community of Chicago expressed itself as follows:

We do not believe in an open-door immigration policy. We are firmly against it . . . there should be a stop to hundreds of aliens who come in monthly through other channels than those prescribed by the Immigration Department . . . stowaways and "human smugglers" are not the kind of people that we want in this country.

Immigrants who have been expelled from their native countries are undesirable if they enter the United States to spread propaganda.

We believe, however, in reuniting families, and that American citizens should be able to bring over to this country their wives, children and parents, their sisters, if single or widows, their fiancées, and their brothers if they are less than 21 years of age.[47]

By this time it was becoming apparent to a growing number of Greek-Americans that political organizations for the promotion of foreign interests could no longer be tolerated. "The American Greeks cannot solve problems belonging to the Greeks in Greece." They had to work on an American basis, "feel thoroughly American," within an organization broad enough to benefit the larger American community. But belonging to a native American organization could also prove ineffective, owing to the language barrier.[48]

During 1925 the political actionists made an abortive attempt to expand their activities by organizing the National League of Greek Voters (NLGV). The sponsors of NLGV made overtures to Republican leaders, asking for their support in exchange for loyalty and votes. The organization promised to function with full force in each presidential campaign and at stated intervals during state elections. State and branch units of the NLGV were expected to sweep the country.[49] But this was a short-lived effort.

If the NLGV failed to attract a national following, the evidence is that the local political clubs grew in number. Chicago became one of the most important of these political centers, presumably because of the large number of active businessmen there. Estimates of the number of Greek voters in Chicago varied: one placed them at twenty-five thousand.[50] Another placed the number of Greek shopkeepers in Illinois at twenty thousand and the voters in excess of fifty thousand.[51]

Those committed to the Republican Party seemed more active and better organized during the 1920s, but it was only a matter of time before the Democrats began picking up lost ground. In 1928 a delegation representing the Alfred E. Smith for President Greek-American Political Club met Smith at the Congress Hotel in Chicago and pledged to him the support of 80 percent of the Greek-American vote in eight midwestern states.[52] The drift toward the Democratic Party in city elections was also unmistakable. During 1931 various political organizations in Chicago united in support of A. J. Cermak for mayor. The Greek-language papers, including *Kathemerini, Hellinikos Astir, Democrat,* and *Saloniki,* joined forces to make the press unanimous for Cermak. *Kathemerini* advised its readers: "Greeks—if you are the descendants of the ancient Greeks and Pericles, the original author of the democratic form of government, you must go to the polls on April 7, raise your voices, and clean up the City Hall of Chicago." [53]

As the presidential election of 1932 drew near, the Democrats made special efforts to win the support of the various ethnic and religious minorities in the United States, including the Greeks. In Chicago the Greek-American political organizations were reorganized to be more in line with the regular party organization. They were assigned a representative who was to cooperate with the Democratic ward committeeman. They were to receive instruction from him, and he in turn was to provide for the needs of his countrymen. In this manner they would obtain recognition and attention from the political leaders of the party, instead of being ignored as they had been in the past.[54]

Franklin D. Roosevelt sought the support of the *National Herald* and its editor, Demetrios Callimachos. Roosevelt extended an invitation to Callimachos to come to Albany or to his Hyde Park home to discuss the national situation, "particularly the outlook among the citizens who read and are influenced by your publication." Roosevelt hoped that he could have the support of Callimachos and his paper—"one that reaches deeper than mere party lines" and one that would command the active approval of thoughtful and forward-looking Americans. The response was quick in coming. The *National Herald* proclaimed: "Why are we supporting Franklin D. Roosevelt? He personifies Greek-American ideals." Continuing in this vein:

Our newspaper, the *National Herald,* knowing well for the last seventeen years of your ideas and moral principles about government and human relationships, has consistently and intensely supported your nomination on the Democratic ticket as the standard bearer of the Periclean and Jeffersonian ideals; and from the day of your nomination we have been doing all we can in order to divulge widely among the Greeks those ideals formulated by you and adapted to our times and our needs.

The Greeks, as a race, have also their own particular reason to love you, Governor, knowing that your family, a hundred years ago, had been instrumental in promoting the success of Greek independence.[55]

Perhaps no agencies better represented the conflicting views on Americanization during the greater part of the 1920s than the American Hellenic Educational Progressive Association (AHEPA), founded in 1922, and the Greek American Progressive Association (GAPA), founded in 1923. The clue to the orientation of each organization is found in the first word of its official name. The first came into existence as a reaction to the antiforeign outbursts of the postwar era, and it espoused a doctrine of Americanization, assimilation, and adaptation. The second was organized as a protest to what many considered an unintelligent program of conformity preached by AHEPA, one that jeopardized the future of the Greek language and church. These rivals, however, did have some things in common. Both were products of the Greek-American efforts to adjust to American society. Both presented positive programs of actions which filled the void left by the demise of the issue of Venizelism versus Constantinism in the United States. For a time, their conflicting philosophies absorbed the energies of sizable segments of the populations in all major communities.

A short résumé of earlier efforts to organize brings into sharper focus the purposes of these two newer bodies. Organizations formed prior to the First World War, such as the Panhellenic Union and the local societies, aimed to satisfy the immediate needs of the immigrants during their temporary stay in the United States, as well as the patriotic interests of the country to which they expected to return. The Panhellenic Union was committed to furthering the nationalistic aspirations of a Greater Greece, while the local societies, or *topika somateia,* dedicated themselves to building roads, schools, churches, and water systems in Greece and providing for the health and medical needs of their members. These groups also paid lip service to such objectives as promoting better understanding between the United States and Greece.

The First World War brought about a remarkable change in attitude regarding the future of the immigrants, and it was reflected itself in their institutions. Instead of satisfying themselves with the temporary and makeshift arrangements of the past, they began to think in long-range terms about their schools, churches, and organizations. This was felt not so much by the local societies as it was by organizations that were nation-wide in character. This called for a de-emphasis, if not a complete abandonment, of the philosophy of the Panhellenic Union, which was committed to the fulfillment of the national aspirations of Greece, and the embracing of a philosophy geared to the needs of people who were to be lifetime residents of the United States.[56]

One of the first postwar groups to reflect this element of permanence was the American Hellenic National Union, an obscure and relatively ineffective organization founded in Massachusetts in 1919. Specifically, the purpose of this association was "to assist those who have selected America for their homes, in learning the English language, in understanding the guiding laws of the United States, enjoying in comfort and happiness the liberty and safety accruing therefrom."[57] At best, the influence of this organization must have been local and minimal.

A comparable but more elaborate philosophy of organization, one which was better led, better financed, and more appealing to the prosperous businessmen and emerging professional classes, was to develop among those who wanted to identify themselves with the American community and stand apart from their less successful compatriots. It was these elements that banded together under the auspices of AHEPA. In part AHEPA responded to a need that could no longer be ignored. Many Greek-Americans, who once believed that the war and its hardships would erase prejudices toward people of different races, religions, and national backgrounds, discovered that they were mistaken. Misguided individuals and groups, some prompted by personal profit and others by bigotry and hate, were preaching a doctrine of national conformity and Americanism that caused immigrant groups to panic. Many Greek-American merchants and businessmen viewed this as a cunning device to drive them out of business. The attacks came at a time when they were bitterly divided in their community affairs. A proud people, they believed that their reputation in the United States had to be defended with the same zeal with which they would defend their liberty.[58]

The idea of organizing a select group of Greek-Americans into an association for the purpose of establishing better relations with non-

Greeks had dawned in the minds of several widely scattered men. But it remained for a small nucleus residing in Atlanta, Georgia, where the Ku Klux Klan was active and the need for positive action was urgent, to assume the leadership. The founding of AHEPA, according to a semiofficial history, followed the proverbial "when Greek meets Greek" pattern. George A. Nicholopoulos—then known as "Poulos"—and John Angelopoulos, both traveling salesmen working out of Atlanta and well known to each other, met by chance in Chattanooga, Tennessee, during the early summer of 1922. Their principal topic of conversation was how best to control the wave of hostility that had developed against members of their nationality.

Nicholopoulos and Angelopoulos agreed that this could best be effected through the formation of a patriotic organization, national in scope, nonpartisan in politics, and nonsectarian in religion. They also believed that such an organization had to be secret and comprised of a select group of individuals, whose purpose would be to unite their fellow countrymen, "inculcate in them an aggressive national conscience," educate themselves in the fundamental principles of Americanism, and aid them to adapt themselves to the social and commercial climate of the country. The practical everyday needs such an organization could fulfill were several. It could bring the Greek-Americans into a closer working relationship with the greater American community. It could be on the alert for the peaceful adjustment of any situation that might disturb friendly relations between Greek-Americans and other groups in society. It would eliminate those turbulent political imbroglios that divided communities and brought ridicule and abuse from unsympathetic quarters.

Nicholopoulos and Angelopoulos, after giving more serious thought to the matter, proposed to present their plan to the Greek-American public. They chose the name of the organization, drafted the rules and regulations, selected titles for the officers, and attended to other details before openly presenting the plan. On July 26, 1922, they met with the most prominent members of the Atlanta Greek community in the classroom of the church and unfolded their plan of organization. Following a lengthy discussion, seventeen of the twenty-five present expressed their approval.

These seventeen men then were called together in a closed session, where they proceeded with the actual formation of the association. It

248

was in this meeting that the American Hellenic Educational Progressive Association was selected as the name and the objectives decided upon. As then stated, the purpose of AHEPA was "to advance and promote pure and undefiled Americanism among the Greeks of the United States, its Territories, and Colonial possessions; to educate the Greeks in the matter of democracy, and [the] government of the United States, and for the general promotion of fraternity, sociability and the practice of benevolent aid among this nationality."

The articles of government provided for a Supreme Lodge, "a self-appointed body with absolute powers of government," and a series of superior and subordinate lodges, later known as districts and chapters. The newly formed Supreme Lodge then established a "propagation department" and adopted a resolution instructing Carl F. Hutchinson, an attorney, to proceed with the incorporation of the organization. The petition for incorporation was filed in the Superior Court of Fulton County and granted on September 25, 1922. AHEPA obtained a twenty-year charter which designated Atlanta, Georgia, as its headquarters.

What in effect was happening was that Greek-American businessmen, who felt the menacing hand of nativist opposition, were organizing for self-protection. Instead of meeting kind with kind and resorting to violent action, marked by bigotry and hate, the Greek-Americans, the immigrants of yesterday, chose the method of peaceful assembly and democratic discussion. They decided upon organization, persuasion, and positive action. If their methods in the past had been inappropriate, they meant to right the situation.

Details of the source the founding fathers of AHEPA drew upon for the structure and complexion of the organization are known only in part. We may assume that they, and the non-Greek friends who counseled them, had been influenced by the ritual of the Masonic and other fraternal orders of which they had some knowledge. But this is of lesser account than the decision to organize, the qualifications they set up for membership, and the rapidity with which the order spread.

An applicant for membership had to be a citizen of the United States or else be eligible to become one. He had to be a member of the Caucasian race and a believer in the divinity of Christ. Special appeals were held out to leading commercial and professional men, as well as to non-Greeks who could lend dignity and status to the order. Its membership, claimed *The Ahepa,* the official organ, stemmed "from a variety of racial stocks including descendants of Mayflower genealogy, but the majority are of Greek birth or American born of Greek descent." [59]

From the outset AHEPA was middle-class in orientation. It appealed to those who were climbing the social and economic ladder of success. It extended recognition to those who craved it but who found it difficult to obtain in "non-Greek" spheres. Its banquets, dances, and meetings furnished an outlet for many a harassed businessman who preferred the company of compatriots facing identical problems. The element of secrecy and exclusiveness also had its charm, for men regardless of race or nationality like to believe themselves among the select. The times were relatively prosperous and the dues were no obstacle to the well-off businessman. AHEPA, after all, represented Americanism in a decade of conformity, when many Greek-Americans, reacting sharply against the politics of the Old World, were desirous of shaking off all traces of foreignism by joining the greater American community. In short, the social climate was favorable to the growth of the order.

As expected, AHEPA made its first great appeal in the states of the south and the southwest. Of the thirty-two chapters organized between the founding on July 26, 1922, and October 14, 1923, the date of the first national convention, only three were in northern cities. The officer rosters of the various local chapters contained the usual polysyllabic Greek names, but an even more interesting assortment of Anglicized ones, such as Coolidge, Wallace, Brown, Davis, Thomas, Perry, Fox, Miller, and Moore.[60]

The membership increased rapidly as the order invaded the north. In 1924 AHEPA had 49 chapters and a membership of 2,800; in 1928, 192 chapters and 17,516 members. In 1956 AHEPA claimed that it had initiated more than 72,000 members and that the membership in the AHEPA family was in excess of 90,000.[61] But these figures, like those of any organization, must be accepted with reservations. Many, perhaps most, who were once initiated and active, dropped out and for all practical purposes could not be considered regular dues-paying members. Still, the leaders of the AHEPA were quick to learn the value of compiling an impressive membership list, especially when it came to swaying legislators and public officials. It appears that once a man joined the order, he was classified as a "duly initiated member," and since the initiated members comprised the largest possible total that could be tabulated, it follows that this figure was the one released for public consumption.

Convention annals and official publications reveal the activities of AHEPA. During the earlier years, the references to "Americanization," "assimilation," and "citizenship" were incessant. Governors, state legislators, judges, lawyers, local politicians, educators, and preachers spoke on a wide variety of subjects, ranging from naturalization to the "wonders of ancient Greece." Often these talks were inspiring, and many derived satisfaction from hearing them. Others were of the kind one could hear from any ward heeler. Perhaps nothing brought greater acclaim than tributes paid to ancient Greece and the part that the immigrants played in perpetuating these traditions in the United States. The spirit of these years can be described most accurately in the words of the official publication: "AHEPA shall never fail to constantly preach the principles of loyalty to the United States of America, advocate and teach the highest form of patriotic sentiments of national honor and national service," and it would continue to serve as "a medium which shall loyally and courageously serve the best interests of the United States, our adopted home and country." [62]

Despite the officially proclaimed objectives, AHEPA to some Greek-Americans was what masonry had been to others.[63] One rather romantic idealist envisioned the order as something that would assume the proportions of a Byzantine revival. More specifically, "The founding of the AHEPA fraternity marks a new era for the Hellenes of the United States—the Hellenic Renaissance . . . In a sense, the founding of this Order is a sequel to the Glorious Age of Pericles—the same Hellenic civic and artistic supremacy." [64] Still others viewed AHEPA from the standpoint of what it might have been instead of what it had become. From a religious source came the plea that AHEPA become the right arm of the Greek Orthodox Church in the United States. Instead of clinging to its policy of nonsectarianism, it was asked to join forces with the church and the Greek school to protect the language and the culture of the mother country. This had been the mission of the Greek church through the years, and AHEPA was urged to contribute to it. Ahepans were advised to view the accomplishments of the Knights of Columbus in behalf of the Catholic church and to decide whether they would serve in an identical capacity and become the militant servants of the Greek Orthodox Church.[65]

Meanwhile, the attacks against AHEPA continued.[66] Its leaders were denounced as opportunists and misguided pseudo-patriots. Objections were voiced against the veil of secrecy that shielded its activities and the immodest prerogatives that had been assumed by some of its more unrestrained leaders. Critics charged that AHEPA was downgrading the Greek school, disassociating itself from the Greek church, and misrepresenting everything worthy among the Greeks in the United States. It was accused of offering a distorted picture of American Hellenism to the outside world.[67] Special emphasis was placed on what AHEPA's foes considered to be the anti-Hellenic features of the society. They saw nothing wrong with the American phase of its program, which had top priority in its activities, but they despaired about the Hellenic portion, which was denied even a secondary role. With indignation they denounced the de-emphasis on teaching Greek. "We do not believe it," remarked one irritated compatriot, "but if it is true, then the AHEPA as an essence of Americanism is an empty boast. Our children, whether we wish it or not, are born American, and it is better they are born so. But Americanism pure and simple is not anti-everything ... The Greek language might not appeal to some of the supreme archons of this order who cannot speak it; nevertheless it is a very valuable tool for every educated man or woman ... And since we are convinced that assimilation is the natural sequence that will follow our race in this country, let us preserve even as a memory a few of the legacies of the past." [68]

Personalities without doubt had a good deal to do with the criticisms of the order. Some of the leaders were officious and even arrogant. Such behavior, one might assume, was probably normal for persons who found themselves in positions of authority they had never before known. And they meant to exercise such authority. Thus the leaders and the activities of the order became common targets. One read in the *American Hellenic World* and the *National Herald* of men who "assumed prerogatives," of "subordinate satraps," "little Napoleons and lesser Kaisers," "the AHEPA mentality," and "the dissecting knife of public opinion" that would "pry open the entrails of the AHEPA organism." Fraternal brotherhood, a mystic ritual, the supporting of a few orphans, the dispensing of a few scholarships, and the adoption of an Olympian attitude in all matters pertaining to Greek-American affairs hardly justified an organization of such pretensions. The order, stated its critics, was crying aloud for an enlightened leadership and a redirection of its policies.[69]

The conformist trend of the 1920s and the determination to eradicate with one mighty blow all vestiges of foreignism were what antagonized many. To them the speed and manner with which AHEPA's program was being imposed were questionable. Genuine Americanism should not be confused with an arrogant chauvinism; it had to come gradually through the slower and orderly process of assimilation. "America . . . does not want new citizens deprived of their valuable nationalistic antecedents. Such citizens will be mechanical, and in the end will add little to the sum total of the civilization of this country." [70]

Much of the furor arose over the use of the English language in all official matters. Critics felt this to be a denial of one's cultural roots. The founders of AHEPA, on the contrary, believed that use of English in its meetings was justifiable, since the United States had become their permanent home. The meetings afforded them the opportunity to use English, strengthen their knowledge of it, and help to adjust themselves to their surroundings. We should recall, in addition, the campaign started after the war to foster the use of English among the foreign-born. This undoubtedly had some effect on AHEPA.

An amusing, but perhaps valid, reason for the use of English might have been to stem the rhetorical proclivities of those who were proficient in Greek. Anyone who attended meetings conducted exclusively in Greek during the earlier years was exposed to endless discourses by would-be philosophers and statesmen. It was suggested, with more earnestness than jest, that the use of English would derail those loquacious individuals who were making endless appeals in Greek for the preservation of Greek ideals, Greek culture, and Greek patriotism, thereby defeating the purpose of the order.[71]

AHEPA, as a rule, refused to answer its critics in public and generally maintained a discreet silence; but periodically one of the more exasperated members would come out in print in defense of the policies of the organization. "The use of the Greek language in our meetings," affirmed one ardent member, "will turn our meetings to coffeehouse pandemoniums." Angrily he accused his adversaries within the order who wanted to use Greek:

you were going to maneuver tactfully and slit open the red veins of the AHEPA and run its pure blood into the veins of the old defunct Panhellenic Union, and declare Greek as the official language of the Brother-hood to please these old fogies . . . sinister propaganda has been started a year and a half ago for the purpose of injecting the old rules and policies of the Panhellenic Union into the virgin, pure, sacred body of our AHEPA.

The fanatical cry of the old Panhellenists, "Pas Hellen Prepei na Einai Orthodoxos" (Every Greek Must Be an Orthodox) is outdated. We are Greeks, but we did not inherit our present religion from our ancestors, the ancient Greeks, as we did our blood and traits. Is Brother no more a Greek because he is a convert to the Episcopalian denomination? Am I What? for being a Presbyterian?

There are thousands of true-blooded Greeks who are members of other churches. Must we deny their race owing to that? Finally the AHEPA is not a doctrinaire cult.[72]

Meanwhile, those who believed that AHEPA had committed itself to a philosophy of de-Hellenization began organizing for the purpose of preserving the Greek church, the language, and traditions. On December 17, 1923, a group met in East Pittsburgh, Pennsylvania, to form the Greek American Progressive Association, known as GAPA. It gave preference to "Greek," as against "American," in its title and advocated the use of the Greek language. (But by no means should this be interpreted to mean that, in times of crisis, first allegiance would be given to Greece.) As the battlelines between royalists and Venizelists became blurred, new ones were formed, pitting Ahepans against Gapans.[73]

The philosophy of GAPA was idealistic, romantic, and somewhat impractical. It was embraced by people who lacked the resources and leadership to implement it with a positive course of action. It made little appeal to the more affluent elements, and its unwillingness to make too radical a break with the past left many potential members cold. It attracted the rank and file, some who felt insecure in an American environment, and others who sincerely believed that an unintelligent brand of Americanism was robbing the Greek-Americans of a heritage worth preserving.

It would be misleading to assume that all Venizelists were sympa-thetic to AHEPA and that all royalists preferred GAPA. This would be an oversimplification, for many ardent Venizelists became ardent Gapans. One of the most eloquent supporters of GAPA, Demetrios Callimachos, was the militant editor of the *National Herald*. Allegiance to either was more a question of national and cultural sentiments than it was of differences over the form of government Greece was to have. The one thing that AHEPA and GAPA accepted in common was that their members were in the United States to remain permanently; they differed over the emphasis that was to be placed on matters Greek. The most notable argument in defense of GAPA is that members refused to be placed into the strait jacket of conformity by going along with the trend against foreignism. Tribute must be paid to a courageous group which waged a relentless, if ineffective, campaign to retain its cultural heritage at a time when many others were discarding theirs.

Another organization, the still-born Knights of St. Constantine the Great, dedicated to the same principles as GAPA, was founded in Chicago, presumably in 1926 or 1927. Named after the first ruler to embrace Christianity, the Knights of St. Constantine aimed to further the spiritual and moral needs of the people by preserving and protecting the tenets of Hellenic Orthodoxy in the United States. The Knights professed special concern over the plight of the second generation and the general indifference of many parents over the spiritual upbringing of their children. Membership was open to Orthodox Greek-Americans, and the ritual and the meetings were conducted in Greek. The Knights, despite their avowed religious purposes, denied having any official ties with the Greek Church. Chapters were planned in all major cities, and expectations expressed that the Knights of St. Constantine would assume Pan-American dimensions.[74]

It remained, however, for GAPA to wage this stormy battle, for it was committed to an identical philosophy and claimed priority. GAPA employed Greek as its official language and gave open support to the Greek Orthodox Church. To a certain extent, GAPA thrived on the mistaken assumption that Americanization meant an abandonment of Greek traditions, which to most meant the language and the church. Many Gapans found it difficult to comprehend the meaning of non-sectarianism or to tolerate the idea of a compatriot's embracing another faith. They were wedded to the belief that to be a Greek one had to be a member of the Orthodox Church; one who deviated from this religious norm was viewed as a traitor to his country, faith, and family. This belief was openly nurtured by the Greek Orthodox Church, and for all practical purposes it still is.

Even though GAPA in 1928 claimed more than fifty chapters in various parts of the United States, it never was able to muster the support its rival had. Its members were honest and dedicated, but they were swimming against the current. The overpowering influences of assimilation, the failure to attract the young, the inability to implement their principles with an effective program of action, and the death of the older and more earnest members made it difficult for the organization to grow. The task of GAPA was as hopeless as that of organizations representing other nationality groups. The most that it could hope for was to provide a social outlet for persons of identical ethnic-religious backgrounds.

Relations between Gapans and Ahepans were hardly cordial, at least during the earlier years. Ahepans were reluctant to recognize that GAPA had a place in Greek-American society; perhaps they were angry that the Gapans reminded them of the very things they wished to forget. Fuel was added to the feud by the ostentatious display of superiority that some Ahepans showed. The breach widened.[75] The opposition assumed new dimensions in 1928 when AHEPA, in its national convention, voted to purge all members of GAPA from its ranks.[76]

AHEPA had begun to de-emphasize the superpatriot activities of its earliest years. By the late 1920s AHEPA appeared reconciled to a program that blended the good features of Hellenism with those of Americanism. It was sponsoring, as we shall see, a junior order for the purpose of perpetuating the Hellenic tradition among the members of the second generation, and it was displaying an interest in the sufferings of compatriots in Greece. Use of the Greek language in meetings also was permitted, and other actions were taken to show that AHEPA was neither anti-Church nor anti-Greek.[77]

The Great Depression marked the start of a new transitional period. By this time the pressure for patriotic conformity had eased; naturalization had been proceeding at a steady pace and the novelty of the organization was beginning to wear off. AHEPA was groping for an issue to keep it alive. Efforts to attract the second generation met with enthusiasm in some quarters, temporary interest in others, and complete indifference in still others. The needs of the second generation were somewhat different from those of the first.

By the mid-1920s, the intense Greek nationalistic feelings of the pre-war era were disappearing. America had been changing the immigrants in ways that nationalists once believed would be impossible. It was eroding Greek customs, traditions, and the Old World heritage. Those who once heard themselves called Greeks and Greek-Americans now found themselves called Americans of Greek origin. The political situation in Greece ceased to be the principal topic of conversation. No longer were compatriots running to newspaper offices on Sunday afternoons to hear the latest reports on the Greek armed forces or the Greek elections. Participation in American affairs had lessened their zeal for Greece. The house lot in Milwaukee, Chicago, or St. Paul was beginning to mean more to them than the vineyard in Arcadia; the American superhighway was becoming more fascinating than the road leading to Eleusis; the towering American skyscrapers were overshadowing the majesty of the Greek mountains. "We are rapidly becoming a part of restless and opulent America," wrote one ebullient man in 1926:

yesteryear we thought of ourselves as . . . foreigners. Today we view with the most ardent exponents of Americanism in excelling them. Along with the rest of the inhabitants of this fair land we proclaim it to be God's country; and since the barring of immigrants increases our well-being we too are in favor of the enforcement of the immigration law. The constitution we revere and uphold, and in order not to be out of line from the rest of the free Americans we too disobey the eighteenth amendment. An American air prevails over most of our social activities; our festivals have lost their purity of their origins; the jazz has replaced our folk-lore song and the radio is sweeping away the last vestige of the connecting link—the phonograph record . . . English is replacing the Greek in nearly all of our assemblies and has become the official language of numerous organizations . . . As for the new generation, the American school will see to it that no hyphenated Americans emanate from it.[78]

13

GREEKS IN BUSINESS

ROM the very outset the Greeks displayed an ability to engage in business and commerce with energy and resourcefulness. This was remarkable in view of their peasant backgrounds. Few had traveled far beyond their native villages or had much contact with people of other ethnic origins. They arrived with no liquid capital and with no experience in the restaurant, confectionery, theater, or any other line of business in which they were to become so conspicuous.[1]

The average Greek businessman was an independent, freedom-loving individual who thrived in a society that honored these qualities. His hard life in the mother country and a willingness to get along with little in the United States, where his earnings were considerably greater, enabled him to husband his resources. A natural-born competitor with a determination to succeed, he reconciled himself quite early to hard work; he accepted the cult of success without ever having heard of capitalism and the Protestant ethic.

Business appealed to the Greeks for a wide variety of reasons. The desire to acquire wealth and status, and perhaps return to their native villages and flaunt this in the faces of detractors, motivated some. Many entered business with the belief that this was the surest way to wealth and success, and certainly preferable to working for wages. In the old country the more discerning observed that the commercial and financial classes were emerging into prominence, and the United States was living proof of what could be accomplished. Wherever one turned, the admonition was to work hard, save, invest, succeed, become independent, and "be your own boss."[2]

Many were attracted by the possibilities for independence as well as the dollar, for being in business represented a form of freedom. Standing behind the counter as the owner of his own business, instead of as an employee working for a monthly or weekly wage, meant freedom from the domination of others.[3] Those confident individuals who owned their own shops found it difficult to work for others. Some preferred working for themselves at a smaller profit than for someone else at a higher wage.[4] Pride, desire for freedom, and a will to succeed dominated their thoughts. As one woman put it: "Oh my, the Greeks are a proud race." Indeed, at times they seemed to have too much of it.[5]

Among the first immigrant entrepreneurs were the street vendors who plied their wares with baskets suspended from their shoulders or necks; the pushcart peddlers who invaded the streets selling fruit, vegetables, and confections; and for a time the itinerant purveyors of short-order lunches. These trades required small initial investments; the vendors were spared the need of a formidable command of the English language; they were their own bosses; and the returns were good. Their biggest problems were the city policemen who sought to enforce the municipal ordinances against itinerant traders or to exact bribes and the neighborhood merchants who complained against this kind of competition.

As indicated, one of the most popular trades, especially among the Peloponnesians, was shoeshining. It was relatively easy for one to transfer these skills from Greece to the United States without having to undergo a period of retraining. After working for a compatriot and saving his earnings, one could branch off for himself or even go into something better. The only competitors were the Negroes and the Italians who found it difficult to match the willingness of the determined Greeks to work long hours.

The more enterprising men established ornate stores near the busy intersections of the major cities. Their shops often assumed the names of the buildings in which they were located, the most popular neighborhood amusement houses, or the district of the city in which they did business. In the more elaborate establishments, one saw long lines of customers sitting in elevated chairs with their feet resting on shiny brass footstands, attended by bootblacks cleaning shoes, applying the polish, swinging brushes, or flipping finishing rags. The principal job of the owner was to remain on guard at the cash register.

In time more and more proprietors of shoeshine parlors expanded their operations so as to include hat cleaning, shoe repairing, and the cleaning and pressing of clothes. This was done by shopowners, large and small, who found that shoeshining was becoming less profitable, especially after the First World War. As a rule the proprietor of this enlarged operation became the principal hat cleaner, shoe-repair man, or both, while the dwindling shoeshine trade was delegated to his less versatile hired help. In this manner the boss also kept his labor costs at a minimum, for it was cheaper to hire a bootblack than a shoe-repair man.

The owner continued to make a point of remaining in his shop most, if not all, of the day. He meant to exercise his authority and make sure that the cash register received all that was coming to it. Experience had taught him the perils of entrusting too much authority to employees. "Unless you are in your store all the time, your employees will eat you alive." [6] This kind of business is usually associated with the earlier immigrant years. The more prosperous an owner became, the more likely he was to shift into something more dignified and in keeping with his new-found status.

The florist was a less colorful personality, but he had in common with the shoeshine boss the small capital requirements of the trade and the ease with which one could enter it. One might begin as a vendor on a street corner or with a pushcart, save a little money, rent a store, and expand activities. The percentage of profit was quite substantial, the work light, the losses slight, the language needs at a minimum. Best of all, he was his own boss. Statistics bear out that New York City became the citadel of the florist trade in the United States, but considerable progress was also made by those who entered the florist trade in Chicago, Boston, Detroit, Washington, San Francisco, and other cities.[7]

The fruit and vegetable business also appealed to the early arrivals. A man needed a minimum amount of capital and little knowledge of the English language, and he had the advantage of working in the open air. Greeks in the Chicago area came into contact with the Italians who had entered the fruit and vegetable trade at an earlier date and in much larger numbers.[8]

The fruit and vegetable peddlers, especially in Chicago where they were numerous, faced their own problems. One was the neighborhood merchant, who resented their competition. Late in March 1904 the Grocers' Association declared war to the finish, accusing the peddlers of being the parasites of the trade and asking that the city council either prohibit them from selling in the alleys and streets or impose a heavy tax on them. The struggle between the grocers and peddlers became quite fierce, for in some cases it was a Greek grocer versus a Greek peddler. The presiding judge in one instance castigated both groups in strong language and then rendered a decision against six newly arrived immigrants for violating a police ordinance. The fruit and vegetable peddlers fought back. They insisted that they rendered a public service to those housewives who preferred produce that was cheap and fresh. They won a temporary victory from the grocers, which encouraged them to organize a fruit and vegetable dealers' association to ward off future attacks.[9]

The peddlers also suffered from the effects of graft-ridden law-enforcement agencies. Often they were intimidated and forced to pay small fees to dishonest policemen. Their ignorance and passive attitude often invited unscrupulous police officers to threaten them with prosecution for the violation of some municipal ordinance.[10]

In 1909 the city of Chicago made plain its intention of raising the license fee for peddlers from $25 to $200 a year, which aroused the Greeks and members of other nationality groups. The Greeks, however, had special reason to believe that this legislation was aimed at them, for they had a firm grasp on the business in certain quarters of the city. This also made clear to them the need of becoming citizens and reinforcing their protests with the vote.[11]

Even the garbage collector became an aggressive competitor. All one needed was a horse, wagon, customers, and an ability and willingness to stand the stench of the garbage. In 1911 one such enterprising individual contracted to haul the garbage of a hundred compatriots who were in the restaurant business. His rate was one dollar a month. As his clientele increased, so did the number of his garbage wagons. His Irish competitors, he claimed, resented his rise in the business and attacked him with the stern warning: "Get out of the garbage business or we will kill all of you Greeks."

The confectionery field was still another area invaded by the early arrivals. The fascination of this particular business may be attributed to many reasons. Some of the newcomers found employment in shops operated by fellow Greeks; they learned the trade, saved their money, and opened stores of their own as soon as circumstances permitted. Or one may have had experience in making candy and pastries in Greece, for the Greeks always have been known as a people with a sweet tooth. Such an individual could open a shop in the Greek colony and supply the needs of the neighboring coffeehouses, restaurants, grocery stores, and other retail establishments. He could always count on finding a ready market when it came to catering to wedding receptions, christenings, or the celebration of name days.

But we shall see that it was the confectioner who catered to the general public, rather than to his countrymen, who came to be most successful. His capital expenditures were greater, and certainly he occupied a higher status in the Greek colony than the man who owned a shoeshine parlor. As a rule he appeared to be more venturesome. His store was located in the congested downtown area near some moviehouse or place of public entertainment. Often he combined the functions of candymaker with those of waiter, and when his business expanded he had to hire help.

The pioneer confectioners were Eleutherios Pelalas of Sparta and Panagiotis Hatzideris of Smyrna, who established a *lukum* (sweet) shop shortly after their arrival in 1869. This partnership was terminated within a brief time; in 1877 Pelalas assumed the management of an American-owned establishment in Springfield, where he later opened a number of stores. Hatzideris, on the other hand, formed a partnership with another associate in New York, which handled more commercialized brands, such as "Turkish Delight" and "Greek Prince." Hatzideris eventually returned to Smyrna, but his partner continued the business under the name of Haggis Greek-American Confectionery Company, with plants in New York, Memphis, and Pittsburgh. The establishments of Pelalas and Hatzideris furnished employment for many of the first immigrants from Sparta, providing an opportunity to learn the skills of the trade.[12]

Chicago became the Acropolis of the Greek-American candy business. "Practically every busy corner in Chicago is occupied by a Greek candy store," reported *Hellinikos Astir* in 1904. At one time it was said that 70 percent of the Greek candy merchants in the United States were or had been residents of Chicago. With Chicago money and Chicago training, they set out in search of cities which suited them and opened up-to-date candy stores. Chicago naturally became the center of supply for all new stores in the states of the south and west. Chicago firms had scores of traveling salesmen to supply the Greek-American confectioners.[13]

Since the great majority were novices in the candymaking trade, they had much to learn about the business of dealing with the general public. The more experienced and community-conscious individuals stressed the need for the constant publicizing of their shops and products, for honesty in all transactions (they were sensitive to the slightest insinuation to contrary), and for the establishing of credit with the leading merchants. At first the majority bought for cash; hence, their credit rating was not listed with a credit bureau and their reliability was unknown to the business world. Worst of all, when they applied for credit, they often gave evasive answers on question forms and refused to declare the value of their businesses lest these facts become known to their competitors.[14]

Problems of this sort and the swelling number of confectioners in Chicago—925 in 1906 according to one estimate—brought forth pleas for the formation of a Greek confectioners' association. These merchants were especially sensitive to the needs of better adjusting themselves to the American community. "Let us Americanize ourselves. We make our bread and butter in America. We deal and trade with American people; we breathe free American air. Let us adopt the best they have, and let us unite ourselves with the best friends that Greeks could ever wish for. America and Americans are our best friends and protectors." [15] This plea for Americanism was but an indication that antiforeign opposition was compounding both business problems and relations with the community.

Many of the small shops suffered from poor management. The overhead costs were high and the owners worked night and day to pay for marble soda fountains and expensive furniture. Salesmen shackled many of the earlier inexperienced storekeepers with debts running into many thousands of dollars for fixtures and equipment, which was obsolete or out of style before it had been paid for. These merchants paid the penalty for trying to operate ornate shops in an unbusinesslike manner. The more successful learned these and other lessons through the trial-and-error method. They discovered that cutthroat competition was disastrous, that it did not pay to establish a candy store next door to that of a competitor, that it was contrary to ethical business practices to force a rise in the rent of a rival and condemn the quality of another confectioner's ice cream or candy, and that it was indecent to heap insults and malicious accusations upon neighbors and competitors in the presence of customers.

For some years the need was felt for an effective organization of all Greek confectioners for the purpose of settling disputes within the business, making more economical purchases of merchandise needed in the manufacture and sale of confectionery, and establishing a corporate industrial concern for the manufacture of machinery and other equipment needed for making candy.[16] Perhaps the major concern of the confectioners was the ten-cent store and the drugstore chain. These were powerful competitors who entered the candy and icecream business successfully and aggressively. They not only captured more and more of the business, but they were determined to crush the smaller independent competitors. In Chicago they made unsuccessful efforts to pass a municipal ordinance that would have required candy stores to be closed on Sundays. The small confectioners felt the impact of this competition. They realized that they were helpless in the face of strong and ruthless chains that had huge capital resources behind them. These experiences drove home the need for burying their petty differences, pooling their economic strength, and purchasing their supplies and needs on a wholesale basis.[17]

At least two efforts were made by the confectioners in Chicago to form a united economic front. A Greek confectioners' association was in existence in 1919,[18] but no record of accomplishment has been found. In 1926 another organization, composed of more than two hundred candy-store owners, chiefly "Tsintsiniotes" or natives of the village of Tsintsina near Sparta, was in existence. Its leaders spoke of Americanizing their methods of doing business, which simply meant the pooling of purchasing strength and buying at wholesale prices.[19]

Statistics on the failures of the small confectioners are unavailable; but it is reasonable to assume that, with the onset of the depression in the late 1920s and early 1930s, most of the marginal confectioners were driven to the wall. Poor management, high overhead costs, the spread of the drugstore chain with its soda fountain and lunch counter, and the cheaper candies of the ten-cent and department stores made it difficult for the small proprietors to survive. Still Chicago, which at one time had as many as one thousand Greek-owned candy stores, remained the

Greek-American center of the candy industry. In 1947, an estimated 350 to 400 shops and eight to ten candy manufacturers were still located in the city.[20]

The trade usually associated with the Greeks is the restaurant business. It represented a milestone in economic progress; for many it was a major step beyond working on the railroad or in the factory, pushing a cart or driving a lunch wagon. Restaurant keeping marked the high point in the careers of many; to others it represented but another rung in the economic ladder, the opportunity to establish a chain of restaurants or to branch off into real estate, the theater business, summer resorts, and related enterprises. The restaurant business represented the first stable economic base on which many ambitious immigrants built their fortunes. The restaurant was important for other reasons as well. It brought the Greek businessman into closer contact with the general public, which in many instances found him to be a hard-driving and industrious person. Commercial, patriotic, and fraternal agencies solicited his services or sought contributions from him for a wide variety of causes. Many students also remember working in one of his restaurants as a means of meeting college expenses.[21]

Success in the restaurant business was hardly the product of a national talent, any more than was the Greeks' entrance into the confectionery business. If this had been so, it would have manifested itself before his arrival in America. There is no evidence that the Greek had a better ability to prepare food than any other foreign-born American. Yet he and thousands of his compatriots became the proprietors of successful restaurants in all parts of the United States.[22] The reason perhaps is that he understood the business, knew what his patrons wanted, and worked hard to satisfy them.

The Greeks began invading the restaurant business in considerable force around 1900, first establishing restaurants that catered chiefly to the culinary tastes and pocketbooks of their compatriots. The early arrivals were as loyal to their stomachs as they were to their native country. In time the more venturesome opened lunchrooms in the crowded parts of lower New York, where they sold frankfurters, quick lunches, and other items at reasonable prices. The general idea was to develop a profitable business that did not call for heavy overhead costs or place too great a reliance on trained skills. These enterprises proved to be a testing ground for the more ambitious, giving them an opportunity to learn the language, ways, customs, and tastes of the people and also to amass savings.[23]

A comparable situation evolved in Chicago, where the Greeks entered the restaurant business in even larger numbers. Some started out by selling "red hots" and tamales from lunch wagons to factory workers. It never appeared likely that the dinner pail of the American worker would be replaced by a restaurant or traveling lunch counter, at least until the Greek operator came along. During the administration of Mayor Carter Harrison II, the city council of Chicago passed an ordinance forbidding the sale of food on the city streets. At first the food peddlers thought of fighting the ban, but they finally agreed to abandon their vehicles for more stationary pursuits. All who could manage to gather funds and pool their resources opened restaurants, thus giving some credence to the saying that "when two Greeks meet, they open up a restaurant." [24]

Many of these first restaurants were family enterprises. Entire families worked long hard hours for the success of the business. The working morale was good and the owners had an advantage over competitors who were forced to rely on hired help. When additional help was needed, some newly arrived compatriot was employed. At one time, according to one report, 564 restaurants were owned and operated by Greeks in San Francisco.[25]

The success of the Greek restaurant man aroused the resentment of rivals who found it difficult to compete with him, of Americans who opposed foreigners, and of an unsympathetic press. There was one case of a native-born American's baiting the restaurant owner and refusing to pay for his meal. When pressed for payment the patron informed the owner that the food was "rotten" and that he would not pay for such a meal. The owner retorted: "How could you finish the meal if it was rotten? The plate is empty." This angered the customer who seized a knife and wounded the proprietor.[26] In another instance a committee of restaurant men visited the office of a Greek newspaper in Chicago, complaining about the use of electric signs by their Greek competitors. Advertising to attract customers would add to their own staggering overhead costs; they asked that the Greeks be urged to discontinue this practice lest they all become slaves to the electric company.[27]

A virulent form of antiforeignism manifested itself against the Greek and Chinese businesses of Phoenix, Arizona, which were accused with imperiling the future of the Phoenix merchants. A headline in a local labor journal read: "Greek Peril Confronts Phoenix Merchants." The ensuing article stated, among other things: "Here we have in Phoenix three individuals, brothers, who have grown from one small little business house until they now own or control FIVE big establishments. These with the Chinese restaurants constitute a menace to the economic possibilities of Phoenix. They are a menace to YOU." [28]

The restaurant men, like their compatriots in the confectionery business, strove to organize on a national basis in order to defend themselves from the attacks of competitors and to economize on their purchases. One of the first such organizations was the Greek Restaurant Keepers' Association (Hermes) of Chicago. But in this as in other instances the greatest obstacle was the rivalry between the Spartans and the Tripolitsiotas; both factions were large and precautions had to be taken to prevent them from converting the association into a battlefield. [29]

Many who once worked as busboys, dishwashers, waiters, cooks, and countermen entered the business as independent proprietors and worked as though there were nothing else in life. The more successful ones moved into the better and more prosperous areas of town—neighborhood communities, shopping centers, and downtown areas. In 1919 one of every three restaurants in Chicago is said to have been operated by a Greek, a substantial number of whom were located in the Loop, the central business district. At the time, the average investment in a restaurant is estimated to have been between three and five thousand dollars. Shrewd business practices impelled these owners to adopt the name of the community or the neighboring theater. They had forsaken the use of classical names, such as the Acropolis, Parthenon, and Hermes, and of family names, which could have some thirty letters, were difficult to pronounce and impossible to remember. [30]

The war years brought new wealth, but they also threw fear into the hearts of the smaller owners, who were menaced by the rising tide of patriotism and antialien sentiments. Late in 1917 a measure was before the city council of Chicago that threatened to deprive thousands of aliens, including many Greeks, of the right to do business in the city unless one had become a citizen of the United States or declared his intentions of becoming one. [31]

The successful restaurant owner insisted that he met competition squarely and openly in all his business dealings, paid standard wages, and subscribed to all the legal requirements of the trade. He denied that he ran an unsanitary place of business, as his enemies sometimes insisted. In Chicago he could cite the letter of Commissioner of Health John Dill of October 11, 1919, which stated: "The Department has no record of Greek restaurants segregated from the records operated by all nationalities, but the experience of the Department of Inspection is such that the claim could not be made that Greek restaurants were different in rank as regards sanitation and methods from other restaurants." If the Greek restaurateur succeeded where others failed, it was because he was a better businessman, worked long hours, and had imagination and foresight. He used standard, nationally advertised foods, but as a rule he did not excel his competitors in the preparation of them. His prices were a trifle lower, but his overhead expenses were about the same. He avoided the establishment of the cabaret eating house, with an orchestra and dancing, even though in Chicago he maintained a thriving trade in the heart of the business district where the cabaret prevailed. This, in essence, was the formula for his success.[32]

Coping with the attacks of business enemies and maintaining a united front in the face of hostility became a major problem. The result was the establishment of the American Association of Greek Restaurant Keepers, incorporated on December 1, 1919. Since its inception it devoted itself to raising the standards of cooking, sanitation, working conditions, and service. It sought to aid members to comply with health regulations; it sponsored a program of naturalization, aiming to have all owners and employees become citizens of the United States; it urged its members to conform to American ideals and institutions; it fought all attempts to prejudice the public against the Greek restaurateur and all attacks based on untruthful statements regarding working conditions.[33] The restaurateurs realized that much more had to be done if they were to become effective. They had to expand nationally. They had to revise their old notion that elected officers had to leave their places of business and work gratis for the association, and a more comprehensive program was necessary. The members of the association had to establish better relations with the public and win friends among prominent bankers, merchants, lawyers, and other professional people.[34]

But during the mid-1920s many still complained of anti-Greek whispering campaigns and, to a lesser extent, of pressure from big chains and other competitors. What they resented most was competitors who, unable to overtake them by fair methods, resorted to unfair competition. They were unjustly accused, they felt, of being dishonest in business dealings, unfair to employees, disrespectful to women, unappreciative of home and family life, and dangerous to the community.[35] I recall as a youth frequently passing a lunchroom on Third Street in Milwaukee called "Twentieth Century Lunch": the sign in its window read "Operated by an American." A Santa Rosa, California, newspaper carried the following advertisement: "John's Restaurant, Pure American. No Rats, No Greeks." [36]

The restaurant keepers became aware of the need to act together to overcome hostility and to use care in handling the public. They continued to press for the perfection of national commercial organizations that would be patterned after those of native Americans. The aim appears to have been to demonstrate they were "more American than the Americans." Nothing infuriated these members of the community more than the proprietor who kept an untidy place of business. It was this "bovine-headed" proprietor, the "hash-slinger"—short and barrel-chested, with the ever-present cigar butt in his mouth, who scurried when he collected the patron's bill but who was immovable when asked for a second piece of butter—that brought criticisms and insults upon innocent people.[37] The personal appearance of the owner and employees became a matter of concern to these sensitive Greeks. One heard complaints about the compatriot who did not shave regularly and who, because of his dark complexion, had the appearance of an underworld character. And as if this were not enough, he made matters worse by wearing a shirt or apron until it was fairly black with dirt. When he entered the tavern business in his new role as bartender, he dressed as if he was selling grog to sailors on some dingy wharf. Equally unfortunate was the proprietor with the perpetual scowl on his face. This might have been caused by overwork and worry, but the customer did not know this and could easily mistake him for one of those wild foreigners he read about in the newspapers.[38]

The problems of the Greek merchant were essentially those of the small businessman, though multiplied by the waves of antiforeignism. During the earlier years, the individual merchant predominated in the confectionery, restaurant, shoe-repair, and other retail businesses. He

THE GREEKS IN THE UNITED STATES

continued to flourish until he felt the menacing hand of the chain store. The chain store, in many instances a miniature department store, began grinding him to bits slowly, through capital strength and efficient management. He recognized the peril, yet his ego caused him stubbornly to pursue an individual course of action and refuse to unite with others.[39]

The advice meted out to the small businessman hemmed in by competitors was a compound of emotionalism, nationalism, and Americanism. One course of action was proposed by the uninformed and nationalistic individuals whose formative years had been spent in Greece and who were guided by what successful Greeks had accomplished in Egypt, Turkey, and other countries. They pleaded for organizations of Greek restaurant men, Greek vegetable men, Greek bootblacks, Greek confectioners. This philosophy of organizing on the basis of nationality prevailed well into the 1920s, on the theory that the Greeks had problems that were peculiar to them. A few of these men apparently were motivated by the belief that they were capable of building a miniature Greek economy within the broader American economy.[40]

A second, more realistic, course of action was that of becoming assimilated to American ways and following the example set by the other small businessmen of the nation. Those possessed with the necessary business skills thought it ludicrous to organize as though they were a persecuted national minority; they cooperated more readily with the non-Greeks, and they succeeded. However, the professional patriot, who was anxious to exploit the feeling of nationality as an article of trade, was always busy in the larger metropolitan area, urging his compatriots to organize as Greeks.[41]

The better informed also realized that poor management, rather than persecution and intolerance, was the cause of many business failures. Many small businessmen simply were incapable of keeping books; they probably knew how to add up profits, but they were unable to calculate their operating expenses and losses. One account portrays a restaurant as a Dantesque inferno—where the waiter's fingers "played piano" on the cash register (restaurant jargon for stealing), the chef's cleaver chopped up the boss's profits, sundry callers came to the back door to deliver unnecessary and underweight merchandise, and employees left with filled pockets to lighten the load of the icebox.[42]

The plight of the unsuccessful small businessman, however, should not obscure the fact that thousands succeeded in various retail fields, and that the more successful became manufacturers and wholesale suppliers of various kinds of merchandise.[43] Prominent Greek names in the restaurant business at one time or another included Raklios, who operated a large chain in Chicago; Foltis, Stavrakos, and Litzotakis in New York; and Lambropoulos in North Carolina, South Carolina, and Virginia.[44] Most well-known is the name of John Raklios, who for a time was the king of the Chicago restaurateurs. Arriving in the United States at the turn of the century with a few dollars in his pocket, Raklios climbed the proverbial ladder of success. Like so many others, he subsisted on bread and water during his first days as a means of saving his meager resources until he found employment. He got his first business idea from a boy he saw carrying a basket of fruit and candy into a building. The following day he had a basket under his arm and was hawking chestnuts and bananas.

For a while it appeared as though an encounter with the law was going to force him into involuntary bankruptcy: he was arrested for peddling without a license. But Raklios managed to pay the fine and continued to peddle. In time he scraped together enough money to set up a fruit stand. He then became part owner of a hamburger stand along Burlesque Row on South State Street. "He mopped floors, waited on customers, pocketed his share of the proceeds and blessed America as the land of opportunity." [45] Raklios finally decided that he had saved enough money to buy a place of his own on the north side of Chicago. He hired a waitress who shared his enthusiasm for work, and together they labored and saved to build "the Raklios empire." A shrewd and thorough man in some respects, he often stayed up all night to take meticulous pedestrian and traffic counts before picking corners to lease. He negotiated many leases, the details of which are unknown. Apparently one of his mistakes was that he leased entire buildings instead of the space he intended to occupy.

When the depression came, Raklios found he had overextended himself. Shrunken pocketbooks meant shrunken appetites. Fewer customers ate less food in the Raklios chain. But the large rent bills for the long-term leases he had signed kept coming in. He tried desperately to retrench his position by selling one restaurant after another. The last few establishments of his once proud empire were sold at an auction to satisfy debts. Then he lost his sumptuous home. Raklios was not only ruined financially but was sentenced to "debtors' row." When he entered the county jail, he requested the warden: "Please don't make me a pearl diver." Raklios was freed after his case was fought in the Supreme Court of Illinois.

On several occasions friends tried to back him in what they hoped would be a new climb to the top, but without success. Each time he failed he fell back on a twenty-five-dollar counterman's job with some previous employee. At last even these menial jobs were no longer offered him. At the peak of his career, Raklios had owned or controlled thirty-two restaurants, operated his own bakery, and was a millionaire. One of his three daughters was christened with water brought to Chicago from the Jordan River, and on one occasion he was host to Prince Paul of Greece. Raklios' own explanation of the causes of his failure was that "he signed his name too many times." [46]

A number of Greeks also gained a foothold in the tobacco business during the early years. This began with the arrival late in the nineteenth century of a number of immigrants who had been skilled tobacconists in Egypt or other parts of the Near East. Egypt at the time was a prominent manufacturer of cigarettes, perhaps the most important in the world. From here, it is claimed, was introduced the aromatic tobacco that was sold in the most exclusive shops of the United States. Greeks have been credited with introducing "Fatima," "Rameses II," "Murad," and other lesser known brand names.

One of the pioneer cigarette manufacturers was a native of the island of Spetsoi, Soterios Anargyros, who helped popularize many brands. After disposing of his business interests to P. Lorillard and Company, Anargyros returned to Greece where he built the Poseidon Hotel and founded a school for the study of English and Greek. He was among the first Greek-Americans to contribute to the welfare of his native country through his experiences and earnings in the United States.

At the start of the twentieth century Miltiades Melachrinos came to the United States from Egypt and founded a factory for the manufacture of Egyptian cigarettes. Later his firm was purchased by a competitor, and the Melachrino brand was sold in limited quantities. Melachrinos also contributed to Greek religious and educational institutions in Egypt. The Stephano brothers of Philadelphia came to the United States from

Egypt during the 1890s, but unlike their compatriots they remained in this country and in the business. During the mid-1940s their factories employed some five hundred workers.[47] Still another was Euripides Kehayas, a native of the Pontus district, the president of the Standard Commercial Tobacco Company and a few other corporations. A philanthropist as well as a businessman, he contributed large sums of money to Greek charities and other popular causes.[48]

The 1920s, as we have seen, witnessed a turning point in the business careers of many. Those who once thought in terms of investing their money in Greece had a change of heart and decided to invest in American enterprises. The incessant wars and political convulsions from which Greece suffered brought a loss of confidence in the economic future of the mother country and a greater appreciation of opportunities in the United States. Many began to diversify their economic holdings, for the war and postwar years brought them new wealth and confidence. In the larger metropolitan areas they invested heavily in real estate, hotels, food-processing plants, catering, restaurant supply firms, furniture factories, metals, and the entertainment industry. The drift was definitely away from the fields normally associated with the earlier immigrant years.[49]

The theater business was one such new area invaded by enterprising Greeks. The names that stand out most conspicuously are those of Alexander Pantages and the Skouras brothers. Pantages, a pioneer in commercial entertainment, became famous as a theatrical manager-owner who built up a far-flung empire of vaudeville houses that embraced most of the western states and the lower provinces of Canada; the Skouras brothers became the owners of a still vaster empire of theaters. One of the three brothers, Spyros, became head of one of the largest motion-picture companies in the country. The careers of these men—Pantages and the Skourases—were strikingly different and represent succeeding generations in the entertainment field. They also illustrate, on a grand scale, the adaptations Greek immigrants made as they became progressively acclimated to America.

The early career of Alexander Pantages was filled with the wanderlust, romance, and adventure that fills the pages of a swift-moving popular novel. He was born—some say in 1864 and others in 1871—on the island of Andros, which had a long and proud maritime tradition. Christened Pericles, he changed his name to Alexander after hearing a story about Alexander the Great. His father was the constable, mayor, and harbor master of the village and thought strongly in terms of a business career for his son.

Alexander was nine years old when his father took him on one of his periodic trading excursions to Cairo. According to all accounts, young Pantages was unimpressed with the bickering and the traffic in goods, and he wandered away from his father to Cairo's center of amusement. Being near the warmth and gaiety of people amusing themselves helped him overcome some of the remorse that had seized him for leaving his father. A little later he obtained a job as a cabin boy on a tramp steamer bound for Marseilles, London, and South America. While on leave from his ship he always managed to visit music halls. He listened to strange tongues and saw people "eating and drinking, trying to be happy." With keen insight he saw from firsthand observations, and very early in life, that people paid handsomely for chances at happiness.[50]

In Panama Pantages got a job swinging a pick and shovel and running a donkey engine while employed by the French company that was attempting to dig a canal through the isthmus.[51] Here he fell sick and almost died from an attack of tropical fever. The young Greek was put aboard a ship bound for the United States. He was convalescing when the ship sailed through the Golden Gate at San Francisco, and at the age of twelve he went ashore never to return to sea again.[52]

In San Francisco he came into contact with the American entertainment world in a rather humble way. He got a job "lugging mugs of beer" and attending to a dozen other duties in the beer garden of Walter Meyer, where Joe Weber and Lew Fields, as youngsters, did a good job of "bladder thwacking." [53] Here he put to good use that "questionable knowledge" he had of foreign languages, and his boss liked him for it because he could communicate with sailors from foreign countries.[54] This job opened up other vistas to Pantages. Here he was near music and food, and he could watch the slapstick comedians and the dancing girls. As he heard the proprietor's till clatter with coins, the idea kept running through his mind that people will pay well for momentary happiness.[55] In San Francisco he also got his first taste of the theater business. He became a theater utility man, passed out programs, worked as an usher, and became acquainted with Eddie Foy, June McCree, David Belasco, and others.[56]

For a time Pantages toyed with the idea of becoming a prize fighter. Short and husky, he fought a few fights as a welterweight in Vallejo, which was a thriving boxing center.[57] But when gold was struck in the Yukon during the late 1890s, with stories circulating of the fortunes awaiting those who dug beneath the snow and ice, the venturesome Pantages joined the trek northward. He withdrew his savings, estimated at a thousand dollars, and boarded a ship that was loaded with some of the cleverest cardsharks in the business. By the time he reached Skagway, a boom town, his major concern was for food. For the time being he had forsaken all thoughts of getting rich and got a job for room and board with a widow with four children.

Here he picked up enough information about the trail to the gold-fields to be able to pass himself off as a guide. Pantages played his new role shrewdly enough to be able to cross the border into Canada, despite the fact he had neither a grubstake nor passage money to show the mounted police. By various devices he contrived to transport his charges on two boats down the Yukon to Dawson City. He knew little about boats, but his compulsion to make the grade and his nerve served him well.[58] His first job in Alaska found him once more behind a pick and shovel. This was hardly his idea of living; he hated physical labor and the nights of the laborer were lonely. So he often found his way to the midway and bright lights of Dawson. He soon got a job as a bartender, which plunged him into the center of the social life of the mining community.[59]

Two things happened in Dawson that were to influence the career of Pantages. He met "Klondike Kate" Rockwell, and he began to act upon the idea that men will pay cash for entertainment. He had the idea, and the woman had the money. He and two associates bought an amusement place, where he demonstrated his adroitness as a purveyor of entertainment. The miners gladly paid $12.50 a seat for his shows. Later in life he was quoted as saying "for five years I never made less than $8,000 a day. And when I came out of the Klondike after making $8,000 a day for five years, I had in my pocket just $4,000. I won't say where the money had gone." [60]

When gold was discovered at Nome, Pantages rushed there. If we are to believe his harshest critics, he would not hesitate to do in a rival and, if there was enough money in it, a friend. He had seen life in the raw; he was tough; he asked no favors and gave none. He was an opportunist with the compulsion to succeed. Pantages found what he was looking for when he came upon a theater in financial trouble. After persuading some of the entertainers to stake him, he took over the management of the theater.[61]

By the time Pantages left the Yukon country, he had become a legendary figure. His experiences as a sailor, laborer, miner, and purveyor of commercial entertainment had equipped him for competitive show business. He was vigorous, venturesome, and determined. He knew the common people and their tastes.[62] Ideas, a grubstake, and confidence born in the Yukon came to fruition in the United States and netted him a fortune. When Pantages arrived in Seattle from the Klondike, he opened up a combination bootblack parlor and fruit store—a typical immigrant enterprise—adjoining the Sullivan & Considine theater. The performers playing the theater patronized his store. After selling it, he rented a vacant store, equipped it with hard benches, bought a movie projector, hired a vaudeville act, and was in the show business. As was the case with other pioneers in the business, he was his own manager, booking agent, ticket taker, janitor, and projector operator. The price of admission was ten cents.[63]

The people of Seattle considered him a "Klondike millionaire," and he did not argue about this with them. He borrowed $35,000 to convert his store-theater into a "beautiful palace." He claimed he was the first to combine vaudeville with movies.[64] Pantages knew how to use every opportunity. On Sundays he sacrificed performance schedules to get as many people into his theater as possible. When throngs sought admission he would cut the time of an act in half and the motion picture would be run so fast across the screen that one barely recognized the scenes. (In those days projectors were made without timing devices.) The idea was to get as many paying patrons into the theater as possible.

From here on the fortunes of Pantages multiplied. Money earned from the first theater were put into a second, a third, and a fourth. In time, theaters in Tacoma, Portland, Vancouver, and Spokane were brought into the Pantages circuit. As this chain grew, a bitter rivalry developed between him and one of his competitors, John Considine.

A mad scramble took place in securing acts, as one group tried to outwit the other. Pantages was a shrewd man who found ways of meeting the competition of his rival, who seemed to have unlimited resources and a knack for outmaneuvering him in bidding for the services of performers. But he could fight fire with fire and better a rival through sheer genius of showmanship. He could stage a comparable performance at half the cost and take the luster out of a rival's star performer by presenting an equal or near equal artist a day or two earlier. He proved to be an indefatigable worker.[65]

This merely marked the start of an amazing period of growth. After the San Francisco fire, he bought six theaters at a very low price and later acquired interests in Colorado and Missouri. Early in 1919 when ground was broken for the Pantages Theater Building, he personally owned fifteen theaters, the beginnings had been made for the sixteenth, and twenty other theaters operated under a Pantages vaudeville franchise. By March 1920, he owned twenty-two showhouses and had a controlling interest in twenty-eight others. All indications were that the end was not in sight.[66] To the outsider the Pantages circuit appeared to be a mushrooming institution dominated by one man. He supervised every phase of the work and was gifted with a retentive mind. It is claimed that he was unable to read, but this is hard to believe. He never had a partner, in part because he found it difficult to accept one. He sold no stock. At the peak of his wealth and power, he owned or had interests in a chain of about eighty theaters, valued between $10 million and $15 million.[67]

The success of Pantages may be attributed to a variety of reasons. He was a man of energy who was dedicated to his business. He had an effective publicity department, got credit when he needed it, studied the public reaction to performers, did a good job in selecting theater managers, and knew how to make business decisions in a hurry.[68]

At the height of success he decided to sell his interests to Warner Brothers and the Radio-Keith-Orpheum circuit. Instead of taking cash he took stock in RKO and Warner Brothers, which suffered during the depression. The declining years of his life were marred by a scandal involving a seventeen-year-old girl. But before Pantages died on February 17, 1936, he had established himself as a pioneer in large-scale commercial entertainment. Finance capital and the chain operation had penetrated into the theater business, as in every other field of business enterprise, and Alexander Pantages was among those who helped make this possible.[69]

At about the time that the star of Pantages began to descend, another brighter one was becoming visible on the theatrical horizon—that of the Skourases. Their beginnings were less flamboyant, more in the Horatio Alger fashion. The Skourases built a theatrical empire geared to the needs of a bigger and more competitive American business scene. But they also engaged in philanthropic activities and acquired a highly esteemed national reputation. As natives of the Peloponnesus, instead of the islands or the unredeemed lands of Greece, they helped shatter the belief that the most ambitious and successful immigrants came from the peripheral more commercial portions of Greece.

Charles, the first of the Skourases to come to the United States, was born in 1889 in Skourohorion, in the northwestern part of the Peloponnesus. He reached this country in 1908 in about as penniless a condition as any other immigrant disembarking in New York. His first employment was in a restaurant for the princely sum of fifty cents a day and meals.[70] After familiarizing himself with his new surroundings and obtaining a surer footing on American soil, he moved to St. Louis. As soon as he saved the price of a steamship ticket, claiming that it took him three years to do so, he sent for his brother Spyros.[71] In an amusing scene at the Federal Communications Hearings in San Francisco in 1948, Charles informed the interrogator: "I sent him the ticket to come over. I came over in steerage, he travelled first class."[72]

In Greece Spyros apparently was as restless with his station in life as his older brother had been. When he was fifteen years old, he began to study for the priesthood in Patras and earned a meager living by working as a part-time journalist. In the afternoons he studied English and accounting, and in the evening he attended a school of theology. He believed, as did his brothers, that his towering ambitions could be satisfied only in the United States. Spyros met Charles in St. Louis and immediately began working as a busboy in the old Planters' Hotel. Before being given a job by the head barman, another adopted son of the United States, Spyros had to promise that he would learn the words of the "Star-Spangled Banner." Every morning he and the barman sang the national anthem "with heartfelt thanks" that they were in America. He worked hard at the hotel, saved his money, and in his spare time studied English, business methods, and business law.[73]

Once reunited the three brothers worked and saved, after the fashion of all immigrants who are determined to succeed; by 1914 they were prepared to step into the business world. According to one account, they heard of three compatriots who were having difficulties in completing the nickelodeon they were building. According to another account, they bought a decrepit old theater which they were going to convert into a profitable enterprise. Anticipating that the hitherto disreputable motion-picture business was the wave of the future, Charles and Spyros bought the theater with the four thousand dollars they had saved and renamed it "Olympia." From 1915 to 1917 the three brothers took turns selling tickets, running the projector, and performing janitorial services. These labors provided them with an invaluable fund of information about running the business. In 1917 their careers were interrupted briefly when Spyros and George joined the United States air force, while Charles remained behind to tend to the business.[74] Honorably discharged from the service in 1919, the brothers returned to St. Louis.

By 1926 the Skouras brothers controlled thirty-seven theaters in St. Louis and had interests in a number of houses in Kansas City and Indianapolis. Spyros in particular specialized in the study of motion-picture finances, real-estate values, and theater management. Their theaters were acquired by Warner Brothers at a time when producers were beginning to show their films in their own houses to increase profits. Spyros is said to have influenced Warner Brothers to acquire the First National Film Company, and he remained with them as general manager of the theater circuit. In 1931 Spyros seized the opportunity to enlarge his motion-picture interests by joining Paramount as president of a subsidiary to operate theaters in a number of eastern states.

Shortly thereafter he became head of the Fox Metropolitan Theaters, which were losing a million dollars a year but which were to show a profit of $200,000 in less than twelve months. With Charles and George, Spyros signed a contract to head the Wesco Corporation, a holding company in which all Fox theater interests were merged. Spyros and Charles toured the country studying their theater holdings during the remainder of 1932. In 1933 they took over the active operation of the Wesco interests and rechristened it the National Theaters Corporation; in the reorganization of 1934, the Chase National Bank secured holdings in the company. By 1942, some 563 theaters had become a part of a chain that was rated as one of the most successful in the country. In 1943, Twentieth Century–Fox gained an option in the Chase National Bank holdings in National Theaters for $13 million. Spyros Skouras became president of Twentieth Century–Fox in April 1942, with Wendell Willkie as chairman of the board. At a yearly salary of about a quarter of a million dollars, Skouras was concerned primarily with finances, the theaters, and business problems.[75]

The Skourases and Pantages were the exception rather than the rule, but they demonstrated that it was possible for newcomers of peasant origins, with no capital and a minimum of formal education, to enter the highly competitive, often ruthless, theatrical world and succeed. Others of Greek birth or descent also entered the entertainment business and prospered, but they never achieved the prominence of a Skouras or a Pantages. Still larger numbers showed a determination to become retailers and wholesalers of products and services because this was a quicker way of obtaining wealth and independence. In time they went into every conceivable kind of business, until it became impossible to identify Greeks with any one particular field, with the possible exception of the restaurant business. Their commercial activities thrust them into closer contact with the American public, accelerated the process of Americanization, and had effects on the church and the various organizations they joined.

THE CIVIL WAR WITHIN
THE GREEK CHURCH

T HE SECOND cycle in the history of the Orthodox Church in America began on July 4, 1918, when the Holy Synod of Greece, presided over by Meletios Metaxakis, Metropolitan of Athens, passed a resolution establishing what was expected to become the "Archdiocese of America." Thus ten inactive years had elapsed since the Ecumenical Patriarchate's delegation of spiritual jurisdiction to the Church of Greece. But instead of peace and stability, the resolution ushered in a new era of internecine strife. This was inevitable as long as the fortunes of the church were tied to the fortunes of rival political factions.

Meletios Metaxakis, a prime figure in the history of the church in the United States from 1918 to 1923, deserves a better fate than the harsh pages of history would suggest. A Cretan by birth, he first distinguished himself as an archmandrite and secretary of the Patriarchate of Jerusalem. In 1910 he became the Metropolitan of Kition of the Autocephalous Church of Cyprus, where for the next eight years he displayed great zeal as an organizer. Interested in politics since youth, he spent a great portion of his life in areas in which the Greek irredentist spirit ran high and where the admirers of Venizelos were legion. After the dethronement of King Constantine in 1917, Metaxakis became the Metropolitan of Athens and the titular head of the Church of Greece.[1]

With characteristic determination and energy, Metaxakis proceeded to reorganize and revitalize the churches of Greece, mindful always of his loyalty to the political philosophy of Venizelos. He became interested in the American churches and was disturbed by the apathy of his predecessors toward them. As Metropolitan of Athens, Metaxakis was granted permission to come to the United States, establish a temporary organization, and appoint a supervising bishop.[2] News of the visit reached official Washington during the summer of 1918. Garrett Droppers telegraphed the State Department in an optimistic vein that: "Meletios, Metropolitan, formerly Archbishop of Cyprus, is much respected. He is a judicious but vigorous reformer of abuses in the church. He occasionally exercises in preaching function, practice almost unknown in Greek Church. In politics he is a Liberal and Venizelist. His intention, I believe, in going to America is to render Greek Church there a better instrument of religious work; also, if possible, to appoint a bishop; also said to be interested in closer union of Christian churches." [3]

Metaxakis reached New York City on August 22, 1918.[4] He was to meet with prominent lay leaders and educators, visit President Wilson and the various church communities, urge the Greeks to buy government bonds, and survey the needs of the Greek-American churches. His major purpose was to establish an organization capable of bringing order out of chaos through the centralization of ecclesiastical authority.[5] Among those accompanying the metropolitan was the learned Chrysostomos Papadopoulos, an archimandrite and professor of theology at the University of Athens. According to Callimachos, whose associations with all Venizelist leaders were close, Chrysostomos was offered the post of Bishop of the Greek Orthodox Church in the United States. But he refused it.[6] What the course of the church woud have been if Chrysostomos had accepted is a matter of conjecture.

Metaxakis, as a consequence, left the Right Reverend Alexander, the Bishop of Rodostolou and his assistant in the Athens see, in charge of the American bishopric. The designation of Alexander as the first American bishop intensified the civil war within the Greek church. Nevertheless, it is safe to say that the conflict would have been intensified no matter who had become bishop. Alexander was cut from the same political cloth as Metaxakis. Like so many other devoted followers of Venizelos, he was born in unredeemed Greece, in Nicodemia, Asia Minor. After completing his studies in the theological school in Chalkis and obtaining the degree of doctor of divinity, he served for five years as dean of the Metropolite of Ephesus. Later he became Suffragan bishop of the Metropolite of Adrianople, Xanthe, and Salonica; then the suffragan bishop in the Archdiocese of Athens and the Bishop of Rodostolou, in which capacity he came to the United States.[7]

Metaxakis left for Greece with the expectation of returning to reorganize the church and appoint an archbishop in a manner consistent with the provisions of the Constitution of the United States. But his return was contingent upon certain changes being made in the laws governing the Church of Greece, and upon the substitution of others that would not interfere with the internal life of the church in the United States. He submitted proposals for changes to the Holy Synod and the Greek government, which, if approved, would then go to the Chamber of Deputies for consideration.

Apparently a major blunder had been committed in attempting to establish an archdiocese in the United States. As first proposed, the selection of an archbishop was to take place in accordance with the procedure used in Greece. Under this practice the Ministry of Public Worship appointed one of the archbishops nominated by the Holy Synod and installed him by royal decree. This kind of a relationship was acceptable in Greece, where there was an official union between church and state. But the United States could not be expected to tolerate the appointment of the head of an American church by the political leaders of another country. Such an ecclesiastical authority was incapable of exercising its spiritual power independent of the state in which it originally was established.

Bishop Alexander from the outset faced insurmountable difficulties. The royalists abused and villified him. His personality and mannerisms won him few friends. The royalist organ urged the parish priests to ignore his instructions and to refuse him the revenue he was seeking.[8] Unhappily for Alexander, conditions took a dramatic turn for the worse during the fall of 1920, when Constantine was restored to the Greek throne. The restoration brought with it the fall of Metropolitan Meletios, who had appointed Alexander, and the abandonment of his plan for organizing the Greek churches in the United States. Theoclitus was reinstated to his former position as Metropolitan of Athens and head of the Holy Synod of Greece.

Bishop Alexander, upon assessing the significance of this upheaval in Greece, invited many, if not most, priests in the United States to come to New York, where they organized the Association of Canonical Hellenic Clergymen. Its stated objectives were to preserve the doctrines of the Greek Orthodox Church and to proclaim the independence of the members of the association. Needless to say, the Holy Synod of Greece ordered Alexander to appear before it in Athens. But Alexander did nothing of the sort. He ignored the summons of Theoclitus on the grounds that he could not communicate with "a degraded clergyman" and suffer the penalty of his own degradation, in accordance with Canon 11 of the Holy Apostles. He also issued a proclamation to the priests on February 20, 1921, stating that he, as a canonical officer, could not enter into any working relationship with the new ecclesiastical regime in Greece, and he added that the Ecumenical Patriarchate was the only body with which he would communicate regarding his jurisdiction. By this he did not infer that he was restoring the original relationship between the Patriarchate and the churches of the United States, for this was beyond his authority.[9]

Alexander's actions were endorsed by the Association of Clergymen. Later the bishop and the executive committee of the association cabled the Locum Tenens of the Ecumenical Patriarchate, Dorotheos, Metropolitan of Proussa, who was in London at the time, that they would continue to recognize him as their canonical officer. The Ecumenical Throne had been vacant for an abnormally long period, and Dorotheos governed in the interim.[10]

The history of the Ecumenical Patriarchate during these troublous years appears to have been as follows. Germanos V, the last Ecumenical Patriarch, had been forced to resign after the 1918 armistice by protests from a large part of the clergy and laity who believed that he had been an ineffective administrator. His successor should have been elected within forty days after his resignation; but owing to conditions stemming from the war, the Patriarchate considered it advisable to postpone the election of a new Patriarch until the treaty between Turkey and Greece had been signed. The hope was that the treaty would include provisions for the protection of the Christians remaining in the new Turkey, and perhaps for the separation of Constantinople from the Ottoman Empire. Prolongation of the peace negotiations also prolonged the election of a Patriarch.[11]

In time the deposed Metaxakis reached the United States for the second time, convinced that the actions of Bishop Alexander were justified. He also issued an encyclical in which he emphasized that he had no intention of disputing the legality of the new political regime in Greece, even though he protested his dismissal and the establishment of what he called "the anti-canonical new Holy Synod." "We deny," he continued, "the right of these legal authorities, i.e., the State, to violate sacred canons, to transcend ecclesiastical privileges and to confound the rights of God with the rights of Caesar."

Metaxakis and Alexander, in accordance with the church regulations of 1918, continued to exercise jurisdiction over the Greek churches in the United States. In keeping with Paul's command, they rendered to the state authorities of Greece that which they were obligated to render: "tribute to whom tribute is due; custom to whom custom; fear to whom fear; honour to whom honour." But the two prelates refused to yield to what they termed the antichurch activities of the Greek state, more specifically to the tendency of the Greek government and its representatives in the United States to meddle in the administration of lawfully created churches which had canonical, but not political, dependence on Athens.

The Holy Synod of Greece responded by declaring Metaxakis, Alexander, and certain of their American followers to be schismatics. They countered by accusing the Holy Synod of being a usurper, which committed another canonical crime in declaring clergymen and laymen *in schisma*. Matters became even more complicated when Bishop Germanos Troianos of Sparta reached the United States, much to the pleasure of the royalists. He came as the representative of the reconstituted Holy Synod of Greece and had the approval of the government to establish synodical authority. Consular officials, acting upon instructions of the Greek legation in Washington, sent circulars to the priests and boards of trustees of the various church communities, asking them to recognize Germanos. In exercising his prerogatives as Synodical Exarch, Germanos appointed and dismissed priests at will and persuaded those unacceptable to Bishop Alexander to occupy pastorates. As a consequence, the civil war within the Greek church spread across the country; secession movements became common in various large cities; and litigation over church property developed as factions in one community after another took their claims to the courts.[12]

The relation of the local church communities to the Church of Greece and the Ecumenical Patriarchate became an issue of grave concern. Each church was a part of a self-governing community, which was recognized as a legal entity by the state in which it was located. The church building belonged to this self-governing community, and as a rule it constituted its first and most important piece of property. The board of trustees appointed and discharged priests who, in effect, were treated as employees. A community, through its board of trustees, could engage the services of any priest, regardless of whether he belonged to the Church of Greece, the Ecumenical Patriarchate, or the Patriarchates of Jerusalem, Antioch, or Alexandria. The exception to this was the community whose constitution provided for the appointment and removal of a priest by the Holy Synod of Greece or some other high church authority.

Most of the disputes within the church in the United States revolved around ecclesiastical government and the struggle for power; differences over dogma and doctrine seldom became issues. Administrative dependence on the Holy Synod of Greece would continue as long as the American churches remained under its jurisdiction. If there was a surplus of priests to draw from in the United States, no power could prevent a community from appointing any priest it desired. Preference naturally was for one who knew the English language and the customs, habits, and needs of the people.[13]

The simultaneous presence of the exiled Metropolitan of Athens, the Exarch of the reconstituted Holy Synod of Greece, and Bishop Alexander was a dramatic exhibition of ecclesiastical politics and emphasized the need for a disciplined authority. Each faction naturally claimed it was following the proper canonical course. But the distant church administration of which they were all a part was also to blame. The churches in the United States had to safeguard themselves by forming an independent church organization that would be immune to political calamities.[14]

Pleas for the establishment of such an organization came from various quarters. Community-conscious individuals, such as Andrew Vlachos (a Chicago attorney) and the irrepressible Speros Kotakis (the editor and publisher of *Kathemerini*), were among its more articulate advocates. Bishop Germanos, who expected to return to Greece when his exarchical mission to the United States came to an end, also saw the need for an archdiocese. Germanos felt that it was impossible to administer the American churches by special legates. "We need not only to establish a diocese here, but we must also have a seminary in which to train priests properly for the Greek communities of America, priests who shall have the opportunity to complete their courses in American universities." [15]

Supporters of Metaxakis naturally believed that he was the only person to assume this task. His stature in the ecclesiastical world of the West and his valuable contacts with Protestant leaders in the United States, coupled with his zeal for organization and modernization, they felt, made him the inevitable choice. He was learned, capable, and better oriented toward the needs of Greek-Americans. His dethronement as the Metropolitan of Athens was irrelevant to the needs of the churches of the United States.[16] Meletios, while an exile in the United States, labored strenuously to organize and strengthen those churches that were committed to his spiritual leadership. He traveled extensively, renewing associations and acquiring new followers. He remained in contact with Venizelos who, we already have seen, visited the United States.[17] He was instrumental in organizing the short-lived seminary of St. Athanasius in Astoria, New York.[18] He was working strenuously to effect a closer working relationship with the Episcopalian Church when news reached him of his elevation by the Holy Synod of the Constantinople Patriarchate to the Ecumenical Throne.[19]

The significance of this dramatic turn of events cannot be exaggerated. Here was the deposed Metropolitan of Athens, finding refuge in the United States, being elected to the most prestigious office that the Eastern Orthodox Church could confer on any of its ecclesiastical leaders. Metaxakis was now the spiritual head of the Church of Greece that had ousted him. A Western-oriented ecclesiast, he had been elevated to a post that for centuries had been turned toward the Orient and the Near East. The broader ramifications of these developments, however, were obscured by the more pressing immediate problems.

Metaxakis' election to the Ecumenical Throne brought considerable satisfaction to him and his followers. The board of directors of the diocese, under the chairmanship of Bishop Alexander, voted to pay their respects to the newly elected Patriarch by delivering their congratulations to him en masse, designating a committee to escort him to Constantinople, collecting funds to help finance the needs of the

Patriarchate, and expressing their appreciation for his efforts in behalf of the American churches. Still more honors were extended. On December 20, 1921, Metaxakis called upon President Harding, this being the second time he had been received by a president of the United States. On the following day special services were held in his honor in the Church of St. John the Divine, with dignitaries of the Episcopalian, the Russian, the Armenian, and the Syrian churches in attendance.[20]

The strategic part that Metaxakis could play in ecclesiastical politics was apparent. As Ecumenical Patriarch he could play a key role in revoking the tome of 1908 that had transferred control of the churches in the United States to the Church of Greece and reassert the authority of the Patriarchate. Some felt that as Patriarch he could strengthen the position of Greece in dealing with the Allies and the Turks, for "this Venizelos in ecclesiastical garments" commanded respect in the Western world. He understood the American temperament better than the average Greek cleric and professed an appreciation for democratic institutions and practices.[21]

But the path of the new Ecumenical Patriarch was strewn with many obstacles. At first the royalist Greek government decided to ignore his election, and the Holy Synod of Greece prepared charges against him for illegal occupation of the Throne.[22] Disaffected members of the Synod of the Ecumenical Patriarchate were demanding his resignation.[23] In London he received a cablegram announcing that the ecclesiastical court in Athens had degraded him and decreed that "the monk Meletios" should be imprisoned for life in the monastery on the island of Zante. This was a high point in anarchy. For here was the governing council of a daughter church, the Holy Synod of Greece, illegally issuing orders to the head of the Mother Church. Needless to say, Metaxakis was enthroned with much ceremony on February 8, 1922.[24]

During his brief reign of under a year, Meletios did help to revoke the tome of 1908 and restored the jurisdiction over the churches in the United States to the Ecumenical Patriarchate. Meletios remained on the Ecumenical Throne until the Greek armies were defeated in Anatolia and the Turks returned to Constantinople. He retired to Mt. Athos and for a time considered transferring the Patriarchate to the "holy mountain," but he concluded that it would be better for the church to retain some semblance of authority in Constantinople.[25] The impact that Meletios had on the Greek churches in the United States was far-reaching. It was under his guidance that the first bishop was appointed, the tome of 1908 revoked, and the Archdiocese of North and South America established. His dismissal as Metropolitan of Athens and elevation to the Patriarchate also aggravated the factional strife.[26]

Perhaps Alexander's major move following the enthronement of Metaxakis was to call the second assembly of clergy and laymen into session in August 1922 to draft a constitution for the archdiocese and submit it to the Patriarchate, which accepted it without any changes. The constitution provided for bishops in New York City, Chicago, Boston, and San Francisco; the conditions under which the delegates for the special ecclesiastical assemblies were to be selected in each diocese; and the procedure to be used in electing bishops.[27]

Plans for an independent church organization also began to emerge. Alexander reasoned that political conditions in Greece rendered the leaders of that country unsuited for this supreme authority. For Greek churches everywhere were viewed not merely as places for the worship of God and the curing of the soul, but also as centers for the promotion of Hellenism. In view of the political turmoil and the restoration of the monarchy, the best interests of the Greek-Americans were endangered. They had to seek their own salvation and relinquish all thoughts of preserving the national unity of Greece. The formation of an independent church organization offered the surest and most practical way of accomplishing this. The more enthusiastic hoped that the new organization would be a success and serve as a model eventually to be adopted by the Greek nation for which they had endured so much.[28]

For a time it appeared as if this chaotic chapter in the history of the Greek church was coming to an end. In September 1922 the Greek government, the king, and the Holy Synod of Greece gave indications that they would recognize Meletios as the Patriarch as a means of healing the breach in Hellenism.[29] The Greeks had been beaten in Anatolia, the Turks were back in Constantinople, and the Patriarch had fled to Mt. Athos. This was a blow to Hellenism, and ranks had to be closed.[30] Greek-Americans appealed to President Harding and American clergymen to intervene and put an end to the Kemalist attacks on the Patriarchate.[31] All indications are that an accord was about to be reached. A telegram from Patriarch Meletios to the archdiocese in New York

City stated that Bishop Germanos soon would be recalled, and a comparable message dispatched by the Greek Foreign Ministry to the Greek legation in Washington told of the rapprochement. All signs pointed to a formal recognition of the revocation of the tome of 1908.[32]

It was in this spirit that Alexander issued the encyclical of December 4, 1922, which publicized the accord between the Ecumenical Patriarchate and the Church of Greece. Priests, members of the boards of trustees of the various communities, and all Christians in the United States were expected to abide by this good news. The *National Herald* lost little time in expressing relief over the reconciliation, acclaimed the single church jurisdiction as most welcome, pleaded with all peace-living Christians to accept it, and expected Bishop Germanos to lend his fullest cooperation.[33] But it appears that Germanos inquired instead of the Greek legation in Washington about what would happen to him and the priests who recognized his authority. The Greek Ministry of Foreign Affairs apprised the Synodical Exarch that the Holy Synod of Greece saw no need of dispatching a note to him. The priests in America were under the jurisdiction of the Ecumenical Patriarchate, which sent the message revoking the tome of 1908.[34]

Meanwhile, a new ecclesiastical storm was brewing. While Alexander was laying plans for the election and consecration of bishops in compliance with the constitution of 1922 and the accord of the same year, communities recognizing the spiritual leadership of Germanos began to lay plans for the organization of their own autocephalous church. Germanos was urged by Alexander and others to abide by the Holy Canons of the church and renounce this latest separatist movement. Clergymen hitherto recognizing the authority of the Synodical Exarch were asked to submit their certificates of ordination and other relevant credentials to the archdiocese, and the boards of directors of the various churches were advised to abide by the rules and submit all ecclesiastical questions to the archdiocese.[35]

Even before Germanos formally announced the termination of his exarchal role on January 22, 1923, the board of trustees of the Holy Trinity Church of Lowell, Massachusetts, the capital of Greek royalism in America, gave evidence that the autocephalous church movement would continue. The Lowell movement had as its goal, if we are to believe an astute observer, the formation of a church in the United

States comparable to the national churches of Greece, Russia, Cyprus, Rumania, and other countries. Sanction for the founding of such a church would have to come from the Patriarchate. Such a church would have to comprise a union of all Orthodox Christians in the United States, regardless of nationality. With national passions running high, the emergence of such a church was virtually impossible.[36]

Archbishop Alexander viewed this separatist movement with shame, for the humiliation of the Greeks in Asia Minor and the appeals to patriotism had failed to unite the Greek-Americans. While the Anglicans and other American church groups were offering prayers and urging their respective governments to protect the Patriarchate from the Kemalists, the leaders of the Lowell movement were seeking to sever those bonds that united all Greek Christians to the Eastern Orthodox Church.[37] These Lowell defectors were worse than the Bulgarians, for the latter had been motivated by their ancient animosity toward the Ecumenical Patriarchate and Hellenism. Degradation and excommunication were the likely ends for the perpetrators of this schism.[38]

The leaders of the Lowell movement insisted that they were merely emulating Alexander in seeking to establish an autocephalous church. But the supporters of Alexander saw little similarity between his actions in 1921 and those of the Lowell schism. The conference in 1921 between the then Bishop Alexander, Metaxakis, and the seventy-seven assembled priests, merely asked for a recognition of the church in the United States. The conference knew that it had no authority to bring an independent church into existence, and it did not attempt to do so.[39]

Formation of an autocephalous church was viewed as futile, suicidal, and contrary to the expressed wishes of the Ecumenical Patriarchate and the Church of Greece.[40] This latest development prompted Patriarch Meletios to state on December 30, 1922, that, according to the Holy Canons, an autocephalous church in the United States could be established only when all Orthodox Christians in the country came together regardless of race or nationality.[41] The sponsors of the Lowell movement faced more than their share of problems. Besides facing the bitter opposition of their canonical foes, they were left without a spiritual leader when Germanos returned to Greece. Matters became more involved after a court declared the Lowell schism illegal and deprived its leaders of the control of the independent community. The presidency was restored to a canonical adherent who fought his adversaries without mercy.[42]

This latest ecclesiastical storm, coupled with the insecure position of the Patriarchate in Constantinople, prompted the Ecumenical See to notify Archbishop Alexander that certain provisions in the archdiocesal constitution of 1922 had to be fulfilled without delay. These provided for the election of at least two bishops, one for the Diocese of Chicago, and the other for the Diocese of Boston. In response to these urgent instructions, the ecclesiastical assemblies of the two dioceses, consisting of the canonical clergymen and the elected representatives of the church communities, were summoned into session. The Ecumenical Patriarchate was pressing for the nomination of candidates and the selection of bishops in order to ensure the independence of the church in the United States, to place it beyond intervention by outside forces, and to prevent its constitution from becoming void owing to a failure to elect bishops.

The first ecclesiastical assembly convened in Chicago on April 18, 1923. Candidates for the bishopry of Chicago were nominated from a catalogue of qualified clergymen. Their names, in accordance with the constitution of the archdiocese, were forwarded to the Ecumenical Patriarchate, which was to select the Bishop of Chicago. The same procedure was used by the ecclesiastical assembly of Boston that convened a week after the Chicago meeting. In time the Patriarchate announced that Archmandrite Philaretos had been chosen Bishop of Chicago, and Archmandrite Joachim, Bishop of Boston.[43]

On June 21, 1923, Philaretos was consecrated as Bishop of Chicago in St. Constantine's Church, in a colorful three-hour ceremony replete with touches of the Old World. According to the traditions of the Greek church, at least two archbishops had to be present for a consecration. But in this instance two archbishops, Alexander of New York and the Metropolitan Theiateron Germanos of London, who came as Patriarchical Exarch, as well as Cappadocian bishops and priests of the Greek and Episcopalian churches, assisted in the ceremonies. The Syrians and Russians abstained because they did not wish to become involved in a Greek dispute. The enthronement of the Bishop of Boston came the following week.[44]

As expected, the consecration of the two bishops was characterized as an extension of the "Venizelist bishopric administrations" by those who refused to recognize Archbishop Alexander. Charges continued to be made that Metaxakis had been responsible for institutionalizing the split in the church communities of the United States.[45] This was a palpable exaggeration, for it implied a unity that never existed. The most superficial examination makes it clear that the church communities were torn with dissension long before Metaxakis and Alexander had appeared on the American scene.

The fault must be laid to a church system which had a tradition of becoming involved in the politics of the state. Metaxakis, whatever his limitations were, was an ecclesiastical leader of the first order who had a burning ambition to identify the Greek church with the Western world. It was his misfortune that he became Metropolitan of Athens and Ecumenical Patriarch during the darkest hours of modern Orthodox history. One can only speculate what his accomplishments would have been had he appeared at a more tranquil time. By the same token, it would be equally misleading to accuse the royalist priesthood and Bishop Germanos Troianos of helping to institutionalize the split. They were merely finding new reasons and applying new techniques in the expansion of old dissensions. If anything, the royalists never enjoyed the benefits of organization and the quality of community leadership that their adversaries did. They always ran a poor second, and when they appeared to be catching up in these areas, something always happened to set them back. Regardless of who was to blame, however, the ecclesiastical hierarchs failed to show the spiritual leadership and the Christian charity that they urged upon their parishioners. Perhaps this was expecting too much even from those who claimed they were preaching the word of God.

One of the major goals of the archdiocese was to support the Seminary of St. Athanasius that had been founded by Metaxakis in October 1921, in the hope of preparing young men for the priesthood in America. The need for such a seminary was felt by all who realized that priests trained for spiritual work in Greece were unprepared for parish work in the United States. Its director was Archmandrite Philaretos, who subsequently became the Bishop of Chicago. As expected, the seminary received little support. Nine of the twenty students applying for admission were accepted, and they were all foreign-born. Available information indicates that five were from the Peloponnesus, one from Crete, one from the Greek mainland, one from Asia Minor. The origins of the ninth student is unknown, for he dropped out shortly after the term began. The new class during the second and final year was even smaller than in the first. It consisted of six students who had completed an American grammar school and had at least the equivalent of one year of high-school study.[46]

This training program came to an inglorious ending with the close of the academic year 1922–23. The seminary suffered from the civil war that was tearing the churches asunder and the inability to raise the necessary funds. Many would-be benefactors had grown weary and refused to honor their promises, while others failed to contribute a solitary nickel. Persons who were in a position to make generous contributions had decided to disassociate themselves, at least for the time being, from all foreign efforts and proclaim their Americanism. Such undercurrents naturally hurt the fund-raising campaign. The several students of the defunct seminary were able to complete their studies in the Episcopalian Seminary in Nashotah, Wisconsin, where Bishop Philaretos obtained his D.D. degree. This was in keeping with the policy of the archdiocese of cultivating friendly relations with the Episcopalian Church and doing everything possible to raise the standards of the Greek clergy.[47]

Late in 1923 Chrysostomos, the new Metropolitan of Athens, sent a special message to the Greek-Americans stating that the Greek hierarchy had never lost its interest in the immigrants and their children. He repeated that those living abroad constituted a large and vital part of the spiritual and ethnic strength of Greece; when reunited they would make the greatest contributions to the mother country. The metropolitan then reiterated what the ecclesiastical and political leaders of Greece had said in the past: Greek-Americans could be good citizens of the United States without ceasing to be Greeks. Their absorption in the crucible of American life, fortified by their Hellenic spiritual strength, made them an invaluable part of the New World. America had much to contribute to their spiritual and economic growth. But they, and their compatriots in Greece, had to cast aside all bitterness and unite behind the leadership of the Greek Orthodox Church in order to preserve their ethnic culture. "No force other than the Orthodox Church will be able to save them in the ocean of the New World . . . Without their Church

294

the Greeks will be unable to find themselves in a genuine spiritual life." [48]

But the immediate fate of the Greek church in the United States was neither one of harmony nor one of statesmanlike leadership; it was a continuation of factional strife. This time the Greek-Americans were jolted by the unexpected appearance of the Metropolitan of Chaldea, Vasileos Komvopoulos. He arrived in this country, with a letter of introduction from John Metaxas, with the intention of filling the vacuum created by the departure of Bishop Germanos Troianos and heading the churches committed to the royalist faction. [49] Metropolitan Vasileos proved to be a formidable foe. Born in Sinope in 1887, he studied theology at Chalkis and completed his studies at the University of Athens in 1904, when he received his D.Th. degree. In 1916 Patriarch Germanos V appointed him Metropolitan of Methmis on Lesbos, but in 1922 Patriarch Meletios reassigned him to the preponderantly Venizelist metropolitanship of Chaldea. Vasileos the royalist refused this assignment and subsequently departed for the United States, without the permission of his superiors.

On September 13, 1923, the much-perplexed Archbishop Alexander, faced once more with a rival ecclesiast, appealed to the Patriarchate for instructions. Vasileos not only refused to return to Athens, as ordered, but he pursued an aggressive campaign of organizing and preaching. Then in the presence of the representatives of thirteen communities and many priests in Lowell, he proceeded to declare himself the "Autocephalous Head of the Greek Churches of the United States and Canada." On February 13, 1924, Archbishop Alexander telegraphed the Ecumenical Patriarchate on behalf of the archdiocese and the bishoprics of Chicago and Boston, asking the severest kind of punishment for Vasileos. On May 10, 1924, the Holy Synod in Constantinople responded by reducing Vasileos to "the ranks of the laity." [50] Instructions also were issued to publicize this decree in at least one Greek and one American newspaper in the United States. [51]

The effects of his degradation were surprising. Vasileos, instead of being shunned, became the martyred hero of a well-organized opposition to the administration of Archbishop Alexander. His vigorous leadership and fine qualities as a liturgist, combined with the growing resentment toward the presumptuous airs assumed by those siding with the archdiocese, aided his efforts immeasurably. Involved was an element of class feeling, as well as ecclesiastical and community politics. Those identified with the canonical churches as a rule were the up-and-coming members of the business community and the professional classes, who adopted a contemptuous attitude toward the "urban peasants" identified with the rival faction. This rekindled discord and the further institutionalizing of the split now prompted the Patriarchate to dispatch to this country the Metropolitan of Veria, Archbishop Chrysanthos, to study local conditions and to ease the friction that had multiplied following the degradation of Vasileos.[52] But nothing came of his efforts.

Most clergymen found the unlimited freedom of their parishioners a hindrance to the kind of spiritual power they exercised in the Old World. Bishop Joachim of Boston complained that any Greek-American, believer or unbeliever, educated or uneducated, could become a member of the community church, expound canons and dogmas, and make decisions regarding priests, bishops, calendars, and sundry other matters about which he was uninformed. He complained about the lack of an effective central authority to which the clergy could appeal.

The parishioners had their complaints, too. Sometimes they quarreled over the introduction of pews and the kind of music to accompany the services. Members of the second generation complained of their inability to understand the language of the liturgy. Others felt offended by the boorishness of the priest, the officiousness of a member of the board of trustees, the irreverent passing of collection trays during the services, the talking of children, and other distractions. These complaints, some justified and some exaggerated, were compounded by others of a more general character. The Greek Orthodox Church sponsored no missionary and little philanthropic work and found itself helpless in rendering the kind of leadership the various communities needed. No community was concerned with the problems and needs of another. One hundred and eighty communities were each governed by a different constitution, bemoaned the Bishop of Boston. Was this Christian brotherhood or anarchy?[53]

Even though the church services were conducted in the native language and even though the spirit of Hellenism was still felt, the Americanization of the Greek church was inevitable. The Greek-Americans enjoyed religious freedom, and an American spirit was beginning to take hold. The members of the second generation, and the more assimilable members of the first, began to loosen the ties with the church of their parents. To the more rebellious, the rancorous civil war within the church was reason for fleeing it. The parish priest had queer notions from the Old World, which inspired ridicule instead of respect. Something had to be done, as the farsighted understood; but no one seemed to know just what to do.[54]

The civil war in the church and the demoralized spirit that gripped the communities caused many to reconsider the wisdom of having revoked the tome of 1908 and designating Alexander as archbishop. Vasileos, a preacher and organizer of the first order, established himself in Chicago where he won over church communities that had previously refused to recognize him. After his success there, he left for New York. Formation of these independent church communities under Vasileos was a protest against the ecclesiastical regime of Alexander. Some feared that the rebellion would spread. For Vasileos, encouraged by the support he received, could easily carry out the program suggested by his league of lay and clergymen, follow the example of Alexander, and ordain three bishops for the independent churches. If this happened, then the reconciliation of the churches in the United States would become impossible.[55]

In Greece the belief persisted that the church question arose from the desire of the American churches to gain their independence. The truth of this cannot be denied, for it was the basic premise on which Alexander and his followers functioned. Greek-Americans wanted to be spared the political convulsions that so hampered Greece.[56] But "this is not true," replied one impassioned compatriot who was speaking for a diehard minority. "We love Greece and her problems are our problems." [57]

Agitation was mounting in some quarters for the Church of Greece to request the Ecumenical Patriarchate to restore its former jurisdiction over the American churches. This heightened speculation over whether the archdiocese of Archbishop Alexander was independent. Some believed that it was and that Alexander employed the Patriarchate as a means of fastening his hold over the communities. Those wishing to reassign the authority of the American churches used some specious arguments. They claimed that American Hellenism did not really believe that its churches were dependent on the Ecumenical Patriarchate—it had never ceased to recognize the Church of Greece as the highest ecclesiastical authority. It was wrong for the Church of Greece to resign its rights so that the Patriarchate might transfer them to a separate church. Furthermore, "the Church of America," if such an independent body existed, had no jurisdiction over those Greek churches that were unwilling to submit to its supervision.[58]

During 1928 the criticisms against Alexander and the Church of Greece became voluminous. Leaders of church and state were attacked for their indifferent or partisan attitudes. Disintegration and demoralization were rampant. The "four hiararchs"—Alexander and his three bishops—through monkish caprices and self-interest were accused of having become calloused to the complaints and needs of the people. Consuls, ministers and other government officials, and church representatives traveled, investigated, and reported; but the alienation of the Greek-Americans continued. Both clergymen and laymen were incapable of seeing how much they were contributing to dissension.[59]

Late in 1928 the ecclesiastical question, including the validity of the rites conducted by irregular clergymen in the United States, became the subject of discussion in the Chamber of Deputies of Greece. This had been triggered by a report from a group of Greek-Americans who were demanding action in resolving the church issue. Obviously, the Chamber of Deputies was the wrong body to appeal to. On a previous occasion a Greek foreign minister entrusted with exploring the church question in the United States had replied that this was something the Greek-Americans would have to settle among themselves. After all, this was an American issue, and the Greek government had no right to meddle in it.[60] Even if the Greek government could inject itself into this controversy without offending international diplomacy, it was unlikely to be of any help. A series of Greek governments had displayed an inability to set their own house in order, let alone come to the assistance of their feuding compatriots thousands of miles away.

Fortunately, events were working toward the solution of the ecclesiastical crisis. A sense of urgency was dawning on all, even on the political leaders of Greece who, as private individuals, were pleading in the name of Hellenic decency to resolve the embarrassing dilemma. The royalists, the divided liberals, all the foes of Venizelos, joined hands in making a final effort.[61]

The Ecumenical Patriarchate, determined to bring an end to the

298

church war, on April 9, 1930, designated Damaskinos, the Metropolitan of Corinth, as Patriarchal Exarch to the United States.[62] An able, respected, and well-educated administrator of high principles, who later served as head of the Greek state during the dark years of the Nazi occupation, Damaskinos responded to the challenge with earnestness.[63] Damaskinos, it developed, came both as an emissary of the Ecumenical Patriarchate and the Church of Greece. This was most encouraging. The head of the Greek church still was Papadopoulos Chrysostomos, who had urged the Greek-Americans to bury their differences and reunite for the preservation and perpetuation of the faith. Designation of Damaskinos as the Exarch of both the Patriarchate and the Church of Greece was ample proof that both jurisdictions had united in their determination to end the crisis.[64]

Damaskinos reached the United States on May 20, 1930; this was his second visit, the first being in 1928 when he arrived in quest of funds for the victims of the Corinth earthquake. Shortly after arriving he left for Washington, where he was received by President Hoover and other dignitaries who wished him well in his mission of peace. After these formalities, he returned to New York, where he busied himself charting his course of action. The reception Damaskinos received from the two dailies in New York was a warm one; both exhibited affection for the man and his mission. At the time *Atlantis* wrote: "We are encouraged to believe that the dream of all Hellenism in America will come true and that it will see days of peace, love, and harmony in all respects. This longed-for guidance will be provided by Metropolitan Damaskinos, not only because he is the personal representative of the highest Greek Orthodox authorities, but because this is such a serious mission and he has been given wide powers to solve the entire problem." [65] This kind of editorializing continued for about three weeks.

On May 31, 1930, Damaskinos sent his first encyclical letter to the priests and executive boards of the church communities. This included reproductions of three important documents. One was the Patriarchal letter designating him Exarch and instructing him to find a means of establishing peace. The second was a letter from the Patriarch to the Greek people of the United States, admonishing them: "As of this day you have endured the hardships of partisanship and disunion. Now try the goodliness of peace and you shall observe the difference between peace and partisanship, love and hate, brotherly affection and fratricidal strife." Finally, there was a letter from the Metropolitan of Athens, urging the people of the United States to give the Exarch the fullest possible cooperation.[66]

The reasons for the delay in the publication of these letters are understandable. Upon his arrival Damaskinos had to visit the President of the United States and the official representatives of the Greek government. Furthermore, he had been put to pressures of various kinds. He was bombarded with telegrams, telephone calls, and resolutions from communities, societies, and fraternal organizations, with recommendations for his consideration. Distraught representatives from many communities had rushed to his side in search of lasting peace.[67] It seems clear that spiritual and lay leaders had united in the common objective of peace: the Ecumenical Patriarchate; the Church of Greece; the rival political heads of Greece representing all shades of opinion; the two Greek dailies of New York that had fought each other so mercilessly; and the organized church communities in the United States. Union and harmony had become the goals.

The reaction of Archbishop Alexander was distressing, however. Without consulting the bishops of Chicago, Boston, and San Francisco, he first procrastinated and then rebelled. At about the time the Patriarchal Exarch issued his first encyclical letter, Alexander dispatched his own communication. He said in effect that the Damaskinos mission was a violation of the constitution of the archdiocese, that it sought to reinforce the position of the royalists, and that it stemmed from the basest motives. Some years later, the always well-informed Callimachos wrote that the charges of Alexander were groundless. The Exarch had not come to aid the opposition, and there was no violation of the constitution of the archdiocese; for without the permission of the Ecumenical Patriarchate, the autonomous church to which Alexander made reference could never have existed.[68]

It soon became apparent that the rebellious attitude of Alexander was nothing new. Well-founded reports indicate that his letters, telegrams, and communications to the Patriarchate had always revealed a contentious and insubordinate spirit. Visitors to the United States who were acquainted with the higher church authorities told of the painful impressions he had made on the Patriarchate and the Church of Greece. Alexander behaved as though the archdiocese was a part of his patrimonial estate. All Patriarchal efforts to remedy conditions in the

United States were viewed as unwarranted interference. He wanted a free rein as archbishop; he would not hesitate, if need be, to separate from the mother church and cast to the wind all rights of the Patriarchate to supervise the archdiocese.

Early in June 1930, after the majority had given indications of rallying to the support of Damaskinos, Alexander dispatched a second communication to the communites. In effect it said: "Do not pay any attention to the malicious reports of the newspapers. Ecclesiastical organization remains unchanged, unshaken. The communities remain loyal to the Archbishop. Always recognize him." This was a move of desperation on the part of a man who had been discredited and who personified disunion and disorder. His plea to the faithful to ignore the authority of Greece was a confession of defeat.

From here on events moved rapidly. Early in June the three bishops reached New York City to obtain firsthand accounts of the latest developments and perhaps to agree on some common course of action. One of the bishops, Joachim of Boston, left little doubt that he would support Damaskinos; the other two, Philaretos of Chicago and Kallistos of San Francisco, decided that, at least for the time being, they would cast their lot with the rebellious archbishop. Within time they, too, discovered that it was folly to resist and they abandoned him.

Even more unexpected was the dramatic rapprochement between the rival bishops Vasileos and Alexander. Just who was responsible for arranging the reconciliation between these hitherto bitter foes is unknown. In Callimachos' account, at a clandestine meeting the canonical Archbishop Alexander and his adversary of seven years—the excommunicated Vasileos—embraced and reached what appeared to be a mutually satisfactory understanding.[69] With the embrace of the two principal antagonists, henceforth all would be *meligala* (milk and honey). The mission of Damaskinos had come to an end; he should pack his belongings and leave the country.[70]

Two other measures were seen as required to round out this amnesty between Alexander and Vasileos. One was to dispatch some trusted person to Athens for the purpose of enlightening Venizelos that the pacification of American Hellenism was contingent upon Alexander and the three bishops, and upon the reinstatement of Vasileos. This would pacify the church communities and terminate the mission of Damaskinos. The second requirement was to neutralize the caustic editorial policies of the *National Herald*. Since *Atlantis* had restrained itself on the issue of the church and the exarch, it was also necessary for the *National Herald* to apply itself to the general peace.

The intermediary in the effort to soften the editorial policy of the *National Herald* was Charalambos Simopoulos, the Greek minister to the United States. Simopoulos probably accepted the role of arbitrator without being aware of what was involved. At any rate Simopoulos, Petros Tatanis, the founder and publisher of the *National Herald,* and Demetrios Callimachos, the editor-in-chief, met in the Pennsylvania Hotel in New York. Alexander and members of his entourage awaited the outcome of this meeting in an adjoining room.

Callimachos refused categorically to yield to any demand to soften his editorials and informed the minister of Greece that he was the innocent tool of a plot he did not understand. He reminded Simopoulos that Alexander had declared an insurrection against the Ecumenical Patriarchate and that he was unwilling to depart for Greece voluntarily and permit Hellenism to cure itself. All communities except one, he said, had accepted the mission of the Exarch. Alexander was aware of this, and he wanted a period of amnesty to reorganize his forces and create "a third situation." Callimachos gave no quarter to the proposal of Simopoulos; he fought to the bitter end in favor of the Damaskinos mission.[71]

Next, mass meetings were called to publicize the support of Damaskinos. On June 17, 1930, all organizations, societies, clubs, and church communities in the greater New York area were invited to a rally. Comparable gatherings occurred in other metropolitan areas, as community after community adopted resolutions vigorously upholding Damaskinos and opposing Alexander and his collaborators. People were speaking in public; they craved peace after years of civil war; they were turning their backs on the rival ecclesiastical empires. Texts of the resolutions and much correspondence from the readers found their way into the columns of the *National Herald*.[72] News of these rallies was relayed to the Ecumenical Patriarchate, which took the next step.

On June 19, 1930, Archbishop Alexander was dismissed without trial and stripped of all authority. Supporters of the deposed Alexander continued their relentless efforts to retain him, but without success. On August 13 Athenagoras, the Metropolitan of Corfu, was designated as the successor of Alexander on the recommendation of Damaskinos. When news of this reached the United States, one critic asked: "Who is this foreign man that is to govern our church? Who asked for him and who asked us whether we wanted him or not?" [73]

Now that Alexander had been deposed and a successor chosen, what was to happen to the deposed church administration and its former foes? Alexander, having been removed without a trial, was unlikely to depart from the United States voluntarily, and no one could force him to leave. Vasileos had established his own hierarchy in defiance of his superiors and had been excommunicated as a result, so he would hardly be naive enough to make a peaceful exit. The only one certain to leave was Damaskinos. If Athenagoras, the archbishop-elect, arrived with the deposed hierarchs still in the United States, the situation could have been worsened.[74]

The Ecumenical Patriarchate could well be placed in a humiliating situation. The populace might have been displeased with Alexander and the turmoil he created, but it was not exactly pleased with the tactics of the ecclesiastical authorities. Opposition to the Damaskinos mission was voiced by others besides *Atlantis* and the supporters of Alexander. *Hellinikos Astir* of Chicago published a sixteen-page issue filled with letters to the editor from all parts of the United States, protesting the methods of the Exarch. The editor himself accused the Patriarchate of trying to Romanize the Greek church and predicted that the people of the United States would not permit this. He warned that an autocratic church organization which made the Ecumenical Patriarchate supreme was likely to be resisted.[75]

But this and other protests turned out to be little more than rear-guard action from the vanquished. The mission of Damaskinos had succeeded. In a stately liturgical ceremony that will remain an historic event in the history of the Greek Orthodox Church in Chicago, Bishop Philaretos solemnly relinquished his authority to the Exarch, who officiated in the services held in St. Basil's Church. In his official pronouncement, Philaretos said that he had made some gains, despite numerous obstacles, during the years he served as Bishop of Chicago. In great detail he listed his accomplishments: he had helped to organize fourteen new communities, thirteen new churches, and catechetical schools that served ten thousand boys and girls; he had officiated in three hundred and twenty-five services, preached the word of God four hundred times, delivered seventy-five lectures, ordained six priests, and cultivated the friendship of "our brothers in Christ, the Episcopalians." Moreover, Philaretos said that he had aspired for the establishment of an orphanage, an old people's home, a free hospital, a cemetery, and a cathedral that would become the symbol of Hellenism in Chicago. But community strife made the attainment of these goals impossible.[76]

Apprehensions were still being felt over the delayed departure of the four hierarchs from the United States.[77] The delays, as it turned out, had been caused by technical difficulties in finding assignments for the rival archbishops and two of the bishops in Greece. Clergymen not belonging to the Church of Greece could not be assigned to the metropolitan districts of Greece, and in order to appoint them to such positions the rule had to be abrogated through legislative action. For the Church of Greece, in order to facilitate matters, had promised assignments for the churchmen to ease the transition for Athenagoras in the United States.[78]

Word finally came through the Greek legation in Washington that the legal hurdles had been overcome and that the hierarchs would be given their new assignments. Archbishop Alexander became the Metropolitan of Corfu and thus the successor of Athenagoras who was replacing him in the United States; Bishop Philaretos of Chicago became the Metropolitan of the islands of Syros and Tenos; Bishop Joachim of Boston became the Metropolitan of Phokidos; and the reinstated Bishop Vasileos became the Metropolitan of Drammas and Philipon. One of the three bishops serving under Archbishop Alexander, Kallistos of San Francisco, remained in the United States.[79]

The Ecumenical Patriarchate, the Church of Greece, and the Greek government had done all they could to terminate the dissension. The new ecclesiastical administration had to arise from among the people in the United States and be responsive to their needs. Past experience had made it clear that decisions reached without community representation would create new tensions.[80] The task facing the new archbishop was formidable; he could not remove the bitter results of a decade of agitation by the mere wave of a hand. Individual communities had to place their own affairs in order and solve those local problems that did not require the sanction of the archbishop. In the larger metropolitan areas, boundaries of the church communities had to be defined more clearly and smaller parishes had to merge with the larger ones.[81] Athenagoras also made it clear that the patriotic sentiments of the Greeks in the United States had to be revitalized if the religion and language of contemporary Hellenism were to survive.[82]

Athenagoras visited community after community, studying local conditions, conferring with local leaders, and receiving their recommendations. In turn he apprised them of the preliminary work that was being accomplished elsewhere.[83] Wherever he went, he made it plain that the administrative system of the Greek Orthodox Church was going to be imposed and that he was not going to retreat from it a single inch. Unlike the Protestant churches in which the clergy withdrew from administrative functions and the Catholic churches in which the laymen withdrew, the Greek Orthodox Church employed the mixed system of cooperation between clergy and laymen.[84]

Reorganization required a degree of cooperation that was not easy to obtain. The parish viewed the entire problem from its own standpoint and found it difficult to accept any broader plan. Having worked singly and against each other for many years, they feared that submerging their local interests would cause harm.[85] In a democratic country such as the United States, and among such a highly individualistic people as the Greeks, the principle of lay representation had considerable appeal. This became part of the ecclesiastical administration of the first archbishop. Obviously, some believed that it was the duty of the clergy to assume the most authority. But it was unlikely that the church communities would tolerate conditions which enabled the clergy to assume control of church and school properties and lay down rules of administration.[86]

One of the first issues to be tackled by the Fourth Conference of Laymen and Clergy that assembled on November 14, 1931, in New York City was the Greek-language school. Meeting amidst the worst depression in history, the conference reaffirmed the principle that the Greek church was "the natural mother and protector of the Greek people abroad," and it appraised the work of the schools in the past. The schools had lacked the necessary personnel, finances, planning, and the most elementary forms of administration and supervision. They had remained open only because of dedicated individuals who struggled hard and bitterly, with little compensation and recognition for their efforts. This would have to be changed. The ultimate goal of the schools was to blend Greek and American ideals with a rich Orthodox spiritual life. But to achieve it, the Greek school had to be an original and special organization, not a carbon copy of the school in Greece.

Besides seeking to reorganize and revitalize the church schools, Archbishop Athenagoras sought to extend and solidify the control of the archdiocese. The new bishops were to be appointed by him, without the vote and consent of the church communities. Such a policy was destined to lead to trouble, unless there was a clearer understanding between the archdiocese and the local communities. The authority imposed by Athenagoras varied from the older and more decentralized ecclesiastical administration which had divided the country into the dioceses of New York, Boston, Chicago, and San Francisco. For all practical purposes, the administration of Alexander had had the equivalent of its own Holy Synod, with the archbishop functioning as a president with no jurisdiction over the bishops.

Under Athenagoras the dioceses were eliminated, and the archdiocese assumed jurisdiction over all the churches of North and South America. Hereafter all bishops were auxiliary bishops who assisted the archbishop in the discharge of his duties. These were his choices, not those of the communities; the bishops had neither dioceses nor rights of administration. The archbishop, in turn, was responsible to the highest church authorities. The members of the faith had the right to carry their grievances to the Ecumenical Patriarchate, while under the previous administration the archbishop and bishops constituted an independent and self-governing body with whose administration even the highest ecclesiastical authorities could not interfere.

In community church matters there were no changes of any consequence, except for the clergy. The local administration, the election of officers, and financial affairs were left in the hands of the constituent bodies. But in matters spiritual and ecclesiastical, such as the appointment and discharge of priests, jurisdiction belonged exclusively to the ecclesiastical administration. Supporters of the new regime tried to make it clear that the powers of the archbishop were confined exclusively to religious matters and, as some were charging, did not infringe upon the rights of the local communities.[87] Once the new constitution of the archdiocese was adopted, the hope was that the factions which had converted the churches into political battlefields would cease their fighting, and that the fundamental law worked out by the assembly of clergy and laymen would meet the special needs of the people. The new constitution was particularly welcomed by those who believed in vesting more authority in the clergy.[88]

Problems other than those of ecclesiastical administration plagued the communities. The depression had eaten heavily into the financial organism of most communities and debts were accumulating. The officers of these churches were in despair; priests feared losing their posts; and the people had doubts about the fate of their religion. The simplest way out was to close the churches that were weak financially and to concentrate on the stronger ones.[89]

Events soon demonstrated that the reorganization of the ecclesiastical administration involved much more than adopting a new constitution, having it approved by the Ecumenical Patriarchate, and accepted by the various communities. New grievances soon took the place of the old ones. Athenagoras was accused of ignoring the Mixed Board of Trustees of the archdiocese, denying it the right to take over property, records, finances, and other obligations. His communications to the communities and the priests, and his releases to the press, were described as inaccurate and as dealing with matters that should have been decided by the board. The archbishop, despite his good intentions, suffered from a lack of information and an inadequate knowledge of the laws, customs, and general conditions of the country. The heavy indebtedness of the archdiocese, the various legal suits against it—the largest being that of former Bishop Philaretos for $19,000—the lack of a systematic system of accounting, the depression, all multiplied the woes of the new administration.

Critics insisted that the Archdiocese of North and South America, a corporation, was governed neither in conformity with the laws of the state of New York nor with those of its own constitution, but in a fashion dictated by the archbishop with the assistance of private counselors. If the various communities desired a centralized administration, the existing organization had to be dissolved and a new one created in its place. Or else the archdiocese, according to the laws of the state, had to be governed by a responsible board which bore full responsibility for whatever the archbishop, as president, did.[90]

The opposition to Athenagoras manifested itself in several forms. At least one member of the Mixed Board of Trustees resigned and another threatened to follow suit. In Detroit anti-Athenagoras riots broke out;

for a time the movement of a Reverend Kontogeorge of Lowell, to establish a new church administration, seemed to be gaining ground.[91] The archbishop was criticized for a lack of administrative ability, for disregarding the appointment and transference of priests, succumbing to a clique of flatterers who directed the performance "from the wings," and imperiling the future of Hellenism in the United States. Some strongly suggested that the learned and affable prelate take the road back to his native land.[92]

In the meantime, the depression continued to take its toll. In the smaller cities the lack of members and funds forced churches to close their doors. Even in the large cities the difficulties were pressing.[93] A circular letter by Bishop Kallistos of Chicago indicated that not one of the churches in his district had been able to meet its operating expenses during the fiscal year 1932–33. Such deficits made it impossible for the churches to continue the services of the past years. All parishioners were obligated to share in the responsibilities by becoming members and paying their dues regularly. Hereafter those who failed to do so within two months would be denied the services of the church, except that of communion. The ecclesiastical authorities regretted having to take such a stern stand, but they felt that it was the only way in which the churches would be alleviated of their economic distress.[94]

The circular letter encountered the fire of critics who charged that the bishop was primarily concerned with protecting himself, his subordinates, and the priests under the pretense of saving the churches and the schools. In all good faith, they asked, what had the Greek church and the Greek priests ever done for the victims of the depression to make such calloused demands on the parishioners? Most other denominations and social organizations had established centers for the care of the poor, except "the glorious Orthodoxy which slept under the mandrake" and satisfied itself with a few appeals and pompous pretensions. And what was one to say when informed that the priests had been neglecting their calling to become real-estate dealers and stock-market manipulators?[95]

During the next conference of laymen and clergy in 1933, the decentralization of the ecclesiastical administration became the principal topic of discussion. Community leaders in various areas had grown restless as a result of the power the archbishop had arrogated to himself. The concentration of power in one individual or a restricted group could not serve the needs of the governed groups. There was a need for a division of the duties and obligations of the clergymen and laymen, so that no one could become the vassal or dictator of the other. If the clergy were viewed with suspicion, it was largely owing to a lack of understanding of the crucial issues of the day, as well as to a lack of tact. Still these clergymen in some instances had to deal with boards of directors who were downright incompetent.[96]

This, then, was the situation by the mid-thirties: the civil war of the twenties had come to an end; a new leadership, energetic and determined to place greater authority in the archdiocese and the parish priests, had emerged. But this leadership was hampered by the toll that had been taken by more than a decade of strife, the worst economic depression in history, and a church orientation that was more Greek than American. The early thirties also witnessed the beginning of a new chapter in church history—that of a steady decrease in the influence of the layman in community affairs and an increase in that of the clergy. The church, in addition, was girding itself for a more aggressive role and making efforts to appeal to the disaffected second generation.

15

THE SECOND GENERATION

THE members of the second generation of Greeks in America did not find themselves in an easy position. Born into families with strong paternal and national ties, and thrust into a society that had as one of its objectives the obliteration of those vestiges of foreignism that proud parents wished to perpetuate, they faced a bewildering and frustrating experience. This was especially true for those who reached maturity between the First and Second World Wars.

These youths lived amid two societies engaged in a tug-of-war. One world was that of their perplexed and admonishing parents, the priests and Greek schoolteachers who as a rule knew more about the Old World than the New, and those impassioned compatriots who bemoaned and bewailed the eventual extinction of their Hellenic identity. The other world was that of the public school and the non-Greek friends and institutions with which they came into daily contact. Nor should one overlook those vocal and ubiquitous individuals and groups that wished to mold all foreigners in their own image of Americanism.

For the most part, the members of the second generation wanted to be accepted by the society into which they were born, rather than become torchbearers in preserving the national identity of their parents. For a time it appeared as though an unbridgeable chasm separated the older generation from the younger, but the trend of events demonstrated that the chasm could be bridged. In appreciating the problems of second-generation Greek-Americans, as well as those of their parents, one must keep in mind the prevalence of strong family ties, the Greek language, the Greek school the child was expected to attend, and the role of and the reaction to the Greek Orthodox Church.

All of these factors significantly shaped the attitude and behavior of the child born of immigrant parents.[1]

Family ties in a Greek family, as we have seen, were quite close. Unquestioned authority was vested in the father who, in keeping with the ancestral tradition, made the laws and administered them. Decisions frequently were made without consulting his wife, who was expected to uphold and defend them. The major concern of the closely regulated family was to preserve the language, faith, and traditions. And deviation from this norm could create a crisis.[2] As long as the children were young and manageable, the stern parental will prevailed. The eldest son, in theory the crown prince of the family, was expected to be at his father's side and to see that his commands were respected. He was to serve as the counselor and guide of his younger brothers and sisters and to make sure they behaved as dutiful children were expected to behave. At least this was the ideal.

Besides being raised in strict obedience, the children had specific chores to perform. Every girl was expected to become an expert in housekeeping; she had to help with the housework, the family wash, the shopping, and the cooking. The boys also had duties outlined for them. There were physical labors to be performed around the house, parents to accompany to the store whenever they needed interpreters or assistance, and errands to run. Moreover, there were the studies in Greek. From the public school the children went home, then to the late afternoon and early evening school, and home again for supper and studies. Leisure time in most families was at a minimum.

The early years in the lives of children born of immigrant parents were hardly joyous ones, for they were exposed to the realities of life at a tender age. They heard parents and their friends tell of their hardships in Greece and the early years in the United States, the unemployment, discrimination, and difficulties with the language. They were told in clear and often blunt language that their principal purpose in life was not to have fun, but to work, take advantage of the opportunities denied their parents, assume responsibilities, make a success of themselves, see their sisters happily married, and provide for their parents in old age. All children did not abide by this regimen, but it was the kind of rhetoric to which almost all were exposed.

The first contacts of the children usually were with peers of identical background, as were the associations of their parents and friends. This is understandable, for they spoke a common language, understood each other's problems, and could be counted upon for sympathy and advice. Some parents made a point of seeing to it that their children associated with children of Greek backgrounds. This was part of the family and cultural discipline, as well as a matter of convenience. In fact, some children felt uncomfortable and insecure in the company of people of non-Greek backgrounds.

This cultural isolation, self-imposed in numerous instances, broke down as the children advanced in the elementary and high-school grades. This is when they began to draw comparisons, complain about having to attend the Greek school and the Greek church, and wonder about the observance of customs and traditions that were so different from those of their classmates. This was a natural reaction for children who were thrown into contact with those reared in other faiths, and who saw other children playing after school instead of performing household chores and attending a second school. This made many skeptical and rebellious. The secondary years of schooling compounded the problems of many parents who worried about their children and the non-Greek path they might travel. The loss of Hellenic identity became a widespread fear, for in the high-school years the young began to assert their independence, crave the company of people of other backgrounds, attend social functions with members of the opposite sex, and downgrade the cultural milieu of their parents.

Few parents in the earlier years thought of encouraging children to bring their friends of non-Greek origin to their homes. Entertainment in the home was rare in Greece, except on the most religious and festive occasions, and it was to remain so in the United States, at least until the Americanization process began to take hold. But there is also another explanation for this. It was a rare thing for parents to make provisions for their children's amusement or recreation; there were more important things to do, and there were enough years ahead for such purposes. The father could always go to the coffeehouse when he had the time, but the children when free were left to play in the streets, the neighborhood playground, or perhaps attend a movie.[3]

Parents were of two kinds. Some realized that they were living in the United States and that their children would have to grow up as Americans; they would satisfy themselves with what few vestiges of Hellenism they could retain. Others insisted on attempting to rear their American-born children as though they were Greeks. Parents who chose the former course, and they were in the majority, had much the easier time. They wanted their children to retain membership in the Greek Orthodox Church and maintain a Greek name and some knowledge of the Greek language; however, in all other respects they were willing that their children be American. The other group of parents proved unyielding, and in extreme cases they chose to return to Greece rather than compromise their ideals of Hellenism.

The "unreconstructed" parent, usually found in cities with large Greek colonies, often attempted to force Old World mores on his children. To him Greek customs regulating courtship and marriage were preferable to the American, and he often meant to have his way. Yielding to American custom, he believed, was yielding to immoral behavior. Such a parent did not understand that there were good and appropriate American standards that parents could seek to uphold. Failure to understand this sometimes led to tragedy.[4]

One of the first major problems arose from dating among teenagers. This, of course, was unknown to most parents who as villagers lived under a closely regulated social code. In the Greek village, when one sought the company of a member of the opposite sex, this conjured up thoughts either of marriage or of loose morals. This pattern of thinking was carried to the United States, and in an era of uncertainty and anxiety it could be carried to extremes. Seeing a daughter with a boy could easily arouse suspicions, even if the boy was of Greek background. Seeing an offspring in the company of one of non-Greek background could be a heartbreaking experience. It was by no means uncommon for a friend of the family to report seeing a son or daughter in the company of a member of the opposite sex. In a tightly knit community such news spread rapidly, and often it was edited as it passed from person to person until it was grossly distorted. It could become gossip in the coffeehouse, the grocery store, the market place, and after church. Some of the more venturesome males scarcely realized the notoriety they acquired as a result of having been seen emerging from a theater crowd or strolling along the street with a girl.[5]

The average father left no stone unturned in stressing the advantages of having a son marry a girl of his ethnic and religious background. He spoke of Greek virtue and morality in a society that seemed to have lost all sense of propriety. He emphasized the advantages of having a wife of the same faith, capable of conversing in the native tongue of the parents, and discharging her true duties to the family. He warned of the dangers of mixed marriage, the loss of his Hellenic identity, the prospects of marrying a domineering woman who would squander his money, associate with other men, and eventually take him into a divorce court. "If you want to eat from the same bill-of-fare your mother prepares," warned one coffeehouse philosopher, "marry a Greek girl and you have nothing to worry about. If you want to open tin cans and eat out of them for the rest of your life, then marry someone else." [6] Marriage outside the group could lead to a form of social ostracism on the part of friends and neighbors, especially in the larger communities. A son who married outside the group could become an outcast and be stigmatized as an ungrateful errant who was setting a bad example for others. The predicament of a daughter who deviated from the matrimonial norm was viewed as something even more tragic. But ostracism, criticism, and exhortation were unable to stem the tide of mixed marriages. Nationalistic preferences were hardly a deterrent to the romantic fancies of the second generation. [7]

The position of the second-generation girl was not an enviable one, especially if she was the first child and born into a family with little money and much respect for tradition. The girl had always been a source of worry to parents in Greece, and she continued to be so in the United States. Her plight was aggravated by the greater degree of subservience to which she was subjected. [8] As a rule, the United States opened up a matrimonial frontier. The demand for wives of Greek background was great in the earlier years when the ratio of females to males was small. The opportunities were so abundant that anyone unable to acquire a husband under such conditions was deemed as being deficient. There were an increasing number of comfortably established middle-aged men to select from, as well as a growing number of males born of Greek parents in the United States. "We often wonder," said one observer, "if the young girls of Hellenic descent realize how much better off they are than are girls of other nationalities. Do they understand and appreciate their increased opportunities for a fine marriage. A girl can become a 'Mrs.' through an 'arranged' marriage or through marriage with the man of her own choice. Few American girls have such an alternative." This offered advantages even to shy or unattractive girls and explains why in the earlier years it was rare to find a spinster in Greek families.[9]

The arranged marriage became known to some girls of the second generation. When women of Greek birth or parentage were scarce and commanded a premium, the parents of an eligible girl found themselves in a very favorable bargaining position; for to them marriage was a serious lifetime partnership that was not contingent upon initial romance. The theory behind the arranged marriage was based on the belief that the parents knew best. They knew poverty firsthand and they craved economic security, which to them was synonymous with happiness, for their children. They made diligent efforts to find a groom with whom their daughter would neither starve nor suffer and welcomed the well-established man who sought her hand. A daughter might be promised comforts hitherto unknown, financial security and perhaps wealth, plus a certain amount of social prestige. It sometimes has been charged that parents arranged such marriages without consulting their daughters; but it is difficult to believe that much could have been accomplished without some degree of assent on the part of the girl.

There does not appear to have been any fixed rules on how such marriages were arranged, although a pattern of sorts did emerge. Sometimes a potential groom of Old World vintage would ask a third party to approach the parents and ask for the hand of the girl. In most cases the initiative was assumed by the men, either the potential bridegroom or the anxious father, which as a rule meant that a third party became convenient if not indispensable. This intermediary could have been a relative, a *koumparos,* or a close friend of the would-be bride or groom. After a sufficient amount of exploratory work had been done, arrangements would be made for the prospective mates to meet; this could be a social function, a family gathering, or even a specially devised meeting. Sometimes the meeting was arranged to the complete innocence of the potential bride and groom; sometimes it was known to both and sometimes only to one. After a sufficient amount of confidence had been gained by one or both sides, a direct inquiry would be made into the prospects for marriage.

Once a matrimonial understanding had been reached, the bride lived through a sort of Cinderella existence. She was showered with gifts, clothing, and personal accessories, and made her appearance at social functions with her future husband. Unlike the custom in Greece, the bulk of the expense was shouldered by the groom-elect, who often made a conspicuous display of his capacity to spend; in many instances he could afford it, but often it was made possible only through borrowing from friends, relatives, and business associates. The expenses of the parents were at an absolute minimum and a far cry from what they might have been in Greece. Often the go-between the groom and the parents was rewarded in one way or another. This was especially true when he had been prodded by the bridegroom to find him a wife.

Occasionally a girl was high-spirited enough to refuse to follow silently the decisions or advice of her parents. Urged on by the idea that she had to shape her own future, one such girl made this protest:

I do not wish by word or action to bring you, my parents, unhappiness or disappointment. But I do believe that I have the right to defend myself. Never shall I sell myself for money, even if by doing so I should become a princess. I prefer to marry a young man with whom I have something in common, and to work side by side with him for the establishment of economic security.

Life with a rich old man is for a lazy woman who has no initiative or ideals and who has no interest in creating something through effort and sacrifice. She is a mere social parasite. I am not of that type and you must wait until I meet someone of my own choice who has a better recommendation than mere money. Age is not so very important because, even if he is ten or twelve years older than I, he is still young. The most important thing is understanding and mutual ideals; when these exist age is of secondary importance. However, when these are lacking, age is an all-important factor.[10]

The proponents of the arranged marriage, normally older and respecters of tradition, minimized the importance of the social relationship that the younger people prized. The tall handsome boy who was a good dancer but lacked the worldly experience of the older husband was not a prize catch. A happy marriage was based not on a good dancing partner or on attending social functions, but on the peace and contentment begotten by economic security. The older husband would not demand that his wife go to work in order to help defray the family expenses, as was likely to be the case with the younger husband. The middle-aged husband possessed maturity and was better prepared to make the necessary sacrifices.

The arranged marriage made less headway among the second-generation males. In fact the boy was more likely to despise and ridicule it as something barbarous and uncivilized. Often he would tease a youthful friend with a query about whether his parents had "lined up" some girl from the Old Country for him. The resistance and rebelliousness of the boy meant that arranged marriage was less common among the members of his sex.[11] By the same token the male was more likely to marry outside his group than the female, especially in the earlier years. The aggressive independence of the youth contributed to this; so did the fact that he was more likely to go to college, where romances frequently blossomed into marriages. The college-going boy tended likely to view arranged marriages as the product of a backward society. The fact that he wanted to divest himself of all traces of foreignism probably was another reason for wanting to marry outside the group. Although the better-adjusted male was likely to enter into a mixed marriage, there is no conclusive evidence that he always did so. However, far more of the successful men married outside the group than parents and concerned compatriots desired. It was by no means uncommon for such a person to be reminded that he should have married a girl of his own background.[12]

The church became the target of many second-generation critics. It was called to account for the meaninglessness of its ritual, the frequent disorders that were associated with it, the unsympathetic priest who spoke openly in coarse and brusque tones about members of the second generation, the absence of spiritual integrity, and all the other complaints that one hears leveled at most religious denominations.[13] The differences between the older and younger generations over the church were real and protracted. Neither group seemed capable of understanding the other. The older generation had taken the church for granted and expected the younger generation to follow in blind obedience. But being born in Greece, where the Orthodox Church held complete sway over the religious beliefs of the people, was not like being born in the United States, where a multiplicity of faiths meant a multiplicity of beliefs. Many of the American-born youth, with amazing perceptiveness and brutal frankness, made no secret of their sentiments.

American-born youth who saw good Christian acquaintances attend churches of other denominations saw no reason why they should be barred from doing likewise. America was a free country and the free-dom to attend or not attend a church was the prerogative of all. They also rebelled against the priest who kept haranguing the parish with the admonition that the only way of preserving Hellenism in America was by supporting the Greek church. What American-born youth cared to preserve Hellenism in America? In fact, the more rebellious could be heard to shout, "The sooner it is stamped out, the better."

A frequent complaint was that the church services were meaningless. The young were unable to understand the numerous blessings and chantings uttered in strange and monotonous tones. To some youths the church was a building where their parents and other older people gathered on Sundays to extend their greetings and exchange gossip. To them religion was an external matter, not the product of a deep inner conviction. The critical felt that the average Greek took his religion in the same routine fashion that he took his egg-lemon soup on Sunday. An inquisitive American-born youth felt that he had to be shown why he should attend the Greek church. Merely saying that this was the proper thing for him to do was insufficient cause.

How can the older generation ask the Americanized Greek youth to support a Church that has so much scandal attached to it, that is so badly mismanaged, that has lost the Christian spirit, and only knows the form and ritual, and that offers nothing spiritually satisfying to youth? How can the Greek Church in America survive when it is common knowledge that it is the football of ecclesiastical politics? How can the Greek Church win Greek-American youth when it offers no cultural guidance, no spiritual warmth and no inspirational leadership?

The Greek Church does not have the backing of Greek-American youth. Youth is indifferent to it. And without youth behind it, the Church is doomed. Immigration has practically stopped, and when the present older generation passes out of the picture, the Church will find itself with very little support in this country. Unless the church wins the younger genera-tion, the church will be dead within twenty years. . . .

The Greek Church is dying along with other Christian Churches. The entire church organization of the Christian religion is dying because it has ceased to preach the word of Jesus and instead is preaching the word of the man who built the church buildings.[14]

Still others, while by no means as caustic in their criticisms, began to turn their backs on things Greek. They started in tentative ways. They would compare the grandeur of the public schools they attended during the day with the Greek community scene they returned to after school.

Today, hindsight would prompt the more mature and appreciative adults to be grateful to their parents for their well-meaning efforts to teach them Greek. But in those hectic and bewildering days, the average youth was no more capable of comprehending what was happening than were the members of the older generation who were trying to guide them. The young heard expressions such as "foreigners" and "Americans," the former being used in a disdainful manner. Often they watched various factions quarreling and wrangling over community problems and "long-distance political issues." Such conditions and comparisons would cause a member of the second generation to conclude that his father's nationality was not of the same fiber as those of his school or playmates. He too, perhaps, would view his parents as foreigners. He might believe that fortune had counted his people among the less competent and that it would be to his advantage to conceal these facts as much as he could.[15]

Nor was this all. In school the youth might have heard a teacher refer to the immigrants from eastern and southern Europe as being cast of a less desirable mold than those from western and northern Europe. This, of course, included his parents. Or he might have been reprimanded by some teacher for coming to school with garlic on his breath or be reminded of the good manners he had to acquire to gain the respect of his classmates. In fact, one schoolteacher, the daughter of an Irish detective, threatened to set aside a special row for all onion and garlic eaters in her class. It was time, she felt, that the pupils of her class were protected from the less considerate ones. And, of course, there was always the teasing and name calling from classmates.

Some recall the embarrassing moments spent as interpreters for their parents. The parent, born in a society where haggling over prices was common, carried these practices with him to the United States. Hence a mother shopping in a department store, after learning the price of a particular article, would command the daughter to ask the clerk whether she could have the article at a lower price. Sometimes the daughter would comply, but on other occasions she was too embarrassed to do so. At times words would be exchanged between the two. Or a son could accompany the father to a neighborhood shoestore operated by an immigrant of another religious faith. Being told that the price of a pair of shoes was $3.50, the father would advise the son to work it down to $3.00. In Greek he woud say, "Next week, I'll bring my family for shoes, but I don't have too much money now," hoping that the prospects of additional business would lower the price. (Normally, a sale for $3.25 could be negotiated.) A parent speaking Greek in the presence of a non-Greek also was a source of embarrassment. To a European or a widely traveled American, hearing a foreign language was a common occurrence. But to youth born of foreign parents this could be an awkward experience, for it would attach to him the stigma of being a foreigner in an era when one boasted of his Americanism.

The pressure put on the second generation by a society that was intolerant of the foreigner took its toll in the form of strained relations between the older and the younger people. The young saw their problems as being those of American youth, and they were anxious to make their way in American society and be accepted by their classmates and associates. Their problems, they felt, were not the problems parents conceived them to be: maintaining the Greek language, the Greek church, and the spirit of Hellenism. The two generations often were poles apart and they often clashed.[16]

Members of the older generation continually raised the question of what was going to happen to children born in the United States. They were reconciling themselves slowly to the idea that they would become good American citizens. But would they also renounce the Greek language, history, and traditions? This issue was raised again and again by priests, parents, patriotic individuals, and even by members of AHEPA who had been actively engaged in Americanizing the first generation. Feeling that their society was well on the way to achieving its primary objective, these concerned Ahepans felt that the time had come to embark on the next phase of their program. This was to instill in the second generation a vestige of understanding and appreciating of the basic elements of Hellenism. In short, the time had come for the two wings of the AHEPA program to work together.[17]

The first important effort to organize the second generation resulted in the formation of the Sons of Pericles on January 30, 1926, in Manchester, New Hampshire. The constitution and by-laws of the Sons of Pericles, which quickly was recognized as the junior order of AHEPA, was comparable to that of the average junior fraternal order, except for one phrase in the preamble which included, "to stimulate the love and admiration of Hellenic culture, traditions, and ideals." Membership was open to "Any male person of Hellenic descent from either parent who has passed his fifteenth year of age, and has not yet completed his twenty-first year." [18] The Sons of Pericles was launched with a good deal of fanfare, but the degree of its appeal is rather obscure. In some communities with large colonies there always were large numbers of youths to draw from, but in others the reverse was the case. It seems that most of the prodding to organize came from the top. Some youths were anxious to join, but far too many were indifferent or disinterested. After they went through the motions of joining the organization, they lost all interest in it.

In some areas, periodic conflicts flared up between the senior and junior members. Sometimes members of the junior order were a bit bemused and outspoken in their remarks about the activities and the English of the members of the senior order; they mimicked and ridiculed their elders over the nature of their social functions, arguments, and long drawn-out meetings. The senior members, in turn, felt that the juniors were ungrateful, undeserving, and even incapable. They resented being criticized for their faulty knowledge of English and the ability to cope with the problems they faced on first arriving in this country. In some cases uncomplimentary epithets were exchanged liberally.

It appears that the Sons of Pericles fell far short of the goals that its illustrious name implied. Often they were denounced as modern-day Janissaries. At best the Sons served as a convenient meeting place for youths of identical backgrounds, and in some communities the best youths joined. However, the Sons failed to serve as a feeder organization to the degree that the senior order had desired. Sometimes the graduates of the junior order became active members in the senior lodge, but most of the time they did not. After all, the youth born in the United States had no passionate feelings about Hellenism. Their problems were the problems of a different age and place. If there was an organization they wished to join, there were many others to choose from, such as the DeMolay. They carried more prestige and were free of the kind of rancor and discord that persisted in the Greek organizations.

One of the most significant steps taken in attempting to heal the breach between the older and younger generations came with the organization of a theological school. Clerical and lay authorities were agreed that the spiritual needs of the people could be better served by training young men born in the United States for the Greek Orthodox priesthood. This was expected to diminish the reliance of the Greek-American communities on the Patriarchal Seminary in Chalkis and the theological school of the University of Athens—most, if not all, priests serving in the American communities had been trained in these institutions. In 1937 Athenagoras, the Archbishop of North and South America, concluded that the time was ripe for the founding of such a school. Appeals naturally were made to the Greek-American public, which responded with its customary generosity, and the columns of the *National Herald* were used with considerable effectiveness. A thirty-seven-acre estate was purchased in Pomfret Center, Connecticut, and a seminary established. Classes began on October 3, 1937, with three instructors and fourteen students recruited from among the members of the second generation born in the United States.[19]

The rise of the second generation to professional, commercial, and intellectual prominence in the United States is part of the American success story. Virtually all were of humble origin, without wealth and friends, and climbed to influential places through sheer drive and dedication. The will to succeed had been deeply ingrained in them at a very early age. The admonition to "be someone better than I am" was heard time and again. Work, we have seen, was something to be sought after. Few parents permitted their children to forget that one of the requisites in life was to learn how to assume responsibility at an early age. An unoccupied and unemployed son in his early teens could be made to feel that he was committing an offense against his family, God, and society by not having something gainful or constructive to do.

During high school, selling newspapers, clerking in a store, selling vegetables, shining shoes, waiting on tables, and bussing dishes were common pursuits. Going out for football was unusual, especially in the earlier days, for the patriarchal father considered it a waste of time. "Will it give you anything to eat, will you get paid for it?" were questions frequently asked by the adamant parent. Shining shoes was a common weekend occupation for high-school boys in the larger cities. By the time the American-born youths were old enough to work, the Greek shoeshine proprietors might not have been as numerous as they once were, but they were conspicuous; and they normally had jobs for the sons of relatives, inlaws, or acquaintances. When jobs were scarce, the proprietor might show preference for the son of a compatriot originating from the same village.

The hours of work were long, twelve to fifteen hours, for each of the weekend days; but the pay, including the tips, could be good, much better than the wages received by most employed teenagers. Shoe-shining was an unpleasant and unforgettable experience for those caught in its clutches. It was hard work, despite the good pay, and especially humiliating to those who strove for something more dignified. It meant no recreation, and it sometimes bred a cynical outlook on life. A meek teenager who was working beyond the limits prescribed by the law, seven days a week, upon asking the boss for some time off every third Sunday, was brusquely reminded that the American motto was: "Business before pleasure." Yet shoeshining, with all its agonies, did instill in the young an appreciation for work and for the value of hard-earned money. Finally, it did have a valuable disciplining effect.

During the summer recess a boy could obtain a job in a brewery, a freight house, a leather factory, a steel mill, a tin plant, or a depart-ment store. Working in a store might have meant a white-collar job, but the wages were lower. Obviously those boys whose fathers were proprietors could often find summer employment in their shops or restaurants or perhaps in those of some business acquaintance. Such a youth had much the easier time when it came to attending college.

Some youths had benefactors in the form of uncles and brothers who, in the spirit of the Greek tradition, took these family obligations very seriously. Such persons helped financially with the education of the sons and daughters of their sisters and brothers, especially if they had no families of their own. This family tradition, although practiced with some degree of irregularity, seems to have died out rather early in the United States.

The position of the second generation was not as hapless as is sometimes imagined. The paths of the males, although at times stormy and unpredictable, were strewn with fewer obstacles than those of the females. A son was more aggressive, independent, and less likely to be cowed by a domineering father. He was more adaptable, capable of self-support, and less victimized by gossip. When one considers the family customs and traditions these children had to fight, in addition to the hostile reception the parents were subjected to and the tre-mendous social disadvantages under which they labored, the number of the second-generation members that entered into the business, professional, and intellectual worlds is impressive indeed. Statistical data bearing this out is unavailable, but it would appear that the ratio of youths entering the professions was quite high.

The professions which mostly appealed to the young were those of law and medicine, and to a lesser degree dentistry, perhaps because of the prodding of parents who remembered only too well that these were the professions that counted in Greece. Teaching, engineering, and other professions gradually acquired more appeal. Success in these fields—and there was a good deal—may be attributed to a combination of factors. For one thing, the compactness of the Greek family was a formidable influence. The parents were good parents by all standards. They viewed marriage and the family as permanent responsibilities that could never be taken lightly. There was a healthy respect for work and a high degree of family esteem. The discipline might have appeared severe, but it was not repressive to the point of smothering the resourcefulness and enterprising nature of the child. Childhood and adolescent years were preoccupied with duties, chores, and menial employment, which was atypical of the lives of most other children. Rarely would the parent shield the child from the hard realities of life. Few found their youthful years enjoyable, and fewer still would care to relive them. But the majority probably were thankful in their later years for the severe tests to which they had been subjected.

Parents assumed responsibilities in a very determined manner. Relying on teachers or counselors was rare; as a rule they believed in their own devices. If anything, a parent was likely to be heard telling a teacher that, if his son was not behaving himself, he should feel free to inflict corporal punishment. The mother, besides rearing and helping to maintain a large family, was forever counseling, advising, and imploring to a degree that the average American youth would find unbearable. Sentiment among the second generation regarding their early upbringing varies. Some prefer to forget about it completely because it brings back memories of hardship, even of humiliation. Others, granted that their early years were difficult, look back on them with certain fond memories. There was something zestful and exciting in that background, which was forever passing from their lives; it had given them a smattering of Greek, a cultural distinctiveness, and a special brand of individualism.

The average member of the second generation rarely concerned himself with issues relating to Greece, except in periods of extreme crisis. If the Greek issue was linked to something preponderantly American, the interest could be keener and perhaps justified. Seldom would he read a Greek newspaper or take seriously Greek issues that filled the columns of the American press. In fact, he might resent the efforts of a patriot to inject such issues into community affairs.

Interest in modern Greek culture was also at a minimum, despite the efforts of the Greek press, church leaders, and influential laymen. The majority of the youth were too absorbed with the American way of life and their own personal problems to give any thoughts to Greek letters and learning. What the Greek church, the Greek-language press, and Greek travel agencies wished to encourage for perfectly obvious reasons, the rank-and-file members of the second generation preferred to avoid. They were in America, and it was their country. They just did not care about Greek culture in any of its forms.[20]

16

THE THIRTIES

T HE 1930s found the Greek-Americans engrossed in the problems of the depression, in educating their children, and in struggling to maintain what semblance of Hellenism they could. With the erosion of nationalist sentiments, their problems became those of the average American family. Except for the larger cities, the early colonies had disappeared and those that survived had been diluted by the passing of the older members from the scene, the dispersal of former residents, and the influx of other nationality groups. Although many still belonged to the Greek Orthodox Church, the years of feuding had taken their toll, and the influence of the clergy and the ecclesiastical authorities had dwindled to a low point. Reconciliation to the idea of permanent residence in the United States had weakened ties with the old country to the point where fewer and fewer corresponded even with their closest relatives in Greece. The major concern was with American issues, American programs, and the future of American democracy in the face of totalitarian advances.

The struggle between the traditionalists and those who favored assimilation continued, but the emotion and ferocity of the earlier years was missing. The traditionalists were headed by the ecclesiastical authorities, the parish priests, GAPA, and those miscellaneous groups who wished to keep alive the flame of Hellenism. These defenders of the nationality viewed with alarm the drying up of all wellsprings of national sentiment and culture. They cited the serious inroads that mixed marriages were making into the ranks of the older and the newer generations, the absence of churches in the smaller cities, and the lack of Greek schools in some of the larger cities. They complained of the persistence of fanatical factionalism, the multiplication in the number of the so-called cosmopolitan Greeks, the mounting divorce rate, the activities of the Jehovah's Witnesses, the spread of communism, and the tendency to downgrade the influence of the church.[1]

Traditionalism was confined pretty much to the preservation of the Greek faith and language. The belief was that this could be accomplished only by strengthening the influence of the Greek Orthodox Church in the United States. They argued that the church had performed such a role during the days of Ottoman rule, and they saw no reason why it could not assume such a responsibility now.[2] The priests, according to ecclesiastical tradition, were obligated to assert their leadership in such matters. The concept that "Christ speaks English," and that the preservation of the Orthodox faith for the new generation was contingent upon the introduction of the English language in the liturgy and sacraments, was unacceptable to the traditionalists. There could be no retreat from this position, especially if the language was to be preserved. Priests who believed that they had to preach in English were advised to establish English churches and recruit their followers from the members of other nationalities.[3]

The "environmentalists" observed that few nationality groups had been able to maintain their cultural identity; and those that did, did so with considerable modification. Compromise was essential; English as well as the Greek language had to be used in the sermons. The path of the older immigrant groups had to be followed, even though the liturgy was to be read in Greek. Persons who were grieved over not hearing Greek in a church had to understand that it no longer was a question of what one preferred, but a question of what had to be.[4]

Education of the young became a byword in community after community. Parents were urged not to force their sons into the business world as soon as they graduated from high school. The small salaries they would earn at this stage of their lives could prove detrimental. All were advised to make sacrifices for a few more years and open the doors to greater opportunities by sending their children on to college or an advanced technical school. The parents of girls were asked to do likewise.[5]

Chicago, or "Chicagopolis" as it was called, in 1938 boasted the largest Greek population in the United States—sixty thousand "Chicago-polites" were to be found in the Delta—the district where Halsted and Harrison Streets and Blue Island Avenue intersected; the Lincoln

Square Section, the near South Side, Grand Boulevard, Pullman, and the Ashland district. It was in the Delta where the most typical Greek stores were to be found with their imported articles, the food and spice shops, the coffeehouses, restaurants, bakery shops, and it was here that the Greek Orthodox religion was preserved with all its ecclesiastical splendor.

The Greeks still had their own clubs, newspapers, and professional organizations, as did the other nationalities. There were some two hundred societies and, while many Greeks were businessmen, they boasted more than two hundred professional men among them, of whom doctors and lawyers were the most numerous. The Athenians, the Spartans, the Arcadians, the Messinians, all had their organizations. Besides the chapters of AHEPA and GAPA, there were the Greek Professional Men's Club, the Hellenic Post of the American Legion, the Plato Students' Association, the Young Women's Philharmonic Society, the Illinois Federation of Restaurant Owners, the American Restaurant Men's Association, the Greek Retail Dealers Association, the Hellenic Benevolent Society, the New Genea, the Hellenic Youth, the Hellenic Women's Club, the Sons of Pericles, and others too numerous to mention.[6]

By and large the Greek-American businessman emerged from the Great Depression injured but not crushed. His recuperative powers were formidable, his business acumen sharpened, and his determination to profit from past mistakes insurmountable. Professions such as teaching, medicine, law, dentistry, and engineering had been broached in all the major metropolitan areas, as well as in the smaller communities. Members of the second generation were attending the professional schools and the institutions of higher learning in impressive numbers. The college and university graduate no longer was the rarity he had been twenty or thirty years earlier.

Professional sports made slight appeal to the rank and file as a career, with but few exceptions.[7] Such activities received little encouragement in the home, at least in the earlier days. Most parents frowned on permitting their sons to participate in high school, intercollegiate, or sandlot sports. Their argument was that sports gave them "nothing to eat" and that they could use their time to better advantage. Equally important is the fact that the members of the younger generation found it easy to gain entry into the commercial and professional fields.

By 1939 the Greek-language press was generally limited to the members of the first generation who remembered the Greece of Constantine and Venizelos. As a rule they were among the least articulate of their respective communities, those found on the outer social and economic fringes of American society. Many of these people had a very poor command of the English language; to them the Greek press was a means of keeping in contact with the outside world. The Greek press continued to represent the sentiments of the older generation, those whose formative years had been spent in Greece. It had a distinctly immigrant bias and made no serious attempt to understand the problems of the second generation. It implored the youth to follow in the footsteps of the older generation and to preserve the customs and traditions of their parents. It did not have any serious influence on the thinking of the second generation. What is more, relatively few of the young were able to read a Greek newspaper, for their command of the language was limited.[8]

Even though integration into the American community was having its effects, one must not assume that all bonds with Greece had been severed. Ahepans and Gapans continued to make their annual excursions to Greece, where they visited relatives, acquired wives, and preached the gospel of American progress. The Greek Orthodox Church and the Greek-oriented clergy were a constant reminder of Greece. Even if most people had wanted to confine themselves to the American scene, there were too many forces at work in Greece that pulled at the heart and mind of American Hellenism. The State Department was fully aware of this. It made repeated attempts to negotiate a naturalization treaty with the Greek government, if for no other reason than to accommodate the numerous naturalized United States citizens who wanted to make periodic visits to their native land. An American legation officer in Athens even thought it advisable for Greek-Americans to organize a campaign to induce the Greek government to extend to them some sort of benefit regarding their military obligations.[9]

But hardly had efforts been made to resume these negotiations than John Metaxas came to power. In view of this, the American legation deemed it advisable to explore somewhat further the reception that such a proposal was likely to receive at the hands of the new government. These exploratory discussions made it clear that the Greek authorities had yielded about as much ground as they cared to with respect to military obligations. Permitting United States citizens of Greek birth to remain in Greece for a period of six months was considered a liberal concession.[10]

The royalist victories in 1934 made inevitable the appointment of a Greek minister to the United States who was sympathetic with the monarchist philosophy of government.[11] This role was filled by Demetrios Sicilianos, a fifty-five-year-old bachelor who had weathered the ups and downs of the royalist-Venizelist struggles from their very inception. Upon his arrival in the country, he told newspapermen that everything was "happily in order" when he left Athens ten days earlier. He said that the revolution was over and that "there will be quiet forever in his country."[12] The main purpose of this affable and energetic person was to advertise the merits of the new regime in Greece. He traveled extensively, attended Greek-American social functions, cultivated friends among editors and newspaper publishers, and sought the good will of all Greek-Americans.

The royalist resurgence in Greece promised to revive the tensions of the postwar era and to have repercussions in the United States, for in 1935 a plebiscite was called to determine whether Greece was to remain a republic. The revival of the monarchy that resulted was only a prelude to the greater totalitarian scheme that was developing.

Meanwhile the royalists, whose optimism had been rising by the hour, started to react to a proposed visit of Alexander Papanastasiou to the United States. This was the former right-hand man of Venizelos and reputedly "the father of Greek democracy," and his trip was viewed as part of a campaign to thwart the restoration of the monarchy in Greece. His mission, according to the royalists, was to collect money from the Greeks in America to bolster the position of the Venizelist republicans in the forthcoming elections. But Papanastasiou said that the purpose of his trip was to visit relatives in Chicago.[13] Shortly after Papanastasiou arrived, he admitted that his principal motive was to persuade the Greek-Americans to use their influence to help perpetuate the republican form of government in Greece. Greece was desperately in need of help to preserve its integrity. A royalist restoration, he predicted, would bring forth waves of opposition, discord, and humiliation to the country.[14] Colonel Zezas, the head of the Greek Secret Service, in the meantime reported that Papanastasiou was collecting large sums of money in the United States for the republican campaign.[15]

Royalist sympathizers lost little time in reacting to the Papanastasiou mission. The Greco-American Delphic Society of New York pledged its support to the restoration. Delegates of twelve chapters of the National Union of Greeks in Chicago resolved to send a cablegram to Premier Tsaldaris, declaring themselves in support of the restoration, and denounced the Papanastasiou mission as a communist- and republican-inspired project.[16] Cleanthes Vassardakis, a former consul general in San Francisco, urged that King George be called back to the throne without a plebiscite, claiming that "American Hellenism stands for the affirmative discipline of an authoritative republic under King George."[17]

The high point of the Papanastasiou mission was a public rally sponsored by his sympathizers in New York. Attended by an estimated crowd of six thousand, the sentiments of the rally were clear. It asked Papanastasiou to transmit to the Greek authorities a declaration stating that the majority of the Greek-Americans favored a republican form of government. It also asked for the reinstatement of those university professors and state employees who were dismissed after the abortive March revolution, a general amnesty for all political prisoners and exiles, the holding of a free election, and the cessation of all acts of oppression against democratic newspapers, organizations, and leaders.[18] In Greece republican leaders, acting on the advice Papanastasiou brought back from the "Greek republicans" in the United States, prepared an open letter to former King George, warning him that he could not count on their support if the plebiscite turned out in his favor. The royalists, in turn, countered by asserting that the Greek Communist Party had requested the American Communists to cooperate with the republican Greeks in the United States in preventing the restoration of the monarchy.[19]

If nothing else, the Papanastasiou mission illustrated conclusively that the republican forces in Greece were counting upon the assistance of the Greek-Americans. Their zeal for the politics of the old country might not have been completely extinguished, especially in the more populous centers of the United States, but it certainly did not burn with the fiery glow of the years directly after World War One.

The rise of John Metaxas to power on August 4, 1936, did not have the repercussions of the old clash between Venizelists and royalists, even though many were shocked by the emergence of a dictatorship in their native country. The rise and decline of Greek governments had always been embarrassing, but the conversion of Greece into a dictatorship was a severe blow. It frightened a people who had survived discriminatory attacks from nativist groups, for now they feared they might find themselves cast into the category of potential subversives and perhaps enemy-alien groups that would bear watching. It alarmed them also to think of what could happen to relatives living under a totalitarian regime.

The positions of the two leading Greek dailies, the *Atlantis* and the *National Herald,* were pretty much what one might have expected. *Atlantis* supported the Metaxas government from the outset because it was the government of Greece and perhaps because the rise of Metaxas, an old royalist, was a vindication of its political preferences. The *National Herald,* on the other hand, lamented the conversion of Greece into a dictatorship and attacked Metaxas for his part in it. Eventually the *Herald* began to detect some good in Metaxas, especially in his reform measures that bore a resemblance to those of the New Deal. It finally accepted the Metaxas regime as the lesser of two evils by pointing to the multiple dangers that Greece faced from her enemies to the north. This was hard-headed realism, even though the shift in attitude ran counter to the principles on which the *National Herald* was founded. As more and more Greek-Americans returned from visits to Greece and reported that conditions had taken a definite turn for the better, the *National Herald* reconciled itself to Metaxas as a "necessary evil." [20]

Marxism made no appreciable progress among the Greek-Americans. The rank and file were bitterly opposed to it and could be counted upon to fight it with all the power at their command. Still it would be foolish to deny that Marxists were active among the Greek-Americans at a time when the Communists were seeking a united front in their all-out campaign against fascism and nazism. The working nucleus was provided by a small but aggressive group of furriers in New York

City, natives for the most part of the area around Kastoria in Macedonia, and there were scattered groups in other metropolitan areas. *Empros* (Forward), the organ of the Greek-speaking Communists in the United States, first appeared in 1923 and was published until October 1939, when it was succeeded by *Eleutheria* (Liberty). The latter suspended publication in April 1941.[21]

Among the first outspoken critics of the Metaxas regime was *Protoporos* (Pioneer), a short-lived organ of the Greek Workers' Federation of America. Its program savored strongly of "popular frontism." Metaxas, it charged, represented "monarchy and plutocracy, Hitlerian fascism and English imperialism" and was the tool of the Greek capitalist class. It was not so much a matter of Metaxas' saving Greece as much as it was of Greece being saved from Metaxas. American Hellenism was urged to resist the fascist peril by supporting the candidates of the American Farmer Labor Party.[22]

Protoporos took upon itself the task of stirring up a discussion against Metaxas and fascism by sending out questionnaires to prominent Greek-Americans, asking for personal opinions regarding the Metaxas dictatorship and for suggestions regarding the possible course of action that might be adopted in combating it. Five of the eight published replies favored a positive program of action to organize American Hellenism in a crusade against fascism. They emphasized the importance of taking a position, organizing the forces of democracy, and the need for viewing the Metaxas issue as one of fascism versus democracy: "We cannot separate it from the war against fascism regardless of country." The most militant response urged all antifascists, democrats, liberals, progressives, and genuine friends of freedom and humanity to form a national organization, rally to the assistance of their brothers in Greece, picket the fascist Greek consulates in the United States, demand the retirement of Metaxas and free elections in Greece, and demonstrate against such "fascist and medieval organs" as the *Atlantis* and the *National Herald*.

Of the three published letters that opposed any affirmative course of action, one evaded the questions by discussing tangential matters, while the other two voiced opinions that were more representative of the views of rank-and-file Greek-Americans. Nicholas Kaltchas wrote: "For us Greeks in the United States it is an academic, or if you wish a traditional, concern, but not a political one. For the majority of us who are

American citizens intervention in the political affairs of Greece, besides being illegal, would be indiscreet." Even closer to the sentiments of the majority of Greek-Americans was the comment of N. Mimopoulos who said: "What else is there for us to do but tend to our affairs and discuss the issue in academic terms? Those patriots who are in a positive position to aid Greece, let them repatriate themselves. Anyone who wishes to save his burning house does not flee to the mountain or fall into a well, but remains nearby and battles the flames." [23]

Protoporos, besides proposing a militant united front against fascism, carried other articles and advertisements that shed light on its ideological affiliations. It drew parallels between Greece of 1821 and Spain of 1937, noted the formation of a Greek phalanx to fight in Spain, and carried an advertisement of the Spartacus Restaurant in New York City (a well-known Communist meeting place).[24]

Among the first Communist front organizations to emerge from the anti-Metaxas agitation was the Greek-American Union for Democracy, organized early in the fall of 1937. Some light on its functioning is provided by P. Kekes, a New York physician, who was invited by Demetrios Christophorides, the associate editor of the *National Herald,* to join the Greek-American Union for Democracy to combat fascism in Greece. Believing that this was a commendable cause, Kekes agreed to do so with the understanding that this organization was to be grounded on democratic and patriotic principles and that Communists were to be barred from assuming even a minor role of influence. He argued that the ideologies of democracy and communism were irreconcilable and that any attempt to fuse the two would be a disruptive and discrediting force. Kekes further suggested that a few well-known and financially independent persons should head this organization until it gained the necessary stability and direction. Two persons were mentioned as being capable of offering this leadership, but neither responded to the invitation. The plan of action called for the issuance of a modest publication and the staging of a public rally against fascism.

On November 12, two days before the rally, Kekes was approached by Christophorides and asked to avoid making any public statements that were likely to offend the Communists. Kekes objected to this in vigorous terms, stating that it was contrary to the understanding originally reached, and he held his ground. Kekes was visited again by Christophorides, but this time in the company of others who asked him once more to refrain from making any disparaging remarks about the Communists. Kekes not only refused to do so, but threatened to resign as chairman of the rally and to disassociate himself completely from the group. Now Kekes was asked to refrain only from making derogatory statements about the Communists in public with the understanding that the complete text would be published without any deletions. Kekes agreed to this, making it clear that the Communists would have to keep "their mouths shut about their ideology," and this too was acceptable to the committee. Despite this, Kekes kept receiving telephone calls from anonymous persons who urged him not to speak harshly about the Communists.[25]

The rally was attended by a respectable number of small businessmen and Communists. Kekes characterized the Metaxas regime as a blight on the ancient traditions of the Greek people and as a danger to the American citizens of Greek ancestry. He named Demetrios Sicilianos, the Greek minister to the United States, as the head of the Metaxas propaganda network that functioned through the Greek consuls in the various cities. He also pointed an accusing finger at the Greek Orthodox Church in the United States, especially the hierarchy and the Greek-born parish priests, the Greek-language press that either openly supported Metaxas or refrained from criticizing him, and the businessmen who tolerated the Metaxas regime as a means of protecting their interests abroad.[26]

Kekes believed that the Greek-American Union for Democracy could serve a good purpose, but that certain changes had to be made. First of all, its meetings had to be held in quarters more representative than those of Local 70 of the CIO; and it had to adopt a positive program of action, for shouting "Down with Metaxas was not enough." Able and dedicated members committed to the principles of democracy had to be enrolled to combat the strong leftist influences within the organization. He found it difficult to cooperate with the Communists. "I knew these men were leftists," admitted Kekes, "but I believed it was possible to reason with them in order to do something for our Mother Country. Unfortunately, however, they are fanatics; they are redder than the eggs of Easter. Reaching an understanding with them is impossible." [27] Kekes had high hopes that the Union for Democracy would become a purely patriotic organization committed to the principles of parliamentary procedure, but the organization was democratic in name only. The men most loudly proclaiming the aims of the organization were Communists, who exploited the Greek issue as a means of winning American Hellenism over to international Communism.[28]

The position of AHEPA toward the Metaxas government was somewhat ambiguous and at times embarrassing to those who believed that the actions and utterances of its highest officers might be interpreted as an endorsement of totalitarianism. Certainly the principles, traditions, and history of the order left little doubt that it was opposed to totalitarianism. However, during the spring of 1937 when AHEPA was heading its eighth annual excursion to Greece, the president dispatched a series of radiograms from mid-ocean to King George II, Prime Minister Metaxas, officials of Athens and Piraeus, the Metropolitan of Athens, and other dignitaries. His cable to Metaxas read as follows: "Hellenism in America hopeful that the Mother Country shall see peace from your strong government sends you through its 800 returning sons under the aegis of Ahepa its heartfelt greetings." [29] Although one can accept this as an endorsement of the Metaxas government by AHEPA, a more intimate knowledge of the opinions of the members would disprove this. At best, these official greetings were a compound of opportunism, emotion, and indiscretion.

The attitude of *The Ahepan,* the monthly magazine of the order, appears to have been one of judicious neutrality. It published periodic brief factual accounts of the Metaxas government, but uttered neither words of praise nor criticism of it. It did, however, print full and lengthy reproductions of the numerous articles from the Athens press on the AHEPA excursionists in Greece, for this was grist for the Ahepa mill.[30] During its national convention in 1938, AHEPA was warned about the perils of both fascism and communism, and its members were urged to uphold democracy as they always had in the past. These pleas were incorporated into resolutions condemning the spread of dictatorships, the suppression of individual liberties, and the persecution of the Jews.[31]

The fact remains, nevertheless, that after the Metaxas coup of August 4, 1936, certain representatives of the Greek-language press, the Greek clergy, some patriotic organizations, the Greek legation in Washington, and the consulates in New York, Boston, Chicago, New Orleans, and San Francisco launched a concerted crusade to gain support for the new regime from the Greeks of the United States. Their activities were diversified—among other things they attempted to collect funds for the Greek air force, which brought protests. This concerted effort was slow in crystallizing at first, but by the late 1930s the Greek minister to the United States, the Greek consuls, and other representatives of the Greek government were frequently seen in the company of members of the Greek-language press, business and professional men, clergymen and dignitaries.[32]

The Greek legation in Washington complained about the unfair treatment that the Metaxas government was receiving from the American press. Special exception was taken to the articles of Constantine Brown, who wrote that those Greeks who incurred the political disfavor of Metaxas were compelled to lie on ice and take large doses of castor oil. These statements were branded as falsehoods and efforts were made to counteract them by writing letters to the editors of the *New York Times* and the *Herald Tribune*. The Greece of Metaxas, according to these sources, had nothing in common with the fascist or Nazi regimes. The observations of the Greek dictator regarding Mussolini indicate that he held the Italian dictator in low esteem. The people of Greece were just as free as they ever had been; and now they were blessed with prosperity, happiness, and contentment. The judiciary was as free as ever. The only group faring badly were the Communists, who were under constant scrutiny in the United States as well as in Greece.

But there was nothing that could be done to silence the press critics of the Metaxas regime. The press in the United States was free, and those who had honest criticisms were free to express them. Furthermore, a very large segment of the Greek population in the United States was hostile to the dictatorship and did not hesitate to say so. It was a grievous error for the Greek diplomats and consuls to assume that the Greek-Americans were sympathetic with dictator Metaxas. One thing was clear. The Greek diplomatic and consular corps in the United States had been instructed to bestir itself and do everything possible to create in public and private circles as favorable an impression as it could of the Metaxas regime.[33]

The official sentiments of the Greece of Metaxas were stated by Sicilianos, the minister to the United States. On July 11, 1938, the *Portland Oregonian* quoted him as telling a Greek-American audience: "Greece has a very wise government—a government of authority, but one in which the people have as many liberties as do the people in America. Our government is called a dictatorship, but it is not. It is a fine government for the benefit of our people." [34]

During 1939 the efforts of the Metaxas government to win the support of the Greek-Americans were accelerated. The Metaxas-controlled press heaped lavish attention on the Greek-American excursionists in Greece, who previously had been treated in rather perfunctory fashion. It did so because Greece wanted their cooperation. The Greek-Americans could spread favorable comments about the progress of Greece when they returned to the United States and might even be employed to rekindle the spirit of Hellenism that was in danger of being completely extinguished in the New World. Perhaps some working relationship could be perfected.

The government of Metaxas sponsored a youth movement comparable to that of most totalitarian governments. The National Youth Organization (Ethniki Organosis Neoleas), known as EON, encountered some resistance at first, but once this was eliminated it sought to extend its hold on "Greekdom abroad." It had agents busy among the large and influential Greek colonies of Egypt, and the Greek-Americans were next in line, according to well-founded reports. Its primary targets were AHEPA and its junior order, the Sons of Pericles, and to a lesser extent GAPA.

This well-calculated plan became apparent during the spring of 1939 when a delegation representing AHEPA and the Sons of Pericles visited Greece to present a monument to the historic town of Missolonghi. During this visit leaders of the EON were embarrassingly attentive to the Greek-Americans, and they made special efforts to win the sympathy and active support of the president of the Sons of Pericles, a thoroughly Americanized and educated young man born of Greek parents in the United States. He was showered with attention by the officials of the EON and provided with a uniformed guard of honor of English-speaking Greek youths. The president of the Sons of Pericles was astonished by the almost complete misunderstanding his indulgent hosts had of the United States and of the Greek-Americans. They seemed to think that naturalized Americans of Greek birth, and even children born in the United States, would display a passionate allegiance to Greece, to the extent of working for the dictatorship. The inability of the impassioned Greek nationalist to comprehend the temper and psychology of Greek-Americans was almost beyond belief.[35]

Apparently overwhelmed by the prospects of forging some kind of a working alliance with the Greek-Americans, the Metaxas government decided to dispatch one of its ace propagandists to the United States. The man selected for this task was Vasileos Papadakis, described by some as the Goebbels of Greece. His trip was described officially as a visit to the World's Fair and perhaps a tour of a few Greek communities as a means of bringing tidings from the mother country. But for all practical purposes he came to act as the agent of a foreign government. News of the Papadakis visit rated a front-page headline in the *Atlantis,* which had never concealed its support of the Metaxas government. A good-sized editorial in the same issue told of the greetings that Metaxas was sending to the United States and the Greek people of the country, and of the wing that Greece had at the World's Fair.[36] Successive issues of the *Atlantis* informed readers of the enthusiasm that the Greeks were displaying for the government of Metaxas and the spiritual ties being forged between Greece and the United States by the Greek-American organizations.[37] A further note added that August 4, the date on which Metaxas seized power, was to be celebrated as a Panhellenic holiday.[38]

This was the atmosphere when Vasileos Papadakis arrived in the United States. A Cretan by birth and forty-five years of age, he had studied law and politics in the universities of Athens and Paris, entered the diplomatic service, was considered extremely well-informed in international law and European politics, and was one of the first to come to the support of Metaxas. A dynamic and rabidly partisan individual, he alienated many who did not care for his extremism. According to *Atlantis,* his mission was to make a firsthand study of the Greek-Americans and their problems and make recommendations to the Greek government.[39] This appears to have been the same stereotyped statement of purpose that had been issued by previous key official representatives.[40] Upon his arrival in New York he was greeted by the Greek consul general, the editor-in-chief of *Atlantis,* and a representative of the Greek Orthodox archdiocese.[41]

In an interview with a representative of *Atlantis,* Papadakis said that he was more anxious to see the Greek people of this country than the United States itself. He came not to seek money or assistance, but to be useful to his compatriots. Who asked him to come and just how he proposed to be useful was never explained, at least in public. But here he was asking the Greek-Americans to take heart, to show "a vigorous concern over the welfare of the Motherland," and to share his enthusiasm for Greece. Being so far distant, they had no idea what had occurred during the past three years: "There is a metamorphosis, a cosmogonia, a basic change, the greatest since March 25, 1821." He said he was speaking the truth when he stated that Metaxas had saved Greece, and he pleaded with the people of the United States to have faith in his government.[42] He also expressed hope that the Greek communities in the United States would want him to speak in greater detail about the latest developments in the mother country.[43]

Although Papadakis was well-received by certain portions of the Greek population, tendered a big reception in New York City, photographed with Mayor La Guardia in one instance, and given the keys to at least one other major city, his critics were numerous and often belligerent. There are good reasons to believe that he was roundly opposed by many, if not most, Ahepans; Callimachos of the *National Herald* wrote a series of articles severely criticizing him for his activities and urged him to pack his personal effects and return to Greece where he belonged.[44] The criticisms of Papadakis must have been widespread, for beginning late in July *Atlantis* began to publish numerous letters from readers who were sympathetic with his mission.[45] The New York daily set aside a special column, entitled "The Greeks Respond to the Unreconstructed Sycophants and Liars," for letters praising the mission of Papadakis and the government of Metaxas.[46]

Just prior to a sudden leave-taking from the United States, Papadakis issued a farewell letter, in which he thanked the Greek-Americans for helping him to accomplish his purpose. He said that he spoke in thirty-six cities and before fifty-one audiences. He admitted that his major concern was for the members of the second generation in the United States. He wanted them to remain as Greek in their sentiments as their parents and grandparents had been before them. He wanted the flame of Hellenism to burn brightly in their everyday thoughts.[47] If the youth of America did not take the mission of Papadakis seriously, there is evidence that the hierarchy of the Greek church in the United States did. Apparently some authority within the church authorized the formation of a new youth group to take the place of the defunct Hellenic

Orthodox Youth Association (HOYA), under the initials of EON which, as we have seen, were the initials of the Metaxas youth organization. This elicited at least some critical editorial comment in the columns of *The Ahepan*.

The editors viewed this as an affront to the integrity and loyalty of the young; for here the church was subscribing to totalitarian ideals and attempting to foist them on the unsuspecting members of the second generation. The editors at first stated that they were in no position to say whether this was carried out under specific instructions from church authorities in America, but they did mention "mysterious forces" which released circulars to the various communities, asking them "to receive the notorious Papadakis, agent of the '4th of August formulas' that were repugnant to democratic ideals."

The belief also was broadcast that the Greek church was encouraging the formation of rival organizations to the Sons of Pericles and AHEPA's women's order, the Maids of Athens. For the church to organize its own national group was viewed as unnecessary and detrimental in its tendency to perpetuate an immigrant psychology. The local churches should devote their energies to the formation of Bible classes "and not to movements very much akin to those sponsored . . . by the discredited Mr. Vasileos Papadakis." In admonishing the church authorities, the editorial concluded:

We venture the hope that this unwise movement will be abandoned forthwith. We express our views on the subject not only as Ahepans but also as member and communicants of the Greek Orthodox Church. Keep alien doctrines and ideas out of the Church, out of the schools, out of all organized social forces.
America does not need them—does not want them.
Is that clear?[48]

This editorial brought forth numerous comments, with only a few unfavorable. Of the latter, one came from the Very Reverend Coucouzes, the vice-dean of the Greek Orthodox Theological Seminary, Pomfret, Connecticut, and later the Archbishop of North and South America, and the other from James Matthews, Jr., the national secretary of the EON. The latter regretted the misunderstanding and insisted that the similarity in initials was an oversight that would be corrected. But the letter of the Very Reverend Coucouzes was belligerent and reprimanding in tone. He insisted that the initials EON stood for Elliniki Orthodoxos Neolaias, or Hellenic Orthodox Youth, and not the Ethniki Organosis Neolaias of Metaxas, and that it was a purely religious organization. Its initials were adopted by representatives of youth from twenty-five cities and towns in Danielson, Connecticut, in July 1941 without any interference on the part of the ecclesiastical authorities. Its objectives were to bring together youth of the Greek Orthodox faith.

But this was far from satisfying to the editors of *The Ahepan,* who charged that Athenagoras, the dean of the Greek Theological Seminary and the Bishop of Boston, had signed the circular urging the churches to open their doors to Vasileos Papadakis, who was registered as an official propagandist with the State Department. The head of the theological school had authorized the Greek churches of the country to receive the messenger of "the new civilization" of "the Fourth of August." If Coucouzes read the daily newspapers, he probably would have noted the dissension and the near physical combat that took place in a number of the communities which "the propagandist" visited. The EON either was a continuation of the old organization or it was not. If it was the former, then it had no place in America. AHEPA, among other things, was dedicated to protecting the name of the Americans of Greek descent from any acts that would create friction between them and their neighbors. If the latter was the purpose of the EON, then it was superfluous; the field was well-served.

What was needed from the church, the paper went on, was religious instruction for the young. Those whose mission was to teach religion had to confine themselves to this purpose and not invade the social and fraternal fields. The various chapters of AHEPA and their auxiliaries helped organize Sunday school classes, encouraged "go to church" campaigns, and gave their undivided loyalty and support to the Greek Orthodox Church. It would be most unwise for the church authorities to encourage the formation of a rival organization simply because it could not dominate the old.[49]

It is apparent that many American citizens of Greek birth were disturbed by their continued sentimental attachment to Greece. They were proud of the United States and they never wavered in their loyalty to it, but still they were disheartened by the totalitarian regime of Metaxas. Those who knew the Hellenic temperament and the loyalty of the people honestly believed that even the most tyrannical ruler would not be able to compromise the nation's freedom and independence. History and tradition were on their side. The more responsible leaders, however, could not take the loyalty issue lightly. Members of AHEPA, the Sons of Pericles, and other groups were asked to give serious thought to such matters as the following.

Was one "better off" if he relinquished all ties with Greece or if he retained an active interest in her affairs and government? Was one obligated to go to the assistance of the government of Greece because his parents and grandparents lived there? In the event that Greece went to war with another country, was a United States citizen of Greek descent justified in enlisting in the armed forces of Greece? Should Greek-Americans contribute to the purchase of munitions and weapons if Greece made a call for such assistance? Was Greece justified in claiming as her citizens all those of Greek birth who resided in the United States?[50]

If there were differences of opinion on these issues, there were none regarding the Greek-Americans' loyalty to the United States. This was their country, and they wanted everyone to know it; plans were made even for the unexpected. Experiences during and after the First World War convinced community and organization leaders that the good name of their people had to be protected from rabble-rousers who preyed on the innocent of foreign birth. AHEPA in its annual convention of 1938 adopted a clear and unmistakable position against fascism, nazism, and anti-Semitism, and reaffirmed its faith in the principles of democracy. Its years of experience in dealing with antiforeign attacks had not been useless. While Greece was still under the rule of the dictator, and there were genuine apprehensions in some quarters that Greece might join the Axis, the rival factions within AHEPA had reached a tacit understanding which was essentially this. If such an alliance was proclaimed, an immediate statement was to be issued that would disassociate AHEPA and Americans of Greek descent from such an endeavor, and their resources would be pledged "to fight Metaxas and his cohorts to free Greece from the miasma of fascism."[51]

17

THE SECOND WORLD WAR

WORLD War Two was a great turning point in Greek-American history. The invasion of Greece by the forces of Mussolini late in October 1940 and the heroic resistance of the Greeks aroused the admiration of the world. For the first time since 1939, a victory was scored against a ruthless dictator; the timetable of the totalitarian aggressors was abruptly halted, and the Allies gained a breathing spell. The prestige this heaped upon the Greeks was great, and much of it affected their kin in the United States. No longer could they be accused of having families and relatives who were sympathetic to the totalitarian powers. But, even more, it brought them a new confidence, which they were shrewd enough to capitalize on.[1]

Greek-Americans who had "washed their hands" of Greek affairs or had lost their earlier enthusiasm for the mother country suddenly wanted the entire world to know that they too were Greeks. An American-born restaurateur echoed the sentiments of many of his contemporaries when he said: "I am proud to be an American and I'm proud today that I am a Greek."[2] Unlike the World War One period, when the American populace viewed Greek-Americans with contemptuous amusement or as undesirable aliens, World War Two brought them status and dignity. Newspapermen, cartoonists, political leaders, poets, scholars, all helped to popularize the Greek cause. Greece had become Belgium of World War Two. Now it was "the glory that is Greece," not "the glory that was Greece."[3]

The Greek-Americans quickly came to the assistance of the mother country. They offered prayers in their churches, and they staged rallies and benefit programs. An international brigade of American and British citizens was formed. The big question was whether the Greek-

Americans could coordinate the efforts of their widely scattered clubs, societies, and national organizations into one effective unit.[4] But the response was unmistakable. Community and church leaders, business-men, professional groups, wage earners, and housewives rallied to the call. More than aiding Greece was involved—there were no conflicting loyalties, for the cause of Greece was the cause of the Allies. "Greece shares with Britain the right to call upon the Americans for help. She needs swift and effective aid," wrote *The Ahepan*. "She has said no in all frankness and must have it now if she is to escape the fate of Finland." [5]

Within two weeks after the invasion of Greece, the formation of the Greek War Relief Association (GWRA) was announced.[6] Headed by Spyros Skouras, the president of the National Theaters Company, the GWRA launched an immediate drive for $10 million. Visiting the Greek communities in the larger cities, often in the company of national or local officers of AHEPA, the theater magnate told his audiences of the urgent needs of Greece and that the Greek-Americans were unable to carry the burden alone. All Americans were asked to aid a small country which, on three hours' notice, had the courage to defy a member of the Axis. Skouras, to the surprise of many, singled out Metaxas for praise as a patriot and a great military strategist, who had anticipated and planned for an Italian attack. His careful preparations, aided by expert observations in Ethiopia and Spain, were bearing fruit. In community after community Skouras urged his compatriots to organize as their compatriots in New York City had. There promi-nent professional men and women were lending their names and efforts to the cause. He also announced plans to raise revenues from charity banquets, balls, and theater parties. All money was to go directly to Greece for the relief of the civilian population.[7]

The first news release of the GWRA on November 20, 1940, an-nounced that more than three hundred local committees had been organized to coordinate the activities of the approximately two thousand Greek clubs and organizations in the United States.[8] The local church communities, the hierarchy of the Greek church in the United States, and chapters of AHEPA, GAPA, the Pan-Arcadians, the Messinians, the Cretans, and other groups lent their support. But the greatest assist-ance came from AHEPA, which provided much, if not most, of the regional and local leadership. Its members usually were among the most

345

active and influential elements in their communities. AHEPA, among other things, had a grass-roots basis; without its local chapters it would have been very difficult for the GWRA to function effectively outside of New York, Chicago, and a few other metropolitan areas.[9] Skouras conceded that AHEPA supplied nearly 90 percent of the manpower needed to handle this enormous task.[10]

Much of the GWRA staff was provided by Americans who had lived in Greece for many years and by Americans of Greek descent. Among the former were Homer W. Davis, the president of Athens College since 1930; Henry A. Hill, who had been in charge of the American Express offices in Greece for more than twenty years and had taken an active part in the affairs of the country; and D. O. Hibbard, a former general secretary of the YMCA in Athens, who had helped to alleviate the refugee problem and rehabilitate Greek soldiers into civilian life after World War One.[11] A few months after the launching of the GWRA, the officers of the supreme lodge of AHEPA made their annual call on President Roosevelt; among other things they discussed the needs of Greece. This was in late April 1941. In what was described as an unusual procedure, the White House issued a statement of the remarks the President had made to the visiting Ahepans. The text in part reads as follows:

During the Hellenic war of independence more than a century ago, our young nation, prizing its own lately-won independence, expressed its ardent sympathy for the Greeks and hoped for Hellenic victory. The victory was achieved.

Today, at a far more perilous period in the history of Hellas, we intend to give full effect to our settled policy of extending all available material aid to a free people defending themselves against aggression. Such aid has been and will continue to be extended to Greece.

Whatever may be the temporary outcome of the present phase of the war . . . the people of Greece can count on the help and support of the government and the people of the United States.[12]

AHEPA also sent invitations to each Hellenic organization in the United States, asking it to send a delegate to the First Pan-Hellenic Congress that was to assemble in Cincinnati from August 17–19, 1941, "so that the voices of the descendants of those who rocked the cradle of Democracy could be heard." The reasons for this congress were presented in one pithy paragraph: "The extension of the German-Italian aggression to the sacred soil of Greece has left only us, Americans of Greek descent, as the sole group free to speak and act ... Our government has pledged and the American nation has endorsed the President's policy, that the aggressors must be annihilated. What, then, can we Americans of Greek descent do to contribute not only to the downfall of dictatorship and the liberation of Greece, but also to its proper restoration and the binding of her wounds? First there must be a program and a unified policy." [13]

The Pan-Hellenic Congress, with 461 delegates, was opened officially by the speaker of the House of Representatives, Sam Rayburn, who read the April 25 statement of President Roosevelt. Resolutions passed by the congress approved of the policy of the United States government to wipe nazism and fascism from the face of the globe, and to extend aid to Great Britain, the Soviet Union, China, and other nations committed in the war against the Axis. The Bill of Rights, the Constitution of the United States, and democracy were hailed as the greatest protectors of the rights of the people. Finally, President Roosevelt was thanked for coming to the assistance of the stricken Greek nation.[14] Apart from this convention, however, little else was heard of the organization other than brief notices of its social functions and rallies. It may be presumed that some of the delegates were motivated by cross-purposes, and that the declaration of war by the United States more or less compelled all ethnic groups to submerge their activities on behalf of the supreme American effort.[15]

Prior to America's entry into the war, the Greek-Americans were thoroughly engrossed in the activities of the GWRA. All indications are that these efforts were handled on a systematic and businesslike basis. The central headquarters of the GWRA issued specific instructions on organizing local fund-raising groups. Key leaders in all communities were urged to make special efforts to see to it that all classes and groups were represented and to enlist the support of prominent Americans in heading fund drives. Particular stress was placed on keeping accounts, acknowledging gifts, and reporting funds. Careful records were to be kept of all receipts and expenditures, including the names and addresses of the donors and the amounts they subscribed; and all contributions had to be acknowledged. Each week the treasurer of the local committee had to forward a check to national headquarters covering the receipts and notify his regional director of the amount forwarded; the names and addresses of contributors of sums over a hundred dollars were also submitted so that the national headquarters might send them notes of thanks. Each local committee was asked to solicit special contributions for this purpose, so that prospective contributors would know that each contributed dollar went toward relief needs.

Advice was also issued on the compilation of lists and the solicitation of gifts. The local committees were asked to limit their pledging to persons, organizations, and businesses within their districts, to avoid duplication of effort. Anyone believing that he had a particularly effective approach to a potential contributor outside his area was to clear the name of such a prospect through the regional office. All gifts were welcomed, but special attention was placed on large gifts. Names of those capable of giving substantial amounts were to be reserved for special solicitation by members of the executive committee, the chairman, and other influential members. Teams of five and ten members were to be formed for the solicitation of small contributions, each with a team captain who enlisted his own members. Benefit balls, entertainment, banquets, and similar events were discouraged until personal solicitation had been completed and permission obtained from national headquarters. Committees were also warned about local regulations regarding the collection of funds. It was unlawful to hire anyone to solicit contributions on a commission or percentage basis. The "remit and return" method of raising money by sale of merchandise or tickets was also forbidden. No entertainment or benefit was lawful if the estimated costs, including compensation, exceeded 30 percent of the gross receipts.[16]

Early reports furnished a good idea of where contributions came from and what the cost was of maintaining the national headquarters. Late in February 1941 Skouras announced that about 90 percent of the money collected by the GWRA came from Americans of Greek descent, and that the cost of operating the national headquarters was slightly more than 2 percent.[17] The Greeks demonstrated that they rarely missed an opportunity to be dramatic when it came to raising funds. In St. Louis some three hundred well-dressed diners launched a $400,000 relief campaign by paying $1.25 for bean soup, cheese, and a bit of rye bread, set before them on bare boards. The chairman informed them that this was a day's ration in Greece. Then the tables were cleared and set with linen and silver for the usual steak dinner.[18]

Within a few months after the formation of the GWRA, some 964 chapters had been organized and $5,263,000 collected. In the five-month interval between the attack on Greece and the occupation by the Nazis, $3,336,700 was cabled to the GWRA committee in Athens.[19] This helped to purchase ambulances, build bomb-proof shelters, set up soup kitchens and workshops for refugees, and furnish financial assistance to the destitute families of slain soldiers. GWRA contributions were supplemented by those of the American Red Cross, which consigned four shiploads of food, medicines, and clothing valued at $2,250,000. This and additional assistance from the GWRA enabled the Athens committee to function up to the last possible moment in supplying clothing and funds to 55,000 veterans and civilians.

When the Nazis overran Greece and the Allies closed the sea lanes, the entire Mediterranean was sealed off. Greece, which normally imported 35 percent of her food needs, was completely isolated from the outside world. The helpless Greek population faced starvation. For a time GWRA leaders worked out a plan with the Allied governments, whereby food purchased in Turkey was shipped to Greece and distributed under the supervision of the International Red Cross. The first cargoes sailed from a Turkish port early in October 1941. These and other consignments totaling 19,000 tons reached Greece between October 1941 and August 1942.[20]

Leaders of the GWRA, after considerable inquiry and planning, devised an "Operation Blockade." They discovered that a large fleet of immobilized Swedish vessels were available to carry cargoes of food, clothing, and medicine, providing that safe conduct could be guaranteed by the warring nations. For assistance they turned to President Roosevelt, Under-Secretary of State Sumner Welles, and the chairman of the American Red Cross, Norman Davis. They suggested that the problem of distribution might be solved if a neutral commission functioning within Greece was appointed to see to it that the supplies were distributed to the starving Greeks. However, the Nazis, as a condition for accepting the plan, insisted that the people of Greece were not to be told that the supplies were donated by the people of the United States and Canada. During the two-and-a-half-year period that the program was in operation, a fleet of fourteen Swedish vessels made more than a hundred trips and carried almost 700,000 tons of food, clothing, medicines, and other vital supplies to Greece. But it was not until after

349

the liberation that the Greek people were informed that supplies valued at more than $100 million were the gift of the American people. The GWRA program is believed to have been the only one conducted by an American relief agency in occupied Europe. According to Archbishop Damaskinos, the Metropolitan of Athens and for a time the head of the Greek government, more than one third of the Greek population, or about two million people, were saved from death because of GWRA efforts.[21]

Entry of the United States into the Second World War marked the beginning of a second and more important phase in the Greek-Americans' activities. The one thing they wanted to make clear was their allegiance to the United States: "So clear that no one will ever be able to impugn the loyalty of even one American of Hellenic descent. So clear that when the judgment is made, no one—official or unofficial—can hesitate even a second in declaring the Americans of Hellenic descent gave fully to the war effort of the United States. Their loyalty was never questioned. They did their part as citizens of this country." [22] This time things were different; the sons and daughters of the immigrants joined the armed forces or were drafted. Since the average Greek family was large, it is reasonable to assume that at least one son in each family was in uniform or engaged in an essential occupation. The drive for Greek war relief continued its unabated course; but after Pearl Harbor the emphasis was on the American effort.[23]

Once the United States entered the war, AHEPA made it clear to its members that "America comes first." It publicized the statements released by the State Department on December 10, 1941, and January 7, 1942, regarding the "free" movements that were multiplying in the United States. These messages acknowledged the natural interest that citizens of various national backgrounds had in the countries of their origin, as well as the cultural, artistic, and spiritual contributions they had made to American life. But now that the United States was at war, activities that tended to divide the allegiance of any group of American residents between the United States and a foreign government were to be avoided. The State Department was aware of the existence of a number of committees representing free movements; but it had not extended any form of recognition to them, nor had it attempted to influence any resident alien or any American citizen in deciding whether he should associate himself with such a movement.[24]

A number of persons of dubious distinction, men who had been rulers of the destinies of Greece until or shortly before the German invasion, had come to the United States. A few of these men indicated their desire to assume the leadership of drives and campaigns for the relief of Greece. Such individuals felt that the Americans of Greek descent lacked culture and leadership and that it was necessary for them to take command. Obviously, those who had been working for the relief and liberation of Greece in the United States resented this intrusion. The lack of "parlor culture" by the Americans of Greek descent did not obscure the fact that they were able to handle their own affairs. These visiting Greeks were told to keep "hands off." [25]

News that King George II was pledging Greece to democracy came as a source of satisfaction to the Greek-Americans. A dispatch to this effect from Jerusalem, carrying a February 7, 1942, dateline, brought expressions of hearty approval. "As Americans of Greek descent all Ahepans can now point to their land of ancestry with pardonable pride for today Greece is reborn a Democracy." [26] Additional laurels came to the struggling Greek nation when official Washington welcomed King George II and Prime Minister Emanuel Tsouderos on their visit to the United States. The monarch spent the first night in the White House and the remainder of his stay in Blair House. In the Capitol he was given a tumultuous ovation when he was introduced to both houses of Congress. In presenting the king to the Senate, Vice President Henry Wallace said, "For centuries Greece has held aloft the torch of freedom, and never more than now."

In New York City the king was given a dinner by AHEPA that was attended by some two thousand Americans. The list of speakers included Cedric Foster, the well-known radio commentator and eminent Philhellene, who electrified his audience when he finished his tribute by reciting in Greek: "Kallitera mias oras / eleutheri zoe / para saranta hronia / sklavia kai filaki." Prime Minister Tsouderos then spoke at length and in moving terms about the struggles in Greece.[27]

In commemorating the second anniversary of Greece's resistance, AHEPA, in cooperation with the Treasury Department, initiated a drive to sell $50 million worth of United States government bonds. This campaign was launched over the Blue Network on October 28, 1942, by Speaker of the House Rayburn and George C. Vournas, the president of AHEPA. In a glowing tribute, Rayburn informed his audience that this broadcast was arranged to demonstrate the unity between Greece and the American war effort: "It is certainly in keeping with the battles of their blood brothers in the mountains of Albania that these Americans of Greek extraction are carrying on the battle on the American front." [28] As a means of publicizing the bond campaign, Speaker Rayburn and officers of AHEPA went to the street corner of the White House to sell a bond to Steve Vasilakos, an obscure vendor who was selling peanuts there. Nearby, cameras were clicking.[29] Vasilakos became a bond salesman himself, giving a bag of peanuts with every purchase; for he believed that if the United States lost the war he might lose the privilege of selling peanuts on his favorite corner.[30]

One doubts whether the representatives of any national group took the matter of selling government bonds with as much determination as the Greek-Americans. With them it was a matter of individual and national pride. In Las Vegas, Nevada, a group of restaurateurs ran an advertisement in the local press which informed potential buyers that they could buy bonds at any of their restaurants and enjoy complimentary dinners at the proprietor's expense.[31] A Moline, Illinois, businessman paid for the use of radio time and advertisements in the newspapers of four Illinois and Iowa cities, and gave away almost 35,000 candy bars as inducements to potential purchasers to buy bonds in the local banks and post offices. Another patriot in the soft-drinks-distributing business offered a case of cola with every purchase of a large bond. A Minneapolis café owner offered one of his famous steak sandwiches "with all the trimmings" with every $1,000 purchase.[32] Many others complained they did not have enough time to organize their respective committees and asked that the bond drive be extended; it was carried over from February 22 to May 21.[33] No sooner had the first bond drive ended when a second one was announced; this time it was for $100 million, or a combined quota of $150 million.[34] The grand total actually sold was $162,012,287.[35]

Some first-generation Greek-Americans displayed rather strong feelings about the war and in at least one city, Rochester, New York, about the money they had made in the United States and how they were going to save it. Ever since the bank failures of the early 1930s, many had developed a strong distrust for banks. Believing that they personally were the best custodians of their own hard-earned savings, they "cached thousands of dollars in chinks in cellar walls, hid money in mattresses, flower pots, old shoes and under the flooring of the attic." A member of the Rochester chapter of AHEPA who was selling war bonds visited the homes of his skeptical compatriots and pleaded with them to pry their money loose and invest it in the security of their adopted country. For a time he had difficulty in convincing some of these people that if the war bonds of the government lost their value, so would the money they had tucked away in their secret hideaways.

One of these hoarders was confronted with the fact that his wife returned from church one Sunday morning after purchasing a $25 bond for $18.75. Exasperated, he informed his wife that she had parted with her good money for a beautifully engraved piece of paper that was worthless. The next day he hurried to the man who sold the bond to his wife to reprimand him. In a patient tone the bond salesman informed him that his wife had performed an intelligent deed. His arguments must have been persuasive, for within a few days the once enraged compatriot became a purchaser himself.

Other purchasers dredged up money from cellar crypts and old socks. One purchaser delivered 700 dollar bills in a shoe box. Another arrived with $7,500 in cash to make his purchase. Nervously the bond salesman hurried to the bank to dispose of the money he had just acquired. This was in 1943. The tellers began to count the bills, many of which were of an oversize denomination that had been formally recalled by the United States Treasury as far back as 1919. One overly meticulous teller had this comment: "Not only did the bills smell badly, but many of them were actually mildewy." [36]

The retreat of the Nazis from Greece opened up the third and final phase of the GWRA program. With characteristic Teutonic thoroughness, the retreating Nazis "dynamited the railroads, telescoped the locomotive and rolling stock, blew up the bridges, burned towns and villages, leaving a million homeless, looted their factories, scorched farmlands, slaughtered the livestock, and stole what was worth taking— including the few remaining food stores." The Allied military forces furnished food for the destitute population, but it was apparent that they were ill prepared to carry this on for too long, much less to rehabilitate the shattered Greek economy. Thus UNRRA took over relief responsibilities in April 1945, and it was joined by GWRA which had also been charting its program for the liberation period.

Both agencies planned their relief strategy together so as to avoid duplication of effort, keep down administrative expenses, and make more effective use of their total resources. GWRA lent trained personnel to UNRRA, especially in the fields of health, child welfare, and transport equipment.

The war and the occupation had taken their toll of the Greek people. More than half a million active cases of tuberculosis were reported, and two million malaria victims. Malnutrition afflicted the entire population, especially the children whose growth had been stunted and whose average weight was thirty pounds less than that of comparable American children. As a means of combating these conditions, the GWRA immediately set its program into operation. It established community and mobile clinics for free medical treatment, especially in the rural areas, inaugurated a mass radiology program to determine active tubercular cases, placed in operation a factory to manufacture artificial limbs, supported the UNRRA anti-malaria program, made available scholarships for the training of doctors and nurses in the United States and Great Britain, furnished hot lunches for about one million children, provided for the orphaned and the needy, and arranged for the sending of food and clothing by individual Americans to specific persons in Greece.[37] In undertakings of such scope and urgency, mistakes were bound to happen. One of the most frequent complaints was that supplies, food packages, and clothing did not reach the people. There were the usual charges of graft, wholesale looting, and incompetence. The truth of these accusations will never be known, but in all likelihood a few were true.

The withdrawal of the Nazis also aggravated the political struggle that had been simmering within Greece. This time it involved the monarchists, as it always had in the past, and a new faction which at first blush seemed to have mass support, the EAM (Ethnikon Apeleutheritikon Metopon), or the National Liberation Front. It is difficult to state what percentage of American Greeks were involved in these struggles, but it is clear that a sizable number of them were. Those most active in spearheading the EAM movement and in mobilizing public opinion were obscure persons who had not been actively engaged in Greek-American affairs. But in time they managed to add to their letterheads, temporarily at least, the names of a number of men who had been closely identified with community affairs. To the more discerning it appeared that the united-front or popular-front techniques of pre-World War Two days were being revived in the postwar era.

The history of EAM would constitute a lengthy and involved study in itself. Reports of its activities began filtering into the United States late in 1943 and early 1944. One of the first accounts was a tract issued under the auspices of the hitherto unknown Greek-American Labor Committee, which claimed that it represented 100,000 trade unionists. Entitled *Greece Fights for Freedom*, it was compiled, according to its sponsors, for the benefit of all fighters for democracy and dedicated to a final victory over fascism and to "a people's peace." [38] In highly partisan fashion the pamphlet described the emergence of the forces of the EAM and the ELAS (Ethnikos Laikos Apeleftherotikos Stratos, or National Liberation Popular Army), the underground movement in Greece, the unity of the Greek people in their determination to rid the nation of fascist and royalist influences, and the disruptive reporting of the *New York Times*. It characterized the goal of the EAM as twofold: to prevent the return of the king to Greece until a plebiscite determined the form of government the people wanted; and to form a provisional government of national unity, comprised of all shades of public opinion, which would assume the liberation struggle and express the will of the Greek people in the matter of constitutional government.[39] The Greek government-in-exile was branded as pro-Nazi and pro-King.[40]

The pamphlet unfolded what was heralded as the EAM program of action: assistance to the Greek people in the spirit of the Atlantic Charter and the Moscow Conference. With the liberation of any part of Greece, a government committed to the National Liberation Front was to be formed that would pledge itself to continue the fight on the side of the Allies, organize relief programs, and proclaim a plebiscite that would decide the nature of the future government: "Conditions no longer exist for the return of the status quo before the German invasion. Promises of a temporary government made by King George cannot be considered satisfactory. Therefore, when they enter Greece, the Allies must seek the cooperation of the resistance movement, the EAM in particular, and must not attempt to impose the King on the Greek people." Finally, the United States, the Soviet Union, and Great Britain had to enter into close cooperation.[41]

During 1944 the EAM campaign was waged through the columns of the *Greek-American Tribune* in New York City. This same publication issued tracts in the Greek and English languages that urged a program of national unity to guide the destiny of Greece after liberation. Months before the war ended, it sought to build on the earlier efforts of the Pan-Hellenic Congress, which had met in Cincinnati during the summer of 1941, by continuing the attacks on King George II, and assailing the *Atlantis* for its monarchical bias.

Little doubt now remains as to the leftist political orientation of the *Greek-American Tribune* or the Greek-American Labor Committee and the groups closely identified with it. These organizations attempted to perpetuate the united-front techniques of the late 1930s through the issuance of literature and the formation of Greek-American labor committees in all major cities; the hope was to weld all these elements into a major national organization. Emphasis was placed on the role that the Greek-American worker was to play in freeing Greece from her oppressor.[42] In due course the name of the Greek-American Labor Committee disappeared from its letterhead and in its place appeared that of the Greek-American Committee for National Unity (GACFNU). Precisely when and in what circumstances this change occurred is unknown, but it resulted in no change in policy. Within a few more months the name of the latter was changed to the Greek-American Council (GAC).[43]

After the Allies landed in Greece, the tempo of the Greek-Americans' interest in the internal politics of the country was quickened. Typical of this was a letter that Basil Vlavianos, the publisher and editor of the *National Herald,* had received from President Roosevelt, who said: "I am glad to have this opportunity to reassure my friends of Greek origin and Greek birth everywhere that it is the desire of the American government to help Greece to the utmost of its capabilities. It is the further desire of our government that the Greek people who have fought so valiantly for democratic ideals, will be able to exercise as soon as possible the right of all democratic people and choose for themselves the form of government under which they will live."[44]

Several days later a rally of twenty-five thousand Greek-Americans was staged in Manhattan Center in New York, in commemoration of the fourth anniversary of Greece's refusal to submit to Mussolini and in celebration of the Allied landing in Greece. The speakers asked the Allies to extend full financial aid to Greece, "not in the form of a business transaction but as a deserved assistance to the nation that gave its all." Kimon Diamantopoulos, the Greek ambassador to the United States, urged his listeners to bury their political differences and work for the rebuilding of their country.[45] On the following day the Athens radio appealed to Greeks abroad for immediate financial aid to relatives in the homeland.[46]

Events quickly bore out that the political differences which had been brewing within liberated Greece were spilling over into the United States. Once more it appeared as though the battle between royalists and parliamentarians was going to be refought. At the same time, charges were voiced that these parliamentary forces were the stalking horse for certain sinister elements at work behind the scenes.

Late in November 1944, the GACFNU, after praising Roosevelt for the assistance given Greece, criticized a section of the Greek and American press, including the *New York Times,* for their news dispatches on the EAM. This EAM-oriented committee did not wish its position misunderstood, for it recognized that the United States had become "not only the arsenal of democracy but its cupboard, wardrobe and pharmacy as well." But it did take exception to the "defamatory dispatches" of correspondent A. C. Sedgwick of the *New York Times* and protested the censorship that permitted the release of slanderous reports and the obstruction of real news. Reports of "anarchy and division" in Greece, according to the GACFNU, tended to disrupt the unity of the Greek-Americans.[47] The truth of the matter is that the political future of Greece had taken on anarchical dimensions. The monarchists, with British support, urged the return of King George II, believing that in the long run this would promote the stability of the country. The anti-monarchists, which included the GACFNU and for a time the *National Herald,* insisted that the British were attempting "to impose upon Greece an unpopular regime." "No one should be fooled into the belief that the resistance movement is communistic. Those in the resistance army could not put down their arms as long as they were not given a guarantee that reactionary forces supported by foreign masters would not become masters of the situation."[48]

Late in 1944 an unrepresentative group of Greek-American societies visited the State Department to protest British intervention and to urge the United States to end the bloodshed in Greece. Stelios Pistolakis, the president of the GACFNU, the son-in-law of Venizelos and a former member of the Greek Chamber of Deputies, declared upon leaving the State Department that officials had given him the assurance that American policy in Greece would remain unchanged. He also believed that American influence would be exerted to check the fighting among the Allies and allow a peaceful settlement in keeping with the wishes of the people of Greece. Later this same delegation was received at the British embassy where it left a protest against the attempt of Great Britain "to impose by force of foreign arms a government opposed to the will of the Greek people." Exception was taken to Prime Minister Churchill's charge that these men were patriots and liberals who were in no way associated with communism.

The delegates, although Greek-Americans, differed from those who had espoused the cause of Greece in the past because of their left-of-center orientation. Besides the Greek-American Committee for National Unity, they included representatives of the Athenian Society of New York; the Cretan Association Omonia of New York; the Greek-American Labor Committee of the Federation of Greek Soldiers of New York; the Food Workers Union, AFL; the Greek Fur Workers Union, Local 70, CIO; and the Greek Seamans Union. Conspicuously absent were representatives of AHEPA, GAPA, the Pan-Arcadians, and various other groups.[49]

Perhaps the position of AHEPA was best presented by Vournas, the president, in a message to the members prior to the liberation of Greece from the Nazis. He said:

In extending a helping hand to the people of Greece, we must constantly bear in mind that the AHEPA is a non-political organization. Whether as individuals or as an organization, we act as Americans of Greek descent, we must do everything we can to help the Greek people in their present plight. But we must never forget that the Greeks take their politics seriously and for us to interfere directly or indirectly in their internal affairs is a breach of duty and a breach of propriety. People who have electrified the world with the Olympian message that "it is better to die on your feet than to live on your knees" are more than competent to determine for themselves how they should live or under what system or form of government they should prosper.[50]

But with the Nazi retreat, the arrival of the British, and reports of violence in Athens, an advertisement of protest appeared in the *Washington Post* on December 9, 1944, bearing the signature of George C. Vournas as supreme president of AHEPA. Making known that this was an advertisement "made by Americans—paid for by Americans," it urged the United States to re-examine its lend-lease program. More specifically, though acknowledging the need for unity to defeat Hitler, it said that the progress of the war was opening up newer and larger horizons for consideration. British policy was singled out for censure. The Atlantic Charter was being ruthlessly trampled upon through power politics and Great Britain was arrogating to itself the right to interfere with European governments. In the process Lend-Lease materials acquired from the United States were being used to crush people who were in disagreement with British policy. Among those being shown "the hilt of Britain's imperialistic sword" were "the Greek patriots—the very men who fought Hitler for 4 years—not Communists—hailed for years as glorious allies and so addressed only a month ago—are being shot down daily by British colonial troops in the city of Athens."[51] Since the guns pointed "at civilian populations in Europe by the British may bear the trademark—Made in the U.S.A.," it was time for Congress to inquire into the postwar purposes of Lend-Lease aid.[52]

But the most persistent and active course was that taken by the Greek-American Committee for National Unity. It left no stone unturned to bring the program of the EAM to the American public. It staged rallies, drafted resolutions, circulated petitions, and distributed literature. In a rally on January 14, 1945, Frank Gervasi, recently returned from Greece, informed a crowd of twelve hundred in New York: "The wind that sweeps through Europe is not a red wind . . . the total number of Communists is 10% . . . The EAM program is quite clear . . . They want the establishment of a republic, after a legal, honest plebiscite. Very simple. They want to purge the country of all fascists, the hangovers from the Metaxas regime, of the collaborationists. They do not want to shoot them all or anything quite so violent."[53]

On January 25, 1945, a delegation of fifteen American trade unionists and members of Greek-American societies visited the State Department and the embassies of Greece and Great Britain. Again conspicuously absent among the delegates were representatives of AHEPA, GAPA, and comparable groups whose voices had been raised loud and often in the past when Greek interests were at stake. In its memorandum to the State Department this delegation asked that Greece and the other liberated countries be treated in accordance with the spirit of the Atlantic Charter, the Moscow Agreement, and the Teheran Accord. British intervention in Greece was assailed. The democratic process had to be restored in Greece at the earliest possible moment and reprisals avoided. But this could be accomplished only when foreign intervention ceased and a representation was given to the EAM that was commensurate with the leadership and authority that it wielded. Traitors and collaborators had to be arrested, brought to trial, and punished for their crimes. Free elections could be guaranteed only under the supervision of a commission of the United Nations, and not under the shadow of British arms. Finally, the United States government was asked to act on a petition from eleven American correspondents to remove the restraints that kept them from transmitting the views of the EAM to the American reading public.

The memoranda to the British and the Greek authorities were in the same vein. The British were advised that intervention in Greece brought catastrophe, bloody warfare, and a "terrorist campaign of vengeance against civilians and prisoners of EAM views." The Allied correspondents had to be permitted to tell the truth about Greece. The Greek ambassador was told pretty much the same thing, with the added suggestion that "the Greek Government would do Greece and the United States a great service in requesting the recall of the Provocateur-reporter A. C. Sedgwick from Greece." [54]

The Greek-American Council came into being in New York City on February 11, 1945, when representatives of the Greek-American Committee for National Unity from San Francisco, Chicago, Philadelphia, Washington, Lynn, and Haverhill assembled for the purpose of organizing on a broader and more effective scale. The program of the GAC was nothing more than a restatement of the programs of its predecessor groups; the only difference was the adoption of a more manageable name. One of its major tasks was to give wider publicity to the reports of Leland Stowe, Frank Gervasi, George Weller, M. W. Fodor, and the eye-witness accounts of Constantine Poulos. In a statement released on February 15, 1945, the GAC declared:

The declaration of Yalta is a stimulating reaffirmation of the allied goals of freedom, democracy, and security . . . This is the program which, if it is fulfilled in Greece, can dissipate the legacy of anxiety and distrust left by the damaging policies of the British government . . . It is the hope of mankind that the new pledges of Yalta for joint measures to guarantee freedom and democracy will be carried through sincerely and unconditionally for all liberated nations.[55]

In the succeeding months, the GAC devoted many of its energies to relating accounts of terrorism and destruction in Greece, the return of the collaborationists to power, the threats to free elections, and eye-witness accounts that portrayed the leaders of the EAM as martyrs to the cause of freedom and the British as ruthless imperialists.[56] In the fall Stelios Pistolakis, one of the prime movers behind the GAC, announced that he was returning to Greece to help in the campaign to unite all antifascist forces into one solid front and establish a democratic government.[57]

The year 1946 saw a worsening of political conditions. Wide publicity was given to the spread of terror and persecutions in Greece, the imprisonment of political rivals, the fascist decrees that were wiping out all vestiges of democracy, and the oncoming civil war.[58] That spring an EAM delegation headed by G. Georgalas, a professor of mineralogy in the University of Athens prior to the Nazi invasion, the representative of the Socialist Party on the central committee of the EAM, and the president of the Greek Youth Movement, along with Nicholas Carvounis, the press director of the EAM in Athens, made a two-month tour of the United States speaking to audiences wherever they could be assembled. Shortly prior to their return to Greece, the American Relief for Greek Democracy came into being for the ostensible purpose of providing assistance to the EAM forces. Its distributing agency in Greece was National Solidarity.

This, then, was the response to World War Two. First, the resources of Greeks in America were thrown behind the campaign for Greek war relief; then they were mobilized with even greater force behind the American war effort. The war had enormous psychological effects on the community. It enhanced the Greek-American's status in American society, accelerated the already well-advanced process of assimilation, and increased the confidence of a long-insecure group of people. Few now were prone to view themselves as Greeks or even as Greek-Americans. In some quarters such designations were roundly resented. They had become Americans of Hellenic descent.

THE ERA OF
RESPECTABILITY

THE era after World War Two was one of continued progress and prosperity for Greek-Americans. The lush war years had brought new wealth and affluence to members of the older generation who were solidly entrenched in business, the hotel industry, and the various professions. Greek names became more and more identified with charitable, educational, and community projects. Thousands of immigrants' sons returned from the battlefield to continue their education or resume careers in business, law, medicine, engineering, teaching, and journalism. And the hierarchy of the Greek Orthodox Church continued its program of centralization at the expense of the secular tradition, making it clear that it meant to become the dominant voice in Greek community affairs.

At the same time, American Hellenism received cultural transfusions from many directions. Displaced persons, refugees, and university students began arriving in increasing numbers. President Truman singled out Greece in 1947 as one of the two countries that was to receive assistance from the United States in the campaign against communism; and the departure of Athenagoras, the Archbishop of North and South America, in the private plane of the President of the United States for Istanbul, where he was enthroned as Ecumenical Patriarch, gave the American Greeks a moral lift. Never before had so much interest been displayed in the American press. Relief packages and financial assistance continued to flow into Greece; and once conditions became stabilized, a mounting number of American and Greek-American tourists found their way into the country. By the late 1950s and early 1960s, popular motion pictures filmed in Greece, and the appearance of Greek tragedy players, folk singers, and dancers on the American stage, helped present both the Greeks and their American kin in a more sympathetic light. This was truly an era of respectability.[1]

Relief was uppermost in the minds of American Greeks after the war, as it had been during the actual fighting. This was apparent in the activities of the Greek War Relief Association, AHEPA, GAPA, the various church parishes, the Greek-language press, the numerous independent societies, EAM and anti-EAM circles, and the correspondence that flowed back and forth between the two countries. During April 1945 UNRRA entered Greece and assumed the responsibilities for feeding the people and providing some of their basic agricultural and industrial supplies. The GWRA joined UNRRA in its work, as we saw in the last chapter.[2]

The relief work of the GWRA, although limited, was quite impressive and reflected the affection that the American Greeks retained for the mother country.[3] Timely and substantial as this aid was, it was insufficient to provide for the rehabilitation of Greece. Newspaper accounts made it clear that UNRRA was organized to bring relief to all the Allied countries of Europe and Asia, not merely to Greece. Furthermore, UNRRA was giving more than it originally had intended, and it was planning to pull out of Greece by the end of 1946.[4]

Sending money to relatives during these critical years was "like throwing the money into the sewer" because the rate of exchange on the black market was considerably higher than the official rate. Consequently, the plan was to send goods and animals. During the spring of 1946, the GWRA inaugurated a "Give an Animal" program for Greece. Conceived, planned, and directed by George P. Skouras, the project called upon relatives and friends in the United States to purchase cows, mules, or mares for relatives and friends in Greece as a practical means of facilitating the recovery of the country.[5]

Rather novel, the "Give an Animal" program was based on sound practical reasoning. Since fully 65 percent of the people lived on the land, it was plain that recovery was contingent upon the rehabilitation of Greek agriculture. Funds were lacking, but many in Greece had relatives among the 400,000 American Greeks who were in a position to be of assistance. If all, or most, of these Americans could be persuaded to contribute toward the purchase of a cow or a horse, a good start toward recovery would be under way. The general plan was to send "a bred cow—a cow that would have a calf four to five months after she [got] to Greece—an ordinary Brown Swiss cow which [gave] enough milk for several families." Or one could send "a mare, also bred, so she could have a colt, a few months after she [got] there."

Realizing that the purchase of bred cows and mares and shipping them to Greece on an individual basis was costly, cumbersome, and inadvisable, Skouras sought the advice of experts in the United States Department of Agriculture. Among other things he was advised that the Brown Swiss heifer was the most suitable cow for the Greek climate, and that he should confine himself to the purchase of ordinary, instead of high-grade, cows. An arrangement finally was made with the Department of Agriculture for the purchase of cows at $180 per head and mares for $98, the price including the cost of transportation to the point of embarkation. The animals were inoculated against all diseases and bred to have offspring within four months after reaching Greece. Once this understanding was reached, an agreement was made with UNRRA, which had many ships for the shipment of animals. This service cost nothing. Once the animals reached Greece, they were delivered by the trucks of the GWRA. Operating on the theory that the plan would catch on "like wildfire," the GWRA established a revolving fund through which it purchased three boatloads of animals that were shipped to Greece immediately.[6] Eventually plows, cultivators, sprayers, hoes, books, kettles, and other badly needed equipment also were to be sent to Greece.[7]

Meanwhile, AHEPA planned an ambitious hospital program. At a conference in 1945 it was resolved to raise millions of dollars for this purpose. Early in 1946 a nation-wide drive was launched, and within five months pledges and cash totaling $1 million were collected. Simultaneously, the GWRA was planning a medical and hospitalization program of its own. Realizing that united action was preferable, AHEPA arranged with the GWRA and the Economic Cooperation Administration (ECA) to pool their resources. As a result of this arrangement, the money raised was quadrupled and $5 million was spent for the AHEPA hospitals in Greece.

A breakdown of fund allocations, according to AHEPA sources, shows that fully $2 million was spent on the AHEPA Pavilion in the Evangelismos Hospital of Athens. The AHEPA General Hospital in Salonika that served all of northern Greece—especially Macedonia— and helped in the training of nurses and doctors, cost about $1.6 million. Seven AHEPA Health Centers costing $1.4 million were located in Chrysopolis, Kalavryta, Meligala, Ierapetra (Crete), Thebes, Farsala, and Filiatra. Needless to say, AHEPA and its auxiliaries, the Daughters of Penelope, the Maids of Athens, and the Sons of Pericles, considered this their greatest effort. They acknowledged the assistance of the GWRA and the ECA in seeing these projects completed.[8]

While the GWRA and AHEPA were attempting to accomplish all they could through private efforts, the Greek government, fully cognizant of the herculean task that lay ahead, requested the Food and Agriculture Organization of the United Nations (FAO) to appoint a special mission to study the agricultural needs of the country. Specifically the FAO was asked to formulate a program for the rehabilitation and future development of the agricultural, land, water, and industrial resources of Greece. The hope was that the FAO would make long-range recommendations and take its initial steps during the crop year of 1947. The Report of the FAO Mission to Greece, one of the most exhaustive studies on the agricultural and land resources of Greece published in the English language, was drafted by administrators of American agricultural colleges and representatives of several United States government agencies and two foreign countries. The members of the mission spent several months in Greece amassing information and conferring with all segments of the population.[9] The FAO Report made it clear that far more than the voluntary efforts of American Greeks were needed to help Greece in her recovery. The task was a gigantic one, as anyone who had firsthand knowledge of actual conditions in Greece knew. The plight of Greece, with Russia and her satellite countries as neighbors, had become the concern of the Western world.

Participation by the United States in the affairs of Greece up to this point had been almost entirely limited to the distribution of some relief by the American military forces. Brigadier General Percy L. Sadler, in a statement to news correspondents, stated that American personnel had been instructed to refrain from taking any action that could be interpreted as intervention in Greek political affairs. American officers delivered medical supplies and food to hospitals, milk to child-feeding centers, and flour to bakeries, but they did not go beyond that.[10]

The American Greeks, in the meantime, had started their campaign to aid Greece in her territorial ambitions, just as they had after the First World War. And they mobilized some rather influential support. Among the most assertive groups was the newly formed Panepirotic Federation, which was founded in 1942 under the "wise guidance and blessing" of Archbishop Athenagoras. This federation had, as expected, the support of *Atlantis,* the *National Herald, Eleutheros Typos,* AHEPA, GAPA, the National Justice for Greece Committee, the Panhellenic Committee for the Defense of Greek Rights, and the more recently formed American Justice for Greece Committee.[11] The campaign of the Panepirotic Federation was launched on a methodical, if not entirely successful, basis. Believing that the Moscow Conference of December 17, 1945, would take up the question of northern Epirus, the federation and its various chapters sent telegrams to the foreign secretaries of the nations that were represented in Moscow, the Allied leaders, the Greek-language press in the United States and Greece, and the Epirotic societies in various countries of the world. A bulletin also was issued and mailed to the American press, congressmen, senators, religious and lay leaders, public libraries, ambassadors of the United States throughout the world, and numerous organizations.[12]

Another group that agitated for Greek territorial claims was the Panhellenic Committee for the Defense of Greek Rights. In a statement presented to the American Academy of Political and Social Science, the committee pointed out that the idea of collective security which originated in ancient Greece also inspired people of modern Greece. The problems of the world would be eased considerably if they were settled amicably on the principle of self-determination. The committee further added that a significant step had been taken by the United States Senate Committee on Foreign Relations on March 27, 1946, when it unanimously adopted the resolution of Senator Claude Pepper asking the award of the Dodecanese Islands and northern Epirus to Greece. Claiming that it was voicing the sentiments of American citizens who were "natives of or descendants of natives of the yet unredeemed lands," the committee felt confident that with the moral aid of the American people "those lands which historically, ethnologically and culturally form part of the Greek heritage will come under the fold of their mother country, Greece." [13]

Perhaps the most influential group during these years, although the scope of its activities remains unclear, was the National Justice for Greece Committee.[14] This committee asked that Greece be granted reparations so that she could restore her economy and rebuild the health of her people; that the Dodecanese Islands and northern Epirus be returned to Greece; and that the boundary line with Bulgaria be corrected so as to provide a natural line of defense.[15]

The editorial columns of the many American newspapers echoed these sympathies and reflected a new high in pro-Greek sentiments in the United States. During 1946 it became common for one to read such editorial captions as "Justice for Greece," "Strange Gratitude," "When Greece Stood Fast," "A Greek Day of Remembrance," "Republicans Stand Up for Greece," "The Greeks in the Middle of It," "Our Obligations To Greece," "We Should Back Greek Claims," "The Claims of Greece," "Greek Freedom," "The Liberty-Loving Greeks," and "Greece under Pressure." [16] Just how much influence editorial opinion had on American foreign policy during these years may be subject to question, but it is beyond doubt that the United States did become involved in the affairs of Greece. On December 19, 1946, the United States, in the first of a series of steps, supported a resolution in the Security Council of the United Nations asking for a commission to investigate incidents along the Greek frontier. In February 1947 the United Kingdom announced that it no longer was able to shoulder the Greek burden alone. Then the Greek government formally appealed to the United States for assistance. Finally on March 12, 1947, President Truman announced to Congress that "it must be the policy of the United States to support free peoples who are resisting attempted subjugation by armed minorities or by outside pressures ... Should we fail to aid Greece and Turkey in this fateful hour, the effect will be far-reaching to the West as well as to the East." [17]

President Truman's call received immediate attention. The measure to aid Greece and Turkey was approved on May 22, 1947, the Greek aid program on June 20, the agreement with Turkey on July 12, and one for $400 million in military and economic assistance to Greece and Turkey on July 30. Some $600 million was extended under this program, about 70 percent of which went for military assistance (owing to the activities of the Communist guerrillas). All told, about one billion dollars was given to Greece and Turkey from 1944 to 1950.[18]

The Truman Doctrine and aid to Greece and Turkey did not become an issue with the American Greeks. This is difficult to understand, especially in view of their usual ceaseless concern with the affairs of Greece. Was it because events had moved so swiftly that they were unable to organize themselves for any concerted expression of opinion? Was it because they were too busy with their various relief efforts to find the time for this ground-breaking development? Was it because Washington failed to sound them out on their views, preferring instead to elicit the opinions of private individuals? Or was it that so many of them opposed the nature of this assistance and dared not speak out in opposition lest this brand them as Communists or Communist dupes? Certainly there is no evidence that organizations such as AHEPA, which had figured so prominently in bond sales and other wartime activities, ever were sounded out for their views. Nor has proof been uncovered that GWRA, GAPA, or other groups were asked for opinions. But this was a time when they could do very little even if they were asked. The United States government had to move swiftly, and sentiment in behalf of Greek assistance was abundant.

Archbishop Athenagoras hailed President Truman as "a man sent from God" to play a leading role in world affairs. Speaking at a memorial service on the eleventh anniversary of the death of Venizelos, the archbishop declared that the fears of Americans of Greek descent that the United States would be unable to find a leader capable of asserting its leadership in world affairs were dissipated by the pronouncement of Truman to Congress. At the same time, Athenagoras announced that the three hundred churches under his jurisdiction were offering prayers for the continued health of the President.[19]

Only two American Greeks appeared before the Senate Foreign Relations Committee when hearings on aid to Greece and Turkey were being conducted. Both of these men expressed their outright opposition to the proposed aid. One was Costa Couvaras, a former officer in the United States army, former chief of a secret OSS mission in Greece, and the secretary of American Relief for Greek Democracy. Couvaras blamed the civil war in Greece on "the successive rightist or Royalist governments," and declared that a one-sided picture was being presented to Congress and the American people. He also said:

Sending military aid to Greece would aggravate a bad situation and in the end, a big section of the Greek population would have to be exterminated by force that would not be of benefit to Greece or the United States . . .

If we bring [the Greeks] guns . . . they are going to hate us, just as they hated the Germans and now hate the British. If we put this aid in the hands of the Royalist Government, we will have to pour in more power instead of a representative government.[20]

A second opponent to aid for Greece was Alex Karanikas, the secretary of the American Council for a Democratic Greece. Speaking on behalf of his organization, Karanikas said that its members, composed of Americans mainly of Greek descent, opposed American intervention in Greece because this constituted unilateral action, sidestepped the United Nations, and afforded assistance to an illegal, unrepresentative, and undemocratic royalist government.[21]

Considerable opposition to the Truman aid program also was voiced by correspondents such as Constantine Poulos, Basil Vlavianos, for a time the publisher of the *National Herald,* and others of non-Greek background. Judging from the articles published in the *Nation,* the *New Republic,* and other periodicals, one might get the impression that a large portion of the American Greek population opposed the Truman program.[22] On the other hand, the Liberal Party of New York, which supported Truman's policy, called upon the President to appoint Dean Alfange, a Liberal Party leader in New York and a former president of AHEPA, as head of the American mission to direct the aid program. Alfange's knowledge of conditions in Greece, his opposition to both communism and fascism, and his six years of experience with the Greek War Relief Association made him an ideal choice.[23]

Of great importance to the American Greeks was the announcement that Athenagoras, the Archbishop of North and South America, had been elected Patriarch of Constantinople. This event was of far greater significance than press reports would indicate. For the first time in the history of the Eastern Orthodox Church, an American citizen had been elevated to the throne of the Patriarchate. The Patriarch of Constantinople was the most exalted ecclesiast in the entire Orthodox Church.[24]

Athenagoras' selection as Patriarch can be attributed in part to his success in uniting the feuding church factions in the United States, the growing international importance of the Greek Orthodox churches in America, and a recognition of the leadership of the United States in world affairs. His being flown to the scene of his enthronement in the private plane of the President of the United States was accepted as recognition that the Eastern Orthodox Church was aligned with the nations of the West.

There were signs that the Greek Orthodox Church was becoming the most influential Greek institution in the United States, which to many was a genuine cause for alarm. This growing influence was manifested by the building of new and opulent parishes; the continued centralization of authority in the archdiocese; the recognition of the Eastern Orthodox Church as a major religion, along with the denominations of the Protestants, Roman Catholics, and Jews; and the belated efforts made to identify the faith with the greater American community.

Perhaps one of the most disturbing trends was the process of centralization that was being made at the expense of the bishops, the parish priests, and the laity. The bishops remained assistants of the archbishop, which tended to complicate the problems of the parishes. First invoked by Athenagoras, implemented by Michael, and finally reinforced by Iakovos, the centralization program encountered resistance from various quarters, especially the followers of the Reverend Christopher Kontogeorge. Part of the program involved efforts to systematize the assignment of priests, regularize and enlarge the revenues of the archdiocese, and enforce the Uniform Parish Bylaws of the archdiocese. The archdiocese, which for all practical purposes meant the archbishop, was accused of employing coercion, threatening to deprive parishes of the services of priests unless they accepted the bylaws, and even to excommunicate rebellious leaders if they continued their resistance to the edicts of the archdiocese.

Despite this trend toward centralization, the administrative machinery of the church was little less than chaotic. Obtaining an answer from the archdiocese to a simple communication was a frustrating experience for both priests and laymen. Few of the hierarchs had any real experience in the Western world. As long as hierarchs continued to be trained in Greece and in the adjoining areas that knew a simpler society, so long would the American churches be lost in an administrative jungle. Matters were aggravated by the unwillingness or inability

of the archdiocese to delegate authority. The American Greek parishioners had not been subjected to this kind of authoritarian discipline
in the past, and it appeared unlikely that they would submit to it very
readily now. The better-educated and conscience-stricken priests who
were upset by the actions of the hierarchy openly expressed dissatisfaction and even spoke of their readiness to resign from the priesthood.[25]

Some of the earliest opposition to the archdiocese stemmed from the
unwillingness of members of the faith to be taxed for church services.
The campaign to levy a tax was inaugurated during the early 1940s as
a means of providing a permanent source of revenue. Down through
1942 the archdiocese depended largely on voluntary contributions and
assessments to meet its expenses. According to an official account, the
contributions for 1942 totaled a paltry $41,000.

As a means of augmenting its slender resources, the monodollarion,
or single-dollar contribution, was inaugurated by the archdiocese in
1943. But collecting this voluntary per-capita contribution of one dollar
annually was hardly as simple as one might have expected, even during
the prosperous war and postwar years. Many parishioners were un-
accustomed to this method of finance and resented it as an unwarranted
imposition, even though it was put on a purely voluntary basis to take
the tax sting out of it. After rumblings of dissatisfaction and outright
opposition, the monodollarion revenues of the archdiocese increased
slowly, as the following figures indicate.

1944	$ 62,657.59
1945	92,001.30
1946	90,536.91
1947	80,649.35
1948	100,320.35
1949	unavailable
1950	81,956.36

The revenues fluctuated from year to year owing to the voluntary
nature of the offerings and the unwillingness of some of the priests to
aid in its collection.[26] As a consequence, periodic campaigns for funds
were conducted to supplement the income from the monodollarion.[27]

The Tenth Biennial Congress of Clergymen and Laymen, as a means
of abolishing the hitherto ineffective methods of raising money,
authorized the collection of the compulsory dekadollarion, or a ten-

dollar levy, from each member.[28] Needless to say this brought more funds into the coffers of the Archdiocese, as the following figures show.[29]

1951	$329,726.23
1952	393,902.11
1953	454,709.98
1954	449,661.53
1955	537,615.36
1956	532,132.02
1957	571,951.51
1958	585,698.99

These figures also indicate that, although the revenue of the archdiocese was increasing, the number of members in good standing had actually decreased. Some parishes made little effort to collect the dekadollarion and refused to be bound by the mandates of the biennial congresses.[30] The collections for the year 1958 indicate that less than 59,000 members of the faith were in good standing, which was a far cry from the figure of a million or more followers which the archdiocese released for public consumption.

Another cause for mounting dissatisfaction was the determined effort of the archdiocese to obtain a firm grip over the parishes by the adoption of the Uniform Parish Bylaws. Designed to achieve a degree of unity, these bylaws, for all practical purposes, aimed to place unparalleled power over lay matters in the hands of the church hierarchy. They made the archbishop the final arbiter in almost all disputes. Some parishes accepted the bylaws without reservation; others ratified them with certain misgivings and apprehensions; and still others refused to be bound by them on the grounds that they were an unwarranted transgression on local autonomy. As a means of hastening their acceptance, the archdiocese resorted to various devices, such as bestowing titles on influential parish leaders and releasing misleading information that led hesitant parishes to believe that they were among the few that had not ratified the bylaws. In extreme cases the archdiocese threatened to deprive parishes of priests and even to excommunicate defiant leaders. In some cases litigation resulted, which threatened to revive those earlier dark days in the history of the Greek Orthodox Church in the United States.

Criticism also was leveled at the archdiocese for its failure to appoint an American-born, American-educated, and American-oriented bishop. This made it extremely difficult for American priests, who as a rule were barred from such assignments because they were pressured into acquiring wives before being ordained as priests. This produced somewhat of a schizophrenic situation whereby the hierarchy, despite denials, was oriented toward Greece and the Ecumenical Patriarchate, while more of the rank-and-file priests veered toward the United States.

These years also witnessed a new trend in church architecture that sought to improve on the unimaginative designs of the past. Most of the parish churches had been built during the peak years of immigration, or just before immigrant bars into this country were raised. Their architectural styles, if they could be labeled as such, were carbon copies of churches built in the Byzantine tradition. Some were box-shaped structures or crude imitations of the Hagia Sophia of Constantinople. But the postwar years brought a change. The emergence of a new generation to positions of influence, combined with the cooperation of the more "progressive" older members and the prosperity of the war years, inspired the building of churches that were more in harmony with their improved American surroundings. A church in the old immigrant neighborhood would no longer do. The parishioners were Americans, in many instances they had carved out successful niches for themselves in the business and professional worlds. They wanted their churches to reflect their new status in American society.

Perhaps the most striking example of the new departure in architecture was that of the Annunciation Church of Milwaukee, designed by Frank Lloyd Wright. To some degree this design reflected the uninhibited individualism of the parishioners of the Milwaukee community. For years its leaders had acquired a reputation for defying the archdiocese and the national and district headquarters of AHEPA. The offspring of the older generation had an enviable record in higher education, and the parish itself had been spared the "ghetto complex" that overtook Greek communities in the larger cities. The social climate of Milwaukee with its many years of unorthodox political behavior, coupled with the more venturesome qualities of some of the church leaders, contributed in an oblique fashion to this situation. Some of the better-educated parishioners who assumed positions of responsibility in church affairs were also identified with the greater Milwaukee community. This, combined with wise and careful planning, business

373

acumen, and faith on the part of the lending agencies in the fiscal soundness of the project, served to make this parish church unique in the country.[31] Among other things, it tended to have a contagious effect on other denominations in the city, which began to realize that their own churches were drab and unimaginative structures.[32]

Still another development was the organization of the younger people into the Greek Orthodox Youth Association (GOYA), in the hope of bringing them closer to the church. The launching of this organization was attended with much fanfare and promise for the future, but the fruits of the effort have remained obscure. If nothing else, GOYA served to bring the young into social relationships that previously were limited.[33]

World War Two witnessed the inauguration of a movement to recognize the Eastern Orthodox Church as a major faith. To the members of the church this was most ironic, for they considered the Orthodox faith as the oldest among the Christian beliefs. But this apparently made no difference to Selective Service officials, who refused to recognize one Reverend John H. Gelsinger, an ordained priest of the Syrian Orthodox Church, as being entitled to the benefits of Class IV-D of the Selective Service Act. The Orthodox Church was not recognized as "a regular church," and furthermore, according to these officials, the priest had failed to present evidence of having attended a regular theological school or seminary to justify his exemption from military service.[34]

Since this case involved the Eastern Orthodox Church as a whole, an all-out effort was made to unite the Syrian, the Greek, the Russian, and the Serbian church jurisdictions in the United States to present a united front in Washington and in the various states. Spearheaded by George E. Phillies, a Buffalo attorney who formerly served as president of AHEPA, the result was the formation of the Federation of Orthodox Churches. This marked the start of a campaign that initiated an amendment to the Religious Corporations Law of March 20, 1943, by the New York legislature, outlining the methods that were to be employed in incorporating Greek churches in the state.[35] The New York measure, the first of its kind, triggered the enactment of a series of comparable measures in the states of Wisconsin, Massachusetts, Louisiana, Indiana, New Hampshire, and West Virginia. By 1955, seven states had made provisions for the incorporation of Greek Orthodox churches in this manner. Since then, however, activities for this form of recognition have come to a standstill.

A more popular, and perhaps more expedient, way of obtaining recognition was to have the individual state legislatures enact resolutions granting the Greek Orthodox Church the status of a major faith. By 1959 twenty states had adopted such resolutions. Of a similar nature was the campaign to have the initials of the Eastern Orthodox Church imprinted on the identification tags of members of the faith who joined the armed forces of the United States. Continued resistance on the part of the Pentagon to do so compelled Senator Leverett Saltonstall of Massachusetts to introduce a special bill providing for the inclusion of "E.O." (Eastern Orthodox) on the tags. On June 6, 1955, three days after the hearings on the bill were scheduled before the Armed Services Committee, Secretary of Defense Charles E. Wilson issued a directive ordering the new E.O. label.[36]

This success of the Eastern Orthodox Church in obtaining recognition, even the appearance of the archbishop or a bishop at an invocation or at a presidential inauguration in Washington, was a heart-warming experience to members of the faith. It was proof that the American Greeks were displaying a talent for learning the fine art of legislative pressure. More members of the second generation had moved into state capitals and into Washington, where they were able to exercise effective political influence. At the same time, the church made strenuous efforts to identify itself with the greater American community, as a means of warding off criticisms that it was an alien faith with a foreign orientation. A tardy realization of the need for such action, in addition to the increase in the number of English-speaking priests, facilitated this effort. As a result, parish priests in various communities sought to participate in all undertakings that furthered civic, educational, and philanthropic causes.[37] But in the larger communities this was accomplished at the expense of the parishioners who had to content themselves with a minimum of pastoral attention.

Criticisms of the church hierarchy and the priesthood, however, continued, despite outward signs of serenity and progress. The archbishop was attacked for behaving as though he were an ethnarch and for treating the parishioners as though they were colonists residing in Cyprus or some other unredeemed part of Greece. The policy of centralization and the levying of a per-capita tax was resented in some parishes. The archdiocese was denounced for pursuing a policy of "rule or ruin" in various communities, despite pious utterances to the contrary.

The problems faced by the American-born and American-educated priests in particular were difficult for many to comprehend. They were led by superiors whose formative years of life had been spent in Greece or Turkish-dominated areas and who were trained authoritarians. Nor were the parishioners docile. They had a reputation for being assertive, uninhibited, and demonstrative; they were individualists who had a tradition to maintain, voices to use, and vocabularies to fit the occasion. Ministering to such parishes was a wearing experience. To serve these communities one had to have forbearance, understanding, and dedication; and many priests did prove themselves dedicated servants of God, who ministered well to the needs of their parishioners.

Still, complaints against the parish priests persisted. For instance, they were prepared for the technical and more routine functions of the priesthood, such as marrying, christening, and burying, but they were lacking in a well-rounded education. Many entered the seminary after graduating from high school. They could hardly be compared with the better-educated priests of the Roman Catholic Church. Some of the less discreet parishioners, and even priests, were quick to point out that while many of the older and better-educated clerics proved themselves dedicated servants at salaries of $100 a month, the new generation of priests was demanding $600 and $700 a month, plus an automobile and a house.

The critics were legion, but many placed much of the blame for the poor educational standards among priests on a power-hungry hierarchy. It seemed evident that the church was determined to consolidate its grip and regulate as many facets of community life as it could. These critics continued that campaigns to satisfy the territorial aspirations of Greece had no part in a church program that ministered to the second and third generations in the United States. No one had suggested that the members of the faith in the United States were living under foreign domination; yet the policies of the archdiocese strongly suggested that it was exercising the prerogatives of an ethnarch. One could often hear members of the faith complaining that they were being treated like colonists.

Much was made of the Lay-Clerical Congresses, which on paper gave a great voice to the laymen in administrative, if not ecclesiastical, matters. But many pointed out that these congresses were priest-ridden, that the hierarchy had its own way through a deliberate policy of dispensing church titles and other honors to influential laymen, manipulating delegates and committees, and the general default of responsibilities on the part of laymen and lay organizations. By encroaching upon the lay tradition, the hierarchy was supplanting authoritarianism for democracy and losing sight of the spiritual values that it was supposed to be fostering.

One of the most controversial issues of the late 1950s revolved around the proposal to build a Hellenic university that would use the Holy Cross Seminary in Brookline, Massachusetts, as its nucleus. Really the brainchild of a minority that was more familiar with ecclesiastical politics and the business world, and less with higher education, this proposal encountered severe criticism. The mere thought of using the Theological Seminary in Brookline was in itself cause for alarm. The seminary suffered from a series of administrative convulsions, loss of accreditation at one time or another, poor library facilities, inadequate instruction, and a lack of confidence. Because many private institutions of higher learning started as denominational colleges years ago was no assurance that the same could be accomplished in 1960 when educational costs had soared. Educational leadership was lacking, the funds few, the staffing problem staggering. One could not help asking who would attend such a school if it were founded and what well-placed professors would care to exchange their places for an educational institution of questionable quality.[38]

While the church hierarchy was seeking to extend the scope of its influence, a substantial number of Greeks entered the United States as nonquota immigrants. A smaller yet unprecedented number of students also arrived to pursue their educational studies. Prior to the Second World War, these students would have chosen some university in France or Germany. Obviously the death and destruction that followed in the wake of the Italian invasion, the Nazi occupation, and the civil war caused many to look to the United States for asylum. Many of these people had relatives who facilitated their entry, and still others

377

had been former residents of the United States who, for one reason or another, had returned to Greece before 1939 and were caught in the throes of war.

AHEPA was active in the effort to liberalize the immigration laws so as to permit the entry of more Greeks into the country. Its representatives appeared before Truman's Commission on Immigration and Naturalization to explain why more of their compatriots should be permitted to enter. In the process they emphasized the poverty in Greece, the homeless and orphaned children, America's need for laborers, and the reputation the American Greeks—the immigrants of yesteryear—had established for sobriety, industry, and integrity.[39]

One of the more singular arguments was presented by Nicholas Cassavetes of New York City, long a well-known figure in Greek-American affairs. Cassavetes estimated that in 1952 about 40,000 restaurants, candy stores, fruit shops, grocery stores, and other establishments were operated by Greek-Americans who were sorely in need of help. The average age of the small merchant, he said, was about sixty, which meant that in a few years he would be ready for retirement. Many of these aging merchants were concerned about what was to happen to their places of business when they were unable to operate them. Many were inclined to believe that, if legislation were enacted permitting some of their destitute relatives to come to the United States, they would be able to aid them and salvage a food industry that had taken years to build.[40]

The McCarran-Walter Immigration and Nationality Act was hardly the answer to Greek prayers. More comforting to them was the veto message of President Truman, which denounced the measure as being more unworthy than the one of 1924:

Today we have entered into an alliance, the North Atlantic Treaty, with Italy, Greece, and Turkey against one of the most terrible threats mankind has ever faced. We are asking them to join us in protecting the peace of the world. We are helping them to build their defenses, and train their men in the common cause. But through this bill we say to these people:

You are less worthy to come to this country than Englishmen or Irishmen; you Italians, who need to find homes abroad in the hundreds of thousands—you shall have a quota of 5,645; you Greeks struggling to assist the victims of a Communist civil war—you shall have a quota of 308; and you Turks, you are brave defenders of the Eastern flank, but you shall have a quota of only 225.[41]

The enactment of the Refugee Relief Act of 1953 offered hope to many. One of its provisions authorized the issuance of immigrant visas without requiring assurances of employment or housing for 15,000 from Italy, almost 2,000 from Greece, and 2,000 from the Netherlands.[42] An amendment to the act in 1954 permitted the allotment of special non-quota visas to Italy, Greece, and the Netherlands in either the refugee or relative preference group.[43]

More than 56,000 entered the United States from 1946 to 1960, chiefly as nonquota immigrants; for the annual quota of Greece, as we have noted, was only 308 during most of this period. Their arrival on a year-to-year basis was as follows.[44]

1946	367	1951	4,447	1956	10,531
1947	2,370	1952	7,084	1957	4,952
1948	2,250	1953	1,603	1958	3,079
1949	1,734	1954	2,127	1959	4,507
1950	1,179	1955	6,311	1960	3,797

For the first time since the 1920s, the Greeks were beginning to arrive in substantial numbers and in a manner reminiscent of the earlier days.

Statistics are unavailable, but it is probable that a number of the postwar arrivals were repatriates who had left the United States before 1939. For various unexplored reasons, the authorities in their anxiety to relieve the distressed country either gave preference to them or were persuaded to believe that they had a better chance of adjusting them-selves to the United States.[45] Such persons often obtained a loan to finance their embarkation. In some instances provisions were made for the arrival of the families of those who had remained in the United States. Such families, upon re-establishing themselves or coming to the United States for the first time, found that they were poles apart cul-turally from the American Greeks.

Those designated as displaced persons as a rule were older persons whose lives had been greatly affected by the war in Greece. They had endured great privations, and they proved to be reliable and adaptable. They seemed to be willing to work as hard as the earlier immigrants had, and in this regard they had much in common. In time they purchased automobiles and homes and became United States citizens. The so-called refugee group was younger, restless, and venturesome; many of them were born during the earlier years of the Metaxas regime. They were processed more readily to facilitate departure for the United

States, on the theory that they would find jobs easily, work hard, and be less likely to become public charges. The members of this refugee classification seemed to know more about the United States and in many instances were more demanding than the displaced persons. Some of them married into the families of the older immigrant group, and their arrogance proved more than their sponsors and relatives could tolerate.

Those who came on student visas represented a distinct element that should not be confused with any of the other immigrant arrivals. As a rule they were educated, poised, and intelligent young men who took special pride in their Greek heritage. Most of them attended colleges and universities throughout the country and seemed to be distributed in all branches of learning. Some were sponsored by relatives who informed them that they had to work their way through college; others were provided for in one fashion or another. A number married girls of non-Greek background and decided to remain in the United States, but when questioned they always replied that they expected to return to Greece. When one compares the opportunities available in the United States with those in Greece, one understands why they did not return to the mother country. Professional positions in Greece were few and far between; and the problems of readjustment, once years had been spent in the United States, were great. In various instances those who chose to remain in the United States did so with heavy consciences.

It is difficult to draw comparisons between the arrivals of recent years and the immigrants of the early twentieth century. Generally the latter-day arrivals were better-educated, more cosmopolitan in outlook, and in many cases allergic to hard work; they seemed to want much for a minimum of effort. Unlike the older arrivals, they had relatives who were in a position to be of some help to them in the critical early months. But too often they failed to realize that what their elder brothers or uncles had acquired came from years of toil, privation, and sacrifice. The "oldtimers" came with the expectation of working hard, saving, and sending money to the members of their families in Greece. Many newcomers came with the idea of receiving—they seemed to resent the prosperity of the older immigrant group, partly because they always stressed how hard they had worked and partly because they lacked a formal education. A few of the more demanding probably came with the idea of sharing the wealth of their relatives. "They found the table all set" and wanted to partake of its delicacies without any effort. In some cases they seemed to want to dominate community affairs, on the theory that they were more Greek than the Americanized Greeks, hence more capable and deserving.

As a rule, the newer arrivals tended to emphasize the boorishness of the older ones, and the fact that so many of them had been bootblacks, dishwashers, and laborers. Their contempt frequently was accompanied by arrogance. Some of them, of course, suffered at the hands of brothers and uncles who exploited and, in some instances, reduced them to a form of temporary peonage. This kind of tension between older and newer arrivals is known to most nationality groups and can hardly be viewed as the exclusive monopoly of any one group. The earlier arrivals often took a dim view of their more recently arrived compatriots. It would have been most unusual had not such tensions prevailed.[46]

The fresh wave of immigrants, despite the wide gulf separating the new from the old, gave a new lease to Greek life in the United States. The wellsprings of Hellenism were replenished by the new arrivals. The circulation of Greek newspapers in the United States increased; Greek dancing was revived; and new matrimonial frontiers were opened up for some of the second-generation girls. The business in Greek products was stimulated; more Greek records and foods were sold. Steamship companies and Greek-American lawyers were attracting new clients. Were it not for the thousands of Greeks coming to the United States annually, and the many thousands of Americans visiting Greece, Hellenism in America might have become extinct.

The Greek-Americans continued to be just as organization-conscious after the war as they had been before it. Still important was AHEPA; of less consequence were GAPA, the Pan-Arcadian Federation, and numerous other regional and local societies. GAPA continued to appeal to the members of the first generation, who were diminishing in number but who retained much of the Old World psychology. The common bond of nationality and religion, coupled with the strong desire to preserve the Greek heritage, kept them together. They generally had had a minimum of outside social contacts and tended to gravitate within a Greek-American orbit. Ideologically, GAPA remained more consistent with the teachings of its founders than AHEPA. However, within recent years it has started to bend in its position on the Greek language as more articles published in English have appeared in its official news media. Its interest in charitable, humanitarian, religious, and educational efforts have continued.

AHEPA remained the most influential of the lay organizations. Now there was no question about the loyalty of the Greeks to the United States or the acquisition of citizenship; there was no need of donning the toga of the superpatriot. The first cycle in the history of the organization, that of identifying it with the greater American community, had been completed. Americanization and integration were having their effects. The next cycle was that of bringing the younger generation in closer touch with Greece and their Greek heritage. To many this appeared inconsistent and contradictory, for it broached upon the program of GAPA that AHEPA had severely condemned during the early years. If consistency were the sole criterion in determining the merits of an organization, obviously this could be a severe indictment. But the organization had to change as the times did. AHEPA in the formative stages sought a practical program to protect its members from indiscriminate attacks by antiforeigners; once this ceased to be a need, the organization sought to foster the kind of cultural links that the members had always thought desirable. This was a novel two-way program, but it was not too well understood, even by those who preached it.

Flexibility in strategy and tactics was mandatory. This flexibility was as great as it could have been, but it was more effective than GAPA's rigid adherence to the principles of its founders, which nearly left it withered on the vine. If anything, AHEPA suffered from the failure to explain its program clearly and to emphasize that it was in keeping with its pragmatic philosophy.[47] By 1960, some thirty-eight years after it was founded, AHEPA was still aiding educational, charitable, and community projects of various kinds. It supported the Theological Seminary first at Pomfret and then at Brookline, St. Basil's Academy in Garrison, New York, and several agricultural schools in Greece. It provided scholarships for students seeking higher education and relief to victims of floods, earthquakes, and hurricanes in the United States, Greece, Turkey, and Ecuador. It rendered assistance to the Patriarchates of Constantinople and Jerusalem and built hospitals and health centers in Greece. It had been a prime force in the work of the

Greek War Relief Association and sold a half billion dollars in war bonds while serving as an official issuing agency for the United States government. More than anything else, through the years it accomplished more in identifying Greek-Americans with the greater American community than did all the other organizations combined.[48]

The weaknesses of most Greek-American organizations were pretty much the same. They failed to attract or retain the active support of the better-educated and more socially active people, who tended to disassociate themselves from organizations that were even remotely Greek. The reasons for this disassociation varied from person to person and organization to organization, but the estrangement was persistent. A common heritage was not enough to bind persons to ethnic or quasi-ethnic organizations—interests and associations changed. If recognition was needed, it could be had more meaningfully elsewhere. As a result, many organizations had to content themselves with inadequate leaders or "leftovers."

Some of these organizations suffered from opportunistic and self-centered leaders, who used their offices for personal aggrandizement. Some identified themselves with questionable projects and unethical practices, which cast a dark shadow over the organizations they headed. Election to office was taken to mean a reward for services rendered instead of a trust and responsibility. Lawyers seem to have had too much influence in molding policies and administering programs, which of course gave too legalistic a twist to many of the actions. Some groups suffered from the launching of well-meaning but poorly administered projects. Some were manipulated in a manner designed to enhance the personal ambitions of those entrusted with authority, instead of the cause they were intended to serve.

The weaknesses of these organizations created a vacuum that afforded an expansive and ambitious church hierarchy the opportunity to move into areas that previously had fallen within a secular sphere. This was regrettable, for the future welfare and interests of the American Greeks rested (as it does today) in perfecting their lay groups, rather than in yielding ground to the church. Although one can criticize these organizations, they did serve a useful purpose. They brought together people who were on the outer fringes of American society and felt uncomfortable in the presence of persons of different backgrounds.

They provided a common meeting ground, and they aided many worthy causes. Their survival, however, was contingent upon projecting worthwhile social and educational programs that would merit support.[49]

Along with these changes, the postwar years witnessed a breakthrough into the political arena. This reflected the persistent interest of the Greeks in public affairs and their acceptance by the electorate. The prejudices of old had been more or less dulled, and they began assuming responsible public offices. Members of the older generation with Anglicized names, and to a much greater extent those of the new, could be found in municipal, county, state, and federal offices.

By the 1960s the American Greeks were well integrated into the broader American community. Their names appeared in greater numbers in the theater as actors, producers, and directors; in the academic world as teachers, authors, and lecturers; in the fine arts as painters, sculptors, and designers; in the social and physical sciences as researchers and teachers. The colonies of old had disappeared; mixed marriages had increased; and their acceptance as a vigorous force in society was recognized. Nevertheless, they still took pride in their heritage, and the members of the second and third generations displayed more than a passing interest in the land of their parents and grandparents. An American-brand of Philhellenism seemed to flourish. But alongside this we must consider the cultural transfusions provided by the arrivals from Greece since 1945, latter-day immigrants, who injected new life into the American Hellenic spirit.

Today many American Greeks are distressed by the questionable role that has been assumed by the church hierarchy in lay affairs, especially in view of the assistance that lay groups have given to the church in the past. The undermining of the secular tradition has caused many to lose confidence in the church leadership and has driven many away from the Orthodox faith. The establishment of a well-coordinated association of local groups of laymen and the revival of the major fraternal organizations would seem to offer the best hope of stopping the steady encroachment of the hierarchy into lay affairs and of correcting the imbalance. Such groups have served communities well in the past, and indications are that, under proper guidance, they can accomplish the same in the future. Well-conceived educational programs, headed by influential and actively concerned laymen, can also help to fill the cultural void that exists in so many localities. Perhaps the church can thereby regain the support of those skeptical members of the second and third generation who have strayed away from the fold.

As we have seen, several distinct periods stand out in the history of the Greeks in the United States. The first encompasses the years from the early 1820s to 1890, when the arrivals consisted of young men coming to the United States to be educated under the auspices of missionary groups; factors representing Greek-owned mercantile establishments; sailors and adventurers in search of fame and fortune in the goldfields of California and elsewhere; a scattering of soldiers and sailors who fought with the Union and Confederate forces; a few professional people, and a few unheralded villagers who began to trickle into the major urban centers of the country. Although this earlier period is little explored, it appeals to those with genealogical and antiquarian interests, as well as to those who, for patriotic and other reasons, wish to date the arrival of the Greeks early in the history of this country.

The period from the late 1890s to about 1922 was one of ultra-nationalism, when the spirit of contemporary Hellenism ascended to mercurial heights. A new Greek nation was in the making. Many, if not most, Greeks had come to the United States with the thought of returning to their native land as soon as conditions warranted. The more forthright conceded that their American experience was intended to be a temporary one. The makeshift quality of their churches, schools, and societies reflected this. Patriotic orators, "apostles of nationalism," and the Greek-language press overextended themselves in seeing to it that the essence of Hellenism remained intact during this American interlude.

The next period saw Americanism making serious inroads on Hellenic sentiments. During the early 1920s, the Greek-Americans made valiant efforts to influence the structure and character of the new Greek government and even the policy that the United States should adopt toward the mother country. This was succeeded by an attitude of hasty retreat. The humiliating defeat of the Greeks in Asia Minor in 1922, the realization that their efforts to influence the American and the Greek governments were a mistake, combined with the mounting tide of antiforeignism within the United States, forced them to withdraw from the affairs of Greece and seek to become part of the American scene. This is when AHEPA, with its program of Americanization and identification with the American community, came into being. This also is the apogee of GAPA, with its policy of undiluted Hellenism and its stress on the Greek church and language. Ties with the mother country dropped to an all-time low until General Metaxas came into power in 1936 and made abortive efforts to regain the good will and cooperation of the American Greeks. During these decades Hellenism was rapidly giving ground to Americanism.

The period after 1940 was one of soaring Philhellenism. It manifested itself in the praise that was heaped on the Greek nation for its courageous stand against the invaders, the work of the Greek War Relief Association and AHEPA, the Truman Doctrine, the Marshall Plan, the revived interest of Greek-Americans in the mother country, with hordes of them visiting their native land. This was also an era of respectability and accomplishment, when Greek names became identified in great numbers with scholarship, the fine arts, scientific achievement, and commercial success.

By way of conclusion, I should point out that this study of the Greek people in the United States suggests some striking parallels between their problems of adjustment and those of the older and even pioneer groups. One is that they never lost interest in the country they left behind, any more than did the English, the French, or the Germans. They became embroiled in the political and religious upheavals of the mother country and on various occasions fought them out with a passion that equaled and even exceeded that of their compatriots abroad. They also brought with them the institutions they had known at home. The main difference is that the problems of the Greeks were compounded by the fact that they came to America later, spoke a strikingly different language, and worshiped in a church oriented toward the East. If the Greeks seemed less adaptable, it was because too much was expected of them. Their detractors never realized that these same criticisms had been hurled at earlier immigrants who were now accepted as respectable members of American society. The Greeks' late immigration was a temporary handicap, but it was no deterrent to a people who took pride in their individualism and national background. They overcame the initial obstacles, put down firm economic roots, and became a well-integrated part of the American community.

BIBLIOGRAPHY
NOTES
INDEX

BIBLIOGRAPHY

MANUSCRIPT COLLECTIONS

Of the relatively few manuscript collections available, the most useful has been the files of Dr. Demetrios Callimachos, an ordained priest and a confirmed Hellenist who spent many years as editor-in-chief of the *National Herald*. This file has been particularly helpful for the years since 1940. The Nicholas C. Culolias collection in Houghton Library, Harvard University, is small, but it contains some interesting data on post–World War One politics in the Boston area. The papers of George E. Phillies of Buffalo, New York, shed considerable light on the campaign to obtain official recognition for the Eastern Orthodox Church during World War Two.

No student can afford to overlook the official correspondence in the National Archives between the United States Department of State and the Greek Legation in Washington for the years 1910–1929. Equally valuable is the exchange of correspondence between the American Legation in Athens and the State Department, which has revealed a good deal on the political situation in Greece and the impact it had on Greek communities throughout the United States. Interspersed in this correspondence are official inquiries and replies from Greek governmental authorities, plus information and queries received by the State Department from a wide variety of sources. A surprising amount of material is to be found here on the activities of the Greeks in the United States.

On the subject of immigration, the United States consular correspondence has been invaluable, especially from the consuls in Athens, 1837–1910; Patras, 1861–1910; Piraeus, 1904–1908; and Salonica, 1870–1910.

Scrapbooks that proved informative were those of George P. Skouras, based on his cross-country trip during the spring of 1946, and George C. Vournas, who amassed a collection of clippings dealing with the Constantinist-Venizelist imbroglio.

GOVERNMENT DOCUMENTS AND REPORTS

There are very few Greek government sources dealing directly with immigration. *E ex Hellados Metanasteuseos, E Ekthesis tis Epitropis tis Voulis* (Emigration from Greece, The Report of the Committee of the Chamber of Deputies; Athens, 1906) is sketchy, but the report of Emmanuel Repouli, *Meleti Peri Metanasteuseos, Meta Schediou Nomou* (A Study of Immigration, With Suggested Legislation; Athens, 1912), is a useful Greek document on early immigration. Most valuable among the United States government documents are the following:

Department of Commerce and Labor, Bureau of Foreign Commerce, *Commercial Relations of the United States,* 1891–1902.

—— Bureau of Naturalization, *Annual Reports of the Commissioner of Naturalization*, 1918, 1923–1932, 1944, 1952, 1960.

—— Bureau of Statistics, *Commercial Relations of the United States*, 1904–1910.

—— —— Special Consular Reports, *Emigration to the United States* (Washington, 1903).

—— Food and Agricultural Organization, *Report of the FAO Mission for Greece* (Washington, 1947).

49th Cong., 2nd sess., House of Representatives, Executive Document No. 157, Emigration and Immigration, *Reports of the Consular Officers of the United States* (Washington, 1887).

61st Cong., 3rd sess., Senate Document No. 747, *Abstracts of the Reports of the Immigration Commission*, II (Washington, 1911).

—— Senate Document No. 753, Reports of Immigration Commission, *Immigrant Banks* (Washington, 1911).

—— Senate Document No. 756, Reports of the Immigration Commission, *Statistical Review of Immigration, 1820–1910*.

67th Cong., 2nd sess., Senate Document No. 86, *Loans to Foreign Governments* (Washington, 1921).

80th Cong., 1st sess., *Hearings before the Committee on Foreign Relations, U.S. Senate, on S. 938*, "A Bill to Provide for Assistance to Greece and Turkey, March 24, 25, 27, and 31, 1947" (Washington, 1947).

—— Senate Document 111, *The European Recovery Program: Basic Documents and Background Information* (Washington, 1947).

81st Cong., 2nd sess., Senate Report No. 1515, *The Immigration and Naturalization Systems of the United States* (Washington, 1950).

82nd Cong., 2nd sess., House of Representatives, *Hearings before the President's Commission on Immigration and Naturalization* (Washington, 1952).

83rd Cong., 2nd sess., *First Semiannual Report of the Administration of the Refugee Relief Act of 1953* (Washington, 1954).

85th Cong., 1st sess., *Refugee Relief Act of 1953, Final Report of the Administrator of the Refugee Relief Act of 1953, As Amended* (Washington, 1956).

86th Cong., 2nd sess., *Greeks in America, Congressional Record* (Washington, 1960).

SECONDARY SOURCES

Of value for background material are Lewis Sargeant, *Greece in the Nineteenth Century* (London, 1897); R. A. H. Bickford-Smith, *Greece under King George* (London, 1893), and Percy F. Martin, *Greece in the Twentieth Century* (London, 1913). Eliot G. Mears, *Greece Today* (Stanford, 1929), is most useful for internal Greek developments down into the 1920s.

On the currant-crop crisis that triggered the migration of the 1890s, see V. Gabrielidis, "The Overproduction of Greek Currants," *Economic Journal*, V (June 1895), 285–288; Theodore Burlami, "Overproduction of Greek Currants," *ibid.*, IX (December 1899), 634–651; and A. Andreades, "The Currant Crisis in Greece," *ibid.*, XVI (March 1906), 41–51.

A handy general account of the modern Greek nation, mostly political, is William Miller, *A History of the Greek People, 1821–1921* (London, 1922).

More useful for World War I and the years that followed is Miller's *Greece* (London, 1928). For those who read Greek the eight-volume work of K. Paparrigopoulou, *Historia tou Hellinikou Ethnos* (History of the Greek Nation; Athens, 1932), is all-important.

Useful for an understanding of the social and religious customs of the Greeks are Rennell Rodd, *The Customs and Lore of Modern Greece* (London, 1892); Lucy M. J. Garnett, *Greece and the Hellenes* (New York, 1914); and William Miller, *Greek Life in Town and Country* (London, 1905). Irwin Sanders, *Rainbow in the Rock: The People of Rural Greece* (Cambridge, Mass., 1962), is a readable contemporary account of Greek rural life.

Secondary works dealing with the policies of King Constantine and Eleutherios Venizelos are marred by partisanship. Constantine and his policies are upheld by: Paxton Hibben, *Constantine I and the Greek People* (New York, 1920); S. P. O. Cosmetatos, *The Tragedy of Greece* (London, 1928); and Adamantios Th. Polyzoides, *E Helliniki Oudeterotis kai o Basileus Konstantinos* (Greek Neutrality and King Constantine; New York, 1917). See also Iannou Metaxa, *E Istoria tou Ethnikou Dichasmou kai tis Mikrasiatikis Katastrophis* (The History of National Dissension and the Disaster in Asia Minor; Athens, 1935). Venizelos and his policies are defended by Herbert Baxter Gibbons, *Venizelos* (Boston, 1915), and Doros Alastos, *Venizelos: The Creator of Modern Greece* (London, 1942). These partisan battles can be followed in even greater detail in the files of the *Atlantis* and the *National Herald* for the years 1916–1923 and after.

Secondary sources in the English and Greek languages dealing with immigration are sparse. The first work in English was that of Henry Pratt Fairchild, *Greek Immigration to the United States* (New Haven, 1911). Its strongest feature is the treatment of the economic causes of immigration. The works of Thomas Burgess, *Greeks in America* (Boston, 1913), and J. P. Xenides, *The Greeks in America* (New York, 1922), on the other hand, are less pretentious and more sympathetic. Burgess, an Episcopalian clergyman, was a member of the American branch of the Anglican and Eastern Orthodox Churches Union, which sought to effect a closer union between these two churches of Christianity. His sources of information were the Greeks themselves, the rank and file as well as the leading members of the larger communities, and secondary works. The Xenides volume appeared under the auspices of the Inter-Church World Movement; apparently he possessed the "deeply sympathetic and broad Christian viewpoint" that the sponsors considered a requisite in selecting the authors for the series on immigration. A clergyman born of Greek parents in Asia Minor, Xenides taught in Marsovan Theological Seminary and Anatolia College for twenty years, traveled extensively in Greece and Asia Minor, and served as secretary of the Greek Relief Committee in New York City. Like Burgess, he extracted much of his information through direct personal contacts. His slender volume does one thing that other works do not: it stresses the contacts between Greek and Protestant groups in the United States.

Other helpful secondary sources in English include the following:

Antoniou, Mary, "Welfare Activities among the Greek People in Los Angeles," master's thesis, University of Southern California, 1939.

Attwater, Donald, *The Christian Churches of the East,* 2 vols. (Milwaukee, 1947–1948).

Boyd, Rosamonde R., *The Social Adjustment of the Greeks in Spartanburg, South Carolina* (Spartanburg, 1949?).

Callinicos, Constantine, *The Greek Orthodox Church* (London, 1918).

Calogeropoulos, N., and G. Stratos, *Notes on the Greek Question Addressed to President Wilson* (n.p., 1920).

Canoutas, S. G., *Christopher Columbus, A Greek Nobleman* (New York, 1943).

Chebithes, V. I., *Ahepa and the Progress of Hellenism in America* (New York, 1935).

Corovilles, Theodora Isaakidou, "Greek Church Schools in America," master's thesis, Presbyterian College of Christian Education, 1933.

Doggett, Carita, *Dr. Andrew Turnbull and the New Smyrna Colony of Florida* (n.p., 1919).

Gorgas, Demitra, "Greek Settlement of the San Francisco Bay Area," master's thesis, University of California, Berkeley, 1951.

Hutchison, Thomas S., *An American Soldier under the Greek Flag at Bezanie* (Nashville, 1913).

Kourides, Peter T., *The Evolution of the Greek Orthodox Church in America and Its Present Problems* (New York, 1959).

Lacey, Thomas J., *A Study of Social Heredity as Illustrated in the Greek People* (New York, 1916).

Maniakes, Constantinos D., *America and Greece* (Athens, 1899).

Mistaras, Evangeline, "A Study of First and Second Generation Greek Out-Marriages in Chicago," master's thesis, University of Chicago, 1950.

Pallis, Alexander A., *Greece's Anatolian Venture* (London, 1937).

Ross, E. A., *Old Worlds in the New* (New York, 1914).

Saloutos, Theodore, *They Remember America* (Berkeley and Los Angeles, 1956).

Seligman, Vincent J., *The Victory of Venizelos* (London, 1920).

Valaoras, Vasileos, *Hellenism of the United States* (Athens, 1937).

Venizelos, Eleutherios, *The Vindication of Greek National Policy, 1912–1917* (London, 1918).

Vlassis, George D., *The Greeks in Canada* (Ottawa, 1953).

Yerocaris, Constantine, "A Study of the Voluntary Associations of the Greek Immigrants of Chicago from 1890 to 1948, with Special Emphasis on World War I and Post War Period," master's thesis, University of Chicago, 1950.

SECONDARY SOURCES IN ENGLISH: ARTICLES

Abbott, Grace, "Study of the Greeks in Chicago," *American Journal of Sociology,* XV (November 1909), 379–393.

Adamic, Louis, "Greek Immigration in the United States," *Commonweal,* XXXIII (January 31, 1941), 366–368.

Anonymous, "Life Story of a Pushcart Peddler," *Independent,* LX (February 1, 1906), 274–279.

——— "Greeks in the United States," *Literary Digest,* LIX (December 7, 1918), 37.

——— "My Heritage," *Atlantic,* CLXII (December 1938), 846–847.

——— "New Land Law in Greece," *Nation,* CX (May 15, 1920), 665.

——— "America's Vest-Pocket Athens," *Literary Digest,* LIV (March 17, 1917), 743.

——— "President Wilson on the Turkish Treaty," *Contemporary*, CXVII (June 1920), 884–886.

——— "Greece Attempts to Impose the Sèvres Treaty," *Current History*, XIV (May 1921), 347–352.

——— "The Problem of Greek Tourism," *Quarterly Review of the National Bank of Greece*, IV (October 1961), 3–23.

Bensill, H. L., "Mr. Phasoulias: Eating in a Greek Restaurant," *Commonweal*, XXXIII (January 31, 1941), 372–373.

Davidson, Thomas, "The Present Condition of Greece," *International Review*, VI (June 1879), 597–615.

Elliott, W. A., "The Modern Greek People," *Chautaquan*, XLIII (1906), 144.

Fairchild, H. P., "Causes of Emigration From Greece," *Yale Review*, XVIII (August 1909), 176–196.

Galloway, M. A. A., "Free Greece," *Nineteenth Century*, XXIII (June 1888), 893–900.

Hartley, H., "Greek Way: Sponge Divers of Tarpon Springs," *Colliers*, CVII (May 17, 1941), 18–19.

Hyde, A. E., "Greek Children," *Charities*, XIX (November 9, 1907), 1027–1029.

International Labor Office, "Remittances of Greek Immigrants," *Monthly Record of Immigration, No. 50* (November 1926), 426.

Kyriakides, Nicholas, "America and Hellenism," *Outlook*, XXXV (June 9, 1920), 284–285.

Mears, E. G., "Unique Position in Greek Trade of Emigrant Remittances," *Quarterly Journal of Economics*, XXXVII (May 1923), 535–540.

Papanicholas, H. L., "The Greeks of Carbon County," *Utah Historical Quarterly*, XXII (April 1954), 143–164.

Phoutrides, A. E., "The Literary Impulse of Modern Greece," *Poet Lore*, XXVI (January–February 1915), 56–67.

Polyzoides, A. T., "Greece's Experiment with Proportional Representation," *American Political Science Review*, XXI (February 1927), 123–127.

——— "Greece Abandons Proportional Representation," *American Political Science Review*, XXIII (May 1929), 459–461.

Quigley, M., "Greek Immigrant and the Library," *Library Journal*, XLVII (October 15, 1922), 863–865.

Roberts, K. L., "They Sometimes Come Back," *Saturday Evening Post*, CXCIV (September 10, 1921), 12–13.

Sills, K. C. M., "Greek-Americans," *Nation*, XCVII (October 2, 1913), 309.

Stycos, Mayone J., "The Spartan Greeks of Bridgetown: Community Cohesion," *Common Ground*, VIII (Spring 1948), 24–34.

——— "The Spartan Greeks of Bridgetown: The Second Generation," *Common Ground*, VIII (Summer 1948), 72–86.

——— "The Spartan Greeks of Bridgetown," *Common Ground*, VIII (Winter 1948), 61–70.

Terhune, L. B., "Greek Bootblack," *Survey*, XXVI (September 16, 1911), 852–854.

Thompson, Maurice S., "Notes on Social and Economic Conditions in Greece," *Sociological Review*, VI (July 1913), 213–221.

Wells, R. R., "American Hellenes," *Nation*, XCIX (July 23, 1914), 102.

Weyl, W. E., "Pericles of Smyrna and New York," *Outlook*, XCIV (February 26, 1910), 463–472.

BIBLIOGRAPHY
SECONDARY SOURCES IN GREEK: BOOKS

Among the most useful secondary sources in the Greek language is Bambi Malafouris, *Hellenes tis Amerikis, 1528–1948* (Greeks in America; New York, 1948). This otherwise useful volume is marred by a large collection of biographical sketches of prominent Greek-Americans who contributed financially to its publication. Seraphim G. Canoutas, *O Hellinismos en Ameriki* (Hellenism in America; New York, 1918), is a pioneering, but at times eulogistic, bilingual account by a prominent lawyer-journalist. It has been drawn upon repeatedly by journalists and others. Lesser known in the United States is *E Helliniki Metanasteusis* (Greek Immigration; Athens, 1917), which has a foreword by the distinguished Greek economist, Andreas M. Andreades. What might have been an eminently useful book has been impaired by redundancy and lack of coordination. A novel feature of the study is the treatment of immigration from various provinces and the unredeemed portions of Greece.

A highly perceptive but slender volume written in demotic Greek is Manolis A. Triantafillides, *Hellenes tis Amerikis* (Greeks in America; Athens, 1952). It is based on a trip to the United States during the fall of 1939, when Metaxas was at the height of his power in Greece. Triantafillides lamented the inroads that assimilation was making on the Greek language and customs here. A series of footnotes and a useful collection of newspaper articles reprinted from the Athens press enhance the book's value. Vasileos G. Valaoras, *O Hellinismos tou Enomenon Politeion* (Hellenism in the United States; Athens, 1937), is a general account by a specialist in the public-health problems of Greece who spent some time in the United States. He confirms the observations of earlier students that the Greek population was being assimilated rapidly. Still another special early study is Christodoulou I. Damiri, *Peri tis ek Zakynthou Metanasteusis* (On Emigration from Zante; Athens, 1911), which deals with one of the islands off the northwestern coast of the Peloponnesus.

The Greek theme in fiction is portrayed by Harry Mark Petrakis, *Lion at My Heart* (Boston, 1959); Joseph Auslander, *The Islanders* (New York, 1951); Warren Tute, *The Golden Greek* (New York, 1961); and Mary Vardoulakis, *Gold in the Streets* (New York, 1945).

Among other useful books in Greek are the following:

Anagnostopoulou, Demetrios H. and George, *Mihael Anagnostopoulos* (Athens, 1923).

Asteriou, Asterios, *Ta Hellinika Scholeia en Ameriki* (The Greek Schools in America; New York, 1931).

Booras, John A., *Ai Ethnikai Thermopylai* (The National Thermopylae; New York, 1910).

Canoutas, Seraphim, *To Provbleema tou Hellinismou tis Amerikis* (The Problem of Hellenism in America; New York, 1927).

Dendia, Michael A., *Ai Ellinikai Parikoiai ana ton Kosmon* (Greek Communities Around the World; Athens, 1919).

Ghortzi, N., *Ameriki kai Amerikanoi* (America and Americans; Athens, 1907).

Janetis, Elias I., *E Autou Megaliotis, O Metanastis* (His Eminence, the Immigrant; New York, 1946).

Krikou, Alexandrou, *E Theshis tou Hellinismou en Ameriki* (The Status of Hellenism in America; Athens, 1915).

Kyriakides, Nicholas F., *Ethniki Odeporia eis tin Amerikin, 1918–1919* (Patriotic Mission to America; Athens, 1924).

Lykoudes, E. S., *E Metanastai* (The Immigrants; Athens, 1903).

Marinou, G. M., *To Kratos tou Ploutou* (The Nation of Wealth; Athens, 1903).

Oikonomidou, Marias S., *E Hellines tis Amerikis opos tous Eida* (The Greeks of America as I Saw Them; New York, 1916).

Papulias, Angelos, *Memoirs of A. Papulias* (San Francisco, n.d.).

Sicilianos, Demetriou, *E Helliniki Katagogi tou Christoforou Kolombou* (The Greek Background of Christopher Columbus; Athens, 1950).

SECONDARY SOURCES IN GREEK: ARTICLES

Doukopoulou, C., "E Katastasis tou Hellinikou Pleetheesmou tis Amerikis" (The Condition of the Greek Population of America), *Archeion Oikonomikon Kai Koinonikon Epistimon* (Archives of Economic and Social Scientists; Athens, 1935), vol. 15.

Dournovo, N. N., "E Helliniki Ekklesia kai e Ethinki Anagennesis" (The Greek Church and National Regeneration), *Hellinismos*, III (January 1900), 200–212.

Nouarou, G. M., "Hellino-Amerikanikai Scheseis" (Greek-American Relations), *Hellinismos*, XXXIV (December 1931), 742–751.

Rozakos, N. K., "E Protoi Lacedaimonoi Metanastes stin Ameriki" (The First Spartan Immigrants in America), *Nea Estia*, XLVIII (August 15, 1950), 1080–1084.

Vlachou, Andrew, "Peri tou en Ameriki Ellinismou apo Emporikis, Koinonikis kai Ethnikis Apopseos" (Regarding Hellenism in America from a Commercial, Social, and National Viewpoint), *Hellinismos*, XII (May 1909), 271–283.

——— "E Helliniki Epanastasis en Ameriki" (The Greek Revolution in America), *Hellinismos*, XXXIII (April 1930), 232–238.

——— "O en Ameriki Hellinismos" (Hellenism in America), *Hellinismos*, XXXIII (February 1930), 90–106.

THE CHURCH

Efforts to gain access to records of the Greek Orthodox Church in the United States and Greece were unsuccessful.

Good background material may be found in Walter F. Adeney, *The Greek and Eastern Churches* (New York, 1908), and in the *Encyclopaedia Britannica*, 11th ed., under the heading "Orthodox Eastern Church." Other accounts are those of William C. Emhardt, *The Eastern Church in the Western World* (Milwaukee, 1928); Reginald M. French, *The Eastern Church* (London, 1951); and Thomas J. Lacey, *A Study of the Eastern Orthodox Church,* 2nd rev. ed. (New York, 1912). A recent popular account dealing with the church in Greece is Peter Hammond, *The Waters of Marah: The Present State of the Greek Church* (New York, 1956). Dean Timothy Andrews, *The Eastern Orthodox Church* (New York, 1953), is also useful.

Most helpful for the American scene is the work of Basil Th. Zoustis, an official of the Archdiocese of North and South America, *O En Ameriki Hellinismos kai e Drasis Tou* (Hellenism in America and Its Times; New York, 1954).

Although the book is poorly organized and rehashes some well-known materials, it contains some basic church documents that are unavailable elsewhere.

The back files of the Greek-language press, especially *Ethnikos Kyrix* (National Herald) and *Atlantis,* contain material relative to the church. Much of it, especially that published during the turbulent 1920s and early 1930s, is highly flavored to satisfy the editorial preferences of the papers; but it is still useful if employed judiciously. *Eleutheros Typos* (Free Press), edited for a period by Demetrios Callimachos, for years the editor of the *National Herald,* contains a good deal of early historical data on the New York churches and Callimachos' version of the struggle to effect a reconciliation of the feuding factions in the United States.

Statistics on parishes, priests, and church membership can be extracted from the report of the United States Department of Commerce, Bureau of the Census, *Religious Bodies, 1936,* vol. 2, pt. 1, pp. 572–573; *Year Book of American Churches,* issued by the National Council of Churches of Christ, U.S.A.; and *Greek Orthodox Year Book,* published by the Archdiocese of North and South America. All these data must be accepted with reservations.

Ekklesiastikos Kyrix (Church Herald), which was edited for a time by Meletios Metaxakis, has been helpful. The first American edition appeared on September 2, 1921 under the auspices of St. Athanasius Seminary. The September 1923 issue was the last published under the sponsorship of St. Athanasius; beginning in October 1923 the editorship passed into the hands of Michael Galanos. Of some help have been the scattered files of the *Orthodox Observer* and the *Voice of Orthodoxy.*

For the scholar wanting primary source materials on Eastern Orthodox churches, of use are: Historical Records Survey, Inventory of the Church Archives in New York City, *Eastern Orthodox Churches* (WPA, New York, 1940); V. Basanoff, "Archives of Russian Church in Alaska in the Library of Congress," *Pacific Historical Review,* II (March 1933), 72–84; and the incomplete files of the *Russian Orthodox Messenger,* 1901–1910. Superficial but of some aid is Basil M. Bensin, *History of the Russian Orthodox Greek Catholic Church of North America* (New York, 1941). A general article by W. G. Tinchon-Fernandez, "Eastern Orthodox Peoples and Churches in the United States," *Christendom,* IV (Summer 1939), 423–436, is also helpful.

Pamphlet material is available on the various efforts made to bring the Eastern Orthodox and Anglican churches into closer contact. See especially William C. Emhardt, *Historical Contact of the Eastern Orthodox and the Anglican Churches* (New York, 1920), a pamphlet; *An Unofficial Programme for Reunion as Contained in a Letter to His Grace, the Metropolitan of Athens,* October 26, 1918, written by Emhardt, who was the secretary of the Anglican and Eastern Association and the Christian Unity Foundation; *The Episcopal and Greek Churches; Report of an Unofficial Conference on Unity . . .* (New York, 1920), a pamphlet; Emhardt, *Recent Contact With Eastern Churches* (New York, 1919), a pamphlet; Emhardt, *The Eastern Church in the Western World* (Milwaukee, 1928); J. A. Douglas, *The Relation of the Anglican Churches with the Eastern Churches* (London, 1921); and Arthur R. Sharpe, *Constantinople First, A Plea for a Second Reunion* (London, 1923). See also the *Second Annual Report of the Anglican and Eastern Orthodox Churches Union* (London, 1908), pp. 37–38, on the organization of the American branch.

Background materials on the fate of the Ecumenical Patriarchate in Constantinople following the Greek disaster in Asia Minor in 1922 may be found in S. Papadakis, "Church in Greece under New Leadership," *Current History*, XVII (March 1923), 943–946; William Miller, "Changing Role of the Orthodox Church," *Foreign Affairs*, VIII (January 1930), 274–281. For an important court opinion on the struggle for supreme ecclesiastical authority in the United States, see "Moustakis v. Hellenic Orthodox Society," *New England Reporter*, No. 159, p. 453.

Within recent years a good deal of pamphlet material critical of the Greek Orthodox Church in the United States has appeared. The first—that of Constantine Cavarnos, *E Orthodoxia en Ameriki* (The Orthodox Faith in America; Athens, 1958), is by an American-born and Harvard-trained Ph.D., who taught briefly at Holy Cross Seminary, Brookline, Mass., and rebelled against the conditions he found. Constantine S. Dukakis has written a series of trenchant leaflets and pamphlets revolving around Holy Cross Seminary, which had difficulties with the accrediting authorities: see especially *Betrayal of a Sacred Trust*, August 18, 1958; *The Fate of the Greek Orthodox Church in America* (Arlington, Mass., 1960); *The Proposed Hellenic University* (Arlington, 1961); and *The Fate of the Greek Orthodox Theological School* (Arlington, 1962).

Callimachos' *Hamos ti Heroikes Pheelis* (Disappearance of the Heroic Race), six mimeographed pages, is a vigorous protest in Greek by a journalist-priest, addressed to Bishop Athenagoras Kokkinakis, then dean of the Holy Cross Seminary. *Helliniko Panepistimio stin Ameriki* (Hellenic University in America) is a severe criticism of the proposed Hellenic University, reprinted from *Argonautis* (New York, 1959). Another able criticism is that of Speros Vryonis, a Byzantine scholar, which appeared in the *Hellenic Chronicle* (Boston), September 20, 1962.

One who has a background knowledge of the activities of the Greek Church in the United States can extract useful bits of information from two pamphlets by John Papas, *The Greek Church in the Courts* (Sanford, Maine, n.d.), and *The Scandals of the Greek Church* (Sanford, n.d.).

GUIDES, ALMANACS, DIRECTORIES

Immigrant guides and almanacs published in the United States and Greece furnish valuable local information on the earlier years of immigration. Especially good for background materials is *Spartiatikon Emerologion* (Spartan Almanac) for the years when emigration from Sparta was at its peak; most valuable are the volumes for 1905–1909.

Perhaps the first guide for Greek immigrants in the United States is that of Socrates A. Xanthaky, the former editor-in-chief of *Atlantis*. His *O Syntrophos tou Hellinos en Ameriki* (The Companion of the Greek in America; New York, 1903) furnishes useful statistical information about the various cities and states in the nation, as well as legal, technical, and vocabulary guides for the immigrant. Similar and perhaps more useful is *O Symboulos kai Proheiros Dikegoros tou Hellinos en Ameriki* (The Adviser and Handy Lawyer of the Greek in America; New York, 1919), by Seraphim G. Canoutas. More valuable for local information is *Hellino-Amerikaninkos Odigos* (The Greek-American Guide), issued annually in New York beginning in 1907. Similar in nature is the work of Hercules N. Papamanoli, *Perilyptiki Historia tou Kanada kai Hellino-*

397

BIBLIOGRAPHY

Kanadikos Odigos (Comprehensive History of Canada and Greek-American Guide; Montreal, 1921–1922). Despite its presumptuous title, this handbook gives a clear picture of the business and social activities of the Greek communities in Canada. The numerous advertisements in themselves are informative.

Other miscellaneous directories and handbooks are:

Associated Greek Press of America, *Greek Business Guide and Directory of the Western States* (San Francisco, 1925).

Canoutas, S. G., *Hellino-Amerikanikos Odigos* (Greek-American Guide and Business Directory [New York] for 1907, 1909, 1910, 1912, and 1913).

—— *Hellinikos Emporikos Odigos* (Greek Business Directory, United States and Canada; New York, 1921).

Demeter, George C., *Ahepa Manual; Official Guide of the Order of Ahepa . . .* (Boston, 1926).

Greek-American Progressive Association, *Fifteenth Annual Convention* (Miami, 1950).

The Greek Blue Book; A Purchasing Guide for 50,000 Greek-American Business Establishments (New York, 1939).

Greek Directory of Chicago and Vicinity (Chicago, 1921).

Greek Directory Publishing Company, *Greek Directory of 1923* (Chicago, 1923).

Holy Trinity Greek Community, *Forty Years of Greek Life in Chicago, 1897–1937* (Chicago, 1937); in Greek.

Prometheus Publishing Company, *The Greeks in California, Their History and Achievements, 1918–1919* (San Francisco, 1919).

GREEK-LANGUAGE NEWSPAPERS

Atlantis (New York). March 2, 1895–December 10, 1897; January 1906–July 31, 1913; January 1919–December 31, 1922; June–August 1939: New York Public Library.

California (San Francisco). January 6, 1908–November 20, 1920: Anastasios Mountanos (former editor), San Francisco.

Democrat (Chicago). 1927–April 1931; New York Public Library.

Eleutheros Typos (New York). August 5, 1944–December 20, 1946: personal possession.

Empros (Forward; New York). January 1925–1927: New York Public Library.

Ethnikos Kyrix (National Herald; New York). April 2, 1915–December 31, 1923: Midwest Inter-Library Center, Chicago.

Hellinikos Typos (Greek Press; Chicago). June 1929–March 1934: Chicago Public Library, WPA Project.

Hellinikos Astir (Greek Star; Chicago). January 28, 1904–April 1, 1910: University of Chicago Library.

Kathemerini (The Daily; Chicago). 1921–1932: Chicago Public Library, WPA Project.

Loxias (The Blade; Chicago). June 1908–November 1918: Chicago Public Library, WPA Project.

Nomotagis (The Loyalist; New York). April 12, 1919–July 10, 1920: New York Public Library and British Museum.

Panhellinios (New York). April 7, 1908–December 31, 1908: Benaki Library, Athens.

BIBLIOGRAPHY

PERIODICALS

Ahepan [or *The Ahepa*]. May 1929–October 1950: New York Public Library.

[*Atlantis.*] *Menea Ekonographemenoi Atlantis* (Illustrated Monthly Atlantis; New York). I (January 1910) to X (December 1919; XIII (January 1922) to XXIII (December 1932): British Museum.

American Greek (New York). I (January 1920–January 1921): New York Public Library.

American Greek Review (Chicago). I (June 1923) to VI (January 1928): Midwest Inter-Library Center, Chicago.

American Hellenic World (Chicago). I (March 28, 1925) to V (December 19, 1931): New York Public Library.

Archon Magazine (Philadelphia). July and August 1927: New York Public Library.

Athene (Chicago). I (1940) to present: Chicago Public Library.

Eastern and Western Review (Boston). Broken files from vols. II (August 1909) to IX (December 1916): Boston Public Library and Harvard College Library.

Greek-American Review (Boston). Broken files from I (March 1917) to II (April 1918): New York Public Library.

Greek-American (New York). I (December 1927) to II (May 1928): New York Public Library.

Greek Review (Chicago). I (June 1923) to II (December 1924): Harvard College Library.

Hellenic Herald (London). I (November 1906) to VI (May 1912): Yale University Library.

Hellenic Spectator (Washington, D.C.). I (February 1940–February 1941): New York Public Library.

[*National Herald.*] *Menea Ekonographemenoi Ethnikos Kyrix* (Illustrated Monthly National Herald). I (July 1915) to IX (December 1923): New York Public Library.

National Union (Springfield, Mass.). I (April 1928) to II (May 1929): New York Public Library.

Protoporos (Pioneer; New York). I (March 1935) to III (June 1937): New York Public Library.

Voice of Orthodoxy (Chicago). I (1925) to III (December 1927): New York Public Library.

PAMPHLETS, LEAFLETS

AHEPA, *The Order of Ahepa, 1922–1961*.
—— *The Ahepa Hospitals for Greece Program* (Washington, 1956).
—— *What Is Ahepa?* (1956).
Cassavetes, Nicholas J., *The Question of Northern Epirus at the Peace Conference* (New York, 1919).
Chartopoulos, Evangelos, *E Phone tou Ipodoulon* (The Voice of the Enslaved; New York, 1914).
Circular of Liberty Loan Committee New England, Massachusetts Committee on Citizens of Foreign Birth or Descent (Boston, 1919).
Greek Government Office of Information, *Tribute To Greece* (Washington, 1943).
Greek-American Committee for National Unity, *Greek Liberation* (New York, 1944).
Greek-American Council, *Bulletin*, 1945–1946.

Greek-American Labor Committee, *Greece Fights for Freedom* (New York, 1944).

Greek-American Union for Democracy, *New American Problem in the Light of Nazi Aggression* (New York, 1939).

Greek Archdiocese of North and South America, *The Historic Decision of the 10th Biennial Ecclesiastical Congress at St. Louis* (New York, ca. 1950).

Greek War Relief Association, *$12,000,000* (New York, 1946).

—— *Address to the Fourth Annual Meeting of the G.W.P.A. by the President, Spyros P. Skouras, October 21, 1944.*

Greek White Book, Supplementary Documents, 1913–1917 (New York, 1919).

Harrisiadou, Panou, *E Ethniki Enotis* (National Unity; New York, 1944).

Joachim, K. K., *E Kindinoi tou en Ameriki Hellinismou kai ta Mesa tis Diasoseous Autou* (The Dangers Facing the Greeks of America and the Means for Their Salvation; Boston, 1926).

Kyriakides, Nicholas, *The Unredeemed Hellenism* (New York, 1918).

Lacey, Thomas J., *Our Greek Immigrants* (New York, 1918).

Michalaros, Demetrios, *Demetrios P. Callimachos* (Chicago, 1953).

Official Minutes and Proceedings of the National Youth Conference of the Greek Orthodox Church in America (Chicago, 1951).

Panhellenic Committee for the Defense of Greek Rights, released April 7, 1946; mimeographed.

Report of Photius P. Kyrisis, Supreme President, to the Fifth Annual Panepirotic Convention, July 2, 1947; mimeographed.

Skouras, George P., speech in behalf of "Give a Farm Animal to Greece Program," 1946.

Vournas, George C., *A Message from the Supreme President* [of AHEPA] (Washington, 1944).

Year Book of St. Constantine Church and Koraes School, 1936 (Chicago, 1937).

SPECIAL STUDIES, REPORTS

American Board of Commissioners for Foreign Missions, *Report,* 1831 and 1839.

Greek War Relief Association, Inc., *Annual Meeting of Members,* 1941–1945.

—— Press Releases, November 20, 1940–1943.

—— *News Letters,* I–VI, December 1941–September 1946.

Hauser, Phillip, and Kitagawa, *Local Community Fact Book for Chicago, 1950* (University of Chicago, 1950).

Koenig, Samuel, *Immigrant Settlements in Connecticut: Their Growth and Characteristics,* WPA Federal Writers' Project for the State of Connecticut (Hartford, State Department of Education, ca. 1940).

Mayer, Albert, *A Study of the Foreign-Born Population of Detroit, 1870–1950* (Wayne University, 1951); mimeographed.

Protestant Episcopal Church in the U.S.A., Domestic and Foreign Missionary Society. Department of New England. *A Report of the Commission Appointed . . . to Consider Cooperating with the Eastern Orthodox Churches, the Separated Churches of the East, and Other Slavs . . .* (Springfield, Mass., 1913).

WPA Adult Education Program, Chicago Board of Education, *A Tour of Greek and Macedonian Communities,* arranged by Ira Latimer, August 19, 1936, Syllabus No. 35; mimeographed, 3 pages.

NOTES

1. THE HELLAS OF THE IMMIGRANT

1. Good English accounts of Greece in the late nineteenth and early twentieth centuries are those of William Miller, *Greek Life in Town and Country* (London, 1905); Lewis Sargeant, *Greece in the Nineteenth Century* (London, 1897); Rennell Rodd, *The Customs and Lore of Modern Greece* (London, 1892); R. A. H. Bickford-Smith, *Greece under King George* (London, 1893); Percy F. Martin, *Greece in the Twentieth Century* (London, 1913); and Lucy M. J. Garnett, *Greece and the Hellenes* (New York, 1914).

2. Bureau of Foreign Commerce, *Commercial Relations of the United States, 1898,* II (Washington, 1899), 373; *ibid.* (1903), I, 475.

3. *Ibid.* (1899), II, 363. The depreciation of the Greek currency was blamed on the war in South Africa and on speculation. *Ibid.* (1902), II, 384; letter from Daniel E. McGinley to Herbert H. D. Peirce, April 26, 1904, Dept. of State, vol. 15, "Greece and Bulgaria." Unless otherwise stated, all diplomatic correspondence is from the U.S. State Department files in the National Archives.

4. Charles S. Wilson to Elihu Root, August 31, 1905.

5. Andreas Andreades in the preface to Martin, pp. 8–9.

6. *Commercial Relations of the United States, 1902,* II (Washington, 1903), 378–379.

7. William Miller, *A History of the Greek People, 1821–1921* (London, 1922), p. 99; Martin, pp. 239–240.

8. *Commercial Relations of the United States, 1902,* II, 378–379.

9. National Bank of Greece, *Ekonomike Epetiris tis Hellados, 1938* (Economic Yearbook of Greece, 1938; Athens, 1939), p. 37. Compare these figures with those of E. Repouli, *Meleti Peri Metanasteuseos, Meta Schediou Nomou* (A Study of Immigration, With Suggested Legislation; Athens, 1912), pp. 40, 43. William H. Moffett, the U.S. consul in Athens, wrote in 1889 of Greece's "exceedingly defective statistical system" (letter to William F. Wharton, September 1889).

10. Bambi B. Alivizatou, *E Georgiki Hellas Kai E Exelixis Tis* (Agricultural Greece and Its Evolution; Athens, 1939), p. 29.

11. "Greece," *New Englander,* V (January 1947), 12–13.

12. "Greece," *Encyclopedia Britannica,* 9th ed. (Chicago, 1892), XI, 87.

13. Rodd, p. 54.

14. P. I. Halikiopoulou, *Diagonisma Peri Veltioseos kai Empschihoseos tis en Helladi Georgias* (Efforts for the Improvement and Encouragement of Greek Agriculture; Athens, 1880), p. 52.

15. N. D. Pappou, *Zitimata Agritikis Ekonomias en Thessalia* (Problems in Rural Economy in Thessaly; Athens, 1906), pp. 20–21; Miller, *Greek Life in Town and Country,* pp. 214–215.

16. Carnegie Endowment for International Peace, *Report of the International*

Commission to Inquire into the Causes and Conduct of the Balkan Wars (Washington, 1914), p. 257; John B. Jackson to Elihu Root, April 1, 1907.

17. *Britannica Year-Book, 1913* (London, New York, 1913), p. 1027.

18. *Report of the International Commission,* p. 257; Garnett, pp. 136–137.

19. Rodd, pp. 53–54.

20. Garnett, pp. 137–138.

21. *Encyclopaedia Britannica,* XI, 88; "Greece and the Greeks," *Westminster Review,* LXXIX (January 1863), 99.

22. Eliot G. Mears, *Greece Today* (Stanford, 1929), pp. 31, 256.

23. Martin, pp. 127–129.

24. 61st Cong., 3rd sess., Senate Document No. 748, Reports of the Immigration Commission, *Emigration Conditions in Europe* (Washington, 1911), p. 413.

25. Repouli, p. 40.

26. Economic Yearbook of Greece, 1938, p. 32.

27. *Commercial Relations of the United States, 1892,* II, 459; *ibid.* (1898), II, 373–374.

28. *Ibid.* (1898), II, 376.

29. *Ibid.* (1901), II, 371–372, 380; *ibid.* (1902), II, 368.

30. Charles S. Francis to John Hay, February 12, 1902.

31. *Commercial Relations of the United States, 1902,* II, 368.

32. De Witt T. Riley to Alvey A. Adee, April 30, 1885.

33. Daniel E. McGinley to David J. Hill, February 26, 1900, Consular Letters (Athens), vol. 7, January 1, 1899–June 30, 1904.

34. McGinley to William R. Day, April 26, 1898, Consular Letters, vol. 6, July 1, 1890–November 30, 1898.

35. George Daskaloyanis to Louis Nikolaides, 7/19 April, 1898, Consular Letters, vol. 6.

36. G. Papadopetros, et al., to Louis Nikolaides, April 1898, Consular Letters, vol. 6.

37. Translation of published circular, dated Athens, April 22, 1898, and signed by D. E. McGinley, Consular Letters, vol. 6.

38. Georgiou Ventiri, *E Hellas tou 1910–1920* (The Greece of 1910–1920), 2 vols. (Athens, 1931), I, 17–20.

39. Sargeant, pp. 212–213.

40. *Ibid.,* p. 214.

41. Ventiri, I, 20–22.

42. Doros Alastos, *Venizelos* (London, 1942), pp. 62–63.

43. Herbert Adams Gibbon, *Venizelos* (Boston, New York, 1920), pp. 80–83.

44. T. Lathrop Stoddard, *Present Day Europe* (New York, 1917), pp. 246–247; see also Miller, *Greek Life in Town and Country,* pp. 40–44.

45. 61st Cong., 3rd sess., Senate Document No. 662, *Dictionary of Races or Peoples* (Washington, 1911), pp. 70–71.

46. Miller, *Greek Life in Town and Country,* pp. 251–252; Bickford-Smith, pp. 333–334.

47. Miller, *ibid.,* pp. 251–252.

48. *Ibid.,* pp. 42–43.

49. John B. Jackson to Elihu Root, March 26, 1906, Dept. of State, vol. 18, "Greece and Bulgaria."

50. Jackson to Root, May 4, 1906.

51. See Frederick Strong, *Greece as a Kingdom* (London, 1842), pp. 348–367, on the early history of the independent Greek Church.

52. *Encyclopaedia Britannica*, 11th ed., XII, 433–434.

53. Theodore Saloutos, "American Missionaries in Greece," *Church History*, XXIV (June 1955), 4; K. Paparrigopoulou, *Historia tou Hellinikou Ethnous* (History of the Greek Nation), 8 vols. (Athens, 1932), VII, 313; Elias Venezi, *Archiepiskopos Damaskinos, E Hronoi tis Doulias* (Archbishop Damaskinos, The Years of Slavery; Athens, 1952).

54. Rodd, p. 51. In 1896 the U.S. consul in Athens reported that there were over 160 fast days on the Greek religious calendar and that dried cod was eaten on most of these days. *Commercial Relations of the United States, 1895 and 1896*, II, 199. Another source reported there were 195 fast days and that the working days during any single year never exceeded 265. *Encyclopaedia Britannica*, 9th ed., XI, 87.

55. Department of Commerce, Bureau of Foreign and Domestic Commerce, *Paper and Stationery Trade of the World*, Special Consular Reports, No. 73 (Washington, 1915), p. 79.

56. Edward A. Steiner, quoted in *American Greek Review*, IV (September 1926), 10; Theodore Saloutos, "The Greeks in the United States," *South Atlantic Quarterly*, XLIV (January 1945), 73.

57. *Encyclopaedia Britannica*, 11th ed., XII, 430–431.

58. Charles Williams, "The Thessalian War of 1897," *Fortnightly Review*, LXVII (June 1897), 961.

2. PREPARING FOR THE UNKNOWN

1. Seraphim G. Canoutas, *Christopher Columbus, A Greek Nobleman* (New York, 1943).

2. Demetriou Sicilianos, *E Helliniki Katagogi tou Christoforou Kolombou* (The Greek Background of Christopher Columbus; Athens, 1950), 3.

3. Bambi Malafouris, *Hellenes tis Amerikis, 1528–1948* (Greeks in America; New York, 1948), p. 26.

4. *New York Times*, September 1, 1957.

5. Thomas Burgess, *Greeks in America* (Boston, 1913), pp. 192–193.

6. *Report of the American Board of Commissioners for Foreign Missions, 1831*, p. 43.

7. Malafouris, pp. 61–62. A list of the various Greek commercial firms is found on these pages.

8. Burgess, pp. 190–225; Demetriou and Georgiou Anagnostopoulos, *Michael Anagnostopoulos* (Athens, 1923).

9. *Report of the American Board of Commissioners for Foreign Missions, Thirtieth Annual Meeting* (Boston, 1839), p. 60.

10. *Spartiatikon Emerologion* (Spartan Almanac), 1909, p. 11.

11. N. K. Rozakos, "E Protoi Lacedaimonoi Metanastes stin Ameriki" (The First Spartan Immigrants in America), *Nea Estia*, XLVII (August 15, 1950), 1080–1084.

12. *Sphaira* (The Globe), May 12, 1882.

13. *Ibid.*, May 12, 1882.

14. *Stoa,* August 25, 1882.

15. *Aeon,* May 12, 1882.

16. *Ibid.,* July 22, 1882.

17. De Witt T. Riley to Alvey A. Adee, March 22, 1885, Consular Letters (Athens), vol. 4, January 1, 1883–March 31, 1887.

18. 49th Cong., 2nd sess., House of Representatives, Executive Document No. 157, Emigration and Immigration, *Reports of the Consular Officers of the United States* (Washington, 1887), pp. 244–245.

19. A. C. McDowell to W. H. Moffett on "Emigration from This District to the United States," May 10, 1887; Moffett to James D. Porter, May 24, 1887, Consular Letters (Athens), vol. 5, April 1, 1887–December 31, 1890.

20. Moffett to G. L. Rivers, April 14, 1888.

21. Worthington C. Ford to Dr. St. Clair, May 8, 1888.

22. *Sphaira,* March 30, 1888.

23. *Ibid.,* October 1, 1886, and May 17, 1888.

24. *Ibid.,* March 30, 1888.

25. Andreas M. Andreades, ed., *E Helliniki Metanasteusis* (Greek Immigration; Athens, 1917), pp. 77–79, 93.

26. E. Repouli, *Meleti Peri Metanasteuseos, Meta Schediou Nomou* (A Study of Immigration, With Suggested Legislation; Athens, 1912), pp. 18–21.

27. *Atlantis,* January 14, 1909.

28. William Miller, *A History of the Greek People, 1821–1921* (New York, 1922), pp. 102–103; V. Gabrielides, "The Overproduction of Greek Currants," *Economic Journal,* V (June 1895), 285–288; Theodore Burlami, "The Over-production of Currants in Greece," *ibid.,* IX (December 1899), 634–651; A. Andreades, "The Currant Crisis in Greece," *ibid.,* XVI (March 1906), 41–51; Frank W. Jackson to the Department of State, March 25, 1903.

29. Henry Pratt Fairchild, *Greek Immigration to the United States* (New Haven, 1911), pp. 76–77.

30. U.S. Department of Commerce and Labor, Bureau of Statistics, Special Consular Reports, *Emigration to the United States* (Washington, 1903), pp. 76–77; U.S. *Consular Reports, 1902,* pp. 379–380.

31. E. S. Lykoudes, *E Metanastai* (The Immigrants; Athens, 1903), p. 12.

32. *Atlantis,* March 31, 1909.

33. F. M. Jackson to David J. Hill, June 29, 1901, Consulate of the U.S. (Patras, Greece), vol. 15.

34. *Nea Ephemeris* (Irakleion, Crete), July 28, 1912.

35. Repouli, *Meleti Peri Metanasteuseos,* p. 43.

36. Andreades, pp. 76–77.

37. Edward I. Nathan to Department of State, February 27, 1908.

38. Laskaris, "The Threatened Depopulation of Greece," *Chambers Journal,* LXXXIII (1906), 40.

39. *Atlantis,* March 24, 1909.

40. Repouli, pp. 82–83.

41. *To Kratos* (The Nation), August 26, 1912.

42. *Ibid.,* September 16, 1912.

43. *Atlantis,* May 13, 1913.

44. *Ibid.,* May 25, 1914.

45. Fairchild, pp. 39–40, 93; *Saloniki* (Chicago), September 6, 1919.

PREPARING FOR THE UNKNOWN

46. *Akropolis* (Athens), June 7, 1901 referred to by F. M. Jackson to David J. Hill, June 29, 1901.

47. U.S. Department of Commerce and Labor, *Emigration to the United States*, p. 77; Repouli, p. 56.

48. *Nation*, LVIII (May 10, 1894), 346.

49. Andreades, pp. 78–79.

50. Repouli, p. 57.

51. Andreades, pp. 77–78.

52. *Ibid.*, pp. 342–343.

53. *Ibid.*, pp. 267–268, 300 and 304.

54. John B. Jackson to John Hay, September 3, 1903, Dept. of State.

55. Charles S. Wilson to Hay, September 30, 1903.

56. John B. Jackson to Elihu Root, June 14, 1906.

57. Wilson to Root, July 15, 1906.

58. W. S. Bennett to H. C. Lodge, July 3, 1907.

59. Jackson to Root, July 2, 1906.

60. *Sphaira*, September 6, 1907; 61st Cong., 3rd sess., Senate Document No. 748, Reports of the Immigration Commission, *Emigration Conditions in Europe* (Washington, 1911), p. 109.

61. *Sphaira*, October 9, 1907.

62. Nathan to Department of State, February 27, 1908.

63. A. Donaldson Smith to Ass't. Secretary of State Huntington Smith, October 27, 1909.

64. Senate Document No. 748, p. 109.

65. F. M. Jackson to David J. Hill, June 29, 1901.

66. John B. Jackson to John Hay, February 26, 1903.

67. Jackson to Hay, May 15, 1903.

68. Jackson to Hay, July 1, 1903.

69. U.S. Department of Commerce and Labor, *Emigration to the United States*, pp. 75–76.

70. Charles S. Wilson to Hay, April 2, 1904.

71. D. J. Tsatsos to John B. Jackson, April 16, 1904.

72. *To Kratos*, May 27, 1907.

73. John B. Jackson to Hay, June 21, 1906.

74. Jackson to Root, July 2, 1906.

75. Wilson to Root, July 24, 1906; *E ex Hellados Metanasteusis, E Ekthesis tis Epitropis tis Voulis* (Emigration from Greece, The Report of the Committee of the Chamber of Deputies; Athens, 1906), pp. 186–191, 194.

76. Jackson to Root, February 19, 1907.

77. *Sphaira*, March 17, 1907.

78. Jackson to Root, April 1, 1907.

79. Nathan to Department of State, February 27, 1908.

80. *Sphaira*, November 17 and 22, December 5, 1907.

81. *Atlantis*, April 12, 1909.

82. *Panhellinios Kratos* (Panhellenic Nation), August 6, 1908.

83. *Atlantis*, April 22, 1909; *California*, May 8, 1909.

84. *Nea Ephemeris*, September 8, 1912.

85. *Ibid.*, September 8, 1912.

86. *To Kratos*, July 19, 1912.

87. *Atlantis,* May 13, 1913 and May 25, 1914.

88. Ripley Wilson, "Emigration from Kalamata, Greece, Quarantine Laws and Regulations," September 13, 1913, Dept. of State.

89. "Emigration to United States, Health Conditions," p. 25.

90. John G. Erhardt and W. L. Lowrie, "Passenger Movement from Piraeus to the United States," Athens, January 12, 1921.

91. 61st Cong., 3rd sess., Senate Document No. 753, Reports of the Immigration Commission, *Immigrant Banks* (Washington, 1911), p. 274.

92. J. W. Gregory, *Human Migration and the Future* (Philadelphia, 1927), p. 30; *To Kratos,* March 23, 1914.

3. EARLY YEARS

1. 61st Cong., 3rd sess., Senate Document No. 748, Reports of the Immigration Commission, *Emigration Conditions in Europe* (Washington, 1911), p. 391.

2. Theodore Saloutos, *They Remember America* (Berkeley and Los Angeles, 1956), p. 9.

3. Senate Document No. 748, p. 393.

4. U.S. Department of Labor, *Report of the Commissioner General, 1931* (Washington, 1932), p. 226.

5. Bambi Malafouris, *Hellenes tis Amerikis, 1528–1948* (Greeks in America; New York, 1948), p. 105.

6. *Ethnikos Kyrix* (National Herald), July 27, 1956.

7. 61st Cong., 3rd sess., Senate Document No. 756, Reports of the Immigration Commission, *Statistical Review of Immigration, 1820–1910* (Washington, 1911), p. 47.

8. Senate Document No. 748, p. 395; *Hellinikos Astir* (Greek Star), September 27, 1907; *California,* October 17, 1908.

9. *Hellinikos Astir,* July 10, 1936.

10. W. E. Weyl, "Pericles of Smyrna and New York," *Outlook,* XCIV (February 26, 1910), 472.

11. *American Greek,* I (February 1920), 1; Malafouris, p. 188.

12. Letter, Frank M. Jackson to David Hill, June 29, 1901, Consulate of the U.S. (Patras), vol. 15.

13. A. C. McDowell to William H. Moffett, "Emigration from This District to the United States" (Piraeus), May 10, 1887; Moffett to James D. Porter, May 24, 1887, Consular Letters (Athens), vol. 5.

14. *Washington Post,* December 17, 1904.

15. Frederick W. Coburn, *History of Lowell and Its People,* II (New York, 1920), 399–403.

16. *Sphaira* (The Globe), November 10, 1907.

17. *New York Evening Sun,* May 2, 1908 quoted in *Atlantis,* May 3, 1908; *Chicago Herald and Examiner,* November 6, 1927; Coburn, *History of Lowell,* II, 399–403.

18. 61st Cong., 3rd sess., Senate Document No. 747, *Abstracts of the Reports of the Immigration Commission,* II (Washington, 1911), 391–392.

19. *Ibid.,* p. 393.

20. *Ibid.,* p. 398.

21. *Ibid.,* pp. 398–399.

22. *Ibid.*, pp. 402–403.

23. *Ibid.*, p. 404.

24. *Ibid.*, pp. 404–405.

25. *Ibid.*, pp. 398–399.

26. *Ibid.*, pp. 398–401.

27. *Ibid.*, pp. 403–404.

28. *Ibid.*, p. 394.

29. *Ibid.*, p. 395.

30. *Ibid.*, p. 396.

31. *Ibid.*, p. 396.

32. *Ibid.*, p. 397.

33. *Ibid.*, p. 402.

34. John B. Jackson to Elihu Root, March 7, 1907, Dept. of State.

35. *Sphaira,* May 19, 1907; Jackson to Root, April 18, 1907.

36. *Atlantis,* November 10, December 26, 1908; January 23, 1909.

37. *Saloniki,* January 8, February 5 and 26, 1916.

38. *Ibid.*, April 8, 1916.

39. *Ibid.*, April 15, May 20, 1916.

40. *Ibid.*, May 20, July 8, 1916.

41. Senate Document No. 747, II, 405–406.

42. *Saloniki,* May 1, 1915.

43. *Atlantis,* April 2 and 3, July 13, 1913.

44. *Saloniki,* October 25, 1913.

45. Senate Document No. 747, II, 393–394.

46. *New York Daily Tribune,* August 30, 1903, carries the story of one such person, usually known as an "interpreter" among the immigrants.

47. *Menea Ekonographemenoi Atlantis* (Illustrated Monthly Atlantis), II (July 1911), 9; *ibid.,* I (October 1910), 20–21. Hereafter cited in English translation.

48. *Ibid.*, III (March 1912), 14–15.

49. N. Ghortzi, *Ameriki kai Amerikanoi* (Athens, 1907?), pp. 69–72.

50. *California,* October 20, 1917.

51. *Ibid.*, October 20, 1917.

52. *Ibid.*, November 24, 1917.

53. *Ibid.*, November 9, 1918.

54. *Ibid.*, October 25, 1919.

55. Malafouris, p. 250.

56. *Hellinikos Astir,* September 29, 1905.

57. *Hellinismos,* June 1909, pp. 341–342.

58. Theodore Saloutos, "The Greeks in the United States," in William B. Hamilton, ed., *Fifty Years of the South Atlantic Quarterly* (Durham, 1952), pp. 308–309.

59. *Hellinikos Astir,* April 15, August 26, 1904.

60. *California,* December 22, 1907.

61. *Atlantis,* January 18, 1908.

62. C. C. Maximos to Elihu Root, July 15, 1907.

63. Claude A. Swanson to Robert Bacon, July 20, 1907. A letter describing what happened is appended to this communication. Joel H. Cutchins to Swanson, July 19, 1907.

64. Cutchins to Swanson, January 13, 1908.

65. Roosevelt to Elihu Root, August 8, 1907.
66. William S. Bennett to Henry Cabot Lodge, July 3, 1907.
67. *Hellinikos Astir,* March 13, 1908.
68. *California,* March 14, 21, and 28, April 4, 1908.
69. *Hellinikos Astir,* May 23, 1908.
70. *Ibid.,* March 13, 1908.
71. *California,* November 10, 1907.
72. *Ibid.,* May 23, 1908.
73. *Atlantis,* February 4, 1909.
74. *Ibid.,* February 4 and 6, 1909.
75. *Omaha Evening Bee,* February 22, 1909; *Evening World-Herald,* February 22, 1909.
76. Memorandum of a discussion between Lambros A. Coromilas and the Assistant Secretary of State, July 1, 1909.
77. "In Re Anti-Greek Riots at Omaha, Nebraska, in 1909," dated February 4, 1910, and signed by J. B. S.
78. *Omaha Evening Bee,* February 22, 1909.
79. *Evening World-Herald,* February 22, 1909.
80. *Omaha Evening Bee,* February 22, 1909.
81. "In Re Anti-Greek Riots at Omaha," pp. 2–3. For Greek-language press versions, see *Atlantis,* February 23–27, March 1, 1909.
82. Coromilas to State Department, February 22, 1909.
83. Wires to President Roosevelt, dated February 22, 1909.
84. Cable of Robert Bacon to A. C. Shallenberger, February 23, 1908.
85. Robert Bacon to Lambros Coromilas, February 24, 1909.
86. *Atlantis,* February 23, 1909.
87. *Hellenic Herald* (London), III (February 1909), 47.
88. "In Re Anti-Greek Riots at Omaha," p. 4.
89. "In Re Anti-Greek Riots at Omaha," p. 4; memorandum of discussion between Lambros A. Coromilas and the Assistant Secretary of State, July 1, 1909.
90. *Ibid.,* July 1, 1909.
91. "In Re Anti-Greek Riots at Omaha," pp. 5–9.
92. *Atlantis,* March 12 and 22, 1909.
93. *Ibid.,* May 25, 1909.

4. SOCIAL AND COMMUNITY LIFE

1. *Hellinikos Astir* (Greek Star), March 15 and 22, 1907.
2. *Ibid.,* March 15, 1907.
3. *Ibid.,* October 21, 1904.
4. *Ibid.,* November 22, 1907.
5. *Saloniki,* December 5 and 26, 1914.
6. *Ibid.,* October 10, 1914, August 21, and September 18, 1915.
7. *Ibid.,* September 18, 1915.
8. *Ibid.,* December 11, 1915.
9. *Ibid.,* March 6, 1915.
10. *To Kratos* (The Nation), July 12, 1907; *Sphaira* (The Globe), November 10, 1907; *Saloniki,* March 6, 1915.
11. Henry Pratt Fairchild, *Greek Immigration to the United States* (New Haven, 1911), p. 156.

12. John D. Black and Constantine Ladas, *Greece* (Washington, 1932); M. M. Davis, *Immigrant Health and Community* (New York, 1921), pp. 101–102.

13. *Hellinikos Astir*, January 10, 1908.

14. *Hellinikos Typos* (Greek Press), December 18, 1929.

15. *California*, February 3, November 17, and December 1, 1917; May 3 and 11, 1918; *Panhellenic Almanac, 1918* (New York, 1920), pp. 229–238; *Saloniki*, November 24, 1917, March 30, 1918, March 29, 1919; *Hellinikos Astir*, March 16, 1906.

16. Vasileos I. Chebithes, *Ahepa and the Progress of Hellenism in America* (New York, 1935), pp. 7–8.

17. *Atlantis*, June 3, 1912.

18. *Saloniki*, March 6, 1915.

19. *Hellinismos*, June 1909, p. 303; *Kathemerini* (The Daily), April 18, 1929.

20. Chebithes, p. 9.

21. *Ibid.*

22. *Atlantis*, February 26 and March 1, 1913.

23. *Atlantis*, February 19, 1913.

24. *Eastern and Western Review*, VII (September 1914), 1; *Ethnikos Kyrix* (National Herald), December 1, 1915, and January 8, 1920; *Deltion tis Panhelliniou Enoseos en Ameriki* (Report of the Panhellenic Union in America), October 3, 1914, pp. 6–7; January 2, 1915, pp. 1–2. Hereafter throughout the volume, *Ethnikos Kyrix* will be cited as *National Herald*.

25. *Saloniki*, September 18, 1915; *Hellinikos Typos*, April 9, 1930.

26. *Atlantis*, January 3, 1912.

27. *Saloniki*, September 18, 1915; Kyotchek S. Christowe, *Outlook*, CLV (May 14, 1930), 48–49.

28. *Saloniki*, September 18, 1915; *Hellinikos Typos*, April 9, 1930.

29. *Ibid.*, March 12, 1924.

30. J. P. Xenides, *The Greeks in America* (New York, 1922), p. 88.

31. *Washington Post*, December 17, 1904.

32. Frederick W. Coburn, *History of Lowell and Its People*, II (New York, 1920), 405.

33. Theodore Saloutos, "The Greeks in the United States," *South Atlantic Quarterly*, XLIV (January 1945), 78.

34. Theodore Saloutos, *They Remember America* (Berkeley and Los Angeles, 1956), pp. 95–96.

35. *Atlantis*, November 17, 1908, January 21, 1909; *National Herald*, December 7, 1915; *Hellinikos Astir*, January 4, February 15, April 5, 1918; January 16, 1920.

36. *Saloniki*, December 19, 1914; October 2, 1915.

37. *Ibid.*, September 18, 1915.

38. Coburn, p. 405; *Saloniki*, August 8, 1914.

39. *Chicago Daily Tribune*, April 15, 1901; Grace Abbott, "A Study of the Greeks in Chicago," *American Journal of Sociology*, XV (November 1909), 381; Thomas Burgess, *Greeks in America* (Boston, 1913), pp. 93–97; Lucy M. J. Garnett, *Greece of the Hellenes* (New York, 1914), pp. 160–170; Rennell Rodd, *The Customs and Lore of Modern Greece* (London, 1892), pp. 149–155.

40. *Hellinikos Astir*, October 4, 1907.

41. *Saloniki*, May 20, 1916.

42. *Ibid.*, May 15, 1915.

43. *Ibid.*, September 6, 1919.

44. *Loxias*, September 16, 1911.

45. *Saloniki*, May 1, 1915.

46. Abbott, pp. 387–389.

47. *Report of the Commission on Immigration on the Problem of Immigration in Massachusetts* (Boston, 1914), pp. 193–194.

48. Dio Adallis, *Twenty-Fifth Anniversary, Cumberland, Md., Greek-American Colony, 1908–1933* (Cumberland, 1933), pp. 7–8.

49. *Immigration in Massachusetts*, pp. 201–202.

50. Seraphim Canoutas, *O Hellinismos en Ameriki* (New York, 1918), pp. 230–232.

51. *Ibid.*, p. 232.

52. *Eleutheros Typos* (Free Press), February 19, 1944.

53. *American Hellenic World*, I (September 26, 1925), 12.

54. See Costas Kerofilas, *Une Familie patricienne cretoise, Les Vlasto* (New York, 1932), in which the publisher traces his family background. *Atlantis*, September 20, 1927.

55. *Atlantis, ibid.*

56. *Ibid.*, March 2 and 9, 1895.

57. N. W. Ayer and Son, *Directory of Newspapers and Periodicals, 1897*, p. 560.

58. Interviews with Adamantios Polyzoides in Los Angeles on May 12, 21, June 2, 1959; *Proodos* (Progress; Chicago), August 1933.

59. *Eleutheros Typos*, February 19, 1944.

60. *Panhellinios*, August 6, November 21, 1908.

61. *Atlantis*, May 2, 1913.

62. *Directory of Newspapers and Periodicals, 1911*, p. 642.

63. *Eleutheros Typos*, February 19, 1944.

64. Interview with Polyzoides, Los Angeles, June 2, 1959.

65. Demetrios Michalaros, *Demetrios P. Callimachos* (Chicago, 1953).

66. *Hellinikos Astir*, January 10, 1908.

67. *Saloniki*, February 26, 1916.

68. *Hellinikos Astir*, January 9, 1920.

69. *American Hellenic World*, I (March 28, 1925), 1; IV (July 1928), 1; V (August 29, 1931), 1.

70. *Ibid.*, March 28, 1925; see entire issue.

71. *Ibid.*, April 11, 1925.

5. FOR GOD AND COUNTRY

1. *Sphaira* (The Globe), May 2, 1907.

2. E. Repouli, *Meleti Peri Metanasteuseos, Meta Schediou Nomou* (A Study of Immigration, With Suggested Legislation; Athens, 1912), pp. 12–21; John W. Brown, *World Migration and Labour* (Amsterdam, 1926), pp. 14–15.

3. N. N. Dournovo, "E Helliniki Ekklesia kai e Ethniki Anagennesis" (The Greek Church and National Regeneration), *Hellinismos*, III (January 1900), 200–212.

4. *To Kratos* (The Nation), December 17, 1909.

5. *Panhellinios Kratos*, May 8, June 28, 1908.

6. Aristides E. Phoutrides, "The Literary Impulse of Modern Greece," *Poet Lore*, XXVI (January–February 1915), 56.

7. Letter, John B. Jackson to John Hay, December 20, 1904, Dept. of State, vol. 15, "Greece and Bulgaria." See also C. K. Tuckermann, *The Greeks of To-Day* (New York, 1878), pp. 119–137, for a discussion of the Great Idea.

8. *Hellinismos*, VI (March 1903), 233–240; May 1903, p. 397; December 1903, pp. 928–930; VIII (May 1906), 380–387.

9. *Hellinikos Astir* (Greek Star), July 8, 1904, November 24, 1905, March 30, 1906.

10. *Sphaira*, May 2, 1907.

11. *Hellinikos Astir*, June 29, 1906.

12. *Ibid.*, September 14, 1906.

13. *Ibid.*, October 5, 1906.

14. *New York Sun*, quoted in *Atlantis*, May 2, 1907.

15. *Sphaira*, October 20, 1907.

16. *Ibid.*, August 28, October 19 and 21, 1907; *Hellinikos Astir*, July 19, September 13 and 27, 1907; *To Kratos*, September 27, October 21, 1907.

17. John B. Jackson to Elihu Root, January 21, 1907; Percy F. Martin, in *Greece of the Twentieth Century* (London, 1913), p. 80, makes passing mention of Gennadius and the Washington secretaryship.

18. Jackson to Root, February 17, 1907.

19. Jackson to Root, September 26, 1907.

20. Jackson to Root, October 12, 1907.

21. *Megali Helliniki Enkyklopaideia* (Great Greek Encyclopedia), XIV (Athens, 1934), 916; Martin, pp. 53–54.

22. *Sphaira*, October 20 and 23, 1907; *To Kratos*, October 25, 1907; *Panhellinios Kratos*, September 4, 11, and 25, 1908.

23. *Atlantis*, January 13, July 7, 1908.

24. *Ibid.*, October 13, 1908.

25. *Ibid.*, October 27, 1908.

26. *Ibid.*, October 29, 1908.

27. *Ibid.*, October 28, 1908; *Hellinikos Astir*, September 25, October 23, 1908.

28. *Atlantis*, October 22 and 31, 1908.

29. *Ibid.*, December 2, 3, 5, 12, and 16, 1908.

30. *Ibid.*, December 26, 1908.

31. *Ibid.*, February 4, 5, and 6, 1909.

32. *Ibid.*, March 6, 1909.

33. *Katastatikon Panhelliniou Enosis* (Constitution of the Panhellenic Union) (Boston, 1910); *Hellinikos Astir*, October 15, 1909; *Loxias*, October 23, 1910.

34. *Megali Helliniki Enkyklopaideia*, p. 778.

35. *Atlantis*, January 5 and 21, 1909.

36. *Ibid.*, July 14, 1909.

37. *To Kratos*, April 8, June 3, 1910.

38. *Hellinikos Astir*, February 25, 1910.

39. *To Kratos*, November 19, 1909.

40. *Hellinikos Astir*, January 28, 1910. This issue gives an historical account of the controversy.

41. *Ibid.*, February 25, 1910.

42. *Sphaira*, January 9, 1907.

43. *Atlantis,* January 15, 1908.
44. *Sphaira,* January 9, 1907.
45. *Atlantis,* January 15, 1908.
46. *Ibid.,* March 25, 1908.
47. *Ibid.,* October 20, November 28, 1908; May 1 and 11, 1909.
48. *Ibid.,* May 25, 1909.
49. *Ibid.,* January 30, 1913.
50. *California,* July 24, 1909.
51. *Ibid.,* August 28, 1909.
52. *Panhellinios Kratos,* August 29, 1909.
53. *Atlantis,* August 13, 1909.
54. *Ibid.,* January 30, 1913.
55. *Hellinikos Astir,* October 22, 1909.
56. *California,* November 20, 1909.
57. *Illustrated Monthly Atlantis,* July 1910, pp. 16–17.
58. *California,* January 15, 1910.
59. *To Kratos,* July 18, October 21, 1910.
60. *Ibid.,* September 16, 1912.
61. *Ibid.,* September 23, 1912; *Empros,* September 22, 1912.
62. *Atlantis,* October 4, 6, 7, and 8, 1912. See also K. C. M. Sills, "Greek-Americans," *Nation,* October 2, 1913, p. 309.
63. *Ibid.,* October 3 and 4, 1912.
64. *Ibid.,* October 6, 1912.
65. *Ibid.,* October 7, 1912.
66. *Ibid.,* October 8, 1912.
67. *Loxias* (The Blade), October 5, 12, 19, and November 2, 1912; *Atlantis,* 11, 1912.
68. *Atlantis,* November 16, 1912.
69. *Ibid.,* October 27, 1912.
70. For an account by an American volunteer, see Thomas S. Hutchison, *An American Soldier under the Greek Flag at Bezanie* (Nashville, 1913); also, *Atlantis,* November 6, 1912.
71. *Atlantis,* November 9, 1912.
72. Hutchison, p. 48.
73. *Ibid.,* pp. 50–51.
74. *Atlantis,* November 14, 1912.
75. *Ibid.,* November 15, 1912.
76. *Loxias,* October 19, 1912.
77. *Atlantis,* November 16, 1912; *Eastern and Western Review,* V (December 1912), 31.
78. *Hellinikos Astir,* October 25, 1912.
79. *Atlantis,* January 7, 1913.
80. *To Kratos,* January 20, May 26, September 1, 1913.
81. *Atlantis,* January 16, 25, 29, 30; March 6 and 10, 1913; Cassaveti, p. 177.
82. *Loxias,* February 3, 1913.
83. *To Kratos,* May 26, September 1, 1913.
84. *Atlantis,* February 4, 1913.
85. *Ibid.,* March 13, 1913.
86. *Chicago Tribune,* September 27, 1913; *New York Times,* March 12, 1914.

87. *New York Times,* October 9, 1915.
88. *Saloniki,* September 13, 1913. See also R. R. Wells, "American Hellenes," *Nation,* July 23, 1914, p. 102.
89. *Atlantis,* December 3, 1913.
90. *New York Times,* March 11 and 12, 1914.

6. THE GREEK ORTHODOX CHURCH: THE BEGINNINGS

1. A. McClure, *Leadership of the New America* (New York, 1916), pp. 133–134.
2. Walter F. Adeney, *The Greek and Eastern Churches* (New York, 1908), pp. 325–339, 434–440, 549–552; Charles T. Riggs, "The Plight of the Greek Orthodox Church," *Missionary Review of the World,* XXXI (March 1908), 169–170; "Orthodox Eastern Church," *Encyclopaedia Britannica* (11th ed.); "The Orthodox Church," *Ekklesiastikos Kyrix* (Church Herald), I (September 9, 1921), 20–22 (hereafter cited as *Church Herald*).
3. U.S. Department of Commerce, Bureau of the Census, *Religious Bodies: 1936,* II, pt. 1, 572–573; *Church Herald,* I (September 2, 1921), 3–9.
4. Right Reverend Innocent, Bishop of Alaska, "The Russian Orthodox Church in Alaska," *Russian Orthodox Messenger,* March Supplement (New York, 1907), p. 65; W. G. Tinchon-Fernandez, "Eastern Orthodox Peoples and Churches in the United States," *Christendom,* IV (Summer 1939), 423–436; Basil M. Bensin, *History of the Russian Orthodox Greek Catholic Church of North America* (New York, 1941), p. 3. See also V. Basanoff, "Archives of Russian Church in Alaska in the Library of Congress," *Pacific Historical Review,* II (March 1933), 72–84, for a brief account of the nature of these holdings.
5. Tinchon-Fernandez, p. 431. *The People of the Eastern Orthodox Churches* . . . , publication of the U.S. Protestant Episcopal Church (Springfield, Mass., 1913), p. 22.
6. See Frederick Strong, *Greece as a Kingdom* (London, 1842), pp. 344–367, for an account of Greek religion at the time of Otho's arrival and for a brief period after the Greek clergy had declared their independence of the Patriarchate.
7. Adeney, p. 336.
8. *Church Herald,* I (September 9, 1922), 21–22; Basil Th. Zoustis, *O en Ameriki Hellinismos kai e Drasis Tou* (Hellenism in America and Its Times; New York, 1954), pp. 151–159.
9. Lucy M. J. Garnett, *Greece of the Hellenes* (New York, 1914), p. 91.
10. Seraphim Canoutas, *O Hellinismos en Ameriki* (New York, 1918), pp. 326, 328, 330.
11. Garnett, pp. 90–91; *The People of the Eastern Orthodox Churches,* p. 21; Thomas Burgess, *Greeks in America* (Boston, 1913), p. 58.
12. Zoustis, pp. 43–51.
13. Burgess, p. 54n; *Saloniki,* December 12, 1931.
14. *Eleutheros Typos* (Free Press), January 15, 1943; Canoutas, pp. 163–166; Zoustis, pp. 56–58.
15. Canoutas, pp. 184–186. For a portrait of the priest, see John H. Barrows, ed., *World Parliament of Religions,* II (Chicago, 1893), 1133.
16. *Saloniki,* December 12, 1931. For a portrait of the Bishop of Zante, see Barrows, I, 357.

17. Holy Trinity Church, *Forty Years of Greek Life in Chicago, 1897–1937* (Chicago, 1937), pp. 19–22.

18. Canoutas, p. 192.

19. *Eleutheros Typos*, February 5, 1944.

20. Canoutas, p. 192.

21. Thomas J. Lacey, *Our Greek Immigrants* (New York, 1918), pp. 17–18; Burgess, pp. 52–58.

22. *Eleutheros Typos*, January 29, 1914; Bensin, pp. 8–13.

23. *To Kratos*, July 12, 1907; *California*, April 25, 1908; *Atlantis*, June 5, 1909.

24. Zoustis, pp. 321–327.

25. Lacey, pp. 17–18.

26. Burgess, 57–58; *The People of the Eastern Orthodox Churches*, p. 21.

27. *California*, May 30, 1908.

28. Letter, Oscar G. Straus to Elihu Root, December 2, 1908, Dept. of State.

29. Militiades Constantinides to George B. Billings, November 21, 1908.

30. Straus to Root, December 2, 1908.

31. Root to Straus, December 12, 1908.

32. Coromilas to Root, December 19, 1908; Alvey A. Adee to Coromilas, December 31, 1908.

33. W. A. Wheeler to Root, January 5, 1909.

34. Root to Straus, January 13, 1909.

35. *Atlantis*, October 31, 1908; *Hellinikos Astir*, February 26, 1909; *To Kratos*, October 28, 1910; *Saloniki*, June 19, July 17, 1915; Meletios Golden, *Conversion of a High Priest into a Christian Worker* (Boston, 1909), pp. 98–108.

36. *Hellinikos Astir*, March 5, 1909; *Saloniki*, July 10, 17, 1915; July 15, 1916.

37. Theodore N. Constant, "The Religion of the Hellenes," *Athene*, VI (March 1945), 12.

38. *Atlantis*, July 21, December 17, 1908, April 17, 1909; *California*, May 30, September 5, 1908.

39. *To Kratos*, December 17, 1909.

40. *Saloniki*, February 28, 1914; November 13, 1915.

41. *Ibid.*, December 4, 1915, December 15, 1917; *Loxias*, March 4, 1911.

42. *Saloniki*, December 4, 1915.

43. *Ibid.*, October 16, 1915.

44. *Ibid.*, July 15, August 12, 1916.

45. Clair Price, "The Greek Ecumenical Patriarchate in Turkey," *Current History*, XVII (March 1923), 944.

46. *New York Times*, October 16, 1916; *Church Herald*, II (October 23, 1923), 857; *Hellinikos Astir*, January 11, 1918; Doros Alastos, *Venizelos* (London, 1942), p. 175.

47. *Eleutheros Typos*, December 18, 1943; *Hellinikos Astir*, January 11, 1918; *California*, January 6, February 3, 1917; *New York Times*, June 7, 1917.

48. *Voice of Orthodoxy*, III (November 15, 1923), 2.

7. OLD-WORLD POLITICS IN THE NEW: VENIZELISTS VERSUS ROYALISTS

1. *New York Times*, October 9, 1915.

2. *Eastern and Western Review*, VII (September 1914), 1.

3. *Saloniki,* October 11, 1913.
4. *Ibid.,* November 15, 1913.
5. *Loxias* (The Blade), January 24, 1914.
6. *Saloniki,* February 7, 1914.
7. *Loxias,* April 25, 1914.
8. *Eastern and Western Review,* September 1914, p. 1.
9. *Deltion tis Panhellinios Enoseos en Ameriki* (Bulletin of the Panhellenic Union of America), I (October 3, 1914), 6–7.
10. *Ibid.,* January 2, 1915, pp. 1–2.
11. *Ibid.,* January 23, 1915, p. 2.
12. *Saloniki,* July 10, 1915.
13. *Ibid.,* May 1, 1915.
14. *Ibid.,* November 6, 1915.
15. *Megali Helliniki Enkyklopaideia* (Great Greek Encyclopedia), "Hellas," X (Athens, 1934), 756; *New York Times,* September 8, 1915: S. P. P. Cosmetatos, *The Tragedy of Greece* (London, 1928), pp. 21–35; Herbert Adams Gibbon, *Venizelos* (Boston, 1920), pp. 208–215, 216–274.
16. *New York Times,* December 27, 1915.
17. *Ibid.,* January 11, 1916.
18. Sympathetic treatments of Constantine and his policies are to be found in Paxton Hibben, *Constantine I and the Greek People* (New York, 1920); Adamantios Th. Polyzoides, *E Helliniki Oudeterotis kai o Basileus Konstantinos* (Greek Neutrality and King Constantine; New York, 1917); and Cosmetatos, *The Tragedy of Greece.*
19. Critical treatments of Constantine and support for the policies of Venizelos are to be found in Herbert Baxter Gibbons, *Venizelos* (Boston, 1920), and Doros Alastos, *Venizelos* (London, 1942).
20. *Dekaetiris Ethnikos Kyrikos* (Tenth Anniversary Edition, Illustrated Monthly National Herald), XI (April 1925), 59–60. Hereafter cited by title in translation.
21. Letter, Garrett Droppers to Robert Lansing, December 10, 1917, Dept. of State.
22. Personal interview with Polyzoides on May 12, 1959, in Los Angeles.
23. *New York Times,* September 8, 1915.
24. *Deltion tis Panhellinios Enoseos en Ameriki,* II (January 23, 1915), 1; *Illustrated Monthly National Herald,* April 1925, pp. 31–32; *Athene,* XIV (Autumn 1953), 24–26, 32.
25. *New York Times,* September 8, 1915.
26. Alastos, pp. 140–169, 171–172.
27. *New York Times,* October 16, 1916.
28. *Illustrated Monthly National Herald,* II (November 1916), 7.
29. *Ibid.*
30. *Loxias,* August 16, 1916.
31. *New York Times,* September 5 and 6, 1916.
32. *Ibid.,* October 19, 21, and 22, 1916.
33. *Illustrated Monthly National Herald,* November 1916, p. 3; *ibid.,* January 1917, p. 3.
34. Lansing to J. J. Jusserand, December 21, 1916; *New York Times,* January 14, 1917; *California,* January 27, 1917; Cosmetatos, pp. 261–267.
35. *California,* January 6, 1917.

36. *Ibid.,* January 13, 1917.
37. *Ibid.,* January 6, 1917.
38. *Ibid.*
39. Cosmetatos, pp. 227–228.
40. Droppers to Lansing, February 11, 1917.
41. *Saloniki,* February 24, 1917.
42. *Ibid.,* February 24, 1917; *Loxias,* February 21, 1917.
43. *Loxias,* March 14, 1917.
44. *Ibid.,* February 28, 1917.
45. *California,* February 24, 1917.
46. *Ibid.,* February 3, 1917.
47. *Ibid.,* February 3 and 10, 1917.
48. *Ibid.,* February 24, 1917.
49. *Ibid.,* March 31, 1917.
50. *New York Times,* April 9, 1917.
51. *Ibid.,* April 20 and 27, 1917.
52. *Ibid.,* June 13, 1917.
53. *Ibid.,* June 7, 1917.
54. Droppers to Lansing, March 30, 1917, telegram.
55. Walter Hines Page to Lansing, April 2, 1917, telegram.
56. Lansing to Droppers, April 4, 1917, telegram.
57. D. J. Theophilatos to F. L. Polk, April 24, 1917.
58. "AP" of Division of Near Eastern Affairs to Carr, May 11, 1917.
59. D. T. Timayenis to Lansing, May 2, 1917.
60. "AP" to Carr, May 11, 1917.
61. Greek Chargé d'Affaires to Lansing, June 16/29, 1917.
62. *New York Times,* June 13, 1917.
63. Iannou Metaxa, *E Istoria tou Ethnikou Dichasmou kai tis Mikrasiatikis Katastrophis* (The History of National Dissension and the Disaster in Asia Minor; Athens, 1935), pp. 313–336; Prince Nicholas of Greece, *Political Memoirs of Greece, 1914–1917* (London, 1928), p. 287; *American Year Book, 1917,* pp. 62–63.
64. Among the resolutions on file asking for a government investigation of the loyalty of *Atlantis* were those of the Liberal Clubs in South Bethlehem, Pa.; Washington, D.C.; New Rochelle, N.Y.; Yonkers, N.Y.; Hartford, Conn.; Lowell, Mass.; and Rockford, Ill. Dept. of State, Record Group 60.
65. Droppers to Lansing, July 23, 1917.
66. Text of resolution adopted by League of Greek Liberals, Marlboro, Mass., July 29, 1917, Record Group 60.
67. Samuel J. Graham to Francis G. Caffey, August 13, 1917.
68. Nicholas G. Psaki to Caffey, October 13, 1917.
69. *Atlantis,* October 14, 1917.
70. Caffey to Thomas Watt Gregory, October 19, 1917.
71. John Lord O'Brien, for the Attorney General, to Caffey, no date.
72. Romanos to Greek Legation, November 26, 1917.
73. Lansing to American Legation, November 23, 1917, telegram.
74. Droppers to State Department, December 8, 1917, telegram.
75. Sir Edward Grogan to American Consul General, Saloniki, October 28, 1917; George Horton to Department of State, October 29, 1917.

76. George Roussos to William Phillips, February 26, 1918.
77. Compton Mackenzie, *First Athenian Memoirs* (London, 1931), pp. 169–170.
78. Horton to Lansing, November 23, 1917.

8. THE FIRST WORLD WAR

1. *Chicago Tribune*, April 22, 1914.
2. *Loxias* (The Blade), April 28 and May 9, 1914.
3. *Saloniki*, July 6, 1916.
4. *Loxias*, February 7, 1917.
5. Constantine Paleologus to the President of the United States, February 6, 1917, in Correspondence of C. C. Mammon included in WPA project of Chicago Greek-language press, Chicago Public Library.
6. *Saloniki*, March 31, 1917.
7. Quoted by *Chicago Tribune*, February 10, 1917. See also "Our Proud Declaration," *Saloniki*, February 10, 1917, March 31, 1917.
8. *Loxias*, May 30, 1917.
9. *Ibid.*, July 11, 1917.
10. *Ibid.*, May 30, 1917; *Saloniki*, June 9, 1917.
11. *Saloniki*, August 11, 1917; *Loxias*, August 8, 1917.
12. *Greek-American Review*, I (September 1917), 27–28.
13. *Saloniki*, May 12, 1917; *California*, December 29, 1917; *New York Times*, December 27, 1917.
14. Newton D. Baker to Robert Lansing, December 8, 1917, War Dept.
15. *Loxias*, December 12, 1917.
16. *Ibid.*, February 28, 1918.
17. Nicholas Politis to Garrett Droppers, December 12/25, 1917, Dept. of State; Droppers to Lansing, January 7, 1918.
18. Droppers to Lansing, January 6, 1918, telegram.
19. *Saloniki*, June 22, 1918.
20. *Ibid.*, June 29, 1918.
21. *Ibid.*, October 27, 1917, January 26, March 16, April 6, 1918; *Loxias*, March 14, May 18, 1918.
22. *Chicago Journal*, April 24, 1918; *Chicago Tribune*, April 26, 1918.
23. *Commercial and Financial Chronicle*, CV (September 29, 1917), 1258–1259; *Literary Digest*, LX (March 8, 1919), 96; *Circular of Liberty Loan Committee New England*, Massachusetts Committee on Citizens of Foreign Birth or Descent (Boston, 1919).
24. *Saloniki*, August 31, 1918.
25. *Loxias*, February 23, 1918; *Saloniki*, August 31, 1918; *Chicago Tribune*, September 18, 1918.
26. *Loxias*, September 4, 1918.
27. *Saloniki*, August 10, 1918.
28. Droppers to State Department, August 29, 1918, telegram; Nicholas Politis to Droppers, August 14/17, 1918.
29. Politis to Droppers, November 30/12, 1918; Droppers to Lansing, Secretary of State, December 19, 1918; Droppers to Lansing, December 21, 1918.
30. *Bulletin for Military Intelligence Officers No. 33*, November 4, 1918.
31. P. C. Harris to Nicholas Culolias, March 6, 1920, Culolias Papers, Houghton Library, Harvard.

32. *New York Times,* November 4, 1923.

33. *Greek Review,* I (June 1923), 18; *New York Times,* October 14, November 4, 1923.

9. GREEK-AMERICANS AND THE GREAT IDEA

1. Letter, Garrett Droppers to Secretary of State Lansing, October 19, 1918, Dept. of State.

2. For an unsympathetic treatment of the demands of the "hyphenated Americans" in the United States after the First World War, see Edward R. Lewis, *America: Nation or Confusion* (New York, 1928), pp. 257–318.

3. Evangelos Chartopoulos, *E Phone tou Ipodoulon* (The Voice of the Enslaved; New York, 1914), pamphlet; *Atlantis,* April 5, 1913.

4. *New York Times,* November 19, 1917.

5. Karl Deterich, *Hellenism in Asia Minor* (New York, 1918), statement on front cover of pamphlet. Other publications issued under the auspices of the American Hellenic Society include those by August Gauvain, *The Greek Question* (New York, 1918); Z. D. Ferriman, *Greece and Tomorrow* (New York, 1918); Carroll N. Brown and Theodore P. Ion, *Persecution of the Greeks in Turkey since the Beginning of the European War* (New York, 1918); Archmandrite Alexander Papadopoulos, *Persecutions of the Greeks in Turkey before the European War* (New York, 1919); American Hellenic Society, *Greece before the Peace Conference of 1919: A Memorandum Dealing with the Rights of Greece,* submitted by Eleutherios Venizelos (New York, 1919); *Reports of the American Red Cross Commissions upon Their Activities in Macedonia, Thrace, Bulgaria, the Aegean Islands and Greece* (New York, 1919); Greek White Book (official papers), *Supplementary Documents, 1913–1917* (New York, 1919).

6. Gauvain, back page of pamphlet; *New York Times,* January 28, 1918.

7. Gauvain, pp. iii–iv.

8. Nicholas J. Cassavetes, *The Question of Northern Epirus at the Peace Conference* (New York, 1919), pp. 116–118. This pamphlet was issued for the Pan-Epirotic Union of America.

9. *Ibid.,* pp. 52–53.

10. *Ibid.,* pp. 64–65.

11. *California,* July 6, 1918.

12. Nicholas F. Kyriakides, *Ethniki Odeporia eis tin Amerikin, 1918–1919* (Patriotic Mission to America; Athens, 1924), pp. 3–4.

13. *New York Times,* September 29, 1918.

14. Nicholas F. Kyriakides, *The Unredeemed Hellenism* (New York, 1918), leaflet.

15. *New York Times,* September 29, 1918.

16. Kyriakides, *Ethniki Odeporio eis tin Amerikin,* p. 95.

17. *New York Times,* September 29, 1918.

18. *Ibid.,* October 25, 1918.

19. Kyriakides, *Ethniki Odeporia eis tin Amerikin,* pp. 155–157.

20. *New York Times,* October 30, 1918.

21. *Ibid.,* December 2, 1918.

22. *Ibid.,* December 21 and 22, 1918.

23. *Boston Herald,* December 30, 1918; *Boston Transcript,* December 30, 1918; *National Herald,* January 1, 1919.

24. *European Wars I, Greek Affairs and Policy, 1918–1919,* a collection of printed articles in the Gennadius Library, Athens; includes a reprint of an article from *Asiatic Review,* January 1919, pp. 1–4.

25. *California,* December 25, 1918, January 11, 18, and February 1, 1919; *Los Angeles Examiner,* January 20, 1919.

26. *New York Times,* February 17, 1919.

27. *Boston Evening Transcript,* March 19, 1919.

28. William E. Strong to Nicholas C. Culolias, March 29, 1919, Culolias Papers, Houghton Library, Harvard.

29. Strong to Culolias, April 7, 1919.

30. Strong to Culolias, April 7, 1919.

31. Culolias to Strong, April 11, 1919.

32. Strong to Culolias, April 14, 1919.

33. Strong to Culolias, April 17, 1919.

34. Edward M. House and Charles Seymour, *What Really Happened at Paris* (New York, 1921), pp. 191–194; Venizelos, *Greece before the Peace Conference of 1919.*

35. *New York Times,* May 12, 1919.

36. *California,* May 31, 1919.

37. H. W. V. Temperley, *A History of the Peace Conference of Paris* (London, 1924), VI, 148–149; Dept. of State, *Paris Peace Conference, 1919,* XII (Washington, 1947), 748.

38. *Paris Peace Conference, 1919,* pp. 838–841.

39. *Boston Post,* August 11, 1919; *Christian Science Monitor,* August 11, 1919; *Boston Herald,* August 11, 1919.

40. *Washington Post,* August 19, 20, 21, 22, 1919.

41. *California,* September 27, 1919.

42. *National Herald,* January 23, 1920.

43. *Nomotagis* (The Loyalist), April 13, 1919.

44. *Ibid.,* April 19 and 26, 1919.

45. *Ibid.,* May 14, 1919.

46. *National Herald,* January 22, 1920; *Illustrated Monthly National Herald,* VI (April 1920), 14–15.

47. *National Herald,* February 8, 1920.

48. *California,* April 3, 1920.

49. *Ibid.,* April 21, 1920.

50. *Ibid.,* May 7 and 14, 1920.

51. *Saloniki,* October 2, 1920.

52. *Ibid.,* October 2, 1920.

10. ROYALISTS VERSUS VENIZELISTS: SECOND PHASE

1. *Nomotagis* (The Loyalist), April 12, 1919.

2. *Ibid.,* May 10, 1919.

3. *Ibid.,* April 19 and 26, 1919.

4. *Ibid.,* April 12, 1919.

5. *Ibid.,* April 19, 1919.

6. *Ibid.,* April 26, 1919.

7. *Ibid.,* May 14, 1919.

8. *Ibid.,* May 14, 1919.

9. *Ibid.,* June 21, 1919.

10. *Ibid.,* June 21, 1919.

11. Paxton Hibben, *Constantine I and the Greek People* (New York, 1920), pp. ix, 492, 496.

12. Letter, Garrett Droppers to State Department, December 24, 1917, Dept. of State.

13. *Nomotagis,* May 29, 1920.

14. *Ibid.,* July 10, 1920.

15. *Ibid.,* July 3, 1920.

16. Doros Alastos, *Venizelos* (London, 1942), pp. 199–200.

17. *Ibid.,* pp. 201–202.

18. *Ibid.,* pp. 202–203.

19. *California,* June 26, 1920.

20. *New York Times,* August 16, 1920.

21. *Saloniki,* October 9, 1920.

22. *National Herald,* October 1, 1920.

23. *Ibid.,* October 11, 1920.

24. *Ibid.,* October 22, 1920.

25. *Ibid.,* October 22, 1920; *Saloniki,* October 23, 1920.

26. *New York Times,* October 18, 1920.

27. *Ibid.,* October 21, 1920.

28. *National Herald,* October 26, 1920.

29. Alastos, p. 203.

30. *Ibid.,* pp. 203–204.

31. *New York Times,* October 31, 1920.

32. *Saloniki,* November 6, 1920.

33. *National Herald,* November 2, 1920.

34. *Ibid.,* November 3, 1920.

35. *Ekklesiastikos Kyrix* (Church Herald), I (October 14, 1921), 100.

36. *National Herald,* November 15, 1920.

37. Alastos, p. 204. For partisan views on the defeat of Venizelos as expounded by Greek-Americans, see A. Th. Polyzoides and Demetrios Michalaros in *Nation,* CXI (December 15, 1920), 688. For a fuller statement of the royalist position, see Polyzoides, "Defeat of Venizelos," *New Republic,* XXV (December 1, 1920), 18–19.

38. *New York Times,* November 22, 1920.

39. *Ibid.,* November 25, 1920.

40. *Ibid.,* November 28, December 4 and 10, 1920.

41. *Saloniki,* December 11, 1920.

42. *New York Times,* December 17, 1920.

43. *Ibid.,* December 27, 1920.

44. William Miller, *Greece* (London, 1928), pp. 63–64.

45. 67th Cong., 2nd session, Senate Document No. 86, *Loans to Foreign Governments* (Washington, 1921), p. 221.

46. Senate Document No. 86, p. 179.

47. *Ibid.,* p. 180.

48. *Ibid.,* p. 221.

49. John Sharp Williams to Norman H. Davis, January 5, 1921, in Senate Document No. 86, p. 222.

50. *Ibid.*, p. 180.
51. *New York Times,* February 14, 1921.
52. *Christian Science Monitor,* February 21, 1921.
53. *Forster's Daily Democrat* (Dover, New Hampshire), February 19, 1921.
54. *New York Times,* February 22, 1921.
55. Charles Evans Hughes to American Embassy, London, September 2, 1921.
56. Hughes to American Embassy, London, September 23, 1921.
57. Hall to State Department, September 20, 1921.
58. Hughes to President Harding, October 12, 1921.
59. *Saloniki,* October 29, 1921; *Chicago Daily Tribune,* October 27, 1921.
60. Mark Bristol to Secretary of State, January 3, 1922.
61. *Illustrated Monthly National Herald,* VIII (January 1922), 11; March 1922, p. 8; May 1922, pp. 5, 14.
62. William Phillips to United States Legation, Athens, January 23, 1924, telegram.
63. D. J. Vlasto and A. Th. Polyzoides to Hughes, January 16, 1922, telegram.
64. N. G. Veniopoulos, Nestor President, Massachusetts Greek American National Union, to Henry Cabot Lodge, January 18, 1922.
65. Hughes to Lodge, January 27, 1922.
66. On these two days, telegrams were sent to the President of the United States by royalist groups in New York, Boston, Springfield, Akron, Nashville, Norfolk, Salem, Pittsfield, Burlington, Hartford, and Lexington, Kentucky.
67. Petros Tatanis to Harding, January 20, 1922, telegram.
68. D. Vlasto and Polyzoides to Hughes, February 16, 1922.
69. Post Wheeler to Secretary of State, November 14, 1921; "H. G. D." to Bliss, November 14, 1921.
70. J. Gennadius to Hughes, April 16, 1922.
71. A. W. Dulles to Gennadius, April 16, 1922.
72. "A. W. D." to Phillips and Harrison, June 30, 1922.
73. Phillips to United States Legation, Athens, January 23, 1924; Phillips to Thomas D. Luce, March 25, 1924.
74. Edward S. Forster, *A Short History of Modern Greece, 1821–1945* (London, 1946), pp. 152–153, 159–192.
75. *Atlantis,* March 30, 1922.
76. *New York Times,* May 4, 1922.
77. *National Herald,* August 19, 1922.
78. *Ibid.,* September 7, 1922.
79. *Ibid.,* September 8, 1922.
80. *Ibid.,* September 14, 1922.
81. *Chicago Tribune,* September 29, 1922.
82. Personal interview with Attorney John Gekas, Chicago, August 15, 1957.
83. *Chicago Daily News,* September 3, 1922; *Chicago Daily Journal,* September 7, 1922.
84. *National Herald,* September 27, October 1, 1922.
85. *Ibid.,* September 29, October 2, 1922.
86. *Ibid.,* October 3, 1922; *Chicago Daily Journal,* September 28, 1922; *Chicago Evening American,* September 28, 1922.
87. *National Herald,* October 3, 4, 6, and 8, 1922.
88. *Ibid.,* November 7, 1922.

89. *Ibid.*, October 27, November 7, 1922.

90. *Ibid.*, November 10, 1922.

91. *Ibid.*, December 8, 1922.

92. Alastos, pp. 225–226; A. Th. Polyzoides, "The Greek Political Executions," *Current History*, XVII (January 1923), 539–543. A stenographic account of the inquiry into the activities of the condemned men is available in the Greek language: *E Dike ton ex* (The Trial of the Six; Athens, 1931).

93. Personal interview with John Gekas, August 15, 1957.

94. *Illustrated Monthly National Herald*, IX (January 1923), 8; *National Herald*, November 29, 1922.

95. *Ibid.*, December 11, 1922.

96. *Ibid.*, January 1, 1923.

97. *Ibid.*, February 20, March 19, 1923.

98. Thalis Koutoupis, "Constantine the Greek Assassin," *Illustrated Monthly National Herald*, IX (February 1923), 12–13.

99. *National Herald*, January 13, 1923.

100. *Atlantis*, January 4, 1923.

101. Interview with John Gekas, August 15, 1957.

102. *National Herald*, January 5, 1923.

103. Interview with Gekas, August 15, 1957.

104. *Saloniki*, February 10, 1923.

105. *National Herald*, February 24, 1923.

106. *Ibid.*, March 7, 1923.

107. *Kathemerini* (The Daily), June 16, 1923; May 5, 1923.

108. *Ibid.*, May 17 and 31, 1924; Miller, pp. 87–110.

11. MILITARY OBLIGATIONS AND THE MOTHER COUNTRY

1. *Atlantis*, March 26, April 23, October 29, 1897.

2. Theodore Saloutos, *They Remember America* (Berkeley and Los Angeles, 1956), p. 52.

3. Department of State, Passport Division, *Information for Bearers of Passports*, February 1, 1952, pp. 71–76 (pamphlet).

4. Letter, Edward S. Boylan to S. H. Williams, December 1, 1915; John E. Mehl to State Department, February 11, 1916, Dept. of State. (P. B. finally was released from military service.)

5. Frank L. Polk to Ensle and Covert, November 27, 1915.

6. "Greece: Notice to American Citizens Formerly Subjects of Greece Who Contemplate Returning to That Country," leaflet issued by Department of State, Washington, September 21, 1916.

7. Breckenridge Long to George Roussos, July 26, 1918.

8. George Roussos to Robert Lansing, July 29, 1918.

9. Memorandum, Office of the Solicitor, Department of State, April 16, 1919; see also Alvey A. Adee to Commercial Union of America, April 19, 1919.

10. Garrett Droppers to Secretary of State Lansing, August 15, 1919.

11. Telegram, A. A. Adee to United States Embassies in London and Paris, August 22, 1919.

12. Droppers to Alexander Grivas, August 21, 1919.

13. Grivas to Droppers, July 29 [August 11], 1919.

14. Droppers to Secretary of State, August 21, 1919.
15. Telegram, Droppers to Secretary of State, August 21, 1919.
16. Telegram, Lansing to Droppers, August 22, 1919.
17. Adee to Droppers, October 10, 1919.
18. Doros Alastos, *Venizelos* (London, 1942), pp. 191–192.
19. Droppers to Secretary of State, September 15, 1919.
20. Adee to Droppers, October 27, 1919.
21. Telegram, Droppers to State Department, November 18, 1919.
22. Charles B. Welsh to D. C. Liveris, January 19, 1920.
23. Telegram, Droppers to State Department, March 13, 1920.
24. Frazier to State Department, May 26, 1920.
25. Telegram, Frazier to State Department, July 22, 1920.
26. Colby to American Legation, Athens, August 2, 1920.
27. Telegram, Edward Capps to State Department, October 14, 1920.
28. Telegram, Capps to State Department, October 15, 1920.
29. Capps to Secretary of State, December 7, 1920. A copy of the form letter is attached to the dispatch of December 7, 1920.
30. Telegram, Capps to State Department, December 22, 1920.
31. Capps to State Department, December 23, 1920.
32. Telegram, Adee to American Legation, January 8, 1921.
33. Hall to State Department, March 17, 1921.
34. Barton Hall to Secretary of State, April 6, 1921.
35. Committee of Fifteen U.S. Army Ex-Service Men to American Legion, Dayton, Ohio, March 21, 1921, Dept. of State.
36. John Taylor to Charles Evans Hughes, May 9, 1921.
37. Hall to State Department, May 12, 1921.
38. Telegram, Hall to State Department, May 25, 1921.
39. Telegram, Hall to State Department, June 7, 1921.
40. R. W. F. to Nielsen, June 18, 1921.
41. Telegram, William Phillips to United States Legation, Athens, January 23, 1924.
42. G. Bie Ravndal to Secretary of State, June 14, 1921.
43. Mark Bristol to Secretary of State, July 18, 1921.
44. Telegram, Hall to State Department, June 17, 1921.
45. Hughes to American Legation, Athens, June 17, 1921.
46. Telegram, Hall to American Legation, Athens, August 9, 1921; G. B. Baltazzi to Hall, March 31, 1921.
47. Hall to Baltazzi, August 16, 1921.
48. Baltazzi to Hall, August 27, 1921.
49. R. W. Flournoy to Nielsen, September 13, 1921.
50. Telegram, Hall to State Department, November 7, 1921.
51. Telegram, Hall to State Department, December 16, 1921.
52. Telegram, Charles Evans Hughes to American Legation, Athens, January 4, 1922.
53. Jefferson Caffrey to State Department, May 2, 1922.
54. Caffrey to State Department, June 20, 1922.
55. Telegram, George Horton to State Department, May 23, 1922.
56. Telegram, Hughes to American Consul General, Smyrna, May 31, 1922.
57. Treat to State Department, June 9, 1922.

58. Memorandum, Office of the Solicitor, Department of State, September 14, 1922.

59. Caffrey to Secretary of State, September 7, 1922.

60. R. W. F. to the Secretary, July 10, 1923.

61. Report attached to Dispatch 234, American Legation, Athens to State Department, January 12, 1925.

62. Ray Atherton to State Department, September 21, 1923. See also *Official Gazette* (Greece), Vol. I, No. 254, August 21, 1923, and No. 263, September 18, 1923.

63. Robert F. Skinner to State Department, March 1, 1929.

64. Skinner to State Department, November 26, 1929.

12. THE EROSION OF HELLENIC SENTIMENT

1. U.S. Department of Labor, *Annual Report of Commissioner of Naturalization, 1918* (Washington, 1918), pp. 25–27.

2. *Panhellinios,* July 9, 11, 16, and 18, 1908.

3. *Atlantis,* January 14, 1918.

4. *Ibid.,* April 1, 1908.

5. *Ibid.,* December 23, 1908.

6. *Ibid.,* March 10, 1909.

7. *Ibid.,* March 1, 1909.

8. U.S. Provost Marshal General, *Second Annual Report to the Secretary of War* (Washington, 1919), p. 101.

9. *Nomotagis* (The Loyalist), April 12, 16, and May 31, 1919.

10. *Ibid.,* May 10, 1919.

11. *Ibid.,* May 31, 1919.

12. *Ibid.,* May 31, 1919.

13. *Ibid.,* June 14, 1919.

14. This was not an unusual reaction for immigrants whose knowledge of the language was limited and whose experience with census takers was nonexistent. Such suspicions were also frequently reflected in the non-Greek rural areas of the United States.

15. Department of Commerce, Bureau of the Census, *Abstract of the Fourteenth Census of the United States, 1920* (Washington, 1923), p. 387.

16. *National Herald,* January 14, 1918.

17. Nicholas G. Kyriakides, "America and Hellenism," *Outlook,* XXXV (June 9, 1920), 284–285.

18. *The Ahepa,* Pre-Convocation Number (Washington), September 1925, p. 26.

19. *Ibid.*

20. *Chicago Tribune,* January 11, 1920, quoted in *Hellinikos Astir* (Greek Star), January 16, 1920.

21. *California,* May 15, 1920.

22. *American Hellenic World,* I (October 3, 1925), pt. 2, p. 1.

23. *Ibid.,* June 6, 1925, p. 1.

24. *Ibid.,* July 11, 1925, p. 4.

25. *National Herald,* November 19, 1922.

26. *Kathemerini* (The Daily; Athens), February 16, 1924.

27. *American Hellenic World,* May 30, 1925, p. 2.

28. *Ibid.*, May 30, 1925, p. 1.

29. Figures from *Abstract of the Fourteenth Census of the United States, 1920,* pp. 339, 341; *Abstract of the Fifteenth Census of the United States, 1930* (Washington, 1933), p. 163.

30. Figures for 1923 to 1932 are taken from U.S. Department of Labor, Bureau of Naturalization, *Annual Reports of Commissioner of Naturalization;* those from 1933 through 1936, from *Statistical Abstract;* those from 1937 through 1942, from *Annual Report of Immigration and Naturalization,* for the year ending June 30, 1944, p. 110; and those for 1943 through 1952 from *Annual Report of the Immigration and Naturalization Service,* for the year ending June 30, 1952, table 39.

31. Thomas Burgess, *The Greeks in America* (Boston, 1913), pp. 196–197.

32. *Atlantis,* March 16, 1895.

33. D. Vlasto and Adamantios Th. Polyzoides to Charles E. Hughes, February 16, 1922; *Atlantis,* November 7, 1908, March 20, 1909.

34. *Hellinikos Astir,* March 31, 1905, March 29, 1907; *Loxias,* January 6, 1909.

35. *Bulletin of Achaian League,* February 20, 1915.

36. A. A. Pantelis to *Kathemerini,* February 17, 1923; *Saloniki,* September 5, 1914; February 26, June 3, 1916; *Loxias,* June 2, 1915.

37. Pantelis to *Kathemerini,* February 17, 1923.

38. Pantelis to Peter S. Lambros, March 4, 1923.

39. *American Hellenic World,* April 4, 1925, p. 4.

40. Nicholas Culolias to A. B. Messer, December 11, 1919.

41. *National Herald,* January 9, February 7 and 17, March 24 and 25, 1920; *Saloniki,* September 23, 1922.

42. *Saloniki,* November 25, 1916; *California,* May 10, 1919.

43. *Saloniki,* June 25, 1921.

44. *Ibid.,* June 5, 1919.

45. *American Hellenic World,* November 21, 1925, p. 1; *National Herald,* November 26, 1922; *Chicago Daily Journal,* December 31, 1926.

46. *Saloniki,* October 27, 1923.

47. *Chicago Daily Journal,* February 18, 1924; *Saloniki,* February 9, 1924.

48. *American Hellenic Review,* June 20, 1925, p. 1.

49. *Ibid.,* November 21, 1925, pp. 1, 4.

50. *Chicago Daily Journal,* December 31, 1926.

51. *Chicago Daily News,* March 25, 1926.

52. *Saloniki,* November 29, 1924, and October 27, 1928.

53. *Kathemerini,* April 2 and 6, 1931.

54. *Proodos* (Progress), October 5 and 12, 1932.

55. *National Herald,* November 5, 1932.

56. *Eleutheros Typos* (Free Press), July 31, 1943.

57. *National Union,* I (April 1928), 5.

58. Vasilios I. Chebithis, *Ahepa and the Progress of Hellenism in America* (New York, 1935), p. 24; also pp. 26–28.

59. *The Ahepa,* III (September 1929), 3.

60. Chebethis, pp. 32–33; also *The Ahepa,* September 1925.

61. *Ibid.,* III (November 1929), 6; *What Is the Ahepa?* (1956), booklet.

62. *The Ahepa,* May 1929, p. 28.

63. *American Hellenic World,* September 5, 1925, p. 4.

64. George Demeter, *AHEPA Manual* (Boston, 1926), p. 18.
65. *The Voice of Greek Orthodoxy* (Chicago), III (October 15, 1926), 4.
66. *American Greek Review*, V (March–April 1927), 25.
67. *American Hellenic World*, III (April 2, 1927), 4.
68. *Ibid.*, April 30, 1927, p. 1.
69. *Ibid.*, April 23, 1927, p. 1; June 4, 1927, p. 1.
70. *Ibid.*, May 7, 1927, p. 1.
71. Personal interview with Dimitri Parry, August 1956.
72. *Archon Magazine*, I (August 1927), 4–5.
73. *Tribune of GAPA*, XXI (May–June 1957), 16.
74. *American Hellenic World*, April 30, 1927, p. 5; *Atlantis*, September 2, 1927.
75. *American Hellenic World*, IV (August 1928), 7.
76. *Ibid.*, September 1928, p. 9.
77. *Ibid.*, July 1928, p. 7.
78. Paul Javaras, "New Tendencies in the Thinking of the Greeks of America," *American Greek Review*, IV (December 1926), 30.

13. GREEKS IN BUSINESS

1. *Saloniki*, September 7, 1918.
2. *Opportunity*, November 23, 1923, pp. 8–10, 36–39; personal interview with Philip Phillips, Van Nuys, California, February 5, 1961.
3. *The Ahepa*, II (November 1929), 6–7.
4. Interview with Phillips, February 5, 1961.
5. *American Greek Review*, IV (September 1926), 11; *Hellinikos Astir* (Greek Star), January 19, 1906.
6. Based on conversations with friends who were proprietors of such enterprises.
7. Bambi Malafouris, *Hellenes tis Ameriki* (Greeks in America; New York, 1948), pp. 272–273.
8. *Chicago Herald and Examiner*, November 4 and 6, 1927.
9. *Hellinikos Astir*, April 1 and 22, 1904.
10. *Ibid.*, September 25, 1908.
11. *Loxias* (The Blade), February 12, June 4, 1910.
12. Malafouris, pp. 272–273.
13. *Hellinikos Astir*, April 1, 1906.
14. *Ibid.*, August 24, 1906.
15. *Ibid.*, June 15, 1906.
16. *Saloniki*, May 29, 1915.
17. *Ibid.*, April 15, May 13, June 3, 1916.
18. *Loxias*, March 7, 1918; *Saloniki*, May 24, 1919.
19. *Kathemerini* (The Daily), August 18, 1926; *Saloniki*, October 15, 1927.
20. Malafouris, p. 273; *American Hellenic World*, I (December 19, 1925), 4.
21. Malafouris, p. 275.
22. *Hellinikos Astir*, November 14, 1919.
23. Malafouris, pp. 272–274.
24. *Chicago Herald and Examiner*, November 6, 1927.
25. *San Francisco Examiner*, December 9, 1923; Malafouris, pp. 273–274.
26. *Hellinikos Astir*, June 22, 1906.
27. *Ibid.*, April 21, 1905.
28. *Arizona Labor Journal* (Phoenix), March 2, 1916.

29. *Loxias,* May 21, October 15, 1910.

30. *Hellinikos Astir,* November 14, 1919.

31. *Saloniki,* March 30, 1918.

32. *Hellinikos Astir,* November 14, 1919.

33. *Restaurant Keepers Guide,* August 1925.

34. *Saloniki,* August 2, 1924.

35. *American Hellenic World,* April 11, 1925, p. 1.

36. *Saloniki,* December 27, 1924.

37. *Ibid.,* May 2, 1931.

38. *Saloniki–Hellinikos Typos* (Salonican Greek Press), September 13, 1934.

39. *Saloniki,* January 25, 1930; *Kathemerini,* July 3, 1929.

40. *Saloniki,* October 16 and 23, 1915, October 23, 1926, November 19, 1927.

41. This is difficult to document, but conversations with businessmen and newspaper editors have borne it out.

42. *Kathemerini,* July 12, 1929.

43. *Hellinikos Typos,* January 15, 1931.

44. Malafouris, pp. 273–275; *American Hellenic World,* April 10, 1926, p. 2.

45. *Chicago Daily Tribune,* August 10, 1937.

46. *Chicago Daily News,* May 29, 1940; *Chicago Sun-Times,* April 21, 1957; *Chicago Herald-American,* April 26, 1952; *Chicago Tribune,* November 20, 1957.

47. Malafouris, pp. 263–264; *American Hellenic World,* December 1925, p. 2.

48. *Archon Magazine,* I (July 1927), 14.

49. See the advertisements of the Greek press in Chicago. Representative illustrations of the commercial activities of the Greeks may be found in *Saloniki,* March 3, 1919; April 27, 1919; February 2, July 5, and September 13, 1924; March 26 and May 16, 1925; June 5 and November 13, 1926; December 3, 1927; November 17, 1928.

50. *Los Angeles Times,* March 5, 1928; Rockwell Hunt, ed., *California and Californians,* III (Chicago, 1926), 259–260.

51. Murray Morgan, *Skid Row* (New York, 1951), p. 151.

52. *Los Angeles Times,* November 28, 1929.

53. *Ibid.,* March 5, 1929.

54. Morgan, p. 151.

55. *Los Angeles Times,* March 5, 1929.

56. Hunt, p. 260.

57. Morgan, pp. 151–152.

58. *Ibid.,* pp. 152–153.

59. Hunt, p. 260.

60. *Los Angeles Times,* March 5, 1928, November 28, 1929.

61. Morgan, p. 154.

62. Eugene C. Eliott, *A History of Variety Vaudeville in Seattle from the Beginning to 1914* (Seattle, 1944), p. 58.

63. Joe Laurie, Jr., *Vaudeville* (New York, 1953), p. 401.

64. *Los Angeles Times,* March 5, 1928.

65. Eliott, p. 60.

66. *Los Angeles Times,* January 24, 1919.

67. *Ibid.,* February 18, 1936.

68. Warren E. Crane, "Alexander Pantages," *System,* XXXVII (March 1920), 502–503.

69. *Los Angeles Times,* February 18, 1936.

70. *New York Times,* October 23, 1954; *Los Angeles Examiner,* October 23, 1954.

71. "Spyros Skouras," *Current Biography,* 1943, p. 702.

72. *Daily Variety,* LIX (June 3, 1948), 12.

73. "Skouras," p. 702.

74. *New York Times,* October 23, 1954; *Los Angeles Examiner,* October 23, 1954; "Skouras," p. 702.

75. "Skouras," pp. 703–704.

14. THE CIVIL WAR WITHIN THE GREEK CHURCH

1. *American Hellenic World,* II (June 19, 1926), 4.

2. *Ekklesiastikos Kyrix* (Church Herald), I (September 2, 1921), 3.

3. Telegram, Garrett Droppers to State Department, June 23, 1918, Dept. of State.

4. The first Greek archbishop to visit the United States was the Most Reverend Dionysios Lattas of Zante. For a portrait of the metropolitan, see John Henry Barrows, ed., *World Parliament of Religions,* I (Chicago, 1893).

5. Metaxakis visited President Wilson on September 5, 1918. *Chicago Tribune,* September 18, 1918.

6. *Eleutheros Typos* (Free Press), November 10, 1945.

7. *American Hellenic World,* I (December 19, 1925), 22.

8. *Nomotagis* (The Loyalist), May 3 and 24, 1919.

9. *Ekklesiastikos Kyrix,* I (September 2, 1921), 3–9; *Greek Orthodox Year Book* (1957), p. 268.

10. *Ekklesiastikos Kyrix,* September 2, 1921, p. 6.

11. *Ibid.,* November 19, 1921, p. 179.

12. *Ibid.,* September 2, 1921, pp. 3–9; *Illustrated Monthly Atlantis,* XII (July 1921), 7.

13. *Kathemerini* (The Daily), September 2, 1921.

14. *Ibid.,* September 3, 1921.

15. *Ibid.,* August 24, 1921.

16. *Ibid.,* September 3, 1921.

17. *Saloniki,* October 29, 1921.

18. *New York Times,* November 7, December 27, 1921.

19. *Ibid.,* December 27, 1921.

20. "The New Ecumenical Patriarch and Hellenism in America," *Illustrated Monthly National Herald,* VIII (January 1922), 7–9.

21. *New York Times,* November 7, December 10, 21, 22, 24, and 27, 1921.

22. *Ibid.,* December 15, 1921.

23. *Ibid.,* December 19, 1921.

24. *Illustrated Monthly National Herald,* VIII (April 1922), 7, 40.

25. *American Hellenic World,* II (June 19, 1926), 4; *National Herald,* August 4, 1935.

26. *National Herald,* March 26, 1922.

27. *Saloniki,* April 14, 1923.

28. *Ibid.,* February 23, 1923.

29. Basil Th. Zoustis, *O en Ameriki Hellinismos kai e Drasis Tou* (Hellenism in America and Its Times; New York, 1954), p. 162.

30. *American Hellenic World*, June 19, 1926, p. 4.

31. D. Callimachos, "The Dangers of the Christians in the Near East," *Illustrated Monthly National Herald*, VIII (May 1922), 6–7, 38; *National Herald*, September 27, 1922.

32. *National Herald*, November 27, 1922; Zoustis, p. 162.

33. *National Herald*, December 6, 1922.

34. Zoustis, p. 164.

35. *Ibid.*, p. 165.

36. *National Herald*, December 15, 1922.

37. *Ibid.*, December 16, 1922.

38. *Ibid.*, December 18, 1922.

39. *Ibid.*, December 19, 1922.

40. *Ibid.*, January 2, 1923.

41. For a copy of this statement, see *ibid.*, January 10, 1923.

42. *Ibid.*, March 13, 1923.

43. *Saloniki*, April 28, May 26, 1923.

44. *Chicago Evening Post*, June 21, 1923; *Kathemerini*, June 16, 1923; Zoustis, pp. 166–168.

45. Zoustis, p. 168.

46. *Ibid.*, pp. 172–176.

47. *Saloniki*, August 2, 1924.

48. *Illustrated Monthly National Herald*, IX (December 1923), 23–24.

49. Interview with Adamantios Th. Polyzoides, Los Angeles, May 12, 1959.

50. Zoustis, p. 187.

51. *Saloniki*, July 5 and 19, 1924.

52. *Ibid.*, September 13, 1924.

53. K. K. Joachim, *E Kindinoi tou en Ameriki Hellinismou kai ta Mesa tis Diasoseous Autou* (The Dangers Facing the Greeks of America and the Means for Their Salvation; Boston, 1926), pp. 12–17.

54. *American Hellenic World*, April 3, 1926, p. 4.

55. *Kathemerini*, August 21, 1927.

56. *Democrat*, August 1927.

57. *Kathemerini*, July 7 and 30, 1927.

58. *Ibid.*, March 11, 1926.

59. *Ibid.*, March 3, 1928.

60. *Ibid.*, December 19, 1928.

61. *Eleutheros Typos*, December 1, 1945.

62. *Ibid.*, November 10, 1945.

63. *Ibid.*, October 27, 1945.

64. *Ibid.*, November 10, 1945.

65. *Ibid.*, October 20, November 3, 1945.

66. *Ibid.*, November 24, 1945.

67. *Ibid.*

68. *Ibid.*, December 1, 1945.

69. *Ibid.*, December 15, 1945.

70. *Ibid.*, October 13, 1945.

71. *Ibid.*, December 22, 1945.

72. *Ibid.*, February 2 and 9, 1945.

73. *Ibid.*, October 13, 1945.

74. *Ibid.*

75. *Chicago Post*, August 2, 1930.
76. *Saloniki*, August 9, 1930.
77. *Kathemerini*, October 23, 1930.
78. *Ibid.*, October 28, 1930.
79. Zoustis, p. 204.
80. *Kathemerini*, November 15, 1930.
81. *Ibid.*, April 13 and 15, 1931.
82. *Ibid.*, April 7, 1931.
83. *Ibid.*, May 14, 1931.
84. *Ibid.*, June 22, 1931.
85. *Ibid.*, May 12, 1931.
86. *Ibid.*, May 23, 1931.
87. *Ibid.*, December 6, 1931.
88. *Proodos* (Progress), July 27, 1932.
89. *Kathemerini*, February 18, 1932.
90. *Proodos*, October 26, 1932.
91. *Ibid.*, September 14, October 26, 1932; *Kathemerini*, December 23, 1934.
92. *Proodos*, December 21, 1932.
93. *Hellinikos Typos* (Greek Press), September 28, 1933.
94. *Proodos*, August 1933.
95. *Ibid.*, September 30, 1933.
96. *Hellinikos Typos*, October 26, 1933.

15. THE SECOND GENERATION

1. For a nationalistic version of this in the Greek language, see *E Panhellinios Enosis* (The Panhellenic Union), II (November 1, 1925), 2, 7.
2. Dio Adallis, *Twenty-Fifth Anniversary, Cumberland, Md., Greek American Colony, 1908–1933* (Cumberland, 1933), pp. 7–8.
3. Based on personal observations and on those of numerous friends and members of professional groups who lived in such surroundings.
4. *Hellinikos Typos* (Greek Press), December 4, 1929.
5. Theodora Isaakidou Corovilles, "The Church School Movement of the Hellenic Eastern Orthodox Church," master's thesis, Presbyterian College of Christian Education (Chicago, 1935), pp. 61–63.
6. Theodore Saloutos, *They Remember America* (Berkeley and Los Angeles, 1956), pp. 40–41.
7. *Hellinikos Typos*, January 11, 1934.
8. *Hellinikos Astir* (Greek Star), March 15, 1934. For a good general account of the Greek conception of marriage, see Lucy M. J. Garnett, *Greece of the Hellenes* (New York, 1914), pp. 193–198.
9. *Saloniki–Hellinikos Typos*, December 20, 1934.
10. *Ibid.*, July 11, 1935.
11. *Ibid.*, December 20, 1934; *Hellinikos Typos*, December 4, 1929.
12. *The Ahepa*, VI (May 1932), 19; Corovilles, pp. 30–31; *National Herald*, May 11, 1916.
13. *Hellinikos Typos*, January 4, 1934; *Saloniki–Hellinikos Typos*, June 6, 1935.
14. Corovilles, pp. 56–58.
15. *The Ahepa*, III (August 1929), 7.

16. Note the despairing articles in *The Ahepa,* VII (March–April 1933), 26–29. Some titles of articles were: "Can Our New Generation Live Without the U.S.?"; "A New Deal of Ahepans for the Sons of Ahepans"; and "The New and the Old."

17. Dean Alfange discusses this in *The Ahepa,* III (August 1929), 7–8. *Hellinikos Typos,* November 2, 1933; *American Hellenic World,* III (July 2, 1927), 2.

18. *Constitution and By-Laws Order of Sons of Pericles,* pp. 3–4.

19. Basil Th. Zoustis, *O en Ameriki Hellinismos kai e Drasis Tou* (Hellenism in America and Its Times; New York, 1954), pp. 245–264; Holy Cross Orthodox Theological School, *Catalogue Issue, 1955–1956,* pp. 10–11.

20. Based on personal interviews, discussions, and experiences. The information given throughout this chapter is a matter of common knowledge among Greek-Americans of the second generation.

16. THE THIRTIES

1. *Year Book of St. Constantine Church and Koraes School, 1936* (Chicago, 1936), p. 47.

2. *Saloniki–Hellinikos Typos* (Salonican Greek Press), June 6, 1935.

3. *Kathemerini* (The Daily), April 23, 1931.

4. *Saloniki–Hellinikos Typos,* June 6, 1935.

5. *Ibid.,* August 16, 1934.

6. *Chicago Herald and Examiner,* May 2, 1938.

7. *Lowell Sun,* July 13, 1936; *National Herald,* July 14, 1935; *The Ahepa Magazine,* XI (March–April 1937), 32; *Los Angeles Mirror,* October 28, 1953.

8. Theodore Saloutos, "Ai Entiposis Mou Peri Hellino-Amerikanon" (My Impressions of the Greek-Americans), *Argonautis* (New York, 1959), pp. 122–123.

9. Memorandum, "Naturalization Treaties," October 26, 1931. From American Legation, Athens, August 28, 1935, Dept. of State.

10. From American Legation, Athens, to Secretary of State, July 23, 1937.

11. Edward S. Forster, *A Short History of Modern Greece, 1821–1945* (London, 1946), p. 190.

12. *New York Times,* April 14, 1935.

13. *Ibid.,* June 20, 1935.

14. *Ibid.,* July 17, 1935.

15. *Ibid.,* August 20, 1935.

16. *Ibid.,* August 21, 1935.

17. *Ibid.,* October 1, 1935.

18. *Ibid.,* September 9, 1935.

19. *Ibid.,* September 29, 1935.

20. Personal interview with Demetrios Callimachos, August 15, 1961.

21. Bambi Malafouris, *Hellenes tis Amerikis* (Greeks in America; New York, 1948), pp. 229, 233–234. Interview with Callimachos, August 15, 1961.

22. *Protoporos* (Pioneer), II (September 1936), 3–4, 21–22.

23. *Ibid.,* December 1936, pp. 4–10, 14.

24. *Ibid.,* November 1936, p. 25; January 1937, p. 1; March 1937, p. 4.

25. P. Kekes to Editor of *National Herald,* November 20, 1937.

26. *New York Times,* November 15, 1937.

27. Kekes to Editor of *National Herald,* November 20, 1937.

28. Kekes to Editor of *National Herald,* November 21, 1937.

29. *The Ahepa Magazine,* XI (May–June 1937).

30. *Ibid.,* March–April 1937, pp. 18–35.

31. *New Orleans Times-Picayune,* August 19–21, 1938.

32. Greek-American Union for Democracy, *New American Problem in the Light of Nazi Aggression* (New York, 1939), leaflet; Andrew Pappas to State Department, July 27, 1937; Charles W. Yost to Pappas, August 2, 1937.

33. Memorandum, State Department, "Unfairness of American Press in Treatment of Greeks," January 13, 1938.

34. *Portland Oregonian,* July 12, 1938.

35. American Legation, Athens, "The Greek Phalange and Its Efforts to Obtain Cooperation in the United States," August 5, 1939.

36. *Atlantis,* June 30, 1939.

37. *Ibid.,* July 2 and 4, 1939.

38. *Ibid.,* July 10, 1939.

39. *Ibid.,* July 14, 1939.

40. *Ibid.,* July 14, 1939.

41. *Ibid.,* July 15, 1939.

42. *Ibid.,* July 25, 1939.

43. *Ibid.,* July 21, 1939.

44. Interview with Callimachos, August 15, 1961.

45. *Atlantis,* July 31, 1939.

46. See *Atlantis,* August 3, 1939, and the succeeding issues.

47. *Ibid.,* August 23, 1939.

48. *The Ahepan,* XV (November–December 1941), 16. It should be noted that AHEPA's publication was variously entitled *The Ahepa, The Ahepa Magazine,* and *The Ahepan.*

49. *Ibid.,* XVI (January–February 1942), 20, 23.

50. *Ibid.,* XIV (July–August 1940), 7.

51. George C. Vournas to the author, October 18, 1961.

17. THE SECOND WORLD WAR

1. *New York Times,* December 1, 1940, and January 19, March 22, 1941; *Life,* December 23, 1940, p. 20; *Commonweal,* January 31, 1941, pp. 368, 370.

2. *New York Times,* October 30, 1940.

3. Greek Government Office of Information, *Tribute to Greece* (Washington, 1943), booklet; *Norfolk Virginian-Pilot,* March 21, 1941; *Birmingham Age-Herald,* March 17, 1941; *Milwaukee Journal,* December 29, 1940, January 12, 1941; *The Ahepan,* XIV (November–December 1940), 14.

4. *San Francisco Chronicle,* November 3, 1940; *The Ahepan,* November–December 1940, p. 6.

5. *The Ahepan,* November–December 1940, p. 6.

6. Formation of the Greek War Relief Association was announced on November 8, 1940. Greek War Relief Association, *$12,000,000* (New York, 1946), pamphlet, p. 2.

7. *Milwaukee Sentinel,* November 26, 1941.

8. GWRA, News Release 1, November 20, 1940.

9. George C. Vournas to the author, October 18, 1961.

10. *The Ahepan*, XV (January–June 1941), 39.

11. GWRA, *News Letter*, II (December 8, 1942), 6; III (January 8, 1943), 1; III (November 23, 1943), 1.

12. *The Ahepan*, January–June 1941, p. 6.

13. *Ibid.*, January–June 1941, p. 13.

14. *Ibid.*, September–October 1941, pp. 8, 30.

15. *Chicago Sun*, October 25, 1942; Vournas to author, October 18, 1961.

16. GWRA, News Release 2, November 19, 1940.

17. GWRA, News Release, February 24, 1941.

18. *St. Louis Post-Dispatch*, February 28, 1941.

19. "Address to the Fourth Annual Meeting of the GWRA by the President, Spyros P. Skouras" (October 21, 1944), p. 2. Carbon copy in New York Public Library.

20. GWRA, *$12,000,000*, pp. 6–7.

21. *Ibid.*, pp. 8–9.

22. *The Ahepan*, XVIII (May–June 1944), pp. 15, 30.

23. *Chicago Tribune*, May 4, 1942.

24. *The Ahepan*, XVI (January–February 1942), 18.

25. *Ibid.*, XV (November–December 1941), 16.

26. *Ibid.*, January–February 1942, p. 24.

27. *Ibid.*, July–August 1942, pp. 12–14.

28. *Ibid.*, November–December 1942, pp. 5–6.

29. Vournas to author, October 18, 1961.

30. GWRA, Press Release, August 24, 1943.

31. *The Ahepan*, November–December 1942, pp. 8, 10.

32. *Ibid.*, January–February 1943, p. 18.

33. *Ibid.*, November–December 1942, p. 5; January–February 1943, p. 15; May–June 1943, pp. 7–9.

34. *Ibid.*, May–June 1943, pp. 7–9.

35. George C. Vournas, *A Message from the Supreme President* (Washington, December 1, 1944).

36. *The Ahepan*, November–December 1943, p. 22.

37. GWRA, *$12,000,000*, pp. 10–11.

38. Greek-American Labor Committee, *Greece Fights for Freedom* (New York, 1944), a pamphlet, p. 3.

39. *Ibid.*, pp. 21–22.

40. *Ibid.*, p. 25.

41. *Ibid.*, pp. 27–29.

42. Panou Harissiadou, *E Ethniki Enotis* (National Unity; New York, 1944), pamphlet. See esp. pp. 3–9, 12–23.

43. Greek-American Committee for National Unity, *Greek Liberation* (New York, 1944); Greek-American Labor Committee, *Greece Fights for Freedom; Bulletin of the Greek-American Council*, II (March 1945), 1.

44. *New York Times*, October 25, 1944.

45. *Ibid.*, October 30, 1944.

46. *Ibid.*, October 31, 1944.

47. *Ibid.*, November 27, 1944.

48. *Ibid.*, December 5, 1944.

49. *Ibid.*, December 12, 1944.
50. Vournas, *A Message*, pp. 5–6.
51. Extension of Remarks of Hon. Leo E. Allen, "Greeks in America," 86th Cong., 2nd sess., *Congressional Record* (Washington, 1960), p. 15.
52. *Bulletin of the Greek Committee for National Unity*, II (February 1945), 3.
53. *Ibid.*, February 1945, pp. 1, 4.
54. *Ibid.*, March 1945, pp. 1–2.
55. *Ibid.*, April 1945, pp. 2–3; July 1945, pp. 1–2; August–September 1945, p. 1.
56. *Ibid.*, November 1945, pp. 1–2.
57. *Ibid.*, February–March 1946, pp. 1–3; July 1946, pp. 1–2.
58. *Ibid.*, July 1946, pp. 1–2.

18. THE ERA OF RESPECTABILITY

1. "The Problems of Greek Tourism," *Quarterly Review of the National Bank of Greece*, IV (Athens, 1961), 3–23. According to the *National Herald*, December 10, 1961, more than 87,000 Americans poured into Greece during the first nine months of 1961.
2. Greek War Relief Association, *$12,000,000* (New York, 1946), p. 10.
3. *Ibid.*, pp. 12–13.
4. From a speech delivered by George P. Skouras during 1946.
5. GWRA, *$12,000,000*, p. 13; *Chicago Sun*, March 3, 1946.
6. From a speech by George P. Skouras, 1946.
7. *Chicago Sun*, April 13, 1946.
8. *The AHEPA Hospitals for Greece Program* (Washington, 1956), brochure.
9. Food and Agricultural Organization of the United States, *Report of the FAO Mission for Greece* (Washington, 1947), pp. 1–2.
10. *New York Times*, December 18, 1944.
11. *Report of Photius P. Kyritsis, Supreme President, to the Fifth National Panepirotic Convention, July 2, 1947*, p. 8.
12. *Ibid.*, pp. 13–14.
13. Panhellenic Committee for the Defense of Greek Rights, released April 7, 1946; mimeographed copy.
14. *New York Herald Tribune*, August 28, 1946.
15. *Ogden Standard-Examiner*, November 12, 1946; *Pittsburgh Post-Gazette*, November 21, 1946.
16. *Buffalo Courier Express*, February 23, 1946; *Cleveland Press*, October 28, 1946; *Birmingham Post*, November 2, 1946; *Cleveland Plain Dealer*, March 24, 1946; *New York Sun*, October 28, 1946; *Newark Star-Ledger* [Ark.] *Gazette*, November 18, 1946; *Christian Science Monitor*, August 29, 1946; *New Bedford* [Mass.] *Standard-Times*, October 20, 1946; *Savannah Morning News*, October 21, 1946; *San Francisco Chronicle*, November 21, 1946; *Tacoma News-Tribune*, April 1, 1946; *Philadelphia Inquirer*, March 24, 1946; *New York Herald-Tribune*, August 29, 1946.
17. Harry N. Howard, "The Development of United States Policy in the Near East, 1945–1951," *Department of State Bulletin*, November 19, 1951, p. 812.
18. *Ibid.*
19. *New York Times*, March 17, 1947.
20. 80th Cong., 1st session, *Hearings before the Committee on Foreign Rela-*

tions, United States Senate, on S. 928, "A Bill to Provide for Assistance to Greece and Turkey," March 24, 25, 27, and 31, 1947 (Washington, 1947), pp. 178–181.

21. *Ibid.,* pp. 206–208.

22. Constantine Poulos, "Report from Athens," *New Republic,* March 17, 1947, pp. 26–27, April 16, 1947, p. 16; "What America Could Do in Greece," *Nation,* March 29, 1947, pp. 356–358; "Fiasco in Greece," *ibid.,* December 6, 1947, pp. 614–617; "Meet Our Greek Allies," *ibid.,* June 28, 1947, pp. 761–763; "Lesson of Greece," *ibid.,* March 27, 1948, pp. 343–345; "Coming Greek Dictatorship," *New Republic,* July 21, 1947, p. 7. See Basil J. Vlavianos, "Greece and Its Allies," *Nation,* September 28, 1946, pp. 344–346; "Exclusive Interview," *U.N. World,* April 1947, p. 18. Also, C. G. Cavouras, "Greece in Purgatory," *Nation,* December 29, 1945, p. 747.

23. *New York Times,* April 9, 1947.

24. *San Francisco Chronicle,* May 16 and November 2, 1948; January 28, 1949.

25. Based on personal interviews with individuals who wish to remain anonymous.

26. Peter T. Kourides, *The Evolution of the Greek Orthodox Church in America and Its Present Problems* (New York, 1959), pp. 29–30.

27. Greek Archdiocese of North and South America, *The Historic Decision of the 10th Biennial Ecclesiastical Congress at St. Louis* (New York, 1950?), leaflet.

28. *Ibid.*

29. Kourides, pp. 30–31.

30. *Ibid.,* p. 33.

31. *Milwaukee Journal,* September 21, 1956, July 3, 1961; *Milwaukee Sentinel,* July 8, 1961.

32. *Milwaukee Journal,* July 10, December 24, 1961.

33. *Official Minutes and Proceedings of the National Youth Conference of the Greek Orthodox Church in America* (Chicago, 1951), pp. 4–21.

34. Boris R. Burden to the Director of Selective Service, October 4, 1942; George E. Phillies to Bishop Dionysius, October 17, 1942. In papers of George E. Phillies, Buffalo, New York.

35. *Buffalo Courier News,* March 24, 1943.

36. Kourides, pp. 46–51.

37. Personal interview with Peter Kourides, December 26, 1961.

38. Representative of slashing criticisms of the church and the Hellenic university are those of Constantine Cavarnos, *E Orthodoxia en Ameriki* (Athens, 1958), pamphlet; Constantine S. Dukakis, *The Fate of the Greek Orthodox Church in America* (Arlington, Mass., 1960), pamphlet; and by the same author, *The Proposed Hellenic University* (Arlington, Mass., 1961), pamphlet.

39. 82nd Cong., 2nd sess., House of Representatives, *Hearings before the President's Commission on Immigration and Naturalization* (Washington, 1952), pp. 216–218, 431–433, 536–537, 622–624, 1238–1242, 1768–1771.

40. *Ibid.,* p. 285.

41. "President Truman's Message to the House on the Veto of Immigration Bill," in Benjamin M. Ziegler, *Immigration, An American Dilemma* (Boston, 1953), pp. 97–103, esp. 99–100.

42. 83rd Cong., 2nd sess., *First Semiannual Report of the Administration of the Refugee Relief Act of 1953* (Washington, 1954), p. 9.

43. 85th Cong., 1st sess., *Refugee Relief Act of 1953, Final Report of the*

Administrator of the Refugee Relief Act of 1953, As Amended (Washington, 1954), pp. 12, 139–142.

44. The figures for 1946–1947 are from *Statistical Abstract of the United States, 1949*, p. 96; for 1947–1950, *ibid., 1951*, p. 94. The figures for 1951–1960 are from *Annual Report of the Immigration and Naturalization Service* (Washington, 1960), p. 43.

45. Interview with welfare worker, who prefers that his name be withheld.

46. See *Fifteenth Annual Convention of the G.A.P.A., July 2nd to July 9th, 1950* (Miami, 1950).

47. Personal interview with Dimitri Parry, August 15, 1957.

48. *The Order of AHEPA, 1922–1961* (Washington, 1961), leaflet.

49. George J. Leber to the author, October 26, 1961.

INDEX

439

Restriction on immigration: criticisms of, 238: drive against, 243
Riley, De Witt T., 9, 26
Robert College, 175
Romaios Metanastis, 90
Roosevelt, Franklin D., 245–246
Roosevelt, Theodore, 64
Roussos, George: on *Atlantis,* 157; places hope in United States, 170
Royalists (United States): form Loyalist Leagues, 144; Greek elections of 1920 and, 190; Greek territorial claims and, 181; on United States citizenship, 185–186; organize in United States, 144; reaction to Papanastasiou mission, 331; resurgence, 1935, 330; seek to overthrow Venizelos, 185; views of Droppers, 187; views of Wilson, 186
Russian-American Orthodox Messenger, 127
Russian church (United States): Bishop Nicholas, 127–128; Greek fear of, 119; Greeks rely on, 122; influence extended, 127; Greeks suspicious of, 128

Sadler, Percy L., 365–366
St. Athanasius Seminary, 293–294
St. Constantine Church (Brooklyn), 136, 151
St. Eleutherios Church, 136
Salopoulos, K., Dr., 90
Salonika government, 143, 152
Saloniki (newspaper), battles padrone system, 55
Saltonstall, Leverett, 375
Sargeant, Lewis, 12
School, Greek-language, 73–74
Second generation: appeal of professions to, 324; attitudes to upbringing, 323–324; females, 314; indifference to Greek heritage, 324–325; life in two worlds, 310; occupations as youths, 322–323; pressures, 320; success, 322; teen-agers, 313
Sedgwick, A. C., 357, 360
Selective Service Act, 161
Sèvres, Treaty of: signing of, 188–189; revision opposed, 196–197
Shoeshining, 48–56, 259
Sicilianos, Demetrios, 330, 335, 337–338
Silhouette performances. *See* Karagiozi
Simopoulos, Charalambos, 302
Skouras brothers, 278–281
Skouras, George P., 363
Skouras, Spyros, 278–279, 345, 346, 348

Smith, Alfred E., 244–245
Smyrna, 169, 172, 178, 228–229
Societies, role of, 76
Society for the Formation of a National Fleet, 17
Solicitor, Office of the, 226, 228–229
Sons of Pericles, 301, 320–321
Sophocles, E. E., 23
Sophia, Queen, 41
South Omaha riot, 66–70
Spanish-American War, 10, 162
Spartans, first immigrants, 23–24
Sphaira (newspaper): alarmed over departures, 28–29; on immigration, 24–25
Steamship companies, as cause of immigration, 33
Stephano brothers, 272–273
Stoa (newspaper), 25
Straus, Oscar G., 131–132
Strike-breakers, 61–62
Strong, William, 176–178
Swanson, Claude, 63
Syrian-Arabic Orthodox Church, 127

Tachydromos, 90
Tariff, Greek, 196
Tatanis, Petros, 200
Territorial claims, Greece: *Boston Herald* and, 197; *Christian Science Monitor* on, 196; Dover liberals and, 196; Greek-Americans press for, 169–170; in U. S. Senate, 181; Lodge on, 181–182; at Paris Peace Conference, 175–176; presidential election, 1920, and, 182–183; rallies in behalf of, 174–175, 179–180; royalists on, 181; *Saloniki* on, 182; Venizelos presses, 217
Theoclitus, 136, 145, 283, 284
Theological Seminary, Pomfret Center, 322
Theophilatos, Demetrios J., 152–153, 186, 191
Thermopylae (newspaper), 89
Thermopylae-Simaia (newspaper), 90
Thessaly, hereditary tenants, 5
Timayenis, Demosthenes, 153–154
Tome of 1908, 288, 297
Traditionalists, position of, 326
Treaty of Sèvres. *See* Sèvres
Trikoupis, Harilaos, 13
Tripartite loan, 195–196
Tripolis, 50
Truman, Harry S., 368, 378
Truman Doctrine, 368–369
Tsakonas, Christos, 24